Six Stages on the Spiritual Path

Six Stages on the Spiritual Path

A Way to Transform Ourselves and Our World

RUTH WHITNEY

RESOURCE *Publications* • Eugene, Oregon

SIX STAGES ON THE SPIRITUAL PATH:
A Way to Transform Ourselves and Our World

Copyright © 2021 Ruth Whitney. All rights reserved. Except for brief quotations in critical publications or reviews, no part of this book may be reproduced in any manner without prior written permission from the publisher. Write: Permissions, Wipf and Stock Publishers, 199 W. 8th Ave., Suite 3, Eugene, OR 97401.

Resource Publications
An Imprint of Wipf and Stock Publishers
199 W. 8th Ave., Suite 3
Eugene, OR 97401

www.wipfandstock.com

PAPERBACK ISBN: 978-1-7252-9317-5
HARDCOVER ISBN: 978-1-7252-9318-2
EBOOK ISBN: 978-1-7252-9319-9

05/20/21

Contents

Introduction		vii
Chapter 1	Awe and Wonder Are the First Stage on the Mystic Way to the Divine	1
Chapter 2	Do We All Have a Spiritual Path?	21
Chapter 3	Mystics Explained Different Versions of Stages on the Spiritual Path	51
Chapter 4	Stage Two Is Parents and Religious Leaders Teaching Children about God	82
Chapter 5	Awakening Is the Third Stage on the Spiritual Path	92
Chapter 6	The Awakenings of Mystics of Eastern Religions	120
Chapter 7	Jewish and Christian Mystics' Awakenings	143
Chapter 8	Muhammad and Islamic Mystics' Awakenings	163
Chapter 9	Love for Our Neighbors and Ourselves Is the Fourth Stage	177
Chapter 10	Illumination and Union with the Holy One Are the Fifth Stage	206
Chapter 11	Transpersonal Images of the Divine during Illumination and Union	238
Chapter 12	Love for All People and All of Creation Is the Sixth Stage on the Mystical Way	267
Endnotes		297
Bibliography		323
Index		331

Introduction

The Purpose of this Book

My Mom and Dad were good people. As a child, I knew and felt that they loved me. They also loved my three sisters. Both my parents were alcoholics. Their alcoholism wounded their four young daughters in different ways.

When I was around three years old with a head full of blond curls before my hair turned brown, I plotted in my mind how to approach my Dad. I did not talk to anyone else about this. The reason for my plotting was that Dad's drinking bothered me so much that I wanted to ask him to stop. At that time, I did not use the word alcoholism, because I did not know that word, although Dad was an alcoholic. Because I did not want to make him angry, I said to him, "Dad, why do you drink?" hoping that my question would tug at his heart strings. Although I don't remember how he answered my question, I know that he did not stop drinking.

When I was in elementary school, I realized that his drinking hurt my mother and my three sisters as well as myself. By this time, my mother's drinking has progressed so that she was also an alcoholic. Because I never knew how drunk my mother would be when I came home, I never invited my friends to my house after school or any other time.

Mom taught us "never to say anything negative." What she really meant was never talk to anyone about the alcoholism. Following my mother's orders, I did not talk to anyone about the drinking or anything else of real importance to me. Not my parents, not my sisters, not my relatives, not my friends, no one. Any troubles I had, I dealt with on my own. Emotionally and psychologically, I was completely self-sufficient. As a young person, I knew that something was wrong that I had no one to help me with my problems. When I was with other people, I acted like everything was fine, when it really wasn't.

Probably since my childhood and definitely in my writings in graduate school and afterwards, I not only raised the following questions, but I also tried to solve them. Why do good and loving people hurt their children? Why do they injure others? This book offers my thoughts on what is spirituality, what are its stages, and how does spirituality help to reduce our suffering and nurture more love.

All over the world there is suffering as well as love. The way these two things come into each of our lives is different. Suffering and love are unique. Selfishness, hate, greed, unfairness, inequality, injustice, abuse, cruelty, and violence lead to individual and global unhappiness, misery, pain, suffering, and despair in both rich and poor countries. Love can bring great happiness and joy. My six stages on the spiritual path are one of the many possible ways to help alleviate our suffering and create more love so that all of us will have a better future.

The writings from ancient to contemporary mystics across the world contain a great deal of spiritual wisdom. Some mystics from around the globe and from 3,000 years ago until today explain different versions of the stages of the spiritual path. Of all the mystics in the past and present, who has the best description of the stages on the mystic way?

So far in history, my answer is Evelyn Underhill. In 1911, this highly respected, English scholar wrote a classic entitled *Mysticism: A Study in the Nature and Development of Man's Spiritual Consciousness*. Her five stages on the mystic way that are still utilized by many contemporary writers are: awakening, purification, illumination, dark night of the soul, and union. These are an improvement on the sixth-century Denys the Areopagite's (also called Dionysius) widely used three stages: purification, illumination, and union and complete perfection. In my way of thinking, Underhill's five stages are best description of stages so far in the history of spiritual writing.

My six stages are based on my own spiritual experiences and my decades of studying the writings of mystics from across the world, including Denys and Underhill. My stages are: (1) awe and wonder; (2) parents and religious leaders teaching children about God; (3) awakening; (4) love for ourselves and our neighbors; (5) illumination and union with the Holy One; and (6) love for all people and all of creation. Although there are some similarities with Underhill's stages, there are also significant, profound differences. The description, content, and essence of my stages are unlike hers. Even when there are similarities, my stages are more thoroughly, distinctly, and clearly explained. My framework presents a more easily understood and more comprehensive explanation of the process that happens as the six stages enfold. While Underhill uses mainly Christian mystics to illustrate her stages, I include mystics from all the world's religions and from over 3,000 years ago until the present. Most important, my six stages show more clearly how spirituality helps decrease our suffering and foster more love.

A Brief Summary of This Book

The introduction explains the purpose of this book. It also provides a brief summary of this book. In the first chapter, awe and wonder are the first stage on the mystic way. Children experience awe, but they do not realize that this is a spiritual experience. Many adults and artists have mystical encounters of awe and recognize them as spiritual experiences. When early indigenous tribes experienced awe and wonder, they created their traditional religions. Chapter two answers multiple, basic questions that are important to understand as we think about the six stages on the spiritual path, such as what does it mean to be spiritual and to be a mystic? What is the source of spirituality? Do we all have a spiritual path? What are the purposes, goals, and results of spirituality? Can spirituality help reduce suffering and promote more love? The third chapter describes stages on the spiritual path that are explained by many individuals, including ancient Hindus, Buddhists, early and later Christians, and Muslims, as well as contemporary mystics. Chapter four explains how parents and religious leaders in the second stage teach children about God in ways that cause their spiritual growth to flourish or to become stunted at an elementary school level.

In the fifth chapter, awakening which is an experience of the Divine is the third stage on the spiritual path. Some examples include Buddha and mystics of traditional religions, including Africans and American Indians. Advanced awakening leads to experiences of Divine love as well as the Divine presence within everyone. Awakened mystics mainly have personal images of God rather than transpersonal ones. Chapter six presents the awakenings of ancient and later Hindu, Chinese, and Japanese mystics. In the seventh chapter, the awakenings of ancient and later Jewish and Christian mystics, including Jesus, are spelled out. Chapter eight discusses Mohammad, the Qur'an, and Islamic mystics' awakenings, including the Sufis. In the ninth chapter, love for ourselves and our neighbors is the fourth stage on the spiritual path. Awakening produces love. Then love creates more awakenings. A definition of love and the steps to become more loving are discussed.

Chapter ten presents illumination and union with the Sacred Spirit as the fifth stage. Illumination is a deeper spiritual experience that Holy One is not only within us and all of creation, but also that we are within the ONE.

Union includes spiritual marriage and divinization, which is also called deification. In the eleventh chapter, while the third stage of awakening leads to personal images of God, the fifth stage of illumination and union with the Divine results in transpersonal images, but not impersonal ones. Chapter twelve explains that love for all people and all of creation is the sixth stage on the spiritual path. Ancient mystics throughout time until contemporary illuminated mystics such as Gandhi taught and practiced love for everyone.

Chapter 1

Awe and Wonder Are the First Stage on the Mystic Way to the Divine

Children Experience Awe and Wonder, But Do Not Know They Are Spiritual Experiences

When three-year-old Josh and I were holding hands and walking around a lovely lake filled with spectacular wild life, he pointed and excitedly said, "that Jacaranda tree is beautiful." He spoke the truth. The bluish-purple flowers were truly gorgeous. It surprised me that he knew the name of a Jacaranda tree and expressed his thoughts. Normally, he would experience joy, be amazed, and perhaps say WOW! It is not often that little children express what they are thinking and feeling about experiences of awe and wonder. They are more likely to express their feelings about being hurt and sad than being happy and joyful. However, their excitement and delight when they experience awe and wonder show in their faces.

Young children experience awe and wonder at beauty, power, magnificence, surprises, newness, uniqueness, intricacy, complexity, order, terror, and the mystery of nature and the universe as well as human achievements and creations. As contemporary theologian Harvey Cox says, "awe is a basic and nearly universal human emotion." Picture several children ages three and five playing outside. A beautiful butterfly causes wonder. Flying birds create awe. Gorgeous flowers amaze. A baby duck enchants. The smell of grass and leaves is sweet. The colors of a stone intrigue. The feel of the sun and breeze brings joy. A dog makes them want to play. Often when they watch an insect or lizard, they are excited and curious so they study it. Happily, they run from one wonderful, awe-inspiring thing to another. Their faces express delight and joy. Their experiences in nature make them feel alive and expansive. Being outdoors is life-enhancing.[1]

Children are not only amazed at nature, but also at the universe. Awe strikes them as they stare at the ocean's waves crashing on shore and its magnificent blue color with the sun making it sparkle. Wonder arises when they view the vastness of the universe, the spectacular multitude of stars, a shooting comet, the snowy peaks of mountains, and the depth of the Amazon forest. They are not only overwhelmed by nature and the universe, but also human accomplishments and creations. Visualize girls' and boys' astonishment when they watch a ballet dancer leaping, a baseball player hitting a home run, a figure skater doing a triple jump, and a tennis player smashing a serve at 135 mph. Envision their thrill at seeing a fire truck speed to its destination, a plane taking off, and an astronauts' space ship roaring into space.

When the scientific researcher Albert Einstein was shown a magnetic compass by his father at age five years old, he experienced awe. In his later years, he often spoke about this experience. "When I was a little boy, my father showed me a small compass, and the enormous impression that it made on me certainly played a role in my life." When he was twelve years old, he experienced wonder when he first looked into a geometry textbook.[2]

These primary experiences of awe and wonder are spiritual experiences. They are the first stage of the mystical way to the Divine. Einstein describes mysticism as being able to marvel, to wonder, and to be rapt in awe. Besides declaring that "awe is the beginning of wisdom" and that "awe precedes faith," Abraham Heschel, a twentieth-century Jewish theologian, defines mysticism as "radical amazement." Contemporary theologian Matthew Fox claims that "mysticism is awe and gratitude." Humans' mystical task is "to be radically amazed." This task "demands that we overcome the temptation to take our existence for granted. Awe is the opposite of 'taking for granted.'" Awe, wonder, and radical amazement at the magnificent universe cause us to feel passionate about it. Underhill said that experiencing beauty is "simply Reality seen with eyes of love."[3]

Contemporary spiritual teacher Eckhart Tolle explains that paying attention to a flower, a crystal, or a bird can be a spiritual experience of awe and wonder and can show you the way back to the Source, to the Divine. "When you look at it or hold it or *let it be* without imposing a word or mental label on it, a sense of awe, of wonder, arises within you. Its essence silently communicates itself to you and reflects your own essence back to you." Thus, "seeing beauty in a flower could awaken humans, however briefly, to the beauty that is an essential part of their own innermost being, their true nature." Looking with awe at the beauty of flowers is intrinsically connected to feelings of joy and love. Although we may not fully realize it, "flowers would become for us an expression in form of that which is most high, most sacred, and ultimately formless within ourselves." Flowers that are delicate, ethereal, and fleeting "would become like messengers from another realm, like a bridge" between the world of physical forms and the realm of the Spirit. "Underneath the surface appearance, everything is not only connected to everything else, but also with the Source of all life out of which it came."[4]

According to Tolle, "since time immemorial, flowers, precious stones, crystals, and birds have held special significance for the human spirit. Like all life-forms, they are, of course, temporary manifestations of the underlying One Life, One Consciousness," that are two of Tolle's many names for Ultimate Reality. Once humans are silent, still, alert, and attentive, "they can sense the Divine Life Essence, the one indwelling Consciousness or Spirit in every creature, every life-form, recognize it as One with their own essence, and so love it as themselves." Thus, "when you don't cover up the world with words and labels, a sense of the miraculous returns to your life." Many of you have lost this sense. When you again start looking deeply at the beauty, miracle, and mystery of life, "a depth returns to your life. Things regain their newness, their freshness. And the greatest miracle is the experiencing of your essential self as prior to any words, thoughts, mental labels, and images."[5]

The German scholar Rudolf Otto, the author of the 1917 classic, *The Idea of the Holy*, describes awe as a feeling that emerges in the mind of primeval people and as a "fact of our nature—primary, unique, underivable from anything else." Awe is "the basic factor and the basic impulse underlying the entire process of religious evolution." God and all the products of myth "spring from this root." The distinction between awe and other feelings is "not simply one of degree and intensity." Awe can be "so overwhelmingly great that it seems to penetrate to the very marrow." It may also come as "the gentlest of agitations, a mere fleeting shadow." There are resemblances when "the soul is merely in a state of pleasure, or joy, or aesthetic rapture, or moral exaltation, or finally in religious bliss."[6]

For Otto, a spiritual experience of awe, which he calls a 'numinous experience,' has "two qualities, the daunting and the fascinating," awful and wonderful, fearful and attracting, that "combine in a strange harmony of contrasts." The quality of awe at the mystery of life that is "uniquely attractive and fascinating" causes wonder and captivates, entrances, and transports us to dizzy heights. 'Graciousness' does not grasp "the profound element of *wonderfulness* and rapture which lies in the mysterious beatific experience of Deity."[7]

The ideas "on the rational side of this non-rational element of fascination are love, mercy, pity, comfort" in an absolute and complete way. As "important as these are for the experience of religious bliss or felicity, they do not . . . exhaust it. . . . Bliss or beatitude is more, far more, than the mere natural feeling of being comforted, of reliance, of the joy of love," no matter how enhanced and heightened. When Otto asked a Buddhist monk what Nirvana is, he answered, "Bliss—unspeakable." At its highest point, fascinating awe "becomes the 'overabounding,' 'exuberant,' and 'mystical moment.'" This unutterable experience of awe "may pass into blissful excitement, rapture, and exaltation."[8]

According to Otto, the second quality of awe is frightening and overpowering. Envision an earthquake shaking your home and damaging it, a hurricane roaring in with winds of 125 mph and flattening your home and shattering it into thousands of pieces. Now imagine what you feel when you watch a hawk flying down to pick up a baby duck, a fox killing a chick, a wolf pack running after a deer, and a killer whale chasing a seal. Picture girls and boys witnessing their parents' alcoholism and drug addiction, their father violently beating their mother, machine guns slaughtering their neighbors, bombs exploding buildings, and land mines tearing off their legs. These experiences cause Otto's second kind of awe that is frightening, daunting, fearful, awful, and overpowering. For many, these experiences produce fear, suffering, and trauma that damage their body, mind, and spirit. However, for others, suffering creates a consciousness of the inscrutable awesomeness and depth of life that leads to compassion and love for all who suffer.

Because of children's young age and lack of knowledge, the vast majority do not recognize the feeling of awe as a mystical experience. Because they do not have the language and concepts, they do not speak about their experiences of wonder as spiritual. This is not surprising, because even the most articulate adults are often unable to put their experiences of awe and their encounters with the Infinite into finite words.

However, some young children realize that their experiences are spiritual. Later in life, Mother Teresa, the twentieth-century founder of the Catholic order of religious nuns called the Missionaries of Charity, revealed that she had a religious experience on the day of her first communion. "From the age of five and half years—when I first received Him (Jesus in holy communion)—the love for souls has been within me.—It grew with the years—until I came to India—with the hope of saving many souls."[9]

Dorothy Day, who in the twentieth century co-founded the Catholic Worker movement that established many hospitality houses for the poor and homeless, described her memories of how her spiritual pilgrimage began. After admitting she did bad behaviors between ages seven and eleven, she said, "I also remember all the *wondering* I did, all the questions I had about life and God and the purpose of things." When Dorothy was a child of seven or eight years, her mother told her about the various problems in the world, including children dying because they did not have enough food. Because she was getting ready to eat a doughnut, Dorothy asked why other children didn't have doughnuts? Her mother said something like, "it's the way the world is." Her face showed that she was sad and troubled because "we keep letting such terrible injustices remain." Dorothy tried to understand why she had a doughnut and many children had no food at all. Deciding to solve the problem of world hunger on her own, she asked her mom to take her doughnut to a child whose stomach was empty. Her mother said she couldn't do that because the children didn't live nearby. That day Dorothy did not eat her doughnut. Her mother said that she kept asking her to find someone who needed her morning doughnut.[10]

When Dorothy was ten or eleven, she walked with her father past some beggars on the street. When she asked her dad if they could buy some food for them, he said no because they were in a hurry. Remembering this, she could still feel her sadness and disappointment. Later she wondered why "some people had so much and some people had so little." When she asked, her mother said that "she was sure God didn't like it, that there was injustice in the world." Later in life, Dorothy said that "in many ways I feel I'm the same person now that I was when I was a girl" of nine, ten, or eleven years. Some of the questions I asked then, "I'm still asking now."[11]

Henry Suso, a fourteenth-century German Dominican mystic, wrote that he began to communicate with God in his childhood about his yearning. "My mind has from the days of my childhood sought something with an earnest thirst of longing, Lord, . . . I have now for many a year been in hot pursuit of it, and never yet have I been able to succeed, for I know not aright what it is. And yet it is something that draws my heart and my soul after it, and without which I can never attain to full repose. Lord, I was fain in the earliest days of my childhood to seek it among created things, . . . And the more I sought, the less I found it, . . . Now my heart rages for it."[12]

Robert Coles, a child psychiatrist and psychoanalyst, spent a lifetime interviewing, studying, and writing about U.S. and foreign children. His 1990 book, *The Spiritual Life of Children*, contains captivating accounts about what children experience, feel, think, and say. "Some young people go through intense visionary moments" in which they are "looking with eager passion, toward a spiritual horizon that escaped my eyes and maybe everyone else's." Sometimes the youngsters conveyed these moments softly and concisely and other times powerfully and eloquently. These "intensely personal visionary moments" are "times when a mix of psychological surrender and philosophical transcendence offers the nearest thing to Kierkegaard's 'leap of faith.'"[13]

Coles interviewed nine-year-old Mary from Tennessee who saw a squirrel that was chasing its tail. When it perceived her, it took a nearby acorn up a tree and put it into a hole. She thought, "I might be a big person, a God, to that squirrel—and I reminded him that he should keep on track and not get caught wasting time. Maybe the Lord wants us to get down to business, like the squirrel did. We're here for something!" In Coles' reporting, children's experiences of awe often get mixed up with the lessons they learned from their parents and religious authorities. Mary also said, "I wonder every once in a while if we're the only ones who think. I guess our dog does, a little. I guess the flowers . . . don't. The trees, they don't. The ants, they don't. The birds, they might." When her kid brother was throwing rocks, she told him, "look at it from the rock's view—they don't like being thrown around and around for no reason!" While walking in the woods, she saw a squirrel staring at her and said, "maybe it's saying: hurry up and get away, so I won't be scared."[14]

Mary was concerned about a neighbor who had been in an accident. The neighbor told her dad that "he'd just as soon die now as later, because of all the pain" in his stomach and back. She thought that the funny thing was that our neighbor smiled despite his troubles. Her mom said that he was glad to see the sun rise. When Mary saw the sun come up, she was happy. She thought that "I should be double glad, . . . I love the way the whole sky becomes lit up, presto, and I don't have any pain."[15]

Spending years studying the Hopi tribe of Native Americans in New Mexico and Arizona, Coles' talk with eight-year-old Natalie about her religion illustrated how adults often take the mysteries of nature and life for granted while children look more deeply. Natalie was engrossed with the land, sky, sun, moon, and stars as well as with the flowers and animals. Once when they sat talking in front of her home, she caught sight of a pair of hawks that circled above them and she watched them carefully. Coles wanted to begin talking again and was concerned about how long they would sit with their eyes following the hawks. Unfortunately, he did not seem to realize that Natalie was having a mystical experience of awe and wonder. Finally, with ever widening sweeps, the hawks left their field of vision. Natalie said, "I guess they'll find something (to eat). I wish they were just going on a ride and not really hungry. I love when they glide, then stop, flap their wings, and continue gliding." After those words, Coles realized "how watchful she had been, how carefully heedful of details I had not noticed." Then as he prepared to ask some questions about her religious and spiritual life, she spotted the returning hawks and again watched them intensely. Having to wait again, he became impatient and irritated because he thought that she was rude. Eventually the hawks went away again and Natalie returned to Coles and their conversation.[16]

A different time when Coles asked her about who God is, Natalie answered with "the word 'Spirit,' the collective Spirit of her ancestors, the particular spirit that was hers," and the spirit of her dog Blackie. Then he asked, "what is Spirit?" Natalie stood up, took a few steps, raised her arm, and moved it around in circles. Blackie ran furiously off, stopped, ran back, and received an affectionate hug. Natalie explained that "the spirit is when you go running for someone. It is when you send signals to someone. It is when you are being as much as you can be. When Blackie ran, her spirit was there for me and you to see! When I used my arm with her, it was my spirit talking to her spirit! Every time I look into her eyes, and think of her, and all she does, and all she has been for us, I am trying to see her spirit!"[17]

Mencius, one of the greatest Confucian philosophers who was born in 370 BCE more than one hundred and fifty years after his leader, believed that people should keep their child's heart. Both Confucius and Mencius taught about the *chun-tzu*. Translations for this Chinese word include a Great man, a man of humanity, a true gentleman, a Superior man, and Manhood-at-its-best. Mencius said, "the Great man is the one who does not lose his child's heart."[18]

Some Adults Realize That Awe and Wonder Are Spiritual Experiences

Almost all children experience awe and delight in it, but most do not realize that it is a mystical experience. Besides their childhood encounters, almost all adults experience awe any number of times in their lives. Many take it for granted or ignore it. Thus, they do not acknowledge it as anything important and they do not view it as a spiritual experience. However, other adults are joyful when they experience awe. When some of them reflect on it, they recognize it as a mystical experience.

In his 1836 essay entitled "Nature," Ralph Waldo Emerson, an American transcendental philosopher, claimed that children perceive nature in a way that many adults don't. Many adults do not see nature or they see it in a very superficial way. "The sun illuminates only the eye of man, but shines into the eye and the heart of the child." The lover of nature is the one "who has retained the spirit of infancy" into adulthood. "In the presence of nature, a wild delight" runs through us. We feel exhilaration. In the woods at any age, we can become like a child again by casting off our years, as the snake removes its skin. "The simple perception of natural forms is a delight." For the mind and body, "nature is medicinal" and restorative.[19]

An animal, a tree, a mountain, or the sky gave Emerson delight and pleasure arising from the loveliness of their shape, color, and movement. As a "lover of uncontained and immortal beauty," he claimed that "the standard of beauty is the entire circuit of natural forms—the totality of nature," whose forms are "innumerable and all different." In the tranquil landscape, he found something more dear than in the villages. In the forest, he beheld something "as beautiful as his own nature." The waving branches in a storm took him by surprise, produced joy, and had an effect that is like "a higher thought or a better emotion coming over me, when I deemed I was thinking justly or doing right." Emerson felt being in nature was a spiritual experience. "Nature always wears the colors of the spirit" and is "a symbol of the spirit." However, "the beauty of nature is not ultimate. It is a herald of inward and eternal beauty." Thus, "my head . . . is uplifted into infinite space—all mean egotism vanishes. . . . I see All; the currents of the Universal Being circulate through me; I am part and parcel of God."[20]

Like children, Emerson and some of us adults experience awe at the beauty and mysteries of nature. We are amazed that some animals such as chimps use tools and that dolphins are thought to have speech and empathy. Many of us sit and contemplate lakes, rivers, and oceans. Flowing water fascinates us. A river flows on and on to the sea day and night without pause. It never ceases and never shows weariness. There is a saying that we can never step into the same river twice, because it is constantly changing. We can stand by a river and the seashore one day and when we return the next day, they are not the same. The color of the river has changed and the seashore has different deposits of sand and shells. Unlike children, when some of us adults have a feeling of wonder about nature, we realize it as a spiritual experience. Recognizing that all streams and rivers flow into the ocean, we may have an insight that all the parts of reality flow into the ONE, the Oneness, the ALL, the One Spirit, the One Ultimate Reality.

Adults' experiences of awe and wonder differ in other ways from youngsters. While both experience awe at the beauty and mystery of nature and the cosmos, we adults also feel wonder about ourselves. I am a mystery to myself. Who am I really? What is my essence? What is my human nature? Why do I behave the way I do? Why do I perform actions that I regret? Why don't I accomplish the good deeds that I want? In *Hamlet*, one of

William Shakespeare's characters says, "to thy own self be true, and it must follow as the night the day, thou cannot be false to any man." However, who is the 'I' that I must be true to? My internal self is just as mysterious as the external universe.

We adults also feel awe at other people. They are mysterious to us. Who are you? Are you a mystery to yourself? Who are these other people? Are they the same as me? Do we all possess the same human nature? Do our race and sex make us different? What causes us to be happy, cheerful, joyous, blissful, and ecstatic as well as anxious, frustrated, sad, depressed, and miserable. Our family and acquaintances can be our best friends and bring us magnificent delight and joy. In the opposite vein, they can be our abusers who disappoint us, put us down, trample on our dreams, betray our confidences, deceive us, lie about us, and abandon us when we need them. They are capable of battering us emotionally, mentally, socially, physically, sexually, and violently as well as doing the worst possible action, murdering us. In *No Exit*, French philosopher Jean Paul Sartre went so far as to say, "hell is other people." They are just as mysterious to us as ourselves.

We also ask more questions than children as we wonder about the incomprehensible universe that envelop all of us. We marvel at its spectacular beauty, tremendous complexity, magnificent order, enormous scope, and utter vastness. In fact, we ask some questions that none of us can answer. When and how did the universe start? Was there a First Cause or Creator? Was there anything before? Where does the cosmos stop? Is there anything beyond it? When will it end? Will there be anything after?

Two-thousand-five-hundred years ago Buddha demonstrated his belief in the importance of awe at nature when he gave the flower sermon. According to the story, he stood silently and held up a flower and gazed at it. Of those present, one monk smiled. It was said that besides Buddha, he was the only one who understood the sermon. The two-and-half-thousand years old Hindu scripture, the *Bhagavad Gita*, distinguishes ignorance from impure and pure knowledge. "When one sees Eternity in the things that pass away and Infinity in finite things, then one has pure knowledge. But if one merely sees the diversity of things, with their divisions and limitations, then one has impure knowledge. And if one selfishly sees a thing as if it were everything, independent of the ONE and the many, then one is in the darkness of ignorance."[21]

When Jesus' disciples asked him, "who is the greatest in the kingdom of heaven?" He answered, "unless you change and become like children, you will not enter the kingdom of heaven," the presence of God. Another time when parents brought their little children to Jesus, his disciples sternly tried to stop them. He said, "let the little children come to me, and do not stop them; for it is to such as these that the kingdom of heaven [the presence of God] belongs." Using nature to teach them, Jesus said, "therefore I tell you, do not worry about your life, what you will eat, or about your body, what you will wear. For life is more than food, and the body is more than clothing. Consider the ravens, they neither sow nor reap, they have neither storehouses nor barns, and yet God feeds them. Of how much more value are you than the birds? . . . Consider the lilies, how they grow, they neither toil nor spin, yet I tell you, not even Solomon in all his glory was clothed like one of these. But if God so clothes the grass of the field, . . . how much more will he clothe you. Do not keep striving . . . and do not keep worrying. . . . Your Father knows that you need them. Instead strive for His kingdom [His presence], and all these things will be given to you as well. . . . Sell your possessions and give alms."[22]

Francis of Assisi, a thirteen-century Italian mystic, experienced awe and wonder about everything in nature. One of his ways of expressing this was to call parts of nature "our brother" and "our sister." The wind and air were our brother, while water was our sister. He gave thanks to God for the gift of creation and "for our brother, the sun, who gives us the day and by whom Thou gives us light. He is beautiful and radiant and of great glory, and bears witness to Thee, O most High." In the thirteenth century, the Islamic Sufi mystic Jalal ad-Din Rumi, hereafter called Rumi, had spiritual experiences of awe and wonder. "The work of religion is nothing but astonishment; not the kind that comes from turning your back on God but the kind that comes from being wild with ecstasy, from being drowned in God and drunk on the Beloved." Furthermore, "gaze in wonder at the infinite rose garden, . . . don't, like the violet, always bow down to the ground. In the stream of your being runs the water of life; . . . put your trust in Him who gives life and ecstasy; don't mourn what doesn't exist, cling to what does."[23]

As an adult, Einstein realized the connection between spirituality and the experience of awe at the mysterious. "The most beautiful emotion we can experience is the mysterious. It is the fundamental emotion that stands at the cradle of all true art and science." All his scientific work was "motivated by an irresistible longing to understand the secrets of nature and by no other feelings." In addition, "everyone who is seriously involved in the pursuit of science becomes convinced that a Spirit is manifest in the laws of the universe—a Spirit vastly superior to that of man, and one in the face of which we with our modest powers must feel humble. In this way the pursuit of science leads to a religious feeling."[24]

Einstein's definition of religiousness was "to sense that behind anything that can be experienced, there is Something that our minds cannot grasp, whose beauty and sublimity reach us only indirectly." Furthermore, "my religiosity consists in a humble admiration of the infinitely superior Spirit that reveals itself in the little that we, with our weak and transitory understanding, can comprehend of reality." Einstein regretted "how much our feelings of awe before the beauty and complexity of nature have been eroded by a cool, objective science and a religion" too wedded to rigid doctrines. Not to experience awe at the beauty and mystery of nature, not to feel wonder, is to be "as good as dead."[25]

Tolle claims that many adults see only the outer physical forms of people and things and are unaware of their inner essence. Many even fail to experience awe when they see puppies, kittens, lambs, and babies. These newly born life-forms are delicate and fragile. "An innocence, sweetness, and beauty that is not of this world still shines through them." For Einstein, not to experience awe at the mystery of the universe, not to feel wonder, is to be "as good as dead." For Tolle, not to experience wonder toward "the miracle of life that continuously unfolds within and around us" is to be shallow, lifeless, and deadened.[26]

The less you look deeply, Tolle says, "the quicker you are in attaching verbal or mental labels to things, people, or situations; the more shallow and lifeless your reality becomes; and the more deadened you become to reality and the miracle of life that continuously unfolds within and around you." Labeling everything and everyone may help you navigate and fit into your in-group and culture, but you lose your creativity, aliveness, wisdom, joy, and love. Of course, you have thoughts and you need words to express them, but you do not need labels. Words can be beautiful. However, "words reduce reality to something that the human mind can grasp," which does not capture the reality. Words cannot fully understand or explain who I am, who you are, what love is, what nature is, what the universe is, who the Holy One, is.[27]

The Jesuit Catholic religious superiors claimed that Pierre de Chardin's writings contained errors of theological interpretation so they barred him from teaching or publishing his writings. Although he was deeply wounded, he submitted. However, "if I didn't write," he told a friend, "I would be a traitor." Thus, he continued to write, because he had an "absolute inability to contain my own feeling of wonderment" at beauty, treasures, and mystery. "A thought, a material improvement, a harmony, a unique nuance of human love, the enchanting complexity of a smile or a glance, all these new *beauties* that appear for the first time, in me or around me, on the human face of the earth—I cherish them like children" do. Besides the beauty, Chardin paid attention to our indebtedness to the treasures of the earth. The world "floods us with its riches—food for the body, nourishment for the eyes, harmony of sounds and fullness of the heart, unknown phenomena and new truths, all these treasures, all these stimuli, . . . cross our consciousness at every moment."[28]

Like other mystics, Chardin was astounded by the mysteries of the universe. Interested in "the unfathomable past," he was amazed at "the mystery of the first cells which were one day animated by the breath of our souls!" He was fascinated by "the profound life, the fontal life, the new-born life" and the fact that "beneath this very spectacle of the turmoil of life, there reappeared . . . the Unknown." This enigma "disguised its presence in . . . the very stuff of which the universe and my own small individuality are woven. Yet it was the same Mystery. . . . Our mind is disturbed when we try to plumb the depth of the world beneath us." For Chardin, "one of the most disturbing mysteries of the universe for both our hearts and our minds" is "the problem of evil, that is to say the reconciling of our failures . . . with creative goodness and creative power."[29]

Like Einstein and Tolle, Chardin believed that it is crucial not to be insensitive, but rather to experience wonder, to be aware, and to see in order to live our full humanity. "It is essential to see—to see things as they are and to see them really and intensely. We live at the center of a network of cosmic influences as we live at the heart of the human crowd or among the myriads of stars, without, alas, being aware of their immensity. If we wish to live our humanity . . . to the full, we must overcome that insensitivity." We can start with our own conscious life and move out from there "to consider the spread of our being. We shall be astonished at the extent and intimacy of our relationship with the universe." Chardin saw these experiences of wonder as spiritual encounters with the Sacred presence, with the Divine milieu.[30]

My interpretation of what the twentieth-century Jewish theologian Martin Buber calls the primary word *I-Thou* is an experience of awe and wonder. For all other experiences, he uses another primary word *I-It* or its alternatives, *I-He* or *I-She*. In an I-Thou experience, "I take my stand in relation," while in an I-It, "the Thou is far away." For Buber, "the primary word I-Thou can only be spoken with the whole being. The primary word I-It can never be spoken with the whole being." When the Thou meets me, "I become through my relation to the Thou, as I become I, I say Thou." When I live on the surface, I am in the realm of I-It. "The realm of Thou has a different basis." When I say Thou, I have no thing for my object. I and Thou are in relation. The three spheres in which the I-Thou relation arises are nature, people, and the Eternal. In all three spheres, "we are aware of a breath from the Eternal Thou, in each Thou we address the Eternal Thou."[31]

Many who read Buber's book are puzzled by his description of having an I-Thou relation with a tree. However, what Buber is explaining is an experience of awe at nature, in this case, a tree. When I encounter a tree as

a Thou, I become "bound up in relation to it. The tree is now no longer It." The tree "has to do with me, as I with it—only in a different way." An I-Thou relation with another person is easier to understand. When I face a person as my Thou, "he is not a thing among things and does not consist of things." He is "whole in himself, he is Thou and fills the heavens." Poems are not only made up of words or melodies of notes. This is also true of a person who is my Thou. "The Thou is more than It realizes. No deception penetrates here; here is the cradle of Real Life."[32]

For Buber, "the relation to the Thou is direct. . . . No aim, no lust, and no anticipation intervene between I and Thou." However, "every Thou in our world must become an It." The Thou becomes an object, an It, when we make people and nature into a means to an end rather than an end in themselves. "The It is the eternal chrysalis, the Thou the eternal butterfly." Tolle says that to awaken and to have experiences of awe, we need to live only in the present, in the NOW, and not in the past or future. Buber claims that in so far as a person is satisfied with things that he uses and manipulates, "he lives in the past. . . . He has nothing but objects. . . . True beings are lived in the present." In addition, "love is between I and Thou. The man who does not know this, with his very being know this, does not know love." From the one who has the smallest love to the one who loves all, "love is responsibility of an I for a Thou. . . . Relation is mutual. My Thou affects me, as I affect it." We mold our students as they influence us. "In each Thou we address the Eternal Thou."[33]

One of Buber's two primary words is an experience of awe and wonder. One of twentieth century, humanistic psychologist Erich Fromm's two words, having and being, can also be an experience of awe and wonder. Having and being are "two basic modes of existence;" "two different kinds of orientation toward self and the world;" and "two different kinds of character structure" which determine a person's feelings, thinking, and acting. Both modes of existence are part of human nature. To have is "a normal function of our life, in order to live we must have things," such as food, clothes, and shelter. We also enjoy having them. Some have more things, others less. Some own luxurious things, while others have merely enough to survive. In the having orientation, my relationship to the world is one of acquiring, possessing, and owning. "I want to make everybody and everything, including myself, my property." Not only so I desire things, but I also want to possess people. Besides my clothes and my house, my spouse and my children are my property.[34]

Fromm claims that many people feel their identity is what they have, own, and possess. Western industrial societies, including the U.S., follow the formula: what I am is "what I have." It seems that "the very essence of being is having; that if one *has* nothing, one *is* nothing." One of the reasons why individuals choose a having orientation as their primary mode of existence is that they live in a culture centered around things, rather than people. Their culture emphasizes the having orientation in which the dominant theme of life is greed for money, property, success, fame, and power. "The supreme goal is to have—and to have more and more." Focusing on having is an obstacle to being spiritual.[35]

While having is simple to understand, Fromm said that being is "more complicated and difficult." Most people know more about having than being. In our culture, having is "the more frequently experienced mode" of existence. Being is an activity, a process, an experience, and a way of relating to the world. I am, I feel, I think, I say, I act, I relate, and I love. Being can be a spiritual experience of awe and wonder as well as awakening and illumination when it is "the process of mutual alive relatedness" with another. "We both participate in the dance of life." To have is to possess. To be is to wonder, to learn, to accept, to forgive, to respect, to support, to empathize, to be thankful, "to share, to give, to sacrifice," to care, and to love. While having is possessing things, being is experiencing the depth of my existence and expressing my true, authentic, real, essential self. It is acting out my inner core of love. It is getting in touch and connect with other people and the Holy One.[36]

According to Fromm, being requires giving up our selfishness and egotism. The prerequisites for being are freedom, independence, and critical thinking. Its fundamental characteristic is "being active, not in the sense of outward activity, of busyness." Being involves inner activity, the productive use of our faculties, and the expression of our talents. It is renewing ourselves as well as growing, giving, flowing out, transcending, and loving. However, the moment I try to capture my being in thoughts and words, it is gone, it is a mere thought. "Being is indescribable in words and is communicable only by sharing my experience." The mode of being can emerge "only to the extent that we decrease the mode of having, that is of nonbeing." We need to stop using our possessions to give us our identity and security. *We are not what we have, but what we are.* Some cultures foster having which includes the greed for possessions, while other cultures promote being, wondering, awakening, sharing, caring, and loving.[37]

Juan Mascaro, a twentieth-century expert on the Hindu scriptures, used two different words to describe his two views of reality, the material and spiritual. The material view reduces all reality to matter. The brain is an incredible machine that is part of the material body. Reality is quantities that can be measured. All things eventually die and turn into dust. In contrast, the spiritual view says that reality is "a universe of eternal beauty" and "a universe of spiritual radiance from which this universe of matter is only a reflection." Reality is more than material objects. People are more than vegetable and animal life. Everything is part of "a world of Spirit."[38]

Early Indigenous Tribes Experienced Awe and Wonder

Otto describes awe as "this feeling which, emerging in the mind of primeval man," is "a fact of our nature—primary, unique, underivable from anything else." All over the world the earliest hunter-gatherer people of indigenous tribes, clans, and ethnic groups lived close to nature. Similar to children, they experienced awe and wonder at the beauty, power, magnificence, order, complexity and mystery of nature and the universe. The experience of awe could be aroused by astonishing occurrences in nature, in the animal world, and in the human world. Like children, they were radically amazed people. Unlike children, they realized that their experiences of awe and wonder were spiritual.[39]

According to Otto, awe is "the basic factor and the basic impulse underlying the entire process of religious evolution." God and all the products of myth "spring from this root." In awe, "there is something non-natural or supernatural." At the earliest level of spiritual development, the essential characteristic was an experience of awe "before something 'Wholly Other,'" whether It was called Spirit or God or It was without any name. Awe showed itself in the "first crude, primitive forms" of early religions and formed "the starting point for the entire religious development in history." The first images were "later overborne and ousted by more highly developed forms."[40]

After "a moment of deeply-felt religious experience" of awe, Otto said that "feelings of gratitude, trust, love, reliance, humble submission, and dedication" do not exhaust the content of that experience. "Spirit, reason, purpose, good will, supreme power, unity, selfhood" do not totally capture the Reality of God. These rational attributes are far from giving a complete picture. As "the mother of rationalism," orthodoxy and its doctrines cannot do justice to the non-rational aspect of Deity. Orthodox Christianity gives the idea of the Holy "a one-sidedly intellectualistic and rationalistic interpretation." This rational bias also prevails in discussing early religions, mythology, and comparative religion. The Divine is not exclusively contained in rational statements.[41]

Geoffrey Parrinder, a contemporary scholar of African and world religions, says that religion has been "a universal, social phenomenon" from the earliest times until today. Around the world at all stages of prehistory and history, humans have expressed their deepest understandings about life and the cosmos through their religious beliefs, rituals, symbols, arts, ethics, and community. African scholar Robert Fisher says that from ancient times, "religion has been inextricably woven into the fabric of sub-Saharan African life." Many African, Native American, and other traditional religions continue today.[42]

Some scholars call these early religions traditional, tribal, indigenous, or folk. Others refer to them as primitive, while still others say they are undeveloped, backward, uncivilized, and even savage. Today some still view these religions and their continuations as inferior to the historical world religions. In contrast, many scholars disagree. Contemporary scholar Thom Hartmann claims that these religions "have important lessons to teach us. Indeed, they may well be the lessons that will save our world."[43]

The experiences of awe at nature that caused the earliest peoples throughout the world to produce their traditional religions also led them to develop other foundational concepts and traits, including spiritual and ethical ones. Hartmann claims that because the indigenous tribes, clans, and ethnic groups lived close to nature, they took as "their most foundational concept" the belief that we are not different or separate from nature. We are not superior or inferior to the natural world. "We are part of it. Whatever we do to nature, we do to ourselves. Whatever we do to ourselves, we do to the world. For most, there is no concept of a separate 'nature'; it's all us and we're all it." In the Native Americans' worldview, "we are part of the world" and we are "made of the same flesh as the other animals. . . . It is our destiny to cooperate with the rest of creation. Every life form has its special purpose" in the ecosystem. "All are to be respected. Each animal and plant has its own unique intelligence and spirit. . . . All life is absolutely as Sacred as is human life." The distinction between 'Sacred' and 'not sacred' "does not exist." Sacred life is "at the very core of all existence."[44]

According to Hartmann, each indigenous tribe was "a politically independent unity." Each had a sense of its own identity, so it did not try to recruit new members. The tribe was egalitarian; everyone, including the leaders, was equal to everybody else. Leadership was "an advisory role, not an authoritarian one." With the leaders being changed often, they had an obligation to serve the people, not to dominate them. Using local and renewable resources, tribal members took only what they needed and nothing else. They had respect for other people and tribes. All over the world, tribes of "all races on all the continents—lived like this . . . for 40, 000 to 200,000 years." The remnants of these indigenous tribal peoples still exist today, such as the Laplander of Europe, the Kogi of South America, the Ik of Africa, and the Navajo of North America. About one to two percent of the world's population still live the way they did over 100,000 years ago.[45]

Hartmann compares "the prime differences" between the tribal and modern ways of life. "The 'primitive' people generally have more leisurely lives, less poverty, almost no crime . . . , a more diverse and healthy diet, less degenerative disease, better psychological health, and a culture that holds as its primary values cooperation (rather than competition), mutual respect (rather than domination), long-term renewable care for resources (rather than exploitation for a quick buck), and equality between people, between the sexes, and between humans and nature (rather than power)."[46] [The early indigenous religions will be discussed again in a later stage.]

Artists Experience Awe and Wonder

Poets, writers, painters, dancers, musicians, composers, and all artists have experiences and sensations of wonder and awe similar to children. As Underhill said, "these persons prejudge nothing, criticize nothing. . . . They live a life in which the emphasis lies on sensation rather than thought." Trusting their senses, they live in a "state of pure receptivity" of the essence of things. While many adults ignore their senses and don't look deeply, artists and mystics have enhanced capacities for truly seeing, touching, tasting, smelling, hearing, feeling, and intuiting. With their simple, deep, direct apprehension of the world, their experiences, feelings, and intuitions are not distorted by their thoughts. The greater the artists and mystics, the deeper the range of their senses, the stronger their feelings, the clearer their intuitions, the sharper their awareness of the loveliness of life, the richer their appreciation of beauty and truth, the greater their experiences of awe and wonder. Mystics and artists always want to dig deeper into the universe to expand their perceptions, until they unite with the whole of Reality.[47]

Artists continually attempt to express in their art what they see, feel, and experience in their spirit. To do this, their emphasis is on their immediate perceptions, because they live in the here and now, not in the past or future. Accepting the messages of the universe that pour into their soul, artists do not concern themselves with interpreting them. They try to create a new reality and escape from the materialistic world where everything is labeled, categorized, commercialized, and sold. Their perceptive eyes and ears help them practice a passionate contemplation of ideal beauty, free from all the meanings that the world imposes. Artists experience the living reality of a person, an animal, a forest, a field, a mountain, and a lake without criticism, without their filtering mind processing it, and with a sense of awe that allows no analysis. They appreciate the unimaginable beauty of every colorful flower, bird singing, horse running as well as the softness of a kitty's fur, the exquisite beauty of a person's body, the smell of turkey cooking, and the pleasurable taste of chocolate. Music touches their souls. These simple but profound experiences amaze and astonish.[48]

For Buber, the I-Thou relation is "the eternal source of art." When an artist views a form, "I behold it, splendid in the radiance of what confronts me, . . . I do not behold it as a thing," but as a Thou. "It affects me, as I affect it." He does not describe the form, but stands in relation to it and tries to express it. When he speaks the primary word I-Thou with his whole being, "then the effective power streams out, and the work arises." The artist gives himself totally and withholds nothing of himself. However, the work of art that he produces is a thing among things. Sometimes a receptive beholder faces it as a Thou, while other times an artistic work "enters the world of things, there to be endlessly active, endlessly to become It, but also endlessly to become Thou again, inspiring and blessing."[49]

Searching for the heart of all things, artists and mystics encounter the richness of the expansive universe rather than allowing themselves to be limited by the views of conventional society that fits everything into a narrow box. They love the ideal, the truth, the goodness, and the beauty that their souls see. Then they express it through their various mediums in color, sound, music, movement, and words. Consciously or unconsciously, many tend to move from the artistic to the mystical state. As Underhill said, "the life of pure sensation is the meat and drink of poetry" and art. It is also one of the avenues to mystical union with the Holy One. Both artists and mystics want to encounter the truth and bring it to people. William Blake, the eighteenth-century English poet, expressed his mystical experience of awe.

> To see a World in a grain of sand,
> And Heaven in a wild flower,
> Hold infinity in the palm of your hand,
> And Eternity in an hour.[50]

In her novel, the *Color Purple*, in a conversation between two poor African American women named Shug and Celie, contemporary feminist Alice Walker writes what Shug says about feeling awe, experiencing awakening, finding God, and describing the Divine. Even though Shug calls herself a sinner, she says, "God loves me." After saying, "God ain't a He or a She, but a It," she states that "God is inside you and inside everybody else. . . . But only them that search for It inside, find It. And sometimes It just manifests Itself even if you are not looking, or don't know what you looking for. Trouble do It for most folks. . . . Sorrow. Feeling like shit."[51]

When Celie asks what God looks like, Shug answers, "don't look like nothing. . . . It ain't something you can look at apart from anything else, including yourself. I believe God is everything.... Everything that is or ever was or ever will be. And when you can feel that, and be happy to feel that, you've found It." God made everything. "God love everything you love—and a mess of stuff you don't." God wants "to share a good thing. I think it pisses God off if you walk by the color purple in a field somewhere and don't notice it." God is "always making little surprises and springing them on us when us least expect.... Everything wants to be loved. Us sing and dance, make faces and give flower bouquets, trying to be loved. You ever notice that trees do everything to get attention we do, except walk?"[52]

Celie admits that she is busy "trying to chase that old white man out of my head. I been so busy thinking about him I never truly notice nothing God make. Not a blade of corn (how It do that?), not the color purple (where it come from?). Not the little wildflowers. Nothing." Celie realizes that "next to any little scrub of a bush in my yard," her man's evil shrinks, although not altogether. As Shug says, "you have to get man off your eyeball, before you can see anything a'tall. Man corrupts everything. He on your box of grits, in your head, and all over the radio. He try to make you think he everywhere. Soon as you think he everywhere, you think he God. But he ain't. Whenever you trying to pray, and man plop himself" there, tell him to get lost. "Conjure up flowers, wind, water, a big rock."[53]

An African proverb says that "no one teaches a child about God." The English author Aldous Huxley says that children have mystical experiences. "Strange openings and theophanies are granted to quite small children, who are often profoundly and permanently affected by these experiences." Unfortunately, Huxley claims that in the modern world, "the child tends to grow out of his direct awareness of the one Ground of things; for the habit of analytical thought is fatal to the intuition of integral thinking."[54]

In contrast, the contemporary author Robert Fulghum explains many of the lessons that children learn from awe and wonder. "All I really need to know about how to live and what to do and how to be I learned in kindergarten." Wisdom is not learned in graduate school, but in a children's sand pile. The lessons you learned in childhood from your experiences of awe include the importance of looking and being aware of wonder. "Share everything. Play fair. Don't hit people. Put things back where you found them. Clean up your own mess. Don't take things that aren't yours. Say you're sorry when you hurt somebody.... Live a balanced life—learn some and think some and draw and paint and sing and dance and play and work every day some. When you are out in the world, watch out for traffic, hold hands, and stick together. Be aware of *wonder*." Be sure to "remember the little seed. ... The roots go down and the plant goes up and nobody really knows how or why, but we are like that. Goldfish and hamsters and white mice ... they all die. So do we. And remember the Dick and Jane books and the first word you learned—the biggest word of all—*LOOK*." Wonder. Somewhere in these lessons is all you need to know. "The Golden Rule and love. . . .. Ecology and politics and equality and sane living." And awe and wonder.[55]

Before going to the second stage on the mystical way, some fundamental questions about spirituality will be discussed in the second chapter. Then in third chapter, other mystics' stages on the spiritual path will be offered for comparison before continuing with the second stage in the fourth chapter.

Chapter 2

Do We All Have a Spiritual Path?

What Is the Source of Our Spirituality?

Do we all have a spirit? If so, what is our spirit? What is the source of our spirituality?

Is our spirit the source? These are debatable questions. My answer is that all of us have a spirit that is the source of our spirituality. What finally convinced me that we all have a spirit was my mother's death. After my father's death at the young age of 54, I thought and strongly believed that the only way my dad lived after death was in the memories of those who loved him on earth. My mom lived much longer to age 70. After surgery to remove cancer from her lungs, she suffered a stroke in the recovery room. The doctor said that she had only three months to live. The left side of her brain was so damaged by the stroke that she was paralyzed on her right side. She could not use her right arm or hand, could not walk or talk. Later she had excruciating pain when the cancer spread to her brain. For over three years she lived. Her spirit kept her alive so that she could watch her youngest daughter be married. With all her daughters at her bedside, she died. Then I realized that her spirit that had struggled so valiantly for years against the stroke and brain cancer could not keep her frail body alive any longer. Her physical body died, but her spirit continued to live and still continues to live today decades after her death.

It is not controversial to say that as infants, we humans begin to develop physically, emotionally, socially, and mentally. Despite the fact that it is controversial and many deny it, I think all of us are born with a spirit that is the source of our spirituality. We are all innately spiritual. As the years pass, our bodies grow, our emotions evolve, our social skills increase, our knowledge expands, and our spiritual abilities mature. However, our growth in all these areas can be interrupted by obstacles. Natural disasters such as tornados and hurricanes as well as human-made tragedies such as poverty, violence, and war can cause trauma. In addition, physical, psychological, social, and sexual abuse can stunt our development. Unfortunately, these disasters and tragedies are extremely widespread. Yet another obstacle is that some authoritarian leaders exist in all religions. They often inhibit our spiritual development by requiring strict, rigid, unquestioning, blind obedience to beliefs and practices. Because of this, while our bodies, emotions, mental abilities, and social skills continue to mature as we move from elementary school into high school and beyond, our spirituality often remains at a grade school level. Knowing and working through the six stages on the spiritual path can help all of us progress to deeper levels.

Many people live on a superficial level when they worry about their possessions, their looks, their status, their money, their power, and their success. They are mainly concerned with what they have; how they look; what pleasure and fun they enjoy; and how much wealth, influence, and success they have. In contrast, spiritual people care about what they are. Meister Eckhart, a fourteenth-century German Dominican priest said, "for the just person, to act justly is to live; justice is her life; her being alive." She is "alive to the extent that she is just." His conclusion was that "people ought to think less about what they should do and more about what they are." We need to concentrate less on our possessions, appearance, money, power, and success, and more on what we are. If we are just, then our deeds will be just. If we are peaceful, then our activities will be peaceful. If we are loving, then our thoughts, words, and actions will be loving.[56]

Besides being born with a spirit, we are all born with an inner core of love. Benjamin Spock, a twentieth-century pediatrician and author, described the core of a three-month-old infant as "loving and sociable." All of us are innately loving. That is the reason why we all need and want to love and be loved. On our death bed, we won't be sorry that we did not buy a bigger car or house, but we will regret that we didn't express more love to our family and friends and perhaps beyond them. Not only do scholars offer multiple definitions of love, but we all have our own ideas. Think about love. How important is it to you? Have you ever thought about what love is and how loving you are to the people in your life? In my definition, love is our creative life force, dynamic power, vital energy, passionate soul, and our vibrant spirit. Thus, our loving inner core can also be called our vibrant spirit, passionate soul, vital energy, dynamic power, and our creative life force. All these words are interchangeable phrases for the same reality, our spirit.[57]

We can become conscious of our spirit, but not through the five senses. We can become aware of our soul, but not through our physical abilities. We can experience the wind, but we cannot see it. Like the wind, we can experience our spirit, although we cannot see it. When we search within ourselves and recognize that our spirit is the very substance and essence of our being, we are able to become aware of the Sacred Spirit within us. When we get in touch with our loving inner core, we can become conscious of Infinite Love within us. When we dive into the depths of our soul, we can become cognizant of the Universal Soul within us. We humans are both physical and spiritual beings. More specifically, we are spirits. Our spirits are the Sacred Spirit within us. We are spirits with physical bodies more than we are physical beings with a spiritual dimension.

Our spirit, our loving inner core, our soul, and our creative life force are the Divine dwelling within us. They are the heart of our human nature, the essence of our existence, and the depth of our being. They are the source of our spiritual life. They give us our spiritual awareness and our cosmic consciousness. Our spirit causes us as children and adults to experience awe and wonder, the first stage and the beginning of our journey on the spiritual path. As we mature, our soul is the origin of our progress through the stages on the mystic way.

Contemporary spiritual teacher Eckhart Tolle says, "there is an eternal, ever-present One Life beyond the myriad forms that are subject to birth and death." While some use the word God, he says that this One Life, this Being, is "immediately accessible to you as the feeling of your own presence." It is beyond and also deep within you as your true nature, your essence, your own deepest self. "Being is not only beyond but also deep within every form as its inmost invisible and indestructible essence." Never can you understand Being mentally. It can only be known and felt when your mind is still, when you are fully present in the moment, in the NOW. When you quiet your incessant mental noise, you find "the realm of inner stillness that is inseparable from Being. . . . underneath the level of physical appearances and separate forms, you are One with All that is." When your actions come out of present moment awareness, "what you do becomes imbued with a sense of quality, care, and love—even the most simple actions."[58]

The English scholar Evelyn Underhill equated the words 'soul' and 'spirit.' Innate within us all, the soul is "the immortal spirit and incorruptible substance" that is its "perfect principle" and highest virtue. It is "the spark of Divine desire, the 'tendency to the Absolute,'" that only finds "satisfaction and true life when united with this Life of God." The spirit is "the eternal spark" and "seed of absolute perfection" that lies in "the deep levels where it sustains and guides our normal existence." The soul is "the holy Dweller in the Innermost, the immanent spark," and the bridge between us and God.[59]

In addition, Underhill asserted that the spirit is the innate "germ of the Transcendent Life . . . latent in all of us, an integral part of our humanity." It has "a capacity for Eternal Life." Bringing the lowest to the highest, the soul is "transmuting the natural to the Supernatural, operating the 'New Birth.'" It is "the Principle of Life" as well as "God's immediate presence in the human heart." The spirit is "Divine Love immanent in the heart" that spurs us on to love and "to union with the Transcendent and Absolute Light." As "the Fount and Source of all true Life," the soul is "the Transcendental aspect of the self which is in contact with God." It is "the union of human and Divine, . . . 'enough to be God and enough to be me.'"[60]

Otto said that the soul is "the ultimate and highest part of our nature" that lies hidden "above and beyond our rational being." Our soul "can find no satisfaction in the mere allaying of the needs of our sensuous, psychical, or intellectual impulses and cravings." As "the Divine image" in humans, the spirit "does not merely consist in the fact that he is reasonable, moral, intelligent, and a person, but primarily in the fact that in its profoundest depths . . . the soul is mystery and marvel." In addition, "what is true of the Divine is true also of its counterpart in the creature—soul and spirit." Since the Holy is incomprehensible, so also is the spirit. "The soul and its bottommost depth lie hidden away, ineffable as God." Our spirit is beyond our understanding and it is "an exact resemblance" to the Divine, "representing by its own unfathomableness the incomprehensible Being of God." Our soul is "properly the thing of marvel and stupefaction, quite undefinable, outsoaring all conceptions 'wholly alien' to our understanding." Insight into "the inmost marvel of the soul . . . comes in an experience as an uprush, an irruption, a burst of illumination, like a flash." To experience the Holy, "this spirit, this inborn capacity to receive and understand, is the essential thing."[61]

In her book *Revelations of Divine Love*, Julian of Norwich, a fifteenth-century English mystic, wrote about humans' "twofold nature." Our sensuality is the "lower part of human nature." Our soul, our substance, "our essential being," and "our natural goodness" are our higher part that is "united with God, peaceful, joyful, and blessed." Our essential nature was made by God "so noble and rich that we always work in His will and for His honor." We do not fail when we are in our essential nature, "it is in the realm of our sensuality that we fail."[62]

Catherine of Genoa, a sixteenth-century Italian mystic, said that the soul is created pure, simple, clean, and unstained as well as endowed with a "capacity for the Infinite" and "a certain natural instinct within it that makes it turn to God." The soul's instinct for God has real power. "There is nothing stronger than the instinct of the soul for God when nothing obstructs it, no force that can surpass it." Nothing on earth fulfills the soul. "Because of its capacity for the Infinite, the soul could not satisfy itself with earthly things; and the more it strained to do so, the further it moved away from the peace and rest that is God. . . . Nowhere on earth did it find what it sought and that impossibility was the ordinance of God." Close to its first creation, the soul's "instinct for beatitude asserts itself with such impetus and fiery charity that any impediment becomes unbearable. The more the soul is aware of that impediment, the greater its suffering." When the soul loses itself in earthly things and moves further away from God, its unhappiness grows proportionately. It sighs with longing because it loses sight of what it seeks. What its natural instinct seeks is "God, who is all good."[63]

Gandhi, the Hindu political activist and mystic, used several different phrases to describe our soul: the Spirit within us, our inherent goodness, our inner basic nature, "the Godliness of human nature," the God within us, "the Divine powers within us," the imperishable *Atman*, "the still small voice" within us, and the Truth which resides in our heart. "The soul is imperishable, changeless, eternal," and omnipresent. "The force of love is the same as the force of the soul or truth." Having "faith in the inherent goodness of human nature," Gandhi said, "I must not suppress that voice within, call it conscience, call it the prompting of my inner basic nature. There is something within me impelling me to cry out my agony. . . . That something in me which never deceives me tells me now: 'you have to stand against the whole world although you may have to stand alone. . . . Do not fear. Trust that little thing in you which resides in the heart.'" Then "we can all become messengers of God."[64]

What Does It Mean to Be Spiritual and To Be a Mystic?

All of us can probably agree that all humans are born with physical, emotional, mental, and social abilities. Although many deny it, others believe that we are also born with spiritual capacities. Those who deny this think that there is only one reality, the material world. This physical dimension is our everyday life; our normal, finite reality and natural existence; the plane of time and space; the world of ordinary people, things, and living creatures.

Hindus call this *maya*, Christians the world, and Buddhist *samsara*. This realm is accessible to us through our five senses.

However, in childhood, many of us experience awe and wonder at the beauty, magnificence, complexity, order, diversity, uniqueness, and mystery of life. Although youngsters usually do not realize it, awe and wonder are the first stage on the spiritual path. When some of us adults experience awe and wonder, we become awakened to something beyond the physical reality. We begin to get in touch with the Divine dwelling within us and outside of us. Then we realize that we are spiritual and perhaps that we are mystics.

Meister Eckhart, the fourteenth-century German Dominican priest, said that being a mystic involves "unself-consciousness." Children have this quality in abundance as long as their parents allow them to be children and do not try to force them to be little adults. Matthew Fox, a contemporary author, defines mystics as being in touch with the Divine, with Being, with the Depth of Existence. "All children are mystics" and "a mystic is a child at play—the mystic within us is the child within us." Furthermore, "a basic teaching of all the creation mystical traditions is this: everyone is a mystic." Thus, mystics are not an elite group of spiritual people. All of us are mystics because we are all born to be in touch with our true self and with the Ultimate Reality. The mystic lying within each of us is just waiting to be awakened.[65]

Our spiritual experiences make it possible for us to strip away the visible façade of reality and see the hidden truth, to go below the surface and experience the awe-inspiring Ultimate Reality. Our spirituality is our mystical consciousness of the Divine within the human, the Holy within the worldly, the Infinite within the finite, the ONE within the many, the Absolute within creation, and the Sacred Spirit within all of life. When we look into the depth of ourselves, other people and the universe, we see the Divine shining through. Our mystical consciousness beholds the luminous splendor of ineffable Goodness and Infinite Love radiating out of all people's hearts and out of the center of the universe.

Spirituality exists outside of religion as well as within it. Mystics are in touch with the spiritual realm that is present at all times, in all places, and in all of creation. The spiritual dimension is the presence of the Divine, Sacred Spirit, Higher Power, Universal Soul, Infinite Love, Ultimate Reality, Being, Eternal Life, and the Holy One within everything. Jews and Christians call the Divine the one God, Muslims Allah, Buddhists Nirvana, Taoists the Tao, and Hindus Brahman and also "*Sat, Cit, Ananda,*" that is translated as "Being, Consciousness, and Joy" or as Existence, Knowledge, and Bliss. The spiritual realm is not available to us through our five senses.

Spiritual persons experience both the temporal and Eternal planes, the physical and Sacred worlds, the natural and Divine existence, becoming and Being, the individual soul and the Universal Soul, finite and Infinite Love, the many and the ONE. Although there are two dimensions of reality, they are not actually two totally different spheres. The two realms are not sealed off from each other. The line between them is not solid and unbreachable. The spiritual realm is not separate from the physical world, but rather it is the hidden dimension within it. The Sacred Spirit is within our spirit. Infinite Love is within us as our inner core of love. The Universal Soul is not divorced from but inseparably connected to our soul. An image of Infinite Love within our inner core is like the mechanism within a light bulb. As the mechanism is the source of light and electricity, so Infinite Love is the source of our life and love. Underhill said that when mystics are asked which dimension of reality is central to their lives, the life of the senses or the life of the Spirit, "mystics, one and all," answer the life of the Spirit.[66]

Underhill described two aspects of being spiritual. "Two forces, the desire to know more and the desire to love more, are ceaselessly at work" within all of us. We try to realize these two desires in all parts of our lives. When we fulfill them, we become mystics. When we hunger for the Divine and struggle to escape the bondage of the material world, we attain union with the Sacred Spirit. Our transition from the world of the senses to the world of the Holy One requires effort, work, stillness, and contemplation. Our business is to get rid of our self-centeredness and become focused on the ONE. When we embrace the Ultimate Reality, our substance and true being are "penetrated by the Divine Life which constitutes the underlying reality of all things." When we experience the Sacred Spirit within everyone and everything, we want to express our universal love.[67]

According to Underhill, while philosophers know by reason, mystics "have perfected that method of intuition, that knowledge by union." For the philosopher, the Absolute is unattainable and impersonal. For mystics, the Holy One is alive, attainable, and lovable. Mystics are "pathfinders of the Spirit," pioneers, adventurers, pilgrims, voyagers, journeyers on the pathway, spiritual geniuses, and "the true lovers of the Absolute." They are "heroic examples of the life of the Spirit; as the great artists, the great discoverers, are heroic examples of the life of beauty and the life of truth." These mystics, these spiritual experts, are "ministers of Goodness, Truth, and Beauty who go up and down between the Transcendent and apparent world." They make the Sacred Spirit the center of their life and they are "putting on Divine humanity."[68]

Underhill's definition is that "*mysticism is the art of union with Reality*," with God. "*The mystic is a person who has attained that union in greater or less degree; or who aims at and believes in such attainment."* Mystics "participate here and now in the real and Eternal Life" in the deepest way. A spiritual encounter is "the fullest all-round experience" of the Transcendent that humans can attain. The mark of the mystic is "this all-round expansion of consciousness, with its dual power of knowing by communion the temporal and Eternal, immanent and Transcendent aspects of reality." Thus, "if this transcendence is the highest destiny of the (human) race, mysticism becomes the crown of man's ascent towards Reality; the orderly completion of the universal plan." This in turn results in the desire to express love. The spiritual experience of the Holy One is "an organic process which involves the perfect consummation of the love for God." The Unitive Life is "the complete and conscious fulfillment here and now of this Perfect Love."[69]

After calling mystics "the poets of the soul" and spiritual geniuses, Fox says that they are "keen on the *experience* of the Divine and will not settle for theory alone or knowing *about* the Divine." Kabir, a fifteenth-century Indian mystic, exclaimed, "I say only what I have seen with my own eyes—and you keep quoting the scriptures!" In addition, "experience, O seeker, is the essence of all things." Mystics must experience the Infinite One for themselves, no one can experience It on their behalf.[70]

While many people live on a superficial level, mystics move beyond this when they experience the deepest levels of the Divine, of Being. According to Fox, mystics are "about being-with-Being: being-with-Being in silence, in experience, in awe, in connection-making, in nondualism, but also about being with suffering beings, with the victims of self-hate and oppression." Several weeks into the Montgomery bus boycott, Martin Luther King, Jr., received several phone calls that threatened his family. As he thought about his children and his loyal wife, he said, "I discovered that religion had to become real to me, and I had to know God for myself." Then he prayed out loud. "I'm faltering. I'm losing my courage." At that moment he heard an inner voice say to him, "stand up for righteousness. Stand up for justice. Stand up for truth. And I will be with you, even until the end of the world."[71]

Around a hundred years ago, cosmic consciousness struck Richard Bucke, a psychiatrist, in "one momentary lightning-flash of Brahmic splendor" that ever after brightened his life. It created "a sense of exultation, of immense joyousness, . . . and an illumination of 'Brahmic bliss.'" This caused a transformation of his consciousness so that he realized that "the cosmos is not dead matter but a living Presence," the human soul is immortal, "the universe is so built and ordered that . . . all things work together for the good of all." In addition, "the happiness of everyone is in the long run absolutely certain." Love is "the foundation principle of the world."[72]

Sarvepalli Radhakrishnan, a twentieth-century Hindu sage, states that the normal condition of humanity is a conscious separation from the Holy One. Then a sudden flame of supreme awareness resulted in his vision and intimately felt presence of union with the Absolute. His whole being was "ablaze with purpose." His union with the Sacred Spirit brought "rapture beyond joy, knowledge beyond reason, a sensation more intense than that of life itself, infinite in peace and harmony."[73]

Does the Divine Exist or Is There Absolutely No God?

One of the commonly used definitions of spirituality says that it is an experience of the Holy One. Thus, before continuing, a basic question needs to be asked: does the Sacred Spirit actually exist or is there absolutely NO God? Our search for the ONE is more essential than our ideas about It. As Toni Morrison, the Nobel Prize winner in literature, said, "the search is always more important than the conclusion." Mahatma Gandhi said that joy comes in the struggle, not in the victory. Our happiness and ecstasy come when we make an effort to search for and experience Infinite Love.[74]

While my belief in the Sacred Spirit is lifelong, I freely admit that I could be totally wrong. It is possible that there is no Ultimate Reality. Most certainly God as an old man with a long white beard sitting on a cloud does not exist. A number of other images of God can also be easily denied. Although I have had serious doubts at different times in my life and it is possible that there is no Holy One, I nevertheless strongly believe in the Divine. What mainly convinces me is that a Creator must have crafted this magnificent universe with all its spectacular beauty, its exquisite complexity, its superb order, its incredible diversity, its growing consciousness, its talented inventors and brilliant geniuses in many disciplines, its loving people, and its spiritual and moral giants. This indescribable, incredible, indefinable, ineffable Infinite Creator is vastly beyond anything out finite minds can imagine, think, and envision. Therefore, we use a multitude of concepts to help us understand.

However, it must be acknowledged that although many including myself believe that the Holy One exists, no one knows for sure. Multiple scholars, scientists, and people in many countries say there is NO God. There is only one reality, the material world. One of my replies is that I believe in the existence of beauty, understanding, knowledge, truth, wisdom, fairness, justice, equality, freedom, forgiveness, thankfulness, trust, goodness, empathy, caring, compassion, and love. These are not physical realities that are measurable, touchable, material things, but rather these are spiritual realities. All of us reside in a physical world, but we also live in a spiritual world. We all have our own unique spiritual path, even a young man who shot and killed twenty small American children at their school, even a suicide bomber, and even Adolf Hitler.

It is crucial to say that we can all be good, moral, and loving without being spiritual, without belonging to any religion, without believing in the Holy One, and without being aware of our own mystical path. Many people are totally unconnected to spirituality or religion and still live caring, ethical, compassionate, loving lives.

What Is the Essence of the Divine?

For decades, an assignment I gave in my university religion classes was to write a description of your own concept of God, Goddess, Divine, Higher Power, Allah, Brahman, Nirvana, Tao, or whatever you called It. If you were an atheist, this was an easy assignment. All my believing students found it extremely difficult. Try it.

Discussing the essence of the Sacred Spirit is enormously problematic. Over 700 years ago, Jalal-id-Din Rumi, an Islamic mystic, asked people to describe God or Allah (the Arabic word for the Divine) and he used an elephant as a symbol for God. In a shed where it was too dark to see, people had to feel an elephant to understand what it was like. Touching the elephant's trunk, one said it was like a water pipe. Feeling its side, another asserted it was like a wall. Grasping its leg, the last stated it was like a pillar. All their answers were accurate, but only partially accurate. Like the people in the shed, our ideas about the Holy One depend on how we personally experience the Divine. Our images contain only extremely limited, partial truth.

As we begin to search for the essence of the Ultimate Reality, it is crucial to acknowledge that the Divine is INFINITE. We humans are finite. Our finite capacities cannot succeed in grasping the Infinite. The Infinite is so far beyond our finite minds that it is impossible for us to even imagine. Attempting to describe the Infinite with our finite intelligence is like trying to put the ocean in a tea cup or attempting to lasso the wind. No finite ideas or images adequately describe the Infinite Reality.

The Ultimate Reality is an Ineffable, Invisible, Infinite Mystery. As visible, finite mysteries, we are out of our depth when we discuss this Mystery, even though we help manifest It. Saying the Divine is a Mystery is not a cop-out that tries to evade the troublesome, difficult task of attempting to explain it, but rather it is an indication of the immensity of the undertaking. Some say the Sacred Spirit is incomprehensible to us. Our finite abilities are totally unable to envision It. This Mystery is not actually incomprehensible, but rather infinitely comprehensible. The Holy One gives us our minds and expects us to use them to ask questions and search for answers in order to understand our world. Where do we come from? Is there a Creator? If so, what or who is this Creator? Why are we here? What is our purpose? What is the meaning of life? Where do we go after we die? Furthermore, we need to ask ourselves many more questions, including whether our yearning for the Holy One is simply an attempt to deal with our fear of death? Thus, we need to think deeply about the nature of ourselves, other people, all of creation, and the Divine, even though we know our answers are not adequate.

Because our finite minds are so limited, it seems that our attempts to describe the Infinite are just speculations. All images of God are symbols, metaphors, analogies. Thus, they are only partially true and cannot be taken literally. When we try to depict the Ultimate Reality, we often minimize It and make It finite. Our images diminish the Divine. Even the Jewish and Christian Bible, the Muslim *Quran*, and the Hindu *Upanishads* with all their spiritual wisdom reduce the magnificence, majesty, and greatness as well as the infinite goodness and love of the Holy One. They do what many of their readers have done throughout history, they humanize the Sacred Spirit. We need to try to stop reducing the Divine to human dimensions.

After acknowledging the severe limits on all our concepts, we need to think about what are the most meaningful images of the Ultimate Reality for you and me? My own are that the Divine is INFINITE, the Creator, the Sacred Spirit, the Holy One, the ONE, and Infinite Love. Since one of my most meaningful images is Infinite Love, my own definition of love leads me to more images. Love is our creative life force, dynamic power, vital energy, passionate soul, and vibrant spirit. Thus, Infinite Love is the Creative Life Force, Infinite Power, Divine Energy, Universal Soul, and Sacred Spirit. Nevertheless, like beautiful music, God is ineffable, indescribable, and inexplicable.[75]

In his book, *The Idea of the Holy*, Otto called God the Holy, the 'Wholly Other,' the *Numen*, '*Mysterium Tremendum*,' and "a Mystery inexpressible and above all." God cannot be rationalized or defined. It can only be felt and experienced as well as grasped and glimpsed by inadequate intuitions. The idea of God cannot "be taught, it can only be evoked, awakened in the mind; as everything that comes 'of the spirit' must be awakened." It "can only be induced, incited, and aroused." The sublime is "the most effective means of representing the Numinous" and it includes nearly everything in the arts. Architectural examples include the pyramids, Stonehenge, and European cathedrals.[76]

Do We All Have a Spiritual Path?

Spiritual growth is a natural process that advances from small to expanded consciousness, from minute to incredible wisdom, from slight to great compassion, from little to vast love. Spiritual maturing goes from simple to complex awareness until it develops into mystical consciousness of the Holy One and expresses itself in love for all people and creation.

Since all of us are innately spiritual, we are born with the ability to progress on our spiritual path from our childhood through our adult and elderly years until our death. We are all on a spiritual journey whether we realize it or not. Like Mother Teresa, even Adolf Hitler had a spiritual path. While she traveled far, he stopped at some very early point. Plotinus, a third-century Greek philosopher, called mystical vision our birthright. Mystical vision is a way of seeing, "a wakefulness that is the birthright of us all, though few put it to use."[77]

Beginning in childhood, awe and wonder are spontaneous, automatic, instinctive, and natural responses to beauty, magnificence, complexity, order, diversity, uniqueness, and mystery. They are the beginning of wisdom, the starting point, and the first stage on the spiritual path. Jesus called attention to this when he said, "truly I tell you, unless you change and become like children, you will never enter the kingdom of heaven," the presence of God. All of us will travel on the mystical way because we can't escape it. Most families and religions try to give us some preparation and help. However, it is our individual responsibility to move from one stage to another. The two purposes of our life are to use all our talents to give the best we have to our world as we proceed on our spiritual journey to experience the Holy One and to express our love for all people and creation. Underhill claims that "we are one and all kindred of the mystics." Moreover, "strange and far away as they may seem, they are not cut off from us by some impassable abyss. They belong to us. They are our brethren, the giants and heroes of our (human) race" for us to study and learn how to travel the spiritual path.[78]

Underhill said that the mystic life is a "process of organic development, . . . a movement of consciousness toward higher levels," a striving for the goal of union, and a growth in love for God as well as for all people and creation. To develop their spiritual life, people use mysticism and its methods: "the steps on the ladder, the substances of the progressive exercises undertaken by the developing self, its education in the art of contemplation," the "steep stairs of love," and "the three 'degrees of prayer or orison.'" Mystics' descriptions of their progress in spiritual prayer and contemplation are "bewildering in their variety" of stages, degrees, phases, steps, stairs, divisions, and states. Their stages are based on individual experience. The sixteenth century Spanish nun Teresa of Avila's description of her own states varied in her three principal works. The division into stages is an attempt to help spiritual seekers. Like life, the mystical process is "one and continuous—not a stairway but a slope." The differences in descriptions of stages and the multitude of terms make it difficult to compare mystics' stages.[79]

Contemporary feminist theologians say that spirituality exists both within and outside of religion and involves self-transcendence and "experiences of the Holy." Susan Schneiders defines it as "the experience of consciously striving to integrate one's life in terms not of isolation and self-absorption but of self-transcendence toward the ultimate values one perceives." Joann Conn defines spirituality as "the totality of human life energized by an inner drive for self-transcendence, that is moving beyond self-maintenance to reach out in love, in free commitment to seek truth and goodness."[80]

A contemporary German feminist scholar Ursula King says, "a mystic is a person who is deeply aware of the powerful presence of the Divine Spirit: someone who seeks, above all, the knowledge and love of God, and who experiences to an extraordinary degree the profoundly personal encounter with the energy of Divine life." These lovers of the Spirit "seek participation in the Divine life, union, and communion with God." These mystical seers have an "intense consciousness of God's love and presence" and a relationship with the Sacred Spirit. These friends of the Holy One answer the "Divine summons to a new life" and respond to "the call to seek God's love above all things." They can be called ambassadors of the Spirit and "troubadours of the love of God." Mystics experience "a supreme adventure," a path, and a journey to the summit or center that involve many stages. After they "meet the Ultimate Mystery of Life," they become "God-centered" and "oriented toward a greater Reality" than themselves.[81]

According to King, spirituality shares "characteristics that are . . . life-enhancing, holistic, and greatly supportive of human well-being." It "permeates all human existence" and is "so embracing" that it touches everything. It is "an age-old quest to seek fulfillment, liberation, and pointers to Transcendence amidst the welter of human experience." King cites the French mystic Chardin who claimed that "the whole process of evolution is a continuously expanding movement of spiritual growth" and "a process of transformation that will bring the universe from the material to the spiritual state." Since we humans are "fragmented, wounded, broken," transformative spirituality helps us become conscious of "the tremendous lack of peace, equality, and justice among the people of the earth." It makes us aware that "we form one humanity" and have a responsibility to radically change ourselves and our world. "A truly holistic, integral spirituality must include both personal and social transformation" and "the search for justice, peace, nonviolence, and ecological harmony."[82]

Contemporary psychotherapist Molly Brown asserts that we move toward experiencing our spiritual self "when we expand our awareness, strengthen our center, clarify our purpose, transform our inner demons, develop our will, and make conscious choices." Brother David Stendl-Rast says that spirituality is not a separate department of life, but rather "it is a vital awareness that pervades all realms of our being. . . . Whenever we come alive," whether it is when we garden or listen to music, "that is the area in which we are spiritual." Then we can try to spread that aliveness. "To be vital, awake, aware in all areas of our lives is the task that is never accomplished, but it remains the goal." Psychiatrist Gerald Mays says that spirituality is "our deepest values and desires, the very core of our being." Liberation theologian Leonard Boff says it is the attitude of putting life at the center of our concern and defending and promoting it. Catholic Bishop Pedro Casaldaliga claims that it is "a measure of our humanity—personal depth, conscience, deep will." Frederic and Mary Brussat describe spirituality as a "journey toward wholeness" and "universal wisdom."[83]

Do We Want to Deepen Your Spirituality?

Do we wish to have more spiritual experiences? But what are they? Many do not understand them. They don't realize when they are happening. A way to approach them is to picture what we feel as we go through an ordinary day. We have a quick breakfast, hastily take care of our family's needs, hurriedly drive to our job, do our work, talk with our colleagues, come home tired, try to listen to our family, fix dinner, attempt to relax, and go to bed. All this is done hurriedly without giving it the concern and attention we would like. Now imagine what we feel as we relax and watch a spectacular, breathe-taking sunset. Now envision our feelings as we talk with our very best friend and share our deepest feelings, thoughts, values, experiences, activities, fears, sorrows, joys, hopes, dreams, and loving relationships.

Watching the sunset and talking with your friend can be spiritual experiences that can also be called mystical encounters, peak experiences, transcendental encounters, experiences of awe, wonder, enlightenment, awakening, illumination, and union. Before going on, it is important to say that spiritual experiences can NOT be put into finite words. However, I'll try my best to describe the indescribable. Many define a spiritual encounter as an experience of the Holy One, but it is only a tiny, or rather minuscule, glimpse of the Infinite. There is more, much much more that we do not experience and do not know.

When we go about our daily life, we do our own thing, think our thoughts, and feel our emotions without paying much attention. When we have a spiritual experience, we get in touch with the Sacred Spirit within us and within the external world. In a mystical experience, our spirit feels alive, fully alive, in the deepest, truest part of ourselves. We are completely present in this moment NOW. In viewing a sunset, we become aware of the Holy One dwelling within us and within all creation. Possibly we experience being within the ONE. In talking with our friend, we become conscious of Infinite Love dwelling within us as our inner core of love and possibly of Divine Love dwelling within our friend, within all people, and within all of creation.

Being in nature can trigger spiritual experiences, such as relaxing on a mountain top and looking down at a beautiful green valley with a sparkling lake and a small village; sitting beside a beautiful lake with ducks, geese, and otters swimming around and wood storks, ibis, squirrels, and dogs walking around; and watching a baby kitten leaping around while playing with toys. After a few weeks living in the woods by Walden Pond, Henry David Thoreau, a nineteenth century American philosopher, had a mystical experience. "I was suddenly sensible of such sweet and beneficent society in nature, . . . an infinite and unaccountable friendliness all at once, . . . sustaining me." This made the advantages of human community insignificant. I was "aware of the presence of something kindred to me" in nature.[84]

Being alone can generate mystical experiences, such as meditating, listening to our favorite music, and gazing at a superb painting. When we have a new insight, we feel high, extremely excited, and a surge of energy. We think our insight is brilliant. Later we may be disappointed when we analyze it. Being with people can create spiritual experiences, such as helping needy individuals; working for justice for oppressed people; greeting a loved one returning home from a war where he risked his life fighting or where she served as a doctor in life-threatening situations near the battlefield; saying goodbye to a loved one as she lay dying; and gazing at a six month old baby playing with toys.

A spiritual experience causes our creative life force to flow within us and produces an up swelling of feelings from very good to extraordinarily, exquisitely magnificent. It creates deep happiness so that we feel like we are walking on air. A mystical encounter changes our heart and mind. It expands our awareness of ourselves, other people, and nature so that we are conscious of the Divine presence within them. It stretches our heart to love all people and creation. It spurs us to grow in ways that make us more conscious, creative, complex, resourceful, resilient, considerate, empathetic, caring, and loving.[85]

Having a spiritual experience puts the events in our lives in perspective. We realize that people and creation are most important. We need to appreciate, care for, and love them. We acknowledge that what had been crucial to us before was our possessions, reputation, status, power, and money. Now we recognize that they are actually much less vital. Instead we want to listen to our inner voice, our gut feelings, our life-promoting intuition, and our loving inner core. Then we become aware that we do not take the time to really make genuine, substantive connections with people and nature. We take them for granted. We are too busy with our technology, computers, cell phones, texting, and Facebook as well as our appearance, possessions, money, power, workloads, and to-do lists. Instead of paying attention to what is happening now, we are emotionally and mentally elsewhere. We are not fully present in this moment.

In contrast, when we have a mystical experience, our capacity to see, really see, opens up. We perceive the beauty, depth, spirit, and loving inner core of our family, friends, and even acquaintances. When we recognize our common humanity, we realize that our differences are springboards for learning. We accept and empathize with their weaknesses and strengths. As we walk in their moccasins, we see ourselves in them. We are on the same wavelength, in sync, and in tune. We experience the boundaries between us disappearing. We experience such a strong connection with all people and nature that we feel at ONE with them and with the Ultimate Reality. We are conscious of being part of something greater than ourselves.

Mystical experiences are not exclusive. They are not reserved for a few spiritual geniuses. They are more ubiquitous than most of us think. They spring up or blossom anytime, anywhere. They occur when we are fully alive and totally aware of this present moment NOW.

Spiritual experiences happen when we become attuned to our spirit, soul, loving inner core, and the Holy One dwelling within us. As psychologist Barbara Fredrickson says after having a spiritual experience, "then slowly, this expansive and transcendent feeling fades away." Wondrous mystical experiences usually sweep through us for only a few minutes. We can try to coax these fleeting feelings to last longer. We can "revive them later through conversation." However, their duration is best measured in minutes, extremely rarely in hours, and not in months or years. Fredrickson claims that most spiritual experiences are brief, but their insights and effects can last a lifetime.[86]

Do the Insights and Effects of Spiritual Experiences Last a Lifetime?

The spiritual experiences of Dr. Jill Bolte Taylor provide a real-life answer to this question. As a brain scientist, she says that "the focused human mind is the most powerful instrument in the universe." Her entire life is dedicated to understanding "how the brain creates our perception of reality." Unfortunately, at age 37, she suffered a stroke that severely damaged the left hemisphere of her brain. The two hemispheres, the left and the right, "communicate with each other through the highway for information transfer" called the corpus callosum. When operating as they were designed, the two parts of the brain are connected to each other, complement one another, and work together to create a single seamless perception of the world.[87]

Taylor's stroke caused her left brain to be flooded with so much blood that it was severely injured. Lacking left hemisphere functions, she could not walk, read, write, think logically, define, analyze, categorize, compare, understand what others said, decipher the meaning of words, judge things as good or bad, and do calculations and mathematics. In addition, she heard "all sounds as chaos and noise" and she could not identify color or see three dimensionally. In her own words, "I could not walk or talk, understand language, read or write, or even roll my body over." Besides being devoid of language and linear processing, she felt she lacked her worldly wisdom. Missing her memory of the past, she "felt disconnected from the life" she had lived. The inner voice that previously was constantly talking to her was silent. Her internal clock was also silent. Devoid of any memories of the past, she had no hopes for the future.[88]

In her book, *My Stroke of Insights*, written after she recovered, Taylor explained the connections between the workings of her right hemisphere, her spirituality, and the Divine. While her left mind did not work, her right brain's functioning gave her evidence that there are two different dimensions, the normal world and the spiritual reality. "I felt suspended between two worlds, caught between two perfectly opposite planes of reality." Instead of the left brain's busy, fast paced doing, she lived the right mind's way of being, "a pervasive and enticing deep inner peace." In addition, "no time exists other than the present moment" which "seems to exist in perfect isolation." Every moment is vibrant with sensations, thoughts, and emotions. "The feeling of peace is something that happens in the present moment" and "all I could see was right here, right now, and it was beautiful." This moment now is abundant and timeless. She was no longer able to determine "the physical boundaries of where I began and where I ended." This absence of physical boundaries is "finer than the finest of pleasures" and an experience of "glorious bliss." She felt fluid rather than solid. Because she "was not capable of experiencing separation or individuality," she no longer felt separated from everything else.[89]

According to Taylor, our right brain realizes that "everyone and everything are connected together as *one*." It experiences "each of us as equal members of the human family. It identifies our similarities. . ... It perceives the big picture, how everything is related, and how we all join together to make up the whole." Our right mind does not act on artificial boundaries like religion and race. Accepting people and things as they are, it does not judge things as right or wrong. It lives in innocent, joyful celebration. The right brain is "the seat of . . . the knower, the wise woman, and the observer. It is my intuition and higher consciousness." It realizes that "life is good and we are all beautiful—just the way we are." Taylor says that "happiness is the natural state of being for my right mind," but she also "wholeheartedly believes that 99.999% of the cells in my brain and body want me to be happy, healthy, and successful." Her right brain "understands that I am the life force power of the 50 trillion molecular geniuses crafting my form" and that "we are all connected to one another." It "sees unity among all living entities." We are "part of it all. We are brothers and sisters on this planet."[90]

While Taylor's damaged left mind and body "failed her miserably in any attempt to interact with the external world," her right brain was "the seat of my Divine mind." It provided her with deep inner peace and tranquil euphoria. "I met a growing sense of peace. . . . I felt enfolded by a blanket of tranquil euphoria. . . . my consciousness soared into an all-knowingness, a 'being at *one*' with the universe." While Taylor prays to the Great Spirit, uses the phrase "something greater than ourselves," and experiences "the peaceful bliss of my Divine right mind," she mostly describes her spiritual experiences as "being at *one* with the universe." However, she also says that spiritual experiences mean being at *one* with the universe, with God, with Nirvana. "The experience of Nirvana exists in the consciousness of our right hemisphere." In addition, "swathed in the enfolding sense of liberation and transformation, the essence of my consciousness shifted to a state that felt" like Nirvana.[91]

Taylor also describes being at *one* with the universe as "being connected to the energy flow of all that is" and blending into the eternal flow. She "loved the bliss of drifting in the current of the eternal flow. It was beautiful there. My spirit beamed free, enormous, and peaceful." She felt the rapture of the engulfing, ecstatic bliss and loved most of all "the feeling of deep inner peace that flooded the core of my very being." She gained "the knowledge that deep internal peace is accessible to anyone at any time. . . . at any moment, we can choose to hook into that part of our brain." Her stroke

Do We All Have a Spiritual Path? 39

of insight is that "peace is only a thought away" and "all we have to do is . . . silence our left brain."[92]

Since Taylor's left mind was now off-line, it "no longer inhibited my innate awareness that I was the miraculous power of life" and "the life force energy within each of us contains the power of the universe." She experienced herself as "simply a beam of light radiating life into the world. . . . I perceived myself as perfect, whole, and beautiful just the way I was." Furthermore, "my consciousness ventured unfettered into the peaceful bliss of my Divine right mind" and experienced "the peaceful tranquility of the Divine bliss." Then "my spirit was free to catch a wave in the river of blissful flow." Moreover, "the energy of my spirit seemed to flow like a great whale gliding through a sea of silent euphoria." While "my consciousness dwelled in a flow of sweet tranquility," she felt that "I would never be able to squeeze the enormousness of my spirit back inside" her cellular body. She was "completely entranced by the feelings of tranquility, safety, blessedness, euphoria, and omniscience. A piece of me yearned to be released completely from the captivity of this physical form, which throbbed with pain."[93]

Taylor's experience demonstrates that being spiritual is a two-step process. If she would pick "one word to describe the feeling at the core of her right mind," she would choose *joy*. If she would select one word to portray the action of her right brain, she would say *compassion*. She describes being compassionate as "considering another's circumstances with love rather than judgment. . . . To be compassionate is to move into the right here, right now with an open-heart consciousness and a willingness to be supportive." She feels awe that she is simultaneously capable of having a spiritual experience of "being at *one* with the universe, while having an individual identity whereby I move into the world and manifest positive change" through expressing love. "The most fundamental traits of my right hemisphere personality are deep inner peace and loving compassion." Thus, "my stroke of insight is that at the core of my right hemisphere consciousness is a character that is directly connected to my feeling of deep inner peace. It is completely committed to the expression of peace, love, joy, and compassion in the world."[94]

According to Taylor, the right mind produces our ability to walk in other people's shoes, to feel their feelings, and thus to be empathetic. Being compassionate rather than judgmental, the right brain "chooses a peaceful and loving mind," sees the glass as half full, and views negative events as "valuable life lessons." Being appreciative, "it is filled with gratitude for my life and everyone and everything in it. It is content, compassionate, nurturing, and eternally optimistic." The more time our right mind works on peace and compassion, the more peace and compassion we project into the world, and ultimately the more that will exist on our planet. "We are all one" and "all people are equal." The right brain does not act on differences such as religion, sex, and race. It not only treats all people as equal but it also accepts them as they are. "Helping people liberate their own inner peace, joy, and magnificent beauty has become my personal agenda." In addition, "we are here to help make this world a more peaceful and kinder place." Furthermore, "my right hemisphere consciousness is eager for us to take the next giant step for mankind and *step to the right* (brain) so we can evolve this planet into the peaceful and loving place we yearn for it to be."[95]

As Taylor was recovering her left brain, she thought that she did not want "to lose my connection to the universe" nor to leave behind being "in touch with my authentic self. Frankly, I didn't want to give up Nirvana" in order to become normal again. However, by standing on the ocean's edge or "by remembering the smells, sounds, tastes, and how I felt inside, I can transport myself back to Nirvana in an instant."[96]

Are There Spiritual Practices, Principles, Virtues, and Laws?

In his 2003 book, spiritual writer Wayne Dyer agrees with Teresa of Avila that our "spirit is the life of God within us." Spiritual practice is "a way of making my life work at a higher level and of receiving guidance for handling problems." His seven basic spiritual practices are the seven ways he defines spirituality. In his order of significance, they are: Surrender, Love, Infinite, Empty Mind, Generosity and Gratefulness, Connectedness, and Cheerfulness. His last practice, the state of cheerfulness, provides "a reliable gauge of my level of spiritual enlightenment at the moment. The more cheerful, happy, contented, and satisfied I am, the more aware I am of my deep connection to Spirit." If we feel depressed, frustrated, anxious, hurt, or upset, then we are spiritually disconnected. When we are spiritually connected, we are not judging, criticizing, and condemning others, but we feel happy and at peace with them. Using Francis of Assisi's famous prayer, Dyer explains that "there is a spiritual solution to every problem."

> Lord, make me an instrument of thy peace.
> Where there is hatred, let me sow love; where there is injury, pardon;
> Where there is doubt, faith; where there is despair, hope;
> Where there is darkness, light; where there is sadness, joy.

Then he offers practical applications to each phrase of that prayer.[97]

In his earlier 1999 book, Dyer presents nine spiritual principles as "a step-by-step program for implementing a spiritual manifestation awareness for yourself." He guarantees that you will begin to see yourself as "a co-creator of your own life" and as "an absolute miracle, an individual who connects to the universal all-pervading Spirit." His first spiritual principle is "becoming aware of your highest self." Second, "trusting yourself is trusting the Wisdom that created you." His third spiritual principle proclaims that "you are not an organism in an environment: you are an environorganism." Fourth, "you can attract to yourself what you desire." Dyer's fifth spiritual principle is "honoring your worthiness to receive." Sixth is "connecting to the Divine Source with unconditional love." His seventh principle is "meditating to the sound of creation" and vibrating yourself to those sounds. Eighth is to "patiently detach from the outcome." His ninth and last spiritual principle is "reacting to your manifestation with gratitude and generosity."[98]

Robert Thurman, a professor of Buddhism, presents seven virtues that develop infinite living. His first virtue is wisdom. You need to accept the simple premise that "life is infinite." Through infinite interconnection, you are connected to all other beings. "With your transcendent wisdom, you grasp your true nature as a selfless being." The second through sixth virtues are generosity, justice, patient forbearance, creativity, and serene contemplation. Once you have practiced these virtues and "opened yourself to experiencing each and every moment," you start on the path to an infinite life, the seventh virtue. To complete the process, you need to "take universal responsibility for exerting maximum effort to bring the spirit of enlightenment's love and compassion to all sensitive beings. . . . Since we are so bound together, *we can only attain happiness when all beings attain happiness*."[99]

Spiritual author Deepak Chopra discusses the same laws in his 1994 *The Seven Spiritual Laws of Success* and his 2004 *The Seven Spiritual Laws of Yoga*. He claims they "could also be called the Seven Spiritual Laws of Life, because they are the same principles that nature uses to create everything." His first Law of Pure Potentiality is "based on the fact that we are, in our essential state, pure consciousness," pure potentiality, and "the field of all possibilities and creativity." As our spiritual essence, pure consciousness has other attributes: pure knowledge, simplicity, perfect balance, infinite silence, invincibility, and bliss. This "could also be called the Law of Unity, because underlying the infinite diversity of life is the unity of the one all-pervasive Spirit. There is no separation between you and this Field of Energy." His second Law of Giving and Receiving operates because "your body and your mind and the universe are in constant and dynamic exchange, stopping the circulation of energy is like stopping the flow of blood." Thus, "the more you give, the more you will receive because you will keep the abundance of the universe circulating in your life. In fact anything that is of value in life only multiplies when it is given." His third Law of Karma means "what you sow is what you reap."[100]

Chopra's fourth Law of Least Effort explains that nature functions without effort. "Grass doesn't try to grow, it just grows." Since "nature is held together by love, . . . when your actions are motivated my love, your energy multiplies and accumulates." His fifth Law of Intention and Desire is based on the fact that at the level of the quantum field or the field of pure consciousness, "there is nothing other than energy and information." These are influenced by desire and intention. In their essential components, a blade of grass, a tree, and a human body are information and energy. His sixth Law of Detachment says that "in order to acquire anything in the physical universe, you have to relinquish your attachment to it." You don't have to give up your intention or desire, but "you give up your attachment to the result."[101]

Chopra's seventh Law of *Dharma* uses a Sanskrit word Dharma that means "purpose in life." Being a part of a Field of Pure Consciousness, which is "Divinity in its essence," you take physical form to fulfill a purpose. The three components of your purpose are first to discover your true spiritual self, your highest self, your Divinity, and second "to express your unique talents." The third component is "to serve humanity." Then "you will begin to experience your life as a miraculous expression of Divinity . . . all the time. And you will know true joy and the true meaning of success—the ecstasy and exultation of your spirit." In addition, "you become carefree and joyful and your life becomes an expression of unbounded love."[102]

What Are the Purposes, Goals, and Results of Spirituality?

The fourteenth-century German mystical treatise, *Theologia Germanica*, said that "when a man neither cares for nor desires anything but the eternal Good alone, . . . he is made a partaker of all manner of joy, bliss, peace, rest, and consolation." In this spiritual state of mind, "the time for tension in the soul is over, and that of happy relaxation, of calm deep breathing, of an Eternal present, with no discordant future to be anxious about, has arrived." This happy state of mind in "its highest flights" is "infinitely passionate." Like hope and love, "it adds to life an enchantment" that comes as a gift of God's grace. Spiritual feeling is "thus an absolute addition" to a person's life that "gives him a new sphere of power."[103]

Ralph Waldo Emerson claimed that spiritual sentiment "makes our highest happiness. Wonderful is its power to charm and to command. It is mountain air. It is the embalmer of the world." It "makes the sky and the hills sublime, and the silent song of the stars is it. This sentiment is Divine and deifying. It is the beatitude of man. It makes him illimitable. . . . when love warms him; when he chooses . . . the good and great deed; then, deep melodies wander through his soul from Supreme Wisdom. Then he can worship, and be enlarged by his worship . . . All the expressions of this sentiment are sacred and permanent in proportion to their purity. They affect us more than all other compositions." William James, an early twentieth century American psychologist, said that a person with a fully developed spirituality accepts the universe with "cheerful serenity and enthusiastic gladness" as well as with "passionate happiness." In addition, "this sort of happiness in the Absolute and Everlasting is what we find nowhere" but in spirituality. "That happiness of a supreme sort is the prerogative" of spirituality. Spirituality is "an essential organ of life" and "the most important of all human functions."[104]

Contemporary Roger Walsh, M.D., Ph.D., says that "some of the most potent 'metaphors of transformation' that guide and describe spiritual growth" are awakening, enlightenment, uncovering, freedom, metamorphosis, unfolding, wholeness, journey, death, and rebirth. John White, a contemporary college professor, describes a number of mystics' names for "the highest state of consciousness." In the New Testament, Paul named it "the peace that passeth understanding." Abraham Maslow, a humanistic psychologist, coined the term peak experience. Thomas Merton, a Trappist monk, used "transcendental unconsciousness." Psychologist Carl Jung spoke of individuation. Martin Buber, a Jewish theologian, referred to "the I-Thou relation." Different branches of Buddhism refer to Nirvana, *satori*, and *kensho*. Hindus say *samadhi* or *moksha*. Taoists speak of the absolute Tao. Islamic Sufis say *fana*. The Quakers use "the Inner Light." Whatever the word used to refer to this ancient and worldwide phenomenon—"enlightenment, illumination, liberation, mystical experience—all are concerned with a state of awareness radically different from our ordinary understanding, our normal waking consciousness, our everyday mind."[105]

White claims that all mystics agree that the highest state of consciousness is "a self-transforming perception of one's total union with the Infinite." Since it is beyond space and time, it is "an experience of timelessness which is eternity, of unlimited unity with all creation." Our socialized sense of 'I' is shattered and "the usual ego boundaries break down, as the ego . . . suddenly becomes One with All that has being. . . . Self becomes selfless." In this state of expanded consciousness, thought and feeling, reason and emotion, merge. This experience of a new self-understanding has happened all over the world and throughout history. Mystics testified that they have experienced the highest state of consciousness, realized the Oneness of all reality, and "felt the deepest sense of peace with others and harmony with the world.... They perceived a cosmic plan, a moral order" in their chaotic world and a joyful meaning in their life.[106]

Tolle says, "the only true liberation" is to "free yourself from your own mind." You realize that "there is a vast realm of intelligence beyond thought.... You also realize that all the things that truly matter—beauty, love, creativity, joy, inner peace—arise from beyond the mind." You go beyond your mind when you are fully present in the moment, in the NOW. This rising above thought is "the beginning of your natural state of felt Oneness with Being," with the One Life, with "the God-essence," with the Source of Life, with "the Unmanifested," with "timeless Perfection," and with pure enlightened Consciousness.[107]

For Tolle, to be enlightened is to rise above thought and "to regain awareness of Being." It is "simply your natural state of felt Oneness with Being" and "a state of connectedness with something ... that ... is essentially you and yet much greater than you." When you direct your consciousness outward, your mind and the world arise. "When you direct it inward, it realizes its own Source and returns home into the Unmanifested," into Being, into the One Life, into God. When you face and accept what is and when you are fully present in the moment, the realm of Being opens. "Suddenly, a great stillness arises within you, an unfathomable sense of peace. And within that peace, there is great joy. And within that joy, there is love. And at the innermost core, there is the Sacred, the Immeasurable, that which cannot be named."[108]

Tolle describes the surface of a deep lake as "the outer situation of your life and whatever happens there." Sometimes the surface is calm and sometimes rough with large waves because of a harsh wind. The depth of the lake is always peaceful and undisturbed. When "you are in touch with your own depth," when you accept the surface and what is, you experience inner peace. "You abide in Being—unchanging, timeless, deathless—and you are no longer dependent for fulfillment or happiness on the outer world of constantly fluctuating forms."[109]

Walsh says that "realizing our spiritual nature is the *summum bonum*: the highest goal and greatest good of human existence." The words for this goal are different in various traditions, "salvation and *satori*, enlightenment and liberation, *fana* and nirvana, awakening and *Ruah Ha-qodesh*." Claiming that we seriously underestimate ourselves, Walsh says that "we are sadly mistaken when we see ourselves as merely temporary bodies instead of timeless spirits; as separate, suffering selves instead of blissful Buddhas." Although religions seem to be different, "their central message is the same:

you are more than you think! Look deep within, and you will find that your ego is only a wave atop the vast ocean that is your real Self. Look within, and at the center of your mind, in the depth of your soul, you will find your true Self, that this Self is intimately linked to the Sacred and that you share in the unbounded bliss of the Sacred."[110]

Underhill said that union with the Divine is the fifth and final stage on the spiritual path. The mystic's aim is "conscious union with a living Absolute." Union is "the true goal of the mystic quest" and "that permanent establishment of life upon transcendent levels of Reality." However, she did not end there. Although she did not call it a stage, Underhill went on to say that for mystics in the West, "the highest forms of Divine Union impel the self to some sort of active, rather than passive life." For the great contemplatives, the ideal was "to become 'modes of the Infinite.' Filled with an abounding sense of the Divine Life, . . . sustaining and urging them on, they wish to communicate the revelation, the more abundant life, which they have received." The reports about mystics' lives are "records of supreme activity." They love and do good works. Besides being wrestlers with the Spirit, they include missionaries, organizers, philanthropists, prophets, poets, and saints with a national destiny, like Joan of Arc.[111]

Fox writes that all mystics have in common the experience of being united and not separated from the Divine. The mystical way leads to communion with the Ultimate Reality and the end of separation, alienation, and dualism. "Compassion unites us." It is the origin, the process, and the goal of the mystical way. "Compassion is our universal heritage, our God-origin, and our God-destiny."[112]

Many scholars agree that union with the Sacred Spirit is the goal of mysticism. The purpose of the spiritual path is to go from simple to more complex mystical consciousness and to experience union with the Holy One. Eckhart stated that to find God is to be "united in the ONE." Many are unaware that mysticism's second aim is love, because spirituality leads to love. As mystics, we become Divine instruments and work to express our love for all people, nature, and the Ultimate Reality. Thus, the purpose of spirituality is twofold, wisdom and love.[113]

Does Having a Deep Spirituality Help Reform a Religion?

To be genuinely religious, we need to be spiritual. However, the reverse is not true. We can find our authentic, valuable spiritual path even when we leave religion far behind. There are as many definitions of religion as there are people. There is no one correct definition, even though some religions falsely claim to be the one and only true religion. In my understanding, the founders of all religions were mystics who had spiritual experiences of the Holy One that caused them to form their religions. Thus, religion is first and foremost spirituality. It starts with a mystical experience. A spiritual experience is the essence, the fundamental meaning, and the basic substance of religion. A mystical experience is the primary, intrinsic, and indispensable foundation and prerequisite of religion. As Ursula King says, a mystical experience is "the heart of all religion, the point of light to which all seekers are drawn." Underhill claims that "no deeply religious man is without a touch of mysticism."[114]

Before his 1993 death, Bede Griffin, an English Christian priest who lived most of his life in India, used an image to show the connection of various religions to spirituality. The separate fingers of a hand are like different religions. However, each religion can be traced back to the palm of the hand which is the spirituality from which they all came and where "they all come together in their depths." In the fourteenth century, Eckhart called "God an underground river of wisdom with many wells tapping into it."[115]

A twentieth-century sociologist of religion, Joachim Wach, whose ideas are used by other scholars, claims that the three forms of religious expression are the theoretical, practical, and sociological. In abbreviation, the theoretical form of religious expression is what is said by a religion. The practical is what is done in a religion. The sociological expression is the kinds of groups formed by a religion.[116]

My revision of Wach's theory starts with the idea that spiritual experiences create love. They produce many loving actions and organizations, including religions. The first essential of religion is spirituality, the founder's mystical experience of the Divine. The founder produces the religion's spirituality, wisdom, teachings, beliefs, and theology. Later other religious leaders may develop scriptures, sacred texts, doctrines, myths, creeds, and more theology. Second, these religious leaders create the practical form of religious expression, the worship services, rituals, rites, ceremonies, devotion, prayers, contemplation, and meditation as well as the ethics, the standards of behavior, and the rules of conduct. The third form of religious expression is the groups, organizations, hierarchies, institutions, churches, synagogues, temples, and mosques that religious leaders produce. All three forms can be tools that help people move forward on the mystical way or they can inhibit them. While religions have beliefs, rituals, ethics, and organizations, their foundation is the spirituality of their founder.

Some religious leaders have mystical experiences but suppress them and also fail to pay attention to the founder's spirituality. Because they teach a religion without any spirituality, they stress unbelievable dogmas, rigid codes of conduct, boring worship services, and a hierarchical, authoritarian institution. The people who are members of this institutional religion that neglects spirituality and its teachings have a second-hand religious life that accepts the tradition as it is handed down by authorities. Their religion is created for them by others. Blindly they believe religious doctrines even though they are totally implausible and unrealistic; practice rituals even though they are tedious and dull; docilely follow strict rules of behavior; and unquestioningly obey the strict, inflexible dictates of authoritarian religious leaders and their institution.

In contrast, when other religious leaders have mystical experiences, they not only learn from them, but they also learn from the founder's spiritual wisdom. Their teaching and worship help members have first-hand spiritual experiences that make it possible for them to get in touch with the founder's mystical experiences and spirituality that lead to awe, wonder, awakening, illumination, and union with the Holy One. The founder's, the leader's, and the members' spirituality help to create a religion that has a passionate soul, vibrant spirit, emotional impact, vital energy, creative life force, dynamic power, and love for all.

Aurobindo, a twentieth-century Indian mystic, said that spiritual life and religious life are quite different and should not be confused. "The religious life is a movement of the same ignorant, human consciousness" that tries "to turn away from the earth toward the Divine," but it is "led by the dogmatic tenets and rules of some sect" which claims to be the way, often the only way. In contrast, "spiritual life . . . proceeds directly by a change of consciousness, a change from the ordinary consciousness . . . to a greater consciousness in which one finds one's true being and comes first into direct and living contact and then into union with the Divine."[117]

The best way to reform a religion is to focus on its spirituality and love for everyone. For example, Christian leaders and laity need to stress Jesus' first essential teaching that "the kingdom of God is within us," which I interpret as the presence of God is within us. Then they need to emphasize his second fundamental message that flows from that: we are to love all people and creation. Any doctrines, worship services, standards of behavior, and institutions that do not stress these two basic teachings need to be reformed or rejected.[118]

Can Spirituality Help Alleviate Suffering and Create More Love?

Today what are the concrete results of being spiritual for billions of us who suffer from life and death problems? Buddha's first Noble Truth says, "all life is suffering." Individuals' suffering is always unique. The lives of most of us are full of troubles that damage our self-esteem, physical health, psychological well-being, social skills, mental capacities, political thinking, economics livelihood, and spiritual life. Many of us are unhappy, sad, discouraged, depressed, desperate, miserable, despairing, and hopeless? Some become suicidal and others violent. Because of our unhappiness, we lose touch with our loving inner core. Many of us whose lives are happy help those less fortunate. Others mainly go our own way, but some wonder, why should we be concerned about the unhappiness of others?

Innocent children are suffering every day somewhere in our world. Why do adults hurt them and allow their injuries to continue year after year?

> children living in dysfunctional families with alcoholic and drug abusing parents,
> children learning that appearance, possessions, status, and money are most important,
> children denied an education or receiving an inadequate one,
> homeless children, hungry children living in inadequate housing without health care,
> children's health ruined by pollution and poor diet,
> children's opportunities destroyed by sexism, racism, poverty, violence, and war
> teenagers killed by drugs and opioids coming from pharmaceutical corporations,
> children psychologically abused, neglected, beaten, and sexually molested,
> girl children having babies,
> girls genitally mutilated and girls forced or sold into unwanted marriages,
> girls forced, sold, and trafficked into sexual slavery,
> boys coerced or forced to be soldiers and to kill,
> children committing suicide and boys killing other children,
> children experiencing fear, trauma, brutality, and loss of limbs because of war,
> children dying of gunshot wounds in a war or in their home or in their school.

Again, why do adults harm children? Although all of us have the potential to be destructive and violent, adults who seriously wound children in these and other ways were probably damaged as children. Love breeds more love. Destructiveness creates further destructiveness. Violence begets additional violence. Children who suffered because of destructive people and life circumstances grow into adults who are more likely to injure themselves, children, other people, and nature.

We need to ask, what are the causes for all these tragedies? Then we can inquire, what are the solutions? Is there a separate cause for each? Or is there a root cause for them all? Are they all branches of one deeper difficulty so that confronting the root cause will lead to solutions for all these individual problems?

My conclusion is that there is a root cause for all these tragedies. When we, children and adults, are hurt and suffer, our inner core of love is damaged or possibly destroyed. To protect ourselves, some of us act like or make ourselves believe that we are more important or superior to others and that we have a right to dominate or have power over others in order to benefit ourselves, even though it disadvantages others. Our priorities are to acquire money, status, and power to protect ourselves and make ourselves feel more powerful. Lacking a moral conscience, empathy, compassion, and love, we don't think about or care that our actions cause others to lose opportunities, to be harmed, to be damaged, to suffer, and even to die.

For example, abusive and neglectful parents control their children. Parents and the culture teach boys to be tough and to dominate women. Some males sexually exploit, harass, batter, rape, and kill females. Women in collusion with men genitally mutilate girl children. Pimps force young girls to become prostitutes and sex slaves. White individuals in the US are prejudiced, discriminate against, and exploit people of color. The executives of large corporations and the wealthy care more about profits than human and environmental needs. Governments spend more on weapons than on the education for their children and the health care for their people. Dictators and their militaries dominate their people and their countries. One religious, racial, ethnic, or national group makes war on another, resulting in many being displaced from their homes, injured, maimed, and killed as well as the environment being devastated. Militaries with the approval of political leaders execute wars that shatter lives.

While all these ways that people dominate and hurt others require educational, community, and governmental solutions that we can be participate in, a true revolution begins with ourselves and spreads outward. Before and when we join with others to find solutions, we need to be sure we practice what we advocate. We can begin to solve the root problem that results in all these tragedies by dealing with our own suffering, so that we can heal our own inner core of love. One of the many ways to do this is to develop our spirituality and travel on the six stages of the mystical way. When we have spiritual experiences of awakening and illumination, we get in touch with the Divine within ourselves and all people. Then we realize that we are all sacred. All of us are connected. We are all one family. Our awakening and illumination lead to love for ourselves and everyone else. Then we realize that we are not more important or superior to anyone else, no matter their race, sex, religion, nationality, and other differences. We do not have the right to dominate or have power over other people. We certainly do not have a right to be abusive or violent toward anyone or anything. We need to treat all people with respect, liberty, equality, justice, and love.

The 2,500-year-old Hindu scripture *Bhagavad Gita,* also called *Gita,* said that when a man knows that a person has the Spirit within him, "when a man knows him as never-born, everlasting, never-changing, beyond all destruction, how can that man kill a person, or cause another to kill?" Moreover, "when a man sees that God in himself is the same God in all that is, he hurts not himself by hurting others, then he goes indeed to the highest path." Gandhi claimed that a human "as animal is violent, but as spirit is nonviolent. The moment he awakes to the Spirit within, he cannot remain violent. Either he progresses toward *ahimsa* (nonviolence) or rushes to his doom."[119]

Our spiritual experiences that the Holy One is within all people and creation make us want to express our love for everyone and everything. We also desire to take action to heal the suffering and create respect, liberty, equality, justice, peace, and love for all. Furthermore, we want transform our communities, institutions, nations, and our world to be more empathetic, compassionate, and loving.

Chapter 3

Mystics Explained Different Versions of Stages on the Spiritual Path

What are the Stages on the Spiritual Path to the Divine?

Mystics' writings cover a range of topics. Some describe their spiritual experiences, others describe the lessons that they learned from their mystical encounters, still others present their own spiritual path and mystical stages on the way to the Divine. Catherine of Genoa, a sixteenth-century Italian mystic, describes an interesting take on her stages in a few sentences. When "the loving-kindness of God calls a soul from the world, He finds it full of vices and sins; and at first He gives it an instinct for virtue, and then urges it to perfection, and then by infused grace leads it to true self-naughting, and at last to true transformation." When the soul is transformed, it feels "immersed in an ocean of utmost peace."[120]

    Most of the ancient and contemporary mystics who formulated stages on the spiritual path to the Sacred Spirit spelled them out more fully than Catherine of Genoa. All the frameworks for mystical stages are artificial, but they can be beneficial. They are intended to help us discover our own spiritual path. They may also assist us in realizing that we are mystics. Over the millennia and around the world, multiple mystics of many different religions offered their thoughts and formulae for finding the Ultimate Reality. What is the difference between stages and ways to the Divine? Stages present different levels, steps, and phases in the process of traveling the mystical path. Ways are different spiritual practices, methods, and techniques to use to reach the ONE. My recommendation is that you read the works of the mystics yourself. Dip into them almost anywhere and you will find spiritual riches.

The Evolutionary Stages of Two Twentieth Century Mystics, Chardin and Aurobindo

Pierre Teilhard de Chardin was a French Catholic Jesuit priest and a paleontologist in China. Aurobindo Ghose was a Hindu mystic, a founder of an ashram, and a worker for Indian independence. Both presented four evolutionary stages that are similar. Their frameworks are much larger and more comprehensive than those of almost all other mystics. Their first stage begins with the evolution of matter. In their second stage, matter evolves into life and in their third, life evolves into humans. In contrast, other mystics start with humans and stop with humans. In Chardin's fourth stage, the human race collectively evolves "forward in some sort of supreme consciousness" and progressive spirituality. In Aurobindo's fourth stage, individuals evolve beyond simply being human to become superhuman and to develop a Supermind.[121]

Defining love as "the affinity of being with being," Chardin said that "the most telling and profound way of describing the evolution of the universe would undoubtedly be to trace the evolution of love." Love is "the most universal, the most tremendous and the most mysterious of the cosmic forces" and "the primal and universal psychic energy." In addition, "love is a sacred reserve of energy; it is like the blood of spiritual evolution." Love "in its full biological reality" is "a general property of all life." When life is scarcely individualized, love in its most primitive form is hard to distinguish from molecular forces. Slowly over a long time, love becomes distinct, but not until the evolution of human beings does love reveal its manifold virtues. "'Hominized' love is distinct from all other love, because the 'spectrum' of its warm and penetrating light is marvelously enriched." Since the world is always unfinished and growing, humans can only achieve the fullness of love by consummating a union with others and the universe.[122]

Chardin claimed that love as the parental instinct, sexual passion, and social solidarity is recognized in mammals as well as humans. Earlier in the tree of life, the drive for union is more obscure but "if there were no real internal propensity to unite, even at a prodigiously rudimentary level—indeed in the molecule itself—it would be physically impossible for love to appear higher up, with us" humans. Love is present "at least in an inchoate form, in everything that is." When we perceive "the confluent ascent of consciousness, we see it is not lacking anywhere.... Driven by the forces of love, the fragments of the world seek each other so that the world may come into being." Besides seeing God as love and love as energy, Chardin called God the Omega, the end of the evolutionary process. He wondered whether love in its essence is "the attraction exercised on each unit of consciousness by the Center of the universe?" Love "calls us to the great Union, the realization of which is the only process at present taking place in nature."[123]

Chardin mentioned many laws and principles, such as "the law of universal concentration," the "law of psychic concentration," "the fundamental law of convergence," and "the fundamental law of union." Some of these imply implicitly or explicitly that love is the heart of reality. Love is "the totalizing principle of human energy." This powerful dynamic for cooperation, interdependency, and relationships with other people moves the evolutionary process forward. There is a structural relationship between complexity and consciousness which Chardin called the cosmic law of growing complexity and consciousness. Consciousness experimentally is "the specific effect of organized complexity." Evolution is the "rise in consciousness." There is no contradiction between spirit and matter, the one and the many, unity and plurality. Each of these is simply two phases of the same reality. "In a concrete sense there is not matter and spirit. All that exists is matter becoming spirit. There is neither spirit nor matter in the world; the 'stuff of the universe' is spirit-matter." Spirit is "the indestructible part of the universe." Evolution, which includes human and spiritual evolution, is the process of matter becoming spirit, the many becoming One, the plurality becoming Unity.[124]

Aurobindo said that the purpose and central motive of evolution is the growth of consciousness. The aim of our earthly existence is "the greater and greater awakening of consciousness and its climb to a higher and higher level and . . . our progress toward that supreme and total perfection." By rising out of our ordinary, ignorant consciousness and transforming our mind, life, and body, "our evolution is secretly moving" toward the Supermind and its Supramental Truth-Consciousness that reveals the Spirit dwelling within us. The Spirit is the Divine Reality, the Infinite Reality, "the Universal Consciousness-Force," and the Nameless that Hindus call Brahman. Brahman is Infinite Existence, Consciousness, and Bliss or *Sat, Chit, and Ananda*.[125]

According to Aurobindo, "there are a series of ascending terms between Spirit and matter." His first stage of spiritual evolution is matter, unconscious matter. "In essence matter is a form of veiled life" and it "hides the Universal Consciousness-Force that works within it." Chardin's first stage is also matter. It is pre-life, what exists before life. Both acknowledge that energy is the first form that the Spirit, the Divine Consciousness-Force, assumes in the physical cosmos. Chardin called the second stage life. It is a pre-reflective process of trial and error groping, combined with the two-fold mechanism of reproduction and heredity, including additive improvements. Aurobindo also named the second stage life, living matter, and conscious animal. Life is "a form of veiled consciousness." It "evolves out of material elements" because "life is already involved in matter."[126]

Aurobindo's third stage of spiritual evolution is mind, a thinking, reasoning, mental being with consciousness. It evolves out of living form because mind is already involved in life. At first, matter "appears to be all together unconscious, then struggles toward mentality in the guise of living matter and attains to it imperfectly in the conscious animal. This consciousness is at first rudimentary, mostly a half-subconscious or just conscious instinct; it develops slowly till in more organized forms of living matter it reaches intelligence and exceeds itself in man, the thinking animal who develops into a reasoning mental being."[127]

Homo sapiens who have the power of reflection and thought are Chardin's third stage. From the threshold of reflection onwards, the evolutionary process reaches "a new form of biological existence." Thus, "reflection is . . . the power acquired by a consciousness to turn in upon itself, . . . no longer merely to know, but to know oneself. . . .. Admittedly the animal knows. *But it cannot know that it knows*: that is quite certain." If animals had the ability to know themselves, they would multiply inventions. Since they do not have this capacity, they are denied access to a whole domain of reality in which humans move freely because they are reflective. Animals are separated from humans by a chasm or threshold which they cannot cross. "It is not merely a matter of change of degree, but of change of nature." The humanizing of people in the depths of themselves by reflection makes it possible for them to recognize themselves as endowed with their own conscience and value. Another result of reflection is that humans are able to raise themselves into a new sphere, another world. "Abstraction, logic, reasoned choice and inventions, mathematics, art, calculation of space and time, anxieties and dreams of love—all these activities of the *inner life*" are consequences of reflection.[128]

Chardin's third stage of the emergence of the human mind and reflection leads to his fourth stage of growing complexity and consciousness. "Evolution is an ascent in consciousness. . . .. Therefore, it should culminate forwards in some sort of supreme consciousness." Beyond the elementary 'hominization' or humanization which is the individual leap in his third stage from instinct to thought, there is in his fourth stage the collective hominization and the progressive spiritualization of the whole species.

Humankind is "far from drifting biologically, under the influence of exaggerated individualism, towards a catastrophe or senility." Instead the human group is developing a higher order, a collective reflection. Chardin called this fourth stage by many names including supreme consciousness, hyper-reflection, hyper-personalization, noogenesis, spiritualization, and planetary spiritual transformation.[129]

For Chardin, the process of spiritual development is not open just to a privileged few to the exclusion of others, but rather it is open to everyone. His vision of the future foresees not only the spiritual union of all people and nations, but also the spiritual perfection and self-realization of each one of us. The combination of technical organization and inward spiritual concentration is "driving us together into a contact which tends to perfect each one of us by linking him organically to each and all of his neighbors." Chardin's 'fundamental law of being' is that "union differentiates." Union with others perfects and fulfills each individual. "In any domain—whether it be the cells of a body, the members of a society, or the elements of a spiritual synthesis—union differentiates. In every organized whole, the parts perfect themselves and fulfill themselves. . . .. According to the evolutionary structure of the world, we can only find our person by uniting together."[130]

Aurobindo admitted that "it is open to doubt . . . whether man has the capacity to develop into a higher evolutionary being." The reason for doubt is "because evolution is still halfway on its journey, is still in ignorance, is still seeking in the mind of a half-evolved humanity for its own purpose and significance." A human is "a transitional being; he is not final." Through spiritual evolution, a person climbs to the fourth stage of Supermind and "Divine Superman." The individual's mental being evolves into Supramental Truth-Consciousness. There are several levels between mind and Supermind. "These gradations may be summarily described as a series of sublimations of the consciousness through Higher Mind, Illuminated Mind, Intuition, and into Overmind and beyond it; there is a succession of self-transmutations at the summit of which lies the Supermind."[131]

For Aurobindo, the Divine Consciousness-Force works within what appears to be unconscious matter until it evolves into living matter. Living matter reaches its climax in intelligence and exceeds itself in the thinking human. "Hampered and burdened, mental man has still to evolve out of himself the fully conscious being, a Divine manhood, or a spiritual and supramental supermanhood which shall be the next product of evolution." With the rise of consciousness, the mental person evolved from matter and life, just as the supramental Supermind is beginning to evolve from the mental human. "Having evolved the mental creator, thinker, sage, prophet of an ideal, self-controlled, self-disciplined, harmonious being," the Divine goes deeper within and calls out your soul, inner mind, and heart to create "the spiritual sage, seer, prophet, God-lover, Yogi," Sufi, mystic, and Truth-Consciousness Spirit. All your existence as a supramental superhuman, your whole being, living, feeling, thinking, and acting, is "fused in Oneness with the Transcendent and Universal Spirit." In the center of your consciousness, in every cell of your body, in every vibration of your life force, you "feel the presence of the Divine."[132]

With this supramental consciousness, according to Aurobindo, you "act in an entire Transcendent freedom, a complete joy of the Spirit, an entire identity with the cosmic Spirit, and a spontaneous sympathy with all in the universe." With this Truth-Consciousness, you have "a new range of activities, new value for all things, a widening of your consciousness and life." You become an instrument of the Spirit, "a true doer of Divine works." There is no difference between your will and the Divine will. There is no action that is not God's "action in you and through you." Being God's instrument, you put everything in the Divine hands, "the thing to be done, the way to do it, and the result."[133]

According to Aurobindo, the change from mind to Supermind "might happen not only in a few, but extend and generalize itself in the race." The fulfillment of this possibility "would mean that the human dream of perfection . . . would be no longer a dream but a truth that could be made reality and humanity lifted out of . . . ignorance." At its highest, a new humanity, a race of mental beings and seekers of Truth-Consciousness, "would be capable of passing into the Supermind and from the new race would be recruited the race of supramental beings who would appear as the leaders of the evolution. Even the highest manifestations of a Mind of Light would be an instrumentality of the Supermind, . . . a stepping beyond humanity into Superhumanity." The extent of this transformation, "whether it would eventually embrace the whole of humanity or only an advanced portion of it, would depend upon the intention in evolution itself, on the intention in whatever Cosmic or Transcendent Will is guiding the movements of the universe."[134]

Aurobindo described the Supermind's "embodiment in a supramental race . . . and a new total action in which the new humanity would find its complete development and its assured place in the new order." The transformation that would establish "the Supermind and a supramental race of beings on the earth" would be "far reaching, even enormous." This race of supramental superhumans would not be molded to a single fixed type and pattern. "The law of the Supermind" is that unity is "fulfilled in diversity." Therefore, there would be an infinite diversity of Truth-Conscious Spirits. Everyone would be "a unique formation of Being" and different from every other, although each would be "One with all the rest." Each would also be "fused in Oneness with the Transcendent Spirit."[135]

Stages of Ken Wilber's Integral Spirituality

Ken Wilber is a contemporary, integral, spiritual author of more than 25 books. At the end of his 2000 book, *Integral Psychology: Consciousness, Spirit, Psychology, Therapy*, he very briefly agrees with Chardin and Aurobindo's four stages in the evolutionary process. "Spirit-in-action originally threw itself outward to create . . . Out of itself, as matter, it began; out of itself, as life, it continued; out of itself, as mind, it began to awaken." Thus, "from subconscious to self-conscious to superconscious, the great Play continues." In his 2017 book, *The Religion of Tomorrow: A Vision for the Future of the Great Traditions—More Inclusive, More Comprehensive, More Complete*, Wilber strongly affirms Aurobindo's fourth stage in which people become superhuman and develop a Supermind. When people go through Wilber's seven stages of human development and his four stages of spiritual consciousness, they can and may become superconscious and superhuman as well as attain a Supermind.[136]

Before describing Wilber's stages of spiritual consciousness that he calls Waking Up and his stages of human development that he refers to as Growing Up, it is important to say that in his Integral theory, he stresses that researchers need to study all four quadrants of a square to have a complete understanding of topics, including spirituality. The four quadrants are:

- the "I" is the Upper Left, "Interior—Individual (Intentional),"
- the "We" is the Lower Left, "Interior—Collective (Cultural),"
- the "It" is the Upper Right, "Exterior—Individual (Behavioral),"
- the "Its" is the Lower Right, "Exterior—Collective (Social)."

Wilber places the spiritual, emotional, and mental in the Upper Left quadrant. "All four of the perspectives from these quadrants need to be included for any truly comprehensive or inclusive account—and the same is true of spirituality."[137]

In his 2000 book, *Integral Psychology*, Wilber presents one hundred charts of stages of human development and spirituality by a multitude of authors, including Aurobindo and himself. These charts outline developmental stages for consciousness, cognition, needs, affects, the good life, psychology, self, ego, identity, self-integration, roles, gender identity, defenses, general characteristics, socio-emotional, social cognition, socio-cultural, social organization, basic structures, communication, actions, worldviews, empathy, ethics, morals, moral character, moral motivation, moral stages, faith, religious systems, contemplation, meditation, mysticism, and spirituality. Wilber studied these charts in developing his own stages.[138]

Waking Up is Wilber's phrase for his stages of spiritual consciousness. His first stage is called waking or gross or "psychic (shaman/yogi)—shamanic, nature mysticism, beginning tantric." Next is dreaming or "subtle (saint)—deity mysticism, yidam, contemplative prayer, advanced tantric." Third is deep dreamless sleep or "causal (sage)—vipassana, self-inquiry, bare attention, centering prayer, Witnessing, formless mysticism." The highest stage is nondual "unity" consciousness or "nondual (siddha)—Dzogchen, Mahamudra, Shaivism, Zen, Eckhart, nondual mysticism, etc."[139]

Going through Wilber's stages of "waking, dreaming, deep dreamless sleep, pure empty awareness or witnessing, and nondual 'unity' consciousness" results in "a full awakening and awareness of all the basic states of consciousness." As you meditate, "your Awareness . . . will begin to open onto vast, seemingly infinite stretches of Consciousness itself, plugged into what seems like all of space-time—vast, open, spacious, utterly dark yet suffused with infinite luminosity. At times it will appear completely unmanifest, a pure endless Abyss." Furthermore, "all of this pours out of your own Consciousness, the creative nexus of your own pure Self and infinite Will, often suffused with a radical Joy, pure Love, infinite Beauty, and unlimited Freedom." When this happens," a thread of this deep center of Awareness or Consciousness" is increasingly seen as "your own truest, deepest, fullest, most open Self, or pure I AMness. . . . With a sudden shock of Recognition, you realize that this is your one and only True Self," that "lives only in the timeless NOW."[140]

Next Wilber explains how we can reach the highest spiritual stage, the nondual "unity" consciousness. "The true Self is the pure Seer. . . . I can no more see the Seer than the eye can see itself. Resting in "this pure Witness or True Self," all I find is "a vast sense of Freedom, of Liberation, of Release, of Vast Expanse, of infinite Depth—a Freedom from identifying with all of these small, finite, puny objects . . . with which I had mistakenly identified my true and infinite Self." Eventually "as I rest in the infinite space of radical Emptiness and pure Freedom, . . . the Seer becomes one with all things seen, the subject and object become 'not two,'. . .. I no longer witness the mountain, I am the mountain. . . . The Empty Witness has become one (or nondual, not-two) with all objects. . . . The same is true of self and Spirit, finite and Infinite, . . . you and the ultimate Divine."[141]

In the highest stage of spirituality, nondual "unity" consciousness, "you experience universal love, or being one with all things, or being drenched in infinite bliss." This highest stage results in experiencing "Enlightenment, Awakening, moksha, metanoia, satori" as well as the "ultimate Reality, ultimate Truth, a Great Liberation," and "the Supreme Identity of the self with the ultimate all-pervading Divine, a union of . . . Infinite and Finite, One and Many, Spiritual and individual." It also leads to the "awakening of their ultimate, nondual, radical Great Perfection or True Nature, unborn and undying, uncreated and unlimited, timeless and eternal, spaceless and infinite—the world seen in its pure . . . Isness." Wilber summarizes this process by saying "mystical truths are found by looking within, focusing Awareness, and following Awareness back to its Source, there to awaken to *a unity with the ALL.*"[142]

Wilber contends that "ultimate Truth is not something that can be rationally demonstrated or proven." Agreeing with the world's religious traditions, he says that "humans have at least three modes of knowing." First, the eye of the flesh is grounded in conventional science with its proofs using sensory experience. Second, the eye of the mind uses reason and logic. Third, with the eye of contemplation, people have spiritual experiences that are "the foundation for the Waking Up realizations—for Enlightenment, Awakening." Scholars of the mystical teachings of the world's religions are "fairly unanimous in saying that although the outer teachings of each tradition are considerably different," the inner teachings, "based . . . on direct spiritual experiences of Waking Up, show a remarkable similarity."[143]

Wilber claims that "this universal core of Waking Up and ultimate Truth is . . . slowly but surely becoming less and less influential everywhere in the world." The two basic reasons are: first, people too often confuse the spiritual teachings based on mystical experiences with the "childish, mythic narratives that constitute probably 90 percent of world's religions," which humanity as it continues to mature increasingly finds "embarrassing and silly." The second reason is that even the schools that teach stages of spiritual consciousness "have become out of touch, out of date, outmoded," because they fail to recognize and utilize the new important facts and truths of the stages of human development involved in Growing Up that would "make Waking Up work even better."[144]

The stages of spiritual consciousness involved in Waking Up, according to Wilber, "have been seen, known, and understood by humans for thousands of years, going back at least 50,000 years to the first great shamans. In contrast, he says that the stages of human development involved in Growing Up "weren't discovered until around one hundred years ago," although people have been living these stages since their first ancestor. These Growing Up stages are an important, modern, and postmodern discovery "that affects Waking Up in profound, far-reaching, and absolutely crucial ways." In addition, evolution was discovered around 150 years ago. "Modern science now believes that evolution touches essentially everything in existence." One thing is certain. "Spiritual and religious systems themselves have undergone, and continue to undergo, evolution."[145]

Wilber states that "the ultimate purpose of spirituality and spiritual practice is to discover one's fundamental Supreme Identity with Spirit, with the Ground of all Being, with the ultimate Reality of the Kosmos itself." Perhaps spirituality's "most important and core functions" is "not just to introduce the human being to Spirit itself," but also to help people move through the stages of human development involved in Growing Up. Thus, it is "to act as a conveyor belt for the developmental levels of increased Spiritual understanding and awareness—actually the development of consciousness itself—all the way from the instinctual mind to Supermind, and every level in between."[146]

Before considering how Wilber's stages of human development involved in Growing Up enhance Waking Up and the Great Religious Traditions, these stages need to be described. "Just as an acorn goes through several universal stages on its way to becoming an oak tree, . . . so a human being goes through several universal stages on its way to maturity." Surprisingly, most of the time particularly in the early stages, individuals "have no idea" that they are following these universal stages, because "the stages of Growing Up can't be seen by merely looking within."[147]

After studying a number of other author's models, Wilber describes his seven stages of human development.

- Archaic is the stage of physiological needs, sensorimotor drives, and little or no boundary between the self and other in children's first year.

- Magic is the stage of fantasy, impulsive, immediate gratification, desire for self-protection, belief in God and/or Power Gods, and becoming a more separate self when children are one to three or four years old. These two earliest stages are egocentric with concern only for "me."

- Mythic-literal is the conformist, conventional, roles and rules, law and order, agrarian, tribal, fundamentalist, and traditional stage. "This is when the search for absolute truth originates." God speaks to special people. This stage is ethnocentric with concern only for "us."

- Rational is the scientific, industrial, postconformist, postconventional, autonomous, desire for self-esteem, demythologizing tradition, God not taken on faith but based on direct personal experience, progressive, and modern stage.

- Pluralistic is the multicultural; informational; postconventional; postmodern; a "keen sense of marginalized, oppressed, and suppressed minorities; a drive to correct injustices;" anti-discriminatory; tolerant; egalitarian; socially engaged; and liberal stage. The last two stages are worldcentric with care for "all of us." This is last of the first-tier stages. Approximately in early adulthood, "the Rational View gives way to the Pluralistic View."

- Integral is a second tier, holistic, unifying, inclusive, non-marginalizing, connective, systematic, post-postmodern, integrative, vision-logic, noticing universal common practices, contemplative, and spiritual stage. "Integral stages tend to emerge in early midlife."

- As "the highest available level so far," Super-Integral is a third tier, "self-transcending," co-creative, "universal/mystical," and "transpersonal" stage that has greater consciousness, "greater capacity for love, care, identity, concern, morals, compassion, creativity," and an understanding of "*the communion of all being*." The continuum of relationships runs from "*communion* to *union* to *identity*." These last two stages are Kosmocentric with care for "all being."

Using the phrase "arrested development, Wilber claims that "now most major religions are stuck at some form of mythic View, while the other intelligences are free to move into rational, pluralistic, holistic, and even integral Views."[148]

According to Wilber, as humans advance beyond the earlier stages of being egocentric with concern only for "me" and ethnocentric with concern only for "us," they become worldcentric with caring for "all of us" and Kosmocentric with caring for "all being." Their individual consciousness undergoes a "global transformation." It is "no longer egocentric or ethnocentric, it is becoming worldcentric and even Kosmocentric in its identity, motivations, desires, viewpoints, perspectives and capacities." The universal human development stages lead to a maturity "that is now in progress of becoming characterized by deep-seated care and integral loving-kindness."[149]

In the Super-Integral stage, "the spectrum of degrees of relationship run from communion to unity to identity." When people are in a communion which is the most common, they will feel an incredible closeness with the Divine, but no direct unity. The Super-Integral stage deals with the difficulty of integrating "heaven and earth, spiritual and conventional, infinite and finite, transpersonal and personal, eternity and time, other-worldly and this worldly. All of these are not only dimensions of a Kosmos out there but dimensions of one's own interior Being." Although "the spirituality of this level is clearly hard to describe 'accurately,'" it recognizes "the infinity and the finitude of every phenomenon, the oneness and manyness of every event."[150]

When around 10 percent of the population reach the Super-integral stage, the highest level of human development so far, Wilber claims that they become the tipping point and "major, profound, and extensive changes occur throughout the overall population, as these new emergent values begin to populate and saturate the culture." It is a fact that "the world . . . has indeed evolved over the last 2,000 years, becoming (as all evolution does) more and more conscious, more complex, more caring, more loving, more creative, and more self-organized." Thus, "the human race, *for the first time ever in history*, is heading toward at least the possibility of a world beyond major and deep-seated conflict, and toward one marked more and more often by mutual tolerance, embrace, peace, inclusion, and compassion."[151]

When Wilber "looks at the direction of overall development" of the evolutionary process from the first until now, "from strings to quarks to atoms to molecules to cells to multi-cellular organisms, each shows an increase in the universe's own sensitivity" and an increase in its awareness of its own being. "Starting with matter," moving to plants, animals, fish, reptiles, to mammals and primates, "each one is more sensitive, complex, unified, whole, conscious, and aware." Then come humans, who move through their own developmental stages and become more aware of themselves and all the world. The Integral stage has evolution's "sensitivity moving into inclusive, comprehensive, embracing forms, and from there into what can only be called superconscious and superhuman" in the Super-Integral stage. Because of evolution and because of "its own stunning self-organization and self-transcendence," the universe has "this overall, absolutely unmistakable direction to greater and greater wholeness, greater and greater sensitivity, greater and greater consciousness, . . . look where it is obviously headed . . . with something like a superhuman Supermind looming on our collective horizon."[152]

The Supermind that develops in the Super-Integral stage, according to Wilber, is "a fountain, flooding humanity with Divinity, leaning always to the unfolding of a genuine superhumanity in the making, the crossroads of a full Growing Up with a total Waking up, . . . a trans-transhumanism scarcely recognizable by any of today's standards or values." It leads to mystical experiences of "the oneness of all being" and to feelings of "a deep affinity, a solidarity, a union with all levels and dimensions of reality." Although the Supermind "lies in the emergent unconsciousness, . . . these features will flesh out considerably as evolution continues. . . . It is an event as startlingly new to the Kosmos, as the widest of the wide, the deepest of the deep, the highest of the high, ready to emerge and refashion the work, . . . waiting to flood the human mind with no less than the mind of God."[153]

As "the radical leading edge of evolution," Supermind is "the highest, widest, deepest, most inclusive" stage of human development. It is the highest stage "yet to emerge in evolution" and it is rare. It is "both the most infinitely complex and the utterly most simple occasion in existence." Furthermore, "Supermind is the radical crossroads where absolute and relative truth are not just exposed to each other, . . . but are deeply and intrinsically one (or not-two) with each other. . . . It is one of the most difficult nondual realizations to master." For example, in a deep sense, "eternity and time are the same, or not-two." When Supermind, the highest stage of human development, is "combined or conjoined" with the highest spiritual stage, the nondual "unity" consciousness, it is "the upper limit of both Growing Up and Waking Up."[154]

According to Wilber, Growing Up and Waking Up as "two very different dimensions or axes of development of the human mind and spirit—have very different forms, follow different paths, use different injunctions or practices for evoking them, and possess different stages." Bringing Waking Up and Growing Up together in theory and practice is "a truly revolutionary development" and "should be included in any genuinely Integral Spirituality." Stages of Waking Up "determine *what* you see" and experience, such as the nondual "unity" consciousness. Stages of Growing Up "determine *how* you see" and interpret it, such as at mythic-literal or rational or pluralistic or Integral stage. Thus, "the overall net effect" is the nondual "unity" consciousness as "the highest, widest, deepest, most infinite" spiritual stage being interpreted by Supermind, as "the highest, widest, deepest, most inclusive" stage of human development. "Any integral or complete spirituality (or simple complete Life Path) would want to include both."[155]

The Stages of the Mystics of Eastern Religions

Ancient Eastern mystics offered spiritual paths to the Divine. Since ancient times, Hinduism taught four yogas or paths to Brahman, the Absolute Spirit, which are names for the Divine. According to contemporary Swami Prabhavananda, "*Yoga* literally means union—union with God." Two Yogas are "*Bhakti Yoga*, the path of love" and devotion and "*Jnana Yoga*, the path of knowledge." The third is "*Karma Yoga*, the path of work" and the fourth is "*Raja Yoga*, the path of realization through meditation." The *Bhagavad Gita*, or *Gita*, a 2,500-year-old Hindu scripture stressed the first three of these paths. According to the Swami, "in and through this triune way of knowledge, works, and devotion, runs the thread of Raja Yoga or the path of meditation."[156]

The *Gita* is a dialogue between God called Krishna and his disciple named Arjuna. The Divine Krishna says, "in this world there are two roads of perfection: . . . Jnana Yoga, the path of wisdom . . . and Karma Yoga, the path of action." In addition, "work not for a reward, but never cease to do thy work. Do thy work in peace of Yoga and, free from selfish desires, be not moved in success or in failure. . . . Seers in union with wisdom forsake the rewards of their work, and free from the bonds of birth they go to the abode of salvation." Furthermore, "even as the unwise work selfishly in the bondage of selfish works, let the wise man work unselfishly for the good of all the world." Besides work, the Divine Krishna advocates wisdom. "Work done for a reward is much lower than work done in the Yoga of wisdom. Seek salvation in the wisdom of reason. . . . In this wisdom a man goes beyond what is well done and what is not well done. Go thou therefore to wisdom. . . . When thy mind, that may be wavering in the contradictions of many scriptures, shall rest unshaken in Divine contemplation, then the goal of Yoga is thine."[157]

Besides work and wisdom, the Divine Krishna in the *Gita* adds the third path of Bhakti Yoga, the path of love and devotion. "There are some great souls who know Me: their refuge is my own Divine nature. They love Me with a Oneness of love: they know that I am the Source of all. They praise Me with devotion, they praise Me for ever and ever." In addition, "he who offers to Me with devotion only a leaf, or a flower, or a fruit, or even a little water, this I accept from that yearning soul, because with a pure heart it was offered with love. Whatever you do, or eat, or give, or offer in adoration, let it be an offering to Me." Furthermore, "those who set their hearts on Me and ever in love worship Me, and who have unshakable faith, these I hold as the best yogis." Moreover, "they for whom I am the End Supreme, who surrender all their works to Me, and who with pure love meditate on Me and adore Me—these I very soon deliver from the ocean of death and life-in-death, because they set their hearts on Me."[158]

Sometime between the fourth century BCE and the fourth century CE, Patanjali was a Hindu teacher who recorded sutras, aphorisms, or sayings about yoga practices. Besides describing the reserve of spiritual energy called *kundalini* and the four yogas as "paths to union with God," he presented the eight spiritual disciplines or the eight limbs of yoga. As soon as all impurities of the mind and the obstacles to enlightenment are "removed by the practice of spiritual disciplines—the 'limbs' of yoga—one's spiritual vision opens to the light-giving knowledge of *Atman*" and *Brahman*. Patanjali's first limb is *yama* that involves "abstention from harming others, from falsehood, from theft, from incontinence (or no chastity), and from greed." The second spiritual discipline is *niyamas* or observances that are "purity, contentment, mortification, study, and devotion to God." The third limb is *asana* or posture that is "to be seated in a position which is firm but relaxed," erect, and absolutely still.[159]

After mastering posture, the fourth spiritual practice is control of *prana* or *pranayama*. Prana can be translated as 'breath.' Contemporary mystic Deepak Chopra describes prana as the life force, the essential life energy. All the functions of the senses and mind as well as all the powers of body are "expressions of the force of prana." We control prana "by stopping the motions of inhalation and exhalation." Patanjali's fifth limb is *pratyahara* which is the withdrawal of the mind from sense objects that results in "complete mastery over the senses." The sixth spiritual discipline is *dharana* or concentration, that is "holding the mind within a center of spiritual consciousness in the body, or fixing it on some Divine form, either within the body or outside it." The seventh limb is *dhyana* or meditation that involves "an unbroken flow of thought toward the object of concentration." Patanjali's eighth and last spiritual discipline is *samadhi* or absorption in and union with Brahman, the Absolute Spirit. The liberated yogi who is "purified by samadhi is freed from all latent impressions of karma and from all cravings." Contemporary authors such as Chopra and Wayne Dyer discuss Patanjali's writings.[160]

Living around 2,500 years ago, Siddhartha Gautama experienced an awakening and was given the title Buddha which meant the Awakened One. For 40 years, he taught what he learned from his enlightenment, the Four Noble Truths and the Eightfold Path to Nirvana. The Buddhist scriptures say that the first Noble Truth is that all life is suffering (*dukkha*) and unhappiness. The second is that the cause of suffering is selfish craving (*tanha*). The third Truth is that suffering can be stopped by ending selfish craving. The fourth is that the eightfold path will destroy selfish craving and thus suffering and unhappiness. The eightfold path is "right views, right intention, right speech, right action, right livelihood, right effort, right mindfulness, and right concentration." Following this path leads to "higher knowledge, enlightenment, Nirvana."[161]

One of the many Buddhist scriptures is the third-century BCE *Dhammapada* that can be translated as the Path of Perfection, the Path of Truth, or the Path of Righteousness. This book speaks about the Four Noble Truths and the Eightfold Path. "The best of the paths is the path of eight. The best of the truths is the path of four. The best of the states, freedom from passions. The best of men, the one who sees. This is the path. There is no other that leads to vision. . . . Whoever goes on this path travels to the end of sorrow." Nevertheless, the Dhammapada stresses two paths, two ways of living. Its first words are: "what we are today comes from our thoughts of yesterday, and our present thoughts build our life of tomorrow: our life is the creation of our mind. If a man speaks or acts with an impure mind, suffering follows him as the wheel of the cart follows the beast that draws the cart.... If a man speaks with a pure mind, joy follows him as his own shadow."[162]

Additional teachings of the Dhammapada include that the person who does good "rejoices on the path of joy." He who does evil "laments on the path of sorrow." The wise student, who knows that "this body is the foam of a wave, the shadow of a mirage," finds the clear path of perfection. The one who is ever thirsty for desires and sensuous passions makes death his end. This scripture contrasts many paths, including the paths of ignorance and wisdom, darkness and light, vice and virtue, earthly wealth and Nirvana. "Better than a hundred years not seeing the Path supreme is one single day of life if one sees the Path supreme."[163]

The Stages of Early Christian Mystics

Perhaps a natural scheme for a journey to the Divine is a progression of three stages from beginning to the middle and finally to the end. As early as the third century, Origen, an Egyptian Christian theologian, attempted to describe the mystical way to God in a threefold pattern. This biblical interpreter showed how the three books ascribed to Solomon, which are Proverbs, Ecclesiastes, and Song of Songs, form the basis for the three stages of a Christian format similar to the Greek philosophical education of moral, natural, and contemplative sciences. Toward the end of the fourth century, Evagrius Ponticus, a Christian monk, organized the process for a life of prayer into a threefold blueprint. The first independent stage is the ascetical life in which the soul overcomes vices, acquires virtues, and gives birth to love (*agape*). The second is the contemplation of the created universe, while the third stage is "the highest and endless contemplation" that attains essential knowledge of God.[164]

In Christianity, the classic formulation was the threefold mystical way to the Divine that was created by an unknown theologian who called himself Denys the Areopagite, after Paul's first Athenian convert. He was also called Dionysius the Areopagite and Pseudo-Dionysius. Thought to be a Syrian monk, he wrote around 500 CE. His three stages were purification, illumination, and complete perfection and union. Using the Bible to illustrate, Denys said that first, Moses purifies himself. In the second stage of illumination, he "does not meet God Himself, but contemplates, not Him who is invisible, but rather where He dwells." The highest and holiest of perceived things presuppose the Transcendent One. "Through them . . . His unimaginable presence is shown." Then in the third stage, renouncing all the mind's conceptions and wrapped in the Invisible and Intangible, Moses "is supremely united to" and "belongs completely to Him who is beyond everything." All who reach union are "truly and supernaturally enlightened."[165]

Many contemporary scholars of mysticism, such as William Johnston and Ursula King, follow Denys the Areopagite in saying there are three stages on the 'ladder of perfection' and the mystical way to union with God. King says, the first stage is "the *purgative life*, the way of purification" in which the mystic moves away from the world of senses by "detachment, renunciation, and asceticism." The second stage of the mystic way is "the *illuminative life* which is reached by loving contemplation." The third and highest stage is "the *unitive life*, the ultimate goal of loving union with God." This is "an ecstatic experience of overwhelming joy." For some mystics, union means "absorption, fusion, utter identity," and Oneness with the Divine. For others, it is "the highest consummation of love" and union in which the lover continues to be the Beloved's creation.[166]

John Climacus wrote *The Ladder of Divine Ascent*. This seventh-century monk who lived in Sinai used the biblical image of the ladder in Genesis. When Jacob went to Haran, "he dreamed that there was a ladder set up on earth, the top of it reaching to heaven; and the angels of God were ascending and descending on it." Climacus' ladder had thirty rungs of the spiritual life. In the contemporary Introduction to Climacus' book, Kallistos Ware claims that the pattern of thirty rungs could be put in a scheme of three main sections. The first section starts with "the initial 'turning' or conversion." This includes "the break with the 'world,' the renunciation both outward and inward" that forms the beginning of any spiritual ascent. The second section continues with "a detailed analysis of the virtues and vices." This presents "the 'active life' or 'practice of the virtues' . . . along with the corresponding passions that must be uprooted." In the third section, "the supreme end of the spiritual way is not contemplation or *gnosis* but love. . . . The final step on love is concerned with both the active and the contemplative life at once; in the context of Divine Love there can be no sharp differentiation between the two."[167]

The Stages of Islamic Mystics

The *Quran*, the seventh-century Islamic scripture, presents two paths. True believers follow the straight path, the right path, the path of salvation, the path of God that leads to Paradise. Unbelievers and sinners follow the path of affliction that leads to "the fierce, tormenting flames" of Hell. The Quran says, "this book is not to be doubted. It is a guide to the righteous, who have faith in the Unseen and are steadfast in prayer; who bestow in charity a part of what we have given to them; who trust what has been revealed to you and to others before you, and firmly believe in the life to come. These are rightly guided by the Lord; these shall surely triumph." In contrast, "for the unbelievers, whether you forewarn them or not, they will not have faith. Allah has set a seal upon their hearts and ears; their sight is dimmed and a grievous punishment awaits them." The Quran also says, "believers, if you help Allah, Allah will help you and make you strong. But the unbelievers shall be consigned to perdition." In addition, "for those who have faith and do good works and humble themselves before the Lord, they are the heirs of Paradise and there they shall abide forever. Can the blind and the deaf ever be compared to those that can see and hear? Such are the unbelievers compared to the faithful."[168]

Sufism is a mystical tradition of Islam. Contemporary Sufi scholar John Baldock says that different authors presented various stages on the Islamic Sufi path. In the eleventh century, Qushairi's *Risala* presented 45 stages. Others described only two stages. "The first is to step out of the self, the second is to step into union with God." The twelfth-century Persian Islamic Sufi Fariduddin Attar's path had seven 'valleys' or stages. In "the Conference of Birds," he told the story of birds realizing that they have no king and deciding to find one. Their guide Hoopoe informs them that "they already have a mysterious King" named Simurgh who lives at the end of world beyond the mountains. To reach Him, they have to pass through seven valleys or stages. Attar's first stage is the Valley of the Quest where they renounce all worldly things and devote themselves to the quest. "Love begins to open their hearts." Second is the Valley of Love. Desiring to reach the Beloved, the seekers are consumed by the flames of love. "They will give up everything they own to spend just one moment in the Divine presence."[169]

The third stage is Attar's Valley of Understanding, also called the Valley of Mystical Apprehension or Gnosis. Each quester takes a different path to gain understanding that is appropriate to his attributes and state. When his understanding is illuminated by the light of Truth, the sense of a separate self disappears and the Divine Unity is revealed within everything. In the Valley of Detachment, the fourth stage, all striving for their desires and meaning cease, their attachment to the world decreases, and their trivial pursuits are abandoned for what is essential in life. The fifth stage is the Valley of Unity. Although many or few things appear, "they are all one."[170]

Attar's sixth stage is the Valley of Astonishment which is a place of sadness and pain. The Unity that the seekers knew is gone and is replaced by uncertainty and sorrowful bewilderment. Words are not adequate to describe the last stage, the Valley of Poverty and Annihilation, because all is forgotten and the mind is gone. When the individual drop of water, symbolizing the purified soul, sinks into the Ocean, symbolizing God, it loses its separate identity and becomes One with the Ocean. When the seekers finished the journey through the seven valleys, a herald greets them, tests them, and opens the door. In Attar's own words, "they were *within*—they were before the *Throne*. Before the Majesty that sat thereon, but wrapt in so insufferable a Blaze of Glory as beat down their baffled gaze." Attar continues, then they looked upon a scroll that flashed back "the whole of the half-forgotten story of their souls." All who reflected, "see themselves in Me, and Me in them" as "individual drops of rain then melt into the Universal Main."[171]

The Stages of Twelfth to Fourteen Century Christian Mystics

The twelfth-century French monk William of Saint-Thierry offered a threefold itinerary. "Just as star differs from star in brightness, so does . . . the way of life of beginners, of advanced, and of perfect." The state of beginners is called the animal stage in which people are concerned with their body. The advanced state is the rational stage; here what matters is to be intellectual and to develop understanding. In the perfect or spiritual stage, they are concerned with the Divine.[172]

In the *Threefold Way*, Bonventure, a thirteenth-century Italian Franciscan friar, outlined several triple paths. "There is a threefold way of exerting oneself in this threefold path, namely, by reading and meditating, by praying, and by contemplating" as one works toward wisdom. Echoing Denys the Areopagite, he said that there is "the triple hierarchical activity that is purgation, illumination, and perfection." We ascend to God through these three steps, "through purgative, which consists of getting rid of sin; through the illuminative, which consists in the imitation of Christ; and through the unitive, which consists in receiving the Bridegroom" who is God. "Purgation leads to peace, illumination to truth, perfection to charity." The knowledge of the whole of scripture and the merit of eternal life depend on knowledge of these three things: "an eternal grasp of the highest peace, an open vision of the highest truth, and the full enjoyment of the highest goodness and charity."[173]

Bonventure was also the author of *The Soul's Journey into God* which presents the first "six steps of illumination that begin with creatures and lead up to God" and that culminate in the seventh stage of "divine contemplation that leads to mystical ecstasy." These seven stages reflect "the threefold existence of things," nature, the soul, and the Eternal. They also reflect the triple movement of the mind, first, outward to external material things; second, inward into the soul; and third, above "to ascend into God so as to love Him." In the first stage, we contemplate God through nature, through His footprints in the universe. "The Creator's supreme power, wisdom, and benevolence shine forth in created things" in their sevenfold properties: "origin, magnitude, multitude, beauty, fullness, activity, and order."[174]

In Bonventure's second stage, we contemplate God in His vestiges in the sense world. Through the five senses, we realize that "everything that is moved is moved by something else," and "we are led to the knowledge of spiritual movers." Through apprehension, the sense world enters the soul. "From this apprehension . . . follows pleasure" and "after this apprehension and pleasure comes judgment. . . . All these are vestiges in which we can see our God." In the third stage, we contemplate "God through His image stamped upon our natural powers" of memory, intellect, and will. These powers lead us to God. In the fourth stage, we contemplate "God in His image reformed by the gifts of grace." The image of our soul needs to be reformed and "clothed with the three theological virtues" of faith, hope, and love. These virtues help the soul be "purified, illumined, and perfected."[175]

In the fifth state according to Bonventure, we contemplate "the Divine Unity through its primary name of Being." Pure Being "cannot be . . . received from another." Primary Being is "eternal, utterly simple, most actual, most perfect, and supremely One." In the sixth stage, we contemplate "the most blessed Trinity in its name which is Good." In thinking about the essential attributes and name of God, "Being itself is the root principle . . . so the Good itself is the principal foundation." When we behold supreme, superexcellent Goodness, we see "the purity of goodness which is the pure act of a principle loving in charity with a love that is both free and due." The seventh stage is most secret and no one but the mystic knows it. When we pass over into "spiritual and mystical ecstasy," all our senses and "all intellectual activities must be left behind." Then, "the height of our affection must be totally transferred and transformed into God." We transcend ourselves and all things "by the immeasurable and absolute ecstasy of a pure mind" and pass over into unity with God, into "the superessential ray of the Divine darkness." We "pass out of this world to the Father."[176]

Marguerite Porete, the French Beguine author of the mystical classic, *The Mirror of Simple Souls*, was burned at the stake as a heretic in Paris in 1310. Her book is a dialogue between Reason, Love, and the Soul about the relationship between humans and the Divine. The Soul says, there are seven stages or states or "degrees by which one ascends from the valley to the height of the mountain, which is so isolated that one sees nothing save God." Porete's first stage is "the life of grace . . . which is born in the death of sin." The Soul is "touched by God through grace and stripped of her power of sin." For the rest of her life, she intends to keep God's commandments to love Him with all her heart and to love her neighbor as herself.[177]

Porete's second stage is "the life of the spirit, which is born in the death of nature." The Soul thinks that God advises His special lovers to go beyond His commandments. The lover tries to please her Beloved, "abandons self and strains self above all to do the counsels of men, in the work of mortification of nature, in despising riches, delights and honors, in order to accomplish the perfection of the evangelical counsel." Porete's third stage includes "those who are dead to the life of the spirit and *live the Divine life.*" The soul "through a boiling desire of love" is sharpened in multiplying works of perfection. Her gift is not prized unless she gives the thing she most loves. To practice martyrdom, "she obliges herself to obey another will," to abstain from the works of goodness that she loves, and "to destroy her own will." She enlarges the place for love by "breaking and bruising the self."[178]

In Porete's fourth state, "the Soul is drawn by the height of love into the delight of thought through meditation." She is so "marvelously filled" and "completely inebriated" with love that she is deceived into believing that there are no more stages and "no higher life." The Soul in the fifth stage thinks about two considerations. "God is Who is, from whom all things are" and she does not exist "if she is not of Him." God who is Being wills that she "who has no being might have being." Divine Goodness places free will within her and she gives this will to God. The Soul sees her own wretchedness and nothingness that are a deep, great "bottomless abyss." Her wretchedness makes the Soul see "the true Sun of the Highest Goodness." This Goodness transforms her and "unites her into Divine Goodness."[179]

In Porete's sixth state, the Soul neither sees herself because of an abyss of humility nor sees God because of the Divine Goodness. "But God sees Himself in her" and "God shows to her that there is nothing except Him." Thus, she "understands nothing except Him, and so loves nothing except Him, praises nothing except Him, for there is nothing except Him." The Soul says that "none know how to speak" about the seventh and last stage. In the sixth state the Soul is "not at all glorified. For the glorification is at the seventh stage, which we will have in glory" when we die. "The seventh stage Love keeps to Herself in order to give It to us in Eternal glory, of which we will have no understanding until our soul has left our body."[180]

The fourteenth-century French Dominican mystic John Tauler said that the path to union with God has three stages. The journey begins when a person is aware of the marvelous signs, works, and gifts that show the hidden Goodness and Love of God. "Everything blossoms, sprouts forth, and is filled with God." When he perceives this through loving insight, he is "flooded with an interior joy," *jubilatio*, "great genuine joy." The Lord "gives him inwardly an embrace of palpable union." Thus, God pulls and yanks him out of himself. In Tauler's second stage, God draws "a person so far away from all things, and he is no longer a child" but a mature adult. Then he is "led onto a terribly wild path" and "God takes back from him everything that He had ever given." Left in this distressed state, "he suffers such incredible pain." Then "he has neither any feeling for nor knowledge of God, and he has no liking for any other things." It seems that "he is suspended between two walls" with a sharp spear in front and a sword in back. There is no way to go. "If there could be hell in this life, this would be more than hell—to be bereft of loving and the good thing loved." The more he formerly felt for God, "the greater and more unendurable are the bitterness and misery of this abandonment."[181]

In Tauler's third stage, "the Lord removes the cloak from his eyes and reveals the truth to him. Bright sunshine appears and lifts him right out of all his misery." Besides making him forget his loneliness and healing all his wounds, "God thus draws the person out of his human mode into the Divine mode, out of all misery into Divine security. Here a person becomes so divinized that everything he is and does God does and is in him." Conscious that he has lost himself, "he is aware of nothing but one simple Being." Achieving true unity of prayer, "a person becomes One with God."[182]

The fourteenth-century Italian mystic and activist Catherine of Siena wrote about *The Dialogue* she had with the Divine. God said that His Son, Christ is the bridge. "He had made a stairway of his body." The soul needs to escape from sin, mount the bridge's three spiritual stairs to go from "the imperfection of slavish fear" to "the perfection of love." The first stair is Christ's nailed feet which symbolize the soul's affections. In this stage, "she stripped herself of sin." The second stage is Christ's open side and heart which symbolize the love in her own heart that seeks union. In this stage, "she dressed herself in love for virtue." Catherine's third stair is Christ's mouth which symbolizes the peace of union and the call to action. In this stage, "she tastes peace." God said to Catherine, "when the soul has climbed up on the feet of affection and looked with her mind's eye into my Son's opened heart, she begins to feel the love of her own heart in His consummate and unspeakable Love."[183]

God also spoke to Catherine about two ways. Those who do not follow the way of truth "travel below through the river." Those wicked sinners, who are "blinded by selfishness," scorn the good and choose sinfulness. They have "no concern for anyone or anything but themselves," so "they have lost Me, the supreme and eternal Good." God said to Catherine that those who follow the way of truth travel over the bridge. They are "harmoniously united... with Me through the movement of love." Those just souls who live in charity "forever rejoice in love at the sight of Me, sharing in that goodness which I have in Myself and which I measure out to them according to the measure of love with which they come to Me" and their neighbors. "All things are good and perfect, since they are made by Me" through My supreme Goodness and unspeakable Love. What God asks is "nothing other than love and affection for Me" and for their neighbors. "This can be done any time, any place, and in any state of life." Then they will have "finished their lives in charity, delighting in Me and filled with good will toward their neighbors."[184]

The Seven Stages of Teresa of Avila's Interior Castle

In Spain in the sixteenth century, Teresa of Avila was a mystic and also an activist who founded and reformed many Carmelite convents and several monasteries. In her book, *The Interior Castle*, she explained the soul's journey to loving communion with God. "Our soul is like a castle made out of a diamond." Although she said that this "shining and beautiful castle" has many dwelling places, she describes only seven rooms. In the center of the soul in the seventh and main dwelling place is God who is "always present in the soul." The gate that provides entry into this castle is "prayer and reflection." The soul that practices prayer and reflection needs to walk through the rooms. In Teresa's first dwelling place, "souls are still absorbed in the world and engulfed in their pleasures and vanities, with honors and pretenses." Besides committing sins, "through our own fault we don't understand ourselves or know who we are." Problems arise, harm is done, and "fears come from not understanding ourselves completely." Thus, "self-knowledge is the most important thing for us." Self-knowledge is the necessary, good, and right road and "never... is anything else more fitting." In addition, "humility, like the bee making honey in the bee-hive, is always at work." When the soul ponders the majesty and grandeur of God, "it will discover its lowliness.... While we are on this earth nothing is more important to us than humility." In Teresa's opinion, "we shall never completely know ourselves if we don't strive to know God."[185]

Souls in Teresa's second stage begin to practice prayer with more effort. While in the first room, they were like deaf-mutes. In the second, they are "able to hear the Lord's callings" to draw near Him. These calls come through sermons, books, prayers, illnesses, and trials. After God gives "this first favor," He waits because He perceives our "perseverance and good desires" that are necessary. "The whole aim for any person who is beginning prayer—should be that he work and prepare himself . . . to bring his will into conformity with God's will. . . . the greatest perfection attainable along the spiritual path lies in this conformity. It is the person who lives in more perfect conformity who will receive more from the Lord and be more advanced on this road." Perfection does not involve "some mystery or things unknown or still to be understood, for in perfect conformity to God's will lies all our good."[186]

In Teresa's third dwelling place, we "who fear the Lord" are on the path to salvation. We "long not to offend His Majesty, even guarding against venial sins," practice penance and recollection, and do works of charity for our neighbors. It is not enough to say we want to possess God but do nothing and take no actions. "Great dryness in prayer comes from this." Our love for God must be proved by our actions. God doesn't need our works, but "He needs the determination of our wills." When we experience dryness, we may find humility. "Where humility is truly present God will give peace and conformity" to His will. Being rulers of our passions lies "in striving to practice the virtues, in surrendering our will to God in everything, . . . and in desiring that His will not ours be done." What usually harms us is doing our own will. Perfection consists "in greater love and in deeds done with greater justice and truth."[187]

"Supernatural experiences begin" in Teresa's fourth dwelling place. They are "the most difficult to explain" so she mentioned the differences between "consolations and spiritual delights." Consolations are experiences such as peace and joy that we acquire from our human nature and our petitions to the Lord as well as through our meditations, virtuous work, and effort. "They end in God." Spiritual delights "begin in God, but human nature feels and enjoys them." Teresa used the image of "two founts with two water troughs" to explain the differences. Consolations that are drawn from meditation are like the trough that is filled from the water that comes through the work of many aqueducts. Spiritual delights are like the trough that is filled from the spring. The water that overflows the trough forms a large stream. No skill is needed and the water always flows. In other words, spiritual delights come from their own source, which is God who grants supernatural favors. "The delight fills everything" and "overflows through all the dwelling places." God who is deep within us expands our heart and "our whole interior being." For us, "the initial thing necessary for such favors is to love God without self-interest."[188]

Continuing in the fourth stage by means of the prayer of recollection, the senses and exterior things lose their hold. The soul "senses a gentle drawing inward, . . . like a turtle drawing into its shell." This recollection "doesn't come when we want, but when God wants to grant us the favor." What is most pleasing and essential to God is that "we be mindful of His honor and glory and forget ourselves and our own profit and comfort and delight." The soul is no longer constrained by fear of hell, penance, poor health, and trials, because it has an "even greater fear of offending God." Because it experiences spiritual delights, it perceives that "worldly delights are like filth." To ascend on the path, "the important thing is not to think much but to love much; and so do that which best stirs you to love." Love "doesn't consist in great delight but in desiring with strong determination to please God in everything, in striving . . . not to offend Him."[189]

In Teresa's fifth dwelling place, the Divine is "joined and united with the essence of the soul. . . .. This union is above all earthly joys, above all delights, above all consolations." While union with God lasts, the soul is without its senses and its faculties are asleep to the world. It has "died to the world so as to live more completely in God." Because God places Himself in the interior of the soul, it can't doubt that "it was in God and God was in it." Teresa presented the image of the silkworm that weaves its cocoon, dies, and a white butterfly comes forth. We are to weave our cocoon "by taking away our self-love and self-will, our attachment to any earthly thing, and by performing deeds of penance, prayer, mortification, obedience." When the soul is doing God's will, it will not go astray. When the soul is dead to the world, it is transformed and joined in union with God. It surrenders into His hands so that "it neither knows nor wants anything more than what He wants." God "asks of us only two things: love of His Majesty and love of our neighbor. . . . the more advanced you see you are in love of your neighbor, the more advanced you will be in the love of God." What God wants is action. The love of God is the root of the love of our neighbor.[190]

Teresa's sixth stage is spiritual betrothal. God wants the soul to desire more union. From union with God comes fortitude for the trials of persecutions, denigrations, illnesses, and spiritual afflictions that lie ahead. The best remedy to endure them is "to engage in external works of charity and to hope in the mercy of God who never fails." Often when the soul is "distracted and forgetful of God, His Majesty will awaken it" and call it. The Spouse wounds the soul with an act of love. While the soul is burning with longing for God, a blow is felt from Him. "The soul will feel pierced by a fiery arrow." This sudden flash of lightning "cause a sharp wound . . . in the very deep and intimate part of the soul" and "reduces to dust everything it finds in this earthly nature of ours." In addition, "this pain reaches to the soul's very depths." While removing the arrow, "God is drawing these very depths after Him," withdrawing the soul's deep love. The flaming fire produces a spark that struck the soul. The spark "doesn't set the soul on fire," but "the fire is so delightful." As the spark burns out, "the soul is left with the desire to suffer again the loving pain the spark causes."[191]

Teresa said that in this sixth stage God has other ways of awakening the soul. One is the many kinds of locutions, where God speaks to the soul. Another way the Lord awakens the soul is by giving it ecstasies or "raptures that draw it out of its senses" so "God carries off for Himself the entire soul." Yet another is intellectual and imaginative visions. The Spouse gives the betrothed three jewels. The first gift is "knowledge of the grandeur of God, because the more we see of the grandeur, the greater is our understanding." The second is "self-knowledge and humility" so we see how low we are in comparison to our Creator. The third gift is "little esteem of earthly things save for those that can be used for the service of . . . God." As the soul "knows ever more the grandeur of its God, . . . the desire for the Lord increases much more; also love increases."[192]

The seventh and final stage of Teresa's mystical journey is spiritual marriage, the inseparable union of the soul and God. This secret union happens in the very center of the soul where God is always present. "God now desires to remove the scales from the soul's eyes and let it see and understand." The great and sublime secret that God communicates is that "the soul, I mean the spirit, is made One with God." While in spiritual betrothal the soul and God can be separated, in spiritual marriage they "cannot be separated." Their union is like rain falling into a river or a small stream entering the sea and becoming one. "There is no means of separating" the soul and God. In emptying ourselves and detaching from all that is earthly, the "Lord will fill us with Himself."[193]

Given by God, some of the effects on the soul of spiritual marriage according to Teresa are "a forgetfulness of self" and "a great desire to suffer." Another effect when you are persecuted is "a deep interior joy" and much more peace without any hostile feelings. Still other effects are "a great detachment from everything" and a desire either to be alone or "to serve Him" by working for the benefit of other souls. "The purpose of this spiritual marriage" is "the birth always of good works." The task at hand is "serving the Lord in all possible things" and not desiring the impossible. "You need not be desiring to benefit the whole world but must concentrate on those who are in your company." Your service and great charity toward all as well as your love for God are no small benefit. "This fire of love in you enkindles their souls" and awakens them. Teresa's conclusion is that "we shouldn't build castles in the air. The Lord doesn't look so much at the greatness of our works as at the love with which they are done. And so we do what we can."[194]

The Stages of Contemporary Mystics

Claiming that there is "the universal formula" in cultures around the globe, Joseph Campbell, an expert on myths around the world, describes the three stages of the mythological hero's journey as "(1) separation, (2) initiation, and (3) return." Campbell's brief summary of this pattern says, "a hero ventures forth from the world of common day into a region of supernatural wonder; fabulous forces are there encountered and a decisive victory is won; the hero comes back from this mysterious adventure with the power to bestow boons on his fellow men." In Campbell's blueprint, first, heroes separate from their familiar life; second, they are initiated by facing challenges, ordeals, and struggles; third, their return home is "a rebirth to a new world," where they are "the reflex of a larger self." Thus, "the ultimate aim of the quest... must be neither release nor ecstasy for oneself, but wisdom and power to serve others."[195]

Many contemporary authors use Campbell's threefold pattern, including Joan Borysenko, who calls it "the transformative process" in which "the person we're becoming is none other than who we really are." In addition, she uses the rainbow as a symbol of hope and a metaphor for the seven paths to God, because as white light goes through raindrops, seven colors are revealed. In an indivisible whole, each color is "a precious reflection of one aspect of Divine consciousness." In developing her seven paths, she draws on the seven directions of the Native American Medicine Wheel, on the accounts of mystics in many traditions, on the ancient yoga science, and on contemporary work on the seven chakras of the ancient Hindu *kundalini*. Her seven paths to God are (1) "earth and home: the everyday mystic," (2) "creativity and abundance: generosity of spirit," (3) "how can I help? The passion to serve," (4) "the way of the heart: bridging earth and heaven," (5) "discipline, ethics, and will: Thy will, not mine, be done," (6) "opening the wisdom eye: contemplation and transformation," (7) "the way of faith: paradox and grace."[196]

Caroline Myss, a contemporary author, explains "seven lessons of the universal spiritual path." Her "new model of the human energy system" is "based on the synthesis of three spiritual traditions: the Hindu teachings regarding the seven chakras, the symbolic meaning of the seven Christian sacraments, and the mystical interpretation of the ten sefirot—or Tree of Life—presented in the *Zohar*," a major text of the Jewish mystical teachings. Myss' merging of her three chosen traditions "symbolizes the seven levels of the human energy system and the seven stages of human development, or the seven essential lessons of the universal spiritual path." Myss' seven chakras are tribal power, the power of relationships, personal power, emotional power, the power of the will, the power of the mind, and "our connection to our spiritual nature." Maria Harris, another contemporary author, offers seven steps to women's spirituality: awakening, dis-covering, creating, dwelling, nourishing, traditioning, and transforming.[197]

Besides his four evolutionary stages that were discussed earlier, Aurobindo created a theory of Integral Yoga. In seeking the Infinite, all different forms of yoga "aim in their own way at a union or unity of the human soul with the supreme Spirit." The process of yoga is "a turning of the human soul from the egoistic state of consciousness absorbed in the outward appearances and attractions of things to a higher state in which the Transcendent and Universal can pour Itself into the individual mold and transform it." The heart's eagerness for the Divine "devours the ego."[198]

Aurobindo described five yogas and the "powers of the mental-soul-life" that each uses. The yoga of knowledge and wisdom uses as its chosen instrument reason and the mental vision to reach God-knowledge and God-vision. "Its aim is to see, know, and be the Divine." The yoga of work and action chooses for its instrument "the will of the doer of works." Its purpose is "contact and increasing unity of the soul of man with the Divine Master of the universe." The yoga of devotion and love chooses "the emotional and aesthetic powers of the soul." Its aim is God-possession and unity with the Divine Being. The chosen instrument of hatha yoga uses the body and life in physical postures and other processes until "it meets with and it becomes One with the Divine consciousness." Raja yoga chooses the mind as its instrument. The mind when it is stilled "can lose itself in the Divine consciousness and the soul be made free to unite with the Divine Being." Different yogas are parallel lines of advance. Their aim is to awaken the soul to the Divine within. "Each therefore offers a sufficient way, for all the 100 separate paths meet in the Eternal." Each causes "a complete lifting of the whole nature of man into a Divine and spiritual existence" and fulfillment. Each of the ways at its height can lead to fulfillment. It is sufficient to start with anyone. It is more difficult to start with several at once. In the end, "all power is soul-power."[199]

In addition, Aurobindo has three stages of Integral Yoga. They are successive but not "sharply distinguished or separate." First is "the effort towards at least an initial and enabling self-transcendence and contact with the Divine." The second stage is "the reception of that which transcends . . . into ourselves for the transformation of our whole conscious being." The third stage is "the utilization of our transformed humanity as a Divine center in the world." As long as the contact with the Divine is not very established, personal effort must be dominant. As this contact is more thoroughly established, the spiritual aspirant becomes conscious that a force transcends his egoistic efforts and abilities, "a force other than his own . . . is at work in him. In the end his own will and force become One with the Higher Power; he merges them in the Divine Will and its Transcendent and Universal Force. . . . Always indeed it is the Higher Power that acts." All the perfection of which humans are capable "is only a realizing of the eternal perfection of the Spirit within him. We know the Divine and become Divine, because we are That already in our secret nature."[200]

Deepak Chopra, a contemporary mystic, offers several different spiritual routes. A spiritual journey has four paths that lead to unity. "Every experience comes to us in one of four ways: as a feeling, a thought, an action, or simply as a sense of being." At one moment we are more present and aware of one way and then later of another. Awareness is "pure, alive, alert, silent, and full of potential." It makes us conscious of the differences between feeling I am safe, thinking I am safe, acting safe, and realizing I am safe. The four Hindu yogas of love, knowledge, work, and meditation "arise from feeling, thinking, acting, and being." On the path of feeling, "your personal emotions expand to become all-encompassing. Love of self and family merges into love of humanity." On the path of thinking, "you silence your internal dialogue in order to find clarity and stillness. . . . Thinking can turn into knowing, which is to say wisdom." The path of action "reaches its fulfillment when your surrender is so complete that God runs everything you do." On the path of being, "you cultivate a self beyond ego. . . . Unity is a state in which nothing is left out of 'I am.'" Chopra also says, a spiritual journey has three stages. In the first stage, our awareness depends on our five senses. Next, it depends on the laws of nature that we arrive at by thinking and experimenting. Finally, we experience pure awareness.[201]

The Foundation for My Stages

Throughout the centuries, thoughtful, wise people around the globe not only wrote about ways to become more spiritual, to become mystics, but they also explained the stages on the spiritual path to the Divine. Two extremely influential mystics were the sixth century unknown theologian who was named Deny the Areopagite and the highly respected, early twentieth-century English author Evelyn Underhill. Although this book utilizes many mystics' writings, it is deeply indebted to both of them. Denys who was also called Dionysius offered three stages: first, purification; second, illumination; and third, union and complete perfection. Underhill's 1911 classic *Mysticism* that continues to be read today has five stages that are an improvement on Denys'. Her stages are: awakening; purification; illumination; dark night of the soul;

and union. In my way of thinking, her five stages are the best description that have been produced so far in the history of spiritual writing.

My six stages are based on my own spiritual experiences and my decades of studying the writing for mystics around the world, including Denys and Underhill. My stages are: (1) awe and wonder; (2) parents and religious leaders teach children about God; (3) awakening; (4) love for ourselves and our neighbors; (5) illumination and union; and (6) love for all people and all creation. Although there are some similarities with Underhill's stages, there are also significant, profound differences. The description, content, and essence of my stages are unlike hers. Even when there are similarities, my stages are more thoroughly, distinctly, and clearly explained. My framework presents a more easily understood and more comprehensive explanation of the process that happens as the six stages enfold. While Underhill uses mainly Christian mystics to illustrate her stages, I include mystics from all the world's religions and from over 3,000 years ago until the present. Most important, my six stages show more clearly how spirituality helps relieve suffering and develop more love.

As Underhill said, stages are "the essential phases of life's response to . . . the conditions of our attainment of Being, the necessary formulae under which alone our consciousness of any of these fringes of Eternity—any of these aspects of the Transcendent—can unfold, develop, attain to freedom and full life." Because our soul is "this immortal spark from the central fire" of the Divine, we are children of the Infinite. "The mystic way must therefore be a life, a discipline, which will so alter the constituents of our mental life as to include this spark within the conscious field; bring it out of hiddenness, from those deep levels where it sustains and guides our normal existence;" and make it the center of our spiritual life. This mystic way is an "arduous psychological and spiritual process" that remakes our character, liberates our consciousness, leads us to union with the Ultimate Reality, produces love for all, and results in peace and joy.[202]

Underhill explained that these stages are "the ordered sequence of states, the organic development, whereby our consciousness is detached from illusion and rises to the mystic freedom." They are the steps to "the mystic act of union, that joyous loss of the transfigured self in God, which is the crown of our conscious ascent toward the Absolute." The testimonies of different schools of contemplatives demonstrate that "the stages of this road, the psychology of the spiritual ascent, . . . always present practically the same sequence of states." Scholars do not find it difficult to reconcile Teresa of Avila's "Seven Degrees of Orison" in the *Interior Castle* with the four types of contemplation of Hugh St. Victor or the Islamic Sufi Attar's seven stages of the soul's ascent to the Holy One. Although each mystic uses different landmarks, "the road is one."[203]

Although Underhill described five stages on the mystic way, she claimed that "no sharp lines, but rather an infinite series of gradations separate the two states" where the earthly existence with all its boundaries passes over into the "Boundless Life." Although Teresa of Avila described seven dwelling places in the interior castle that was her symbol for the soul, she was not wed to seven stages. In fact, there were more rooms in the castle. In another book, she also wrote about a different way of perfection. A reason I am not rigid about six stages is that the actual number of levels or gradations of mystical consciousness and spiritual truth are endless.[204]

While my stages are organized in an ordered sequence, they do not occur in a way that one terminates before the next commences. We swing back and forth between the third stage of awakening and the fourth of love. Then we oscillate between the fourth and the fifth stage of illumination. As we progress gradually from one stage to another, we still continue to live and develop simultaneously on the previous levels. Each step provides spiritual lessons. We can continue to learn and hold on to the mystical teachings of one level throughout our lives as we add the new spiritual truths of the next stage.

Although all people are born with spiritual capacities, many do not experience all six stages on the mystic way to the Divine. Atheists deny all the spiritual stages. However, I believe that almost all people including agnostics and atheists experience the first stage of awe and wonder. When atheists experience it, they do not acknowledge that it is a mystical experience. People who are in love with technology and science but don't call themselves atheists often don't even think about spirituality. However, they have many experiences of awe and wonder. People whose parents don't teach them about religion skip from the first stage to the third. Everyone's spiritual path is unique.

Chapter 4

Stage Two Is Parents and Religious Leaders Teaching Children about God

Abraham Maslow's Theory of Peak Experiences

The first stage of the mystical experience of awe and wonder is followed by the second stage of parents and religious leaders teaching children about the Divine. However, some parents do not inform their kids about any religion or God, so their youngsters skip this stage. Abraham Maslow, a twentieth-century American humanistic psychologist, had a theory about peak experiences that helps explain what happens in this second stage. "The very beginning, the intrinsic core, the essence, the universal nucleus of every known high religion . . . has been the private, lonely, personal illumination, revelation, or ecstasy of some acutely sensitive prophet or seer," such as Moses, Lao Tzu, Buddha, Jesus, and Mohammad. Maslow referred to these mystical experiences as peak experiences and these mystics as peakers, people who have peak experiences. The original founders of religions and all people's mystical experiences, revelations, ecstasies, or transcendental encounters were and are "perfectly natural, human peak experiences" which are described in the concepts and language of their culture, time, place, and sometimes in supernatural terms.[205]

Maslow claimed that "all or almost all people have or can have peak experiences." Furthermore, "all mystical or peak experiences are the same in their essence" and in their messages. "Whatever is different about these illuminations can fairly be taken to be localisms both in time and space, and are, therefore, peripheral, expendable, not essential." This mystical experience, "this intrinsic core-experience is a meeting ground" not only for all the different religions, "but also for priests and atheists, . . . for conservatives and liberals, . . . for thinkers and doers." Mystics, transcenders, and prophets who are peakers can be distinguished from legalists, ecclesiastics, and organizers who are non-peakers. Of course, mystics can also be leaders in religious institutions, while ecclesiastics can also be peakers.[206]

According to Maslow, the characteristic mystic, prophet, or peaker is a person who has spiritual experiences, who accepts and values them, and who "discovers his truth about the world, the cosmos, ethics, God, and his own identity from within, from his own personal experiences, from what he would consider to be a revelation." Peakers consider their mystical experiences and the spiritual messages that they learn from them of first importance. They are the "essential, intrinsic, basic, and the most fundamental" part of religion. "All the paraphernalia of organized religion—buildings and specialized personnel, rituals, dogmas, ceremonials, and the life—are to the peaker secondary, peripheral, and of doubtful value in relation to the intrinsic and essential religious or transcendental experience." Almost all mystics develop their own private, personal spirituality which they create out of their own peak experiences. "Each peaker discovers, develops, and retains his own religion" and spirituality.[207]

Non-peakers

Non-peakers are not people who never have mystical experiences. As children and adults, they have spiritual experiences of awe and awakening, but they are afraid of them, turn away from them, reject them, forget them, suppress them, and deny them. They are fearful and repress their mystical experiences, because they can't control them. Since they lack self-love and feel powerless, they want to have control. The less self-love, the lower their self-esteem, the greater their powerless feelings, the more insecure they feel, the more they need to have control. Being pessimistic, non-peakers often believe the world is a hostile, competitive jungle where many lose, while only a few win. They think that people are selfish, power-hungry, greedy, and want to dominate others. Because of these attitudes, they tend to mistrust and be highly critical of others. Non-peakers consider a hierarchy with a chain of command the best structure and prefer an authoritarian leader to help ensure obedience. Since they feel threatened by those who disagree and oppose them, they often turn them into a devil to be hated. They believe the end justifies the means. Since they are afraid and fear change, they crave certainty and want to have control. They need either to follow a strong leader or have power over others.[208]

Non-peakers are often conformists. Elizabeth Liebert, a contemporary professor of spiritual life, says that some of the positive traits of conformists are that they actively promote the goals of their religious groups, including acting with niceness, helpfulness, and generosity toward other members. The negative aspects are that they lack their own inner, self-chosen identity; take their scriptures literally; are authoritarian and rigid; make harsh judgments; and are prejudiced against out-groups. Conformists "feel warmth and trust from and extend co-operation and helpfulness to groups" like themselves, such as their family and religious congregation. Since they lack "a broad and inclusive social worldview," their "niceness and loving concern" is only for their in-group, while they have thoughtless and malignant prejudices about out-groups. "Being outside the pale should merit God's judgment." This "helps explain why some religious groups, typically those that attract a large number of conformist persons, can be among the most prejudiced in our society."[209]

When legalists or ecclesiastics or church members are non-peakers, they want to conserve the religion that gives them certainty and security. Their conservatism and need for certainty often work at cross purposes with a religion that was "built up on the basis of the prophet's original revelation" and was meant "to make the revelation available to the masses." When the religious leaders are non-peakers, they produce their own version of the mystic's vision to create a role for themselves in which they can be a leader and have power over others. They also tend to take literally their religion's scriptures and doctrines, create elaborate rules and laws that are to be strictly obeyed, require church attendance, and judge harshly all who fall short. They make the religion's scriptures, dogmas, rituals, and laws more important than the founder's mystical experiences and spiritual teachings.[210]

When mystics, prophets, and peakers become part of the institutional structure of their religion, they try to communicate to their members the founder's mystical experiences and spiritual teachings and how they themselves can have spiritual experiences and learn from them. An example is Pope Francis. In contrast, legalists, ecclesiastics, and organizational leaders who are non-peakers have trouble understanding the deep meaning of the founder's mystical experiences and spiritual messages. Thus, non-peakers cannot begin to communicate what they don't really comprehend. Because they can't understand the heart of their religion, they stress its secondary parts, such as doctrines and rules. Unfortunately, the examples of these leaders are abundant. Many of us have dealt with them.

Some call mystics and peakers liberals and left wing, while the legalists and non-peakers are referred to as fundamentalists, conservatives, and right wing. At times throughout religious history, some legalists and non-peakers declared some mystics and peakers heretics. Religions need to help the peakers and non-peakers learn to understand and love each other.[211]

Peakers Encourage and Non-peakers Suppress Children's Experiences of Awe

Maslow's ideas illustrate why parents and religious leaders who are peakers and who appreciate the value their own spiritual experiences are able to encourage children to remain peakers by helping them treasure their own mystical experiences of awe and wonder and keep them alive and joyful. Then they are able to assist them in understanding that these are spiritual experiences that produce teachings about the Divine. When they begin to teach them about their own religion and its image of the Holy One, they communicate the founder's mystical experiences and spiritual messages. Next, they are able to explain to youngsters why they need to learn about and take seriously their own religion, study other religions, and develop their own spiritual beliefs and practices from their own mystical experiences and the spiritual teachings that derive from them. All these lessons will make young people open to the mystical experience of awakening in the third stage.

In contrast, parents and religious leaders who are non-peakers often suppress children's spiritual experiences of awe and wonder. Since youngsters usually do not recognize their experiences of awe and wonder as mystical encounters, they themselves aren't concerned about protecting them. Parents and religious leaders who are non-peakers don't protect their children's experiences of awe and wonder either. When their kids come to them overwhelmed with excitement about their experiences, they are often too busy or don't care so they push them away and squash their experiences. Thus, they tend to ignore, put down, suppress, reject, deny, and destroy children's spiritual experiences of awe and wonder. Over time, kids learn to devalue their own experiences.

The nineteenth-century English author John Ruskin said that in his youth he had delightful, joyful mystical experiences of awe and wonder in the natural world that faded away when he was in his late teens. He did not report whether his parents and religious leaders influenced their fading away. "Although there was no definite religious sentiment mingled with it, there was a continual perception of Sanctity in the whole of nature, from the slightest thing to the vastest; an instinctive awe, mixed with delight; an indefinable thrill, . . . I could only feel this perfectly when I was alone; and then it would often make me shiver from head to foot with the joy and fear of it." Mountains, hills, rivers, forests, and distant sunsets gave him these experiences. "I cannot in the least describe this feeling; . . . for I am afraid no feeling is describable." As he could not explain hunger and starvation to a person who has never felt them, he could not put these feelings into words. "The joy in nature seemed to me to come as a sort of heart-hunger, satisfied with the presence of a Great and Holy Spirit." For years, "these feelings remained in their full intensity till I was 18 or 20, and then, as the reflective and practical power increased, and 'the cares of this world' gained upon me, they faded gradually away."[212]

Because parents and religious leaders who are non-peakers repress their own spiritual experiences, they stress that children must not only suppress their own, but they must also take their religious scriptures literally, learn and believe all the doctrines, practice all the rituals, and obey all the rules and laws as well as obey the parents and the church leaders who teach them. These youngsters are in danger of becoming non-peakers and are in dire need of the mystical experience of awakening in the third stage.

Contemporary feminist theologian Rosemary Ruether discusses "authentic Catholicism" which she describes as "the church we need now, the church we have always needed" as well as ways to change ourselves and our church. "We need to *grow up*. Traditional Catholic socialization breeds a spirituality of infantilism. We have great difficulty really liberating ourselves from the residue of a spirituality of childlike dependence that has been deeply bred into our psyches. Catholicism, like all patriarchal hierarchical institutions, recreates relationships of domination and submission, modeled on relations of male over female and parent over child. We learn to dominate those below us and submit to those above us, but we do not learn to be equals in mutually affirming relationships." Because of this, "we are not encouraged to become genuinely autonomous adults, but rather to remain always a dependent child under some kind of higher authority. These patterns of relationship are central to clerical culture, in which priests are literally called 'Father,' even by those older than they are."[213]

Parents and Religious Leaders Teach Children about God

When their parents and religious leaders begin to teach youth about God, it often seems to be a foreign concept that is not meaningful to them. Non-peakers teach them to honor and revere their religion's image of God more than their own experiences. Peakers teach children to respect their religion's concept of the Divine as well as to honor and value their own experiences of awe and wonder. With open and appreciative conversations, they try to gently coax them to tease out what their experiences mean to them. Possibly they are able to help them realize that these were spiritual experiences from which they can learn something about the Sacred Spirit.

Parents teach children to pray to God at meals and bedtime. When they take them to religious services, they help them see that this is a way to worship God. Parents teach children to believe in God, say their prayers, attend religious services, and avoid wrongdoing. Along the way they impart their religion's image of a personal God. Parents and religious leaders who are peakers and non-peakers teach similar lessons about God and their religion, but peakers are more open and focus on spirituality, while non-peakers stress believing in doctrines and obeying rules.

Karen Armstrong, a contemporary scholar of world religions, says that "inevitably our understanding of our personal Lord is colored by the religious tradition into which we were born. But the mystic knows that this 'God' of ours is simply an 'angel' or a particular symbol of the Divine which can never be confused with the Hidden Reality Itself." In contrast, nonpeakers believe their religion's teaching literally, blindly, and unquestioningly.[214]

Religious leaders' teachings often make such a strong impression on youngsters that they continue to portray their spiritual life in their religion's language and images for the rest of their lives. Throughout her life, Mother Teresa described her spiritual experiences in the language and concepts she was taught by Catholic leaders. "From childhood the Heart of Jesus has been my first love." At age twelve, she wanted to be a missionary. "I first knew I had a vocation to the poor, in 1922. I wanted to be a missionary, I wanted to go out and give the life of Christ to people in the missionary countries." Between twelve and eighteen, she did not want to be a nun, because she came from a very happy family. When she was eighteen, she decided to become a nun. "Since then, this 40 years, I've never doubted even for a second that I've done the right thing; it was the will of God. It was His choice."[215]

Spiritual growth, like physical and intellectual development, follows a natural process. Our spiritual awareness and knowledge start small and grow until they reach mystical consciousness. When we are young, we are taught religion through simple stories, pictures, images, rituals, music, and prayers that are appropriate for our age. For example, young Christians are taught that God is our Father who loves us. Our spiritual development is much more likely than our physical, psychological, social, and intellectual growth to become stunted at the childhood level, especially if we are taught by non-peakers. One reason that the teachings of religious leaders have a more powerful effect than those of leaders in all other fields is because they are considered to have an expertise about, to be representative of, and to have a relationship with the Holy One, the highest authority. When they tell children to obey their teachings without any questions, many do and thus they stop growing spiritually. Today this lack of mature mystical development contributes to our serious contemporary problems, because a shallow spirituality often goes along with prejudiced attitudes, superficial values, rigid dogmatism, blind unquestioning obedience, and conformity to authoritarianism. The enrichment of our spirituality is a crying need.[216]

What causes our spiritual development to stagnate at the childhood level? When religious teachers who are non-peakers tell us to stop questioning, many of us obey them. They teach us that God is our Father who loves us. Since we are born sinners, He punishes us for our sins. Some of us picture God as an old man with a long white beard sitting on a cloud in heaven. Practicing blind unquestioning obedience, many of us use our religion as an insurance policy that will get us into heaven. We live in fear of going to hell. We not only take our religious scriptures and doctrines literally, but we also defend them against those who question them. We consider other religions inferior and reject their images of the Divine as idolatry.[217]

Often our church leaders who are non-peakers "claim that the founding revelation was complete, perfect, final, and eternal." When they teach that our religion is the one and only truth, many of us believe them. Then we affirm that our religion's teachings are the only way to God, our doctrines are the only right beliefs, and our rituals are the only correct worship. In 2000, the Vatican Congregation for the Doctrine of the Faith issued a declaration entitled "Lord Jesus" that Pope John Paul II ratified. It said that all other religions, even Protestant Christianity, are defective. Today fundamentalist Christians say that people who do not believe in their version of religion, even other Christians, will go to hell.[218]

From at least back to St. Cyprian in the third century, most Catholics believed and took literally their religion's teaching that "outside the church there is no salvation." The word church meant the Catholic Church. In the fifth century, a disciple of Augustine said that "you can be certain and convinced beyond any doubt: not only all pagans but also all Jews, all heretics and schismatics, who die outside the Catholic Church, will go into everlasting fire which has been prepared for the devil." In the thirteenth century,

Stage Two Is Parents and Religious Leaders Teaching Children about God

Pope Boniface VIII said in his encyclical *Unam Sanctam* that "there is but only one Holy, Catholic, and Apostolic Church outside of which there is no salvation or remission of sins. . . . We declare, announce, and define that it is altogether necessary for salvation for every creature to be subject to the Roman Pontiff." Vatican Council II in the 1960s presented a different, more affirmative attitude toward other religions. When we do not question and discard outmoded religious doctrines as we mature, our spiritual knowledge, consciousness, and image of the Divine becomes stunted. Our spirituality remains at an elementary school level, while we live the rest of our lives at a much higher, more complex level.[219]

Currently most of us are taught by our parents and religious leaders to believe in God. It is difficult to experience the Divine because our culture emphasizes materialism and technology. It is like living in a world where the smog is so thick that we cannot see the stars. It is not that the Holy One retreated, it is we who turn away and busy ourselves with our consumerism, fun, and games. We are so engrossed in our search for success, money, power, status, and pleasure, that we do not take time to deal with our spiritual needs. Our elementary image of the Divine is often unbelievable and meaningless since the remainder of our lives is lived at a much more complex, sophisticated level.

Some of us break free from outdated images of the Holy One. In a novel, the *Color Purple*, by Alice Walker, Shug, a poor black woman, explains to another named Celie the steps that she took to stop believing in the God that she was taught in childhood. She went from believing in an old white man with a beard sitting on a cloud to experiencing the Divine and affirming her own image. "My first step from the old white man was trees. Then air. Then birds. Then other people. But one day when I was sitting quietly and feeling like a motherless child, which I was, it come to me: that feeling of being part of everything, not separate at all. I knew that if I cut a tree, my arm would bleed. And I laughed and I cried and I run all around the house. I knew just what It (God) was. In fact, when it happens, you can't miss it."[220]

Two of the many ways to symbolize the Divine are personal and transpersonal images. Hindus have over 300 million personal Goddesses and Gods, but they also have a transpersonal Brahman. Chinese religions have many personal Goddesses and Gods, but they also have a transpersonal Tao. Buddhists have a transpersonal Nirvana, but Goddesses and Gods are also popular and some consider Buddha a God. The vast majority of Divine images of Judaism, Christianity, and Islam are personal.

Most parents and religions teach children to believe in a personal God, because this is easier for them to understand. A popular personal Christian image is that God is our Father who loves us. This personal concept is usually carried over from the second stage on the mystical way into the third stage. In the fifth stage, mystics usually express their spiritual experiences in transpersonal images, such as the Infinite Love and the Ultimate Reality. In a transpersonal image, the Divine is not less than personal, but beyond the personal. Both personal and transpersonal images are useful as long as they continue to provide life-promoting meaning for individuals and religions.[221]

No matter what we are taught by our parents and religious leaders, we need to keep our minds open to our own questioning, exploring, reading, schooling, studying, and our own mystical experiences. We also need to recognize that finite words are totally inadequate to describe the Infinite Reality. The unknown author of the fourteenth-century English classic, *The Cloud of Unknowing*, said that although we have knowledge of almost everything, "nobody can think adequately about God's essential Being." The Divine "can be grasped and held by love but never by thought."[222]

Writing in the fifteenth century, Nicholas of Cusa, a German mystic, referred to the Divine as Infinity, a transpersonal image. "I behold Thee as Infinity. By reason of this, Thou may not be attained, or comprehended, or named, or multiplied, or beheld." Furthermore, "Thou cannot be grasped because Thou are Infinity. To understand Infinity is to comprehend the incomprehensible. . . . Thou cannot be known, unless the unknowable can be known, and the invisible beheld, and the inaccessible attained." Nevertheless, he used a variety of gender-free transpersonal names for the Divine, including Almighty, Eternal, Being, All in all, and "the Absolute and Infinite God."[223]

If we claim to have exact knowledge of God, it would mean that the Infinite Reality is finite. There is no absolutely correct way to speak about the Sacred Spirit. NO images, symbols, concepts, or names can be accepted as literal descriptions of the Holy One. Attempting to capture the Infinite Reality in finite words is like trying to pour the entire ocean into a tea cup. A tea cup catches a tiny fraction of the ocean. Is a verbal description of an enormous dinosaur like an actual one? Is a verbal picture of the sun like the real sun? Can a rope lasso the wind?[224]

All our images of the Infinite One are finite and imperfect. To take literally any image of the God is totally inadequate. Liebert says that for conformists, "God can be a separate person" with whom their dualistic relationship is hierarchical and authoritarian, like a parent and dependent child. Many feminist theologians claim that exclusive use of male images of the Divine, like Father and King, is not only idolatry, but it also legitimizes male domination in society and religion. Mary Daly said, "if God is male, male is God." Male concepts need to be used alongside female and other symbols to ensure against taking them literally.[225]

Some atheists are never exposed to religion. Other atheists were taught about God by their parents and their religion, so they believe in Him for a time, but the outdated, unbelievable images of God cause them to become an atheist. Most people who end up totally rejecting God find that the image of the Divine that they were taught by their religion is inferior and unacceptable. Therefore, they claim that God does not exist.

In summing up, Maslow said that "the two religions of mankind tend to be the peakers and the non-peakers," those who have Transcendent "experiences easily and often and who accept and make use of them, and those who have never had them or who repress and suppress them." Whether we are peakers or non-peakers, a spiritual experience of awakening will help us enter the third stage on the mystical way to the Divine.[226]

Chapter 5

Awakening Is the Third Stage on the Spiritual Path

We Are Finite, But We Unconsciously Yearn for the Infinite

All of us have desires. When our wishes are not met, we are frustrated and sad. When our desires are realized, we are happy. However, we are also strangely dissatisfied and depressed when our desires are achieved. An example is a man who works hard to earn enough money to buy a new car that he craves. In his happiness, he washes it until it shines. Driving at high speeds at first gives him a thrill that slowly wears off. After buying a different new car, he is again excited, but little by little his joy disappears. To deal with his unhappiness, he buys a boat. Gradually his exhilaration turns to frustration because it involves so much work. Similarly, a woman finally has enough money to buy a new expensive coat she yearns for. After wearing it a number of times she tires of it. Seeing a costly house, she longs for, she eventually has enough to purchase it. Again, it loses its appeal. On a larger scale, millionaires are not content with their millions and all the luxuries that they possess. They lust after more luxuries and more millions. They want billions, but even billions do not stop their cravings. No matter how many material things they possess, they still look for something more.

Even when our desires are met and we are blessed with a wonderful, beloved partner; happy, healthy children; fantastic, good friends;

meaningful, worthwhile work; and an adequate amount of success, power, status, wealth, and pleasure, we continue to thirst for something more. Nothing finite can totally please us. Many of us continually try one possession or one cell phone or one game or one activity or one occupation or one spouse after another. Nothing provides lasting happiness. As Richard Rolle, a fourteenth-century English mystic, said, "since the human soul is capable of receiving God alone, nothing else than God can fill it, which explains why lovers of earthly things are never satisfied." Jan van Ruysbroeck, the fourteenth-century Flemish priest, said, "there begins an eternal hunger, which shall never be satisfied. It is the inward craving and hankering of the affective power and created spirit after an Uncreated Good."[227]

The fifteenth-century English mystic Julian of Norwich said that "the reason why we have no ease of heart or soul" is that "we are seeking for rest in trivial things which cannot satisfy and not seeking to know God, Almighty, All-wise, All-good. He is true rest. . . . Nothing less will satisfy us." In the seventeenth century, an English nun Dame Gertrude More, said, "nothing can satiate a reasonable soul, but only Thou." Thou are "the only thing which is necessary and which alone can satisfy our souls." Denys the Areopagite, a Christian mystic writing at the beginning of the sixth century, made the claim that all people and even all animals and all things seek God, the Good, the One that is referred to here as It. "Everything with mind and reason seek to know It, everything sentient yearns to perceive It, everything lacking perception has a living and instinctive longing for It, and everything lifeless and merely existent turns . . . for a share of It."[228]

Many of us continue to seek materialist possessions to make us happy even though we meet with frustration. Some of us use religion to find the Divine, while others utilize spirituality. Both spirituality and religion help us search for the Holy One. We are finite, but we unconsciously yearn for the Infinite. Many of us consciously desire the Sacred Spirit. Some of us seriously take up the quest. Rumi, the thirteenth-century Islamic Sufi mystic, said that the core of a human has "such a passion and longing that even if he owned a hundred thousand worlds, he would never find peace." People dabble in many different activities and occupations. "They study astronomy and medicine and all kinds of other things, and never find peace," because they never reach the goal of their search which is God. "The authentic human being, then, is one who is never free from striving, who turns restlessly and endlessly about the Light of the Majesty of God." Although people seem to be children of the earth, they are "the faithful guardian of the treasure of the Divine Light." It is "the Beloved alone that is called the "heart's ease."[229]

Huston Smith, a contemporary expert on world religions, says about all of creation, "from the lowest level of reality, . . . to the highest heavens,

94 Six Stages on the Spiritual Path

...a single breath and motion sweeps through existence, the search of each existent for the Good," the True, and the Beautiful; for the Divine, Infinite Love, the Holy One, and the ONE. Karen Armstrong says that "the desire to cultivate a sense of the Transcendent may be *the* defining human characteristic."[230]

What Is an Awakening?

Often, we cannot relate to or find any meaning in our parents and religious leaders' teaching about God. Their messages do not help us overcome our consumerism and materialistic desires. When we have a mystical experience of the Divine, we are awakened to our own meaningful image of the Holy One. Awakening is the spiritual experience of becoming conscious of the Ultimate Reality. We encounter the Sacred Spirit as real, alive, and sometimes as loving. No longer do we believe that there is a God just because we were taught by our parents and religious leaders. Now we believe because of our own mystical experiences of the Divine. This becoming awakened to Infinite Love is the third stage on the mystical way to the Ultimate Reality. My own mystical experience of the Holy One happened when I reflected on the magnificence of humans, nature, and the universe. Then I became conscious that there must be a Creator who created this universe with its spectacular beauty, complexity, order, diversity, consciousness, and love. Another word for awakening is enlightenment. It can also be called a spiritual experience, cosmic consciousness, a transcendental encounter, conversion, a religious experience, and a mystic encounter with Infinite Love.

For most of us, awakening comes slowly. When we try a number of different spiritual practices, enlightenment still comes gradually. For some, it happens abruptly. Buddha had both experiences. First, he tried a number of mystical methods for years. Then he was suddenly awakened under the Bodhi tree. Most mystics experience the third stage by itself. However, a few mystics encounter all at once the third mystical stage of awakening along with the fifth stage of illumination and union with the Divine. Still most of us experience these stages one at a time, at a snail's pace, little by little, over years. This is the way it happened to me.

Our experience of awakening transforms our awareness into a mystical consciousness. Eventually many of us realize that we ourselves are mystics. Other new spiritual insights and possible interpretations of our awakening result. The first way that we attempt to deal with our enlightenment is to describe our actual mystical experience of awakening. We make an effort even though spiritual encounters are ineffable. In the second way, we do not depict our actual experience of enlightenment, but we explain our interpretation of it. The third way we deal with it is to share the mystical insights and teaching that we gained from our awakening.

What is most important to us mystics is not our religion's beliefs and rituals, but our own spiritual experiences and our new awakened mystical consciousness. We move from being concerned about our world of materialistic desires to entering the heart of the Ultimate Reality, from being self-centered and selfish to experiencing Divine consciousness. Centering ourselves on the Sacred Spirit, we undergo changes that give new life to our thoughts, feelings, words, values, actions, and love. When we lift our hearts to the Divine, we are filled with a more vibrant, dynamic, spiritual life. The Holy One is our true source of happiness that floods our consciousness with rapturous moments of unspeakable joy. Our spirits delight in Divine Goodness, Truth, Beauty, Consciousness, Wisdom, and Love. We experience Eternal Peace. Our mystical experiences of Infinite Love create ecstasy and bliss. It is springtime for the awakened.

Buddha's Awakenings

Buddha provides an excellent example of the third mystical stage since he experienced an awakening. The Buddhist scriptures state that Siddhartha Gautama did spiritual practices for six years before his sudden awakening. Afterward he was given the title Buddha which means the Awakened One, Enlightened One, and Illumined One. No writings by Buddha have been discovered. The earliest Buddhist scriptures were written hundreds of years after his death. Thus, the stories about his life in those scriptures are viewed more as legend than as history.[231] Siddhartha Gautama was born in northeast India, that is now Nepal, in the warrior caste around 560 BCE and lived eighty years. Because he was a Hindu prince of the Shakya tribe, one of his names was *Shakya-muni* which meant the sage or wise person of this tribe. According to the Buddhist scriptures, while Siddhartha was still an infant, Hindu religious experts predicted that the king's son was "to be the perfectly Enlightened One or a universal monarch." Later Asita, a great Hindu seer, told the king that his son will achieve his true destiny. He "will abandon the kingdom in his indifference to worldly pleasures; he will obtain the Truth," he will attain enlightenment, and he will proclaim the path to salvation. Because the monarch wanted his son to follow him as king, he provided him with a life of luxury and worldly pleasure. Because he didn't want him to see anything to perturb his mind, he orders that all common folk with afflictions be kept away from the royal road that the prince traveled.[232]

The stages for Hindu men were first to be students and then householders with wives and children. After the first grandchild, they were to withdraw into the forest to achieve spiritual consciousness. Siddhartha followed these stages by being a student and then becoming a householder by marrying Yashodhara and having a son, Rahula. However, when he saw a diseased body, an old man, and a corpse, he was shocked, dismayed, and discontented. This caused the prince to abandon his life of luxury and his wife and young son. Then he searched for religious truth by practicing austerities and asceticism for six years as his body steadily became emaciated.[233]

The Buddhist scriptures say that after trying both a life of luxury and asceticism, Siddhartha said, "I stand above these two extremes, my heart is kept in the Middle Way," in balance with the universe. In explaining the Middle Way, he described as foolish both ascetics and materialists. "Those foolish people who torment themselves, as well as those who have become attached to the domains of the senses, both these should be viewed as faulty in their method, because they are not on the way to deathlessness." Of ascetics depriving themselves, Siddhartha said, "those so-called austerities but confuse the mind which is overpowered by the body's exhaustion." On the other hand, the minds of the materialists, "who are attached to the worthless sense-objects, are overwhelmed by passion and darkening delusion." Thus, he chose the Middle Way. "So I have given up both these extremes, and have found another path, a Middle Way. It leads to the appeasing of all ill."[234]

According to Buddhist scriptures, Siddhartha then sat and meditated under the Bodhi tree for seven days until he had a mystical experience of awakening, enlightenment, and Nirvana. Thereafter he was called "the Awakened One." In attaining this different state of consciousness, "he had reached perfection" and he "found freedom" from reincarnation, from the cycle of birth, death, and rebirth. The lessons that he learned from his awakening were the Four Noble Truths and the Eightfold Path to Nirvana. In his first sermon and for 40 years after his enlightenment, he taught this message.[235]

Although the content is the same, the Buddhist scriptures present several different descriptions of the Four Noble Truths. The thinking behind these truths is that being born and living create suffering. The more we suffer, the more we crave things and people to alleviate or distract us from our suffering. The more things and people we possess, the more we fear losing them which produces more suffering. Buddha's Four Noble Truths break this vicious circle. His first Noble Truth is that all life is suffering (*dukkha*) and unhappiness. Buddha said, "birth is ill, death is ill. To be conjoined with what one dislikes means suffering. In short, all grasping . . . involves suffering."[236]

Buddha's second Noble Truth is that the cause of suffering is selfish craving (*tanha*), desire, grasping, clinging, and attachment. The origin of suffering is "that craving which leads to rebirth, accompanied by delight and greed, seeking its delight now here, now there, i.e., craving for sensuous experience, craving to perpetuate oneself." His third truth is that stopping craving will end suffering. Buddha said that "it is the complete stopping of that craving, the withdrawal from it, the renouncing of it, throwing it back, liberation from it, non-attachment to it." His fourth Noble Truth is that the way to stop craving is to follow the Eightfold Path. "It is this holy Eightfold Path, which consists of right views, right intention, right speech, right action, right livelihood, right effort, right mindfulness, right concentration." Some scholars, both Buddhists and others, divide the Eightfold Path into three aspects: wisdom, morality, and meditation. Wisdom includes the first step, right views, and the second, right intentions. Morality involves the third step, right speech, the fourth, right conduct, and the fifth step, right livelihood. Meditation includes the sixth step, right effort, the seventh, right mindfulness, and the eighth, right concentration.[237]

Buddha's Four Noble Truths and the Eightfold Path lead to Nirvana, the ultimate goal of all Buddhists. Some scholars say that Nirvana is the extinction of craving; a life beyond birth, death, and rebirth; and the realization that there is no separate self. However, since Buddha's awakening was a mystical encounter, his experience of Nirvana was beyond words, incomprehensible, ineffable, indescribable, unutterable, and inconceivable. Nevertheless, Buddha said that "bliss, yes bliss, my friends, is Nirvana." Because Buddha's spiritual experience of Nirvana was not only an awakening in the third stage, but also an illumination and union with the ONE in the fifth stage on the mystical way, it will be explained more fully in a later chapter.[238]

A More Advanced State of Awakening

We experience a more advanced enlightenment when we progress beyond being aware of and experiencing the Sacred Spirit. We develop our mystical consciousness when we go beneath our surface self to become conscious that the Divine presence is within us. Some of us then become aware that Infinite Love is within us as our inner core of love. Our spiritual consciousness is deepened even further when it goes beneath the surface of the normal world and becomes awakened to the Eternal, Absolute, Infinite, Ultimate Reality within all people and all things.

In her book *Revelations of Divine Love*, the fifteenth-century English mystic Julian of Norwich described her experiences of awakening in the third stage. She also presented mystical experiences of illumination and union with God in the fifth stage that will be explained later. Julian was a Christian anchoress which means that she was a recluse who was shut away from ordinary social life in a parsonage. Her life was primarily praying. She received her sixteen revelations or showings from God in three ways. First, she was shown by actual physical sight, but "obscurely and mysteriously." When she wanted to see more clearly, the answer came to her mind, "if God wills to show you more, He will be your Light. You need none but Him." The second way was "by imaginative understanding." She explained that "words formed in my intellect" that "our Lord showed me." The third way was by spiritual sight. "Our Lord gave me greater insight," but "I can never describe it fully."[239]

In the third stage of awakening, Julian saw that "God the blessed Trinity is everlasting Being" with "three attributes: Fatherhood, Motherhood, and Lordship—all in one God." Her revelations described God within us. "Our soul can never find its rest in lesser things. When it is lifted above created things . . ., all its gaze is set blessedly on God its Maker who dwells therein. For man's soul is God's true dwelling." Furthermore, "our Creator . . . lives eternally in our soul." He sits "at ease in our soul dwelling there" forever. "God never leaves the soul in which He dwells." Moreover, "our good Lord showed Himself to me in various ways both in heaven and on earth. But the only *place* I saw Him occupy was in man's soul." It is God's will "that we should trust that He is always with us. . . . He is with us in our soul, eternally dwelling, guiding, and keeping us" alive. "God is working in us, helping us to thank and trust and enjoy Him." In addition, "our good Lord, the Holy Spirit, who is everlasting and who securely dwells in our soul, keeps us alive and by His grace procures a real peace" for us. God is "here with us, leading us on, and staying by us until He brought us all to the blessedness in heaven." This highest blessedness is "to have God in the clear light of eternity, seeing Him in truth, experiencing His sweetness, and possessing Him in utter perfection and fullest joy."[240]

Julian said that God "often showed Himself as reigning . . ., but chiefly in man's soul." Not only is He within our soul, but He is also within all of creation. "God is in man and God is in everything." Furthermore, "when the gracious presence of the Lord is felt," people not only experience it within their own souls, but they also experience "His presence in all things." Moreover, "God functions in His creatures. . . . God is the focal point of everything, and He does it all" and "everything that is done is well done."[241]

Another Aspect of Advanced Awakening Is Experiencing Divine Love

Another ingredient of advanced awakening is experiencing Divine Love. We mystics feel blessed by all that Infinite Love has bestowed on us: our life, health, and talents as well as our family, friends, community, nation, nature, and universe. Julian of Norwich saw that "God is Love" and "eternal sovereign Love uncreated." She experienced God's love. He "showed me spiritually how intimately He loves us." He "loves all that He has made." His love is abundant, merciful, compassionate, and unending. "God who made everything because of His Love, by the same Love sustains it in being, now and forever." In short, "everything owes its existence to the Love of God." Before we were made, "God loved us; and His Love has never slackened nor never shall. In this Love all His works have been done; and in this Love He has made everything serve us; and in this Love our life is everlasting." Since the first of sixteen revelations, Julian "often wanted to know, what was our Lord's meaning?" More than fifteen years later, she received an answer. "Love was His meaning. Who showed it to you? Love. What did He show you? Love. Why did He show it"? For Love." Thus, she learned that "Love was our Lord's meaning . . . before ever He made us, God loved us; and that His Love has never slackened, nor ever shall. . . . In this Love our life is everlasting."[242]

George Fox, the seventeenth-century British founder of the Society of Friends, also called the Quakers, experienced Divine Love. "The Lord gently led me along, and let me see His love, which was endless and eternal, surpassing all the knowledge that men have in the natural state, or can obtain from history or books." Then "another time I saw the great love of God and was filled with admiration at the infiniteness of it."[243]

Matthew Lee, Margaret Poloma, and Stephen Post in their 2013 book, *The Heart of Religion: Spiritual Empowerment, Benevolence, and the Experience of God's Love*, give empirical evidence of people's experiences of God, His presence, and His love. Their random survey of 1,208 Americans is called "the Godly Love National Survey (GLNS)." It is "supplemented by hundreds of more targeted survey responses" and interviews with 120 Christians whom they refer to as exemplars. Their purpose is to discover the relationship of experiencing God's love and doing acts of benevolence to help others. They present the statistic that "half of Americans claim to have experienced a life-altering spiritual event" that stands out in their minds.[244]

Lee and associates are less concerned with the externals of religion such as beliefs, rituals, and organizations. They are more focused on the heart of religion, "the inner experience of lived religion" that they describe as "the dynamic and emotionally powerful experience of a radically loving, radically accepting God" and "the experience of Divine Love that fosters benevolence." What they describe as the heart of religion are the two components of their spirituality. Using their scale for "measuring the frequency and intensity of experiencing God's Love," 95% of Christians who identify as Pentecostals "scored either moderate or high on experiencing God's Love, while 73% of Christians who do not identify as Pentecostals scored the same way. A common theme in their interviews with Christian exemplars is that "powerful experiences of spiritual transformation . . . lead to a deeper sense of God's Love."[245]

A Spiritual Experience of Awakening to God through Prayer

Some people have experiences of God when they pray. In doing their empirical study, Lee and associates looked at various polls about prayer. For over 60 years, a Gallup poll said that over 85 percent of Americans claim that they pray once in a while. According to the 2009 GLNS survey, 68 percent say that they pray at least once a day. This number is the same as the 2007 Pew Research survey. The authors describe three types of prayer. The first type, 'Devotional prayer,' means a one way reaching out and talking to God in your own words, such as thanking Him or asking Him to meet the needs of the self and others. 95 percent of pray-ers do this. 'Prophetic conversation," the second type of prayer, means a dialogue with God in which people hear and respond to God in a two-way conversation. It is "a two-way interaction with God, in which pray-ers reach out to God, wait for a response," and experience "a sign, a feeling, or perhaps an audible voice." Examples of hearing God include having "a sense of a Divine call to do some actions, a sense of hearing the voice of God, a sense of stillness as they listen with their own spirit for the Spirit of God, and a sense of calm and peace that prayer brings."[246]

Lee and associates call the third type of prayer 'mystical communion.' This means "feeling the presence of God or experiencing union with God (e.g., sensing God in a way that cannot be expressed)." Like spiritual transformation, prayer is "journey toward union with the Divine." It is a process that begins with talking to God. Some progress to the other two types of praying. Their statistical analysis "found a strong relationship between these three prayers measures and knowing God's Love." Over half of those who score high on talking to God also score high on hearing from God. Even more 62 percent of those who score high on talking to God score high on the mystical scale of feeling the Divine presence. "God is always present despite the illusion of His absence." At the center of a spiritual experience is a 'loving presence' so that "the striving for power, pleasure, and wealth becomes replaced by spiritual growth and generosity."[247]

According to Lee and associates, as with the other two types of prayer, "experiences of mystical prayer have been reported by a majority of our respondents—at least on occasion." In presenting the mystical scale's three items, they surprisingly give the statistics for the people who did *not* have the three spiritual experiences rather than for those who did. 39 percent of GLNS survey said "they had *never* experienced 'everything seemingly disappear except the consciousness of God,' 36 percent reported they have *never* had 'an experience of God that no words could possibly express,' and 33 percent reported they have *never* felt the 'unmistakable presence of God during prayers.'" A positive statistic on the last item is that "one in four (25 percent) claim to experience the 'unmistakable presence of God' on most days or even 'several times a day.'"[248]

Irregular Spiritual Experiences Are Not Essential

Lee and associates present a number of examples of what I call irregular spiritual experiences. They claim that "one common marker of religiosity . . . is the experience of being 'born again.'" Although definitions vary, this commonly means "accepting Jesus as one's personal savior and receiving assurance of salvation." Being born again is much more common among Protestants. 82 percent of Evangelical, 80 percent of Hispanic, 71 percent of African American, and 33 percent of mainline Protestants are born again. In contrast, these experiences are much less common among Catholics. Only 11 percent of Euro-American and 41 percent of Hispanic Catholics are born again.[249]

The authors describe irregular spiritual experiences among Pentecostals who are centered in a small number of Christian denominations. "Pentecostals often feel they are empowered through the Holy Spirit" and have "paranormal experiences attributed to the Holy Spirit." They "are likely to be involved in a dynamic and personal relationship with God" and have transforming spiritual experiences since God is "miraculous and unexplainable." Their "initiation into the realm of the spirit" is known as 'baptism of the spirit' or 'baptism of love' or being 'bathed in love' or the 'flame/fire of love.' Other markers are speaking and "praying in tongues (glossalalia), receiving Divine emotional or physical healing, being baptized in the Holy Spirit." The holistic, spiritual healing treats the body, emotions, mind, and soul.[250]

More Pentecostal markers are "prophecy, healing, miracles, deliverances," and "signs and wonders." Acts of spiritual transformation are "new birth, indwelling of the Spirit, awakening, epiphany." Some even include "heavenly music," visits by Jesus or angels, and "emotionally powerful visions of God" that are rarely "associated with involuntary convulsions and shouting." Some have "fallen to the ground during the time of public worship—what old Pentecostals called 'going under the power' or being 'slain by the spirit' and Pentecostals now refer to as 'resting in the Spirit'." Some years ago, "stories of paranormal Pentecostal events" and "walking in the supernatural and eschewing involvement in 'heathen' society were normative."[251] Julian of Norwich, Underhill, Armstrong, Lee, and others describe unusual spiritual experiences that are rare. However, they can happen more frequently if perhaps they are encouraged or praised as they are in Pentecostal circles. While the experiences that are based on the physical senses *cannot* be totally ignored, discounted, and denied, in my thinking these do not teach us as much about the Ultimate Reality as less exceptional spiritual encounters. However, if mystics interpret their experiences, they can be valuable. Examples of these interpretations include the mystical messages heard and reported by Julian of Norwich and Catherine of Siena. The danger of these irregular types of spiritual experience is that some people devalue their own experiences because they do not have this extraordinary quality. In fact, some mistakenly define mystical experiences as only these nonessential events.

Underhill mainly studied "the mystical life-process in man, the organic growth of his transcendental consciousness." She wrote about "the by-products of that process, its characteristic forms of self-expression: the development of its normal art of contemplation, and the visions and voices, ecstasies and raptures which are frequent—though not essential—accompaniments of its activity." Thus, she said that contemplation is normal, but the visions, voices, ecstasies, and raptures are *not* essential. "'Voice' or 'vision' is often the way in which the mystical consciousness presents its discoveries to the surface-mind." However, "when apprehension of the Divine comes by way of vision or audition, this is but a concession to human weakness; a sign, they (the mystics) think that 'sensitive nature' is not yet wholly transcended." Thus, "the true contemplative, coming to the plane of utter stillness, does not desire 'extraordinary favors and visitations,' but the privilege of breathing the atmosphere of Love." To reach mystical consciousness and deeper degrees of prayer, people need to get rid of selfhood and pride, "the most fertile of all sources of deception," by "a cutting off of all their possible encouragements" and by "a steady abolition of sense imagery."[252]

According to Armstrong, the Christian theologians who were concerned about the ineffable Divine and silence, such as "Origen, Gregory of Nyssa, Augustine, Denys, Bonaventure, Aquinas, and Eckhart," were suspicious of the type of experiential spirituality that Pentecostals practiced. "Pentecostals relied on the immediacy of sense experience to validate their beliefs. But the meteoric explosion of this type of faith indicated their widespread unhappiness with the modern rational ethos;" their fears of science, technology, and modernity; and their reaction against other conservative "Christians who were trying to make their Bible-based religion entirely reasonable and scientific." Her own thought is that "perhaps the only viable 'natural theology' lies in religious experience," but not in "fervid emotion" or "exotic raptures" or looking for God outside ourselves in the universe. We should turn within and be aware of how ordinary responses help us find transcendence.[253]

Mystics' Images of the Divine after Awakening

We are conscious of God's existence and presence before we ponder what the Divine is. First, we become awakened that there is a real, alive, dynamic Holy One. Then we become enlightened about the Divine presence within us. Next, we realize that this presence is within all people and nature. Only later do we begin to wonder what the Sacred Spirit is? What is the essence of the Ultimate Reality? Is It like us? Is It totally separate from us? How is It different from us? Can we relate to It? Does It help us with our lives? Do prayers help It to be more involved with us? As the twentieth century Jewish theologian Abraham Heschel said, a person is "aware of His presence before he thinks of His essence."[254]

Once individuals begin reflecting on what the Holy One is, there are numerous concepts of the Divine. In fact, there are as many images of the Sacred Spirit as there are people because even atheists and agnostics have ideas about what they are doubting and denying. Everyone's notion is different because each is personal and often passionate. The language for Infinite Love that we tend to use to describe our mystical experience in the third stage is usually what we are taught by our parents and our religious leaders. The images of the Ultimate Reality that we are taught tends to be a personal God who has human traits.

Awakened mystics mostly view God as a Person and describe Him with personal qualities. Among the multitude of His personal qualities, God is good, mighty, powerful, wise, understanding, knowing, just, liberating, faithful, trustworthy, truthful, and peaceful. The Divine is caring, responsive, sharing, accepting, forgiving, generous, empathetic, benevolent, compassionate, and loving. Around the world, the earliest traditional religions worshipped the Great Mother Goddess. She had many different names, including Isis, Astarte, Oshun, Kali, Venus, Gaia, and Amaterasu. Later they also worshipped God as male. Other images include the High God as well as the sun, earth, rain, storm, stars, rivers, mountains, animals, and more. For Hindus, there were over 300 million different Goddesses and Gods, including Kali and Shiva.

In the Jewish scriptures, personal images were far more prevalent. Male concepts were much more common than female ones. God was Yahweh, King, Father, Husband, Shepherd, Creator, Warrior, Savior, Liberator, Redeemer, Lawgiver, and Judge. Their personal God formed a loving relationship and made a covenant with Abraham, Moses, and the Jews. God tested Abraham's faithfulness by asking him to sacrifice His only son. Because He gave Moses the ten commandments, God was a lawgiver and judge who rewarded those who obeyed His commandments and punished those who disobeyed. As the Hebrew Bible said, He showed "steadfast love to the thousandth generation of those who love Me and keep My commandments," but He also punished children for the wrongdoing of their parents down to the third and fourth generation. Many times He questioned the Jews' faithfulness in obeying His commandments. God is also described as the savior, redeemer, and liberator who delivered the Jews out of oppression and slavery in Egypt and brought them to "a land flowing with milk and honey." Although He taught them to love God and their neighbor, He was also a warrior who told the Jews to kill people who worshipped other Gods and Goddesses. Several prophets viewed God as a husband and the people as His unfaithful wife or harlot.[255]

According to a contemporary Biblical scholar, Marcus Borg, an important and striking fact is that the Bible contained multiple images of God that were drawn from a number of areas of human experience. God was also represented as natural and inanimate objects, such as a burning bush, fire, wind, spirit, eagle, bear, lion, rock, and shield. Borg claims that "God cannot literally be all of these." These images are evocative and suggestive of more than one meaning. "They have multiple associations and cannot be translated into a single equivalent literal statement." An example is Moses hearing God in the fire of the burning bush. "There the angel of the Lord appeared to him in a flame of fire out of a bush; he looked and the bush was blazing, yet it was not consumed. . . . God called to him out of the bush." This image is not literally true. However, it suggests that God as fire is burning but not consuming, hidden but available, light-producing but mysterious, enlightening but disappearing, nonmaterial but real, constant but fleeting, purifying but fear-provoking, warm but dangerous, and protective but destructive.[256] In the Christian scriptures, Jesus presented a variety of personal and transpersonal images, metaphors, analogies, and symbols for the Divine. Most frequently, he chose the personal image of "our Father." His parables presented multiple personal images of God that were female and male as well as could be either female or male, including the woman who lost one of her ten coins, the father who lost his prodigal son, and the shepherd who lost one of his hundred sheep. Much less often Jesus used transpersonal images. "God is Spirit, and those who worship Him must worship in spirit and truth."[257]

Since Jesus never wrote his spiritual teachings, Paul's epistles were the earliest Christian writings included in the New Testament. Jesus spoke in parables about the Divine. Paul wrote without parables and pictured the Divine in personal images. God was the Father who had personal qualities. He was loving, merciful, kind, graceful, faithful, just, righteous, truthful, knowing, wise, powerful, almighty, wrathful, and the "God of love and peace." Frequently, he used the transpersonal image of God as Spirit and Holy Spirit. "The Spirit of God dwells in you." In his epistles, John referred to God as Father. He also used the transpersonal image that "God is Love." John said, "whoever does not love does not know God, for God is Love." In addition, "God is Light and in Him there is no darkness." God is "the Holy One."[258]

Traditional, orthodox Christianity teaches that God is Trinity, a transpersonal image, even though the word Trinity never appeared in the Bible. The Trinity is also a multi-personal image. The Trinity is the Father, Son, and the Holy Spirit, three persons in one God, three persons in one Divine nature. All three persons have human qualities. The Father loves us so much that He gave us Jesus, His only son. As John's gospel said, "God so loved the world that He gave His one and only Son." Jesus loves us so much that He died on the cross to save us from our sins. The Father sent us the Holy Spirit, "another Counselor, the Spirit of Truth, to be with us forever." The Holy Spirit teaches us all things and reminds us of everything that Jesus said to us. In addition, the Holy Spirit lives with us and will be in us.[259]

According to Borg, throughout their history, Christians found two personal models of God in the Bible. The first is "the monarchical model" that draws its name from God as king and lord. "As king, God is both the lawgiver and judge." This image of God as "a lawgiver and judge who loves us" is softened somewhat when father is substituted for king. "God did love us—but it was a conditional love." God accepted us if we did not sin and forgave us if we repented. In this model, the central Christian dynamic is "sin, guilt, and forgiveness." Borg's second Christian model for God is "the Divine Lover model." This image of God as Lover is deeply rooted in the

Bible. Jesus is "the embodiment or incarnation of God as Lover." In addition, "the God of Love is also the God of Justice." God is the Liberator of the oppressed, compassionate toward all, and "passionate about social justice." Borg answers yes and no to the question, are the two models mutually exclusive? Although some people affirm both, "one will always be subordinate to the other." As Divine Lover, God practices unconditional love, while as lawgiver and judge, God's love is always conditional. Conditional love is "a terrible form of love, but it is better than no love at all."[260]

If contemporary scholar Jack Nelson-Pallmeyer was asked "to choose one word that best describes the character of God in the Bible, it would be violence." Idolatry and other kinds of unfaithfulness triggered God's punishing violence. Thus, God was "the violent judge and executioner." If he was asked to "choose a second word, it would be justice. . . . Justice was foundational to the post-Exodus covenant." The just God heard the cry of the oppressed Jewish people, knew their sufferings, freed them, and brought them to a good "land flowing with milk and honey." The just God urged people to "give justice to the weak and the orphan; maintain the rights of the lowly and the destitute. Rescue the weak and needy; deliver them from the hand of the wicked." Islam is the seventh century religion that teaches in the Quran God's revelation to Mohammed. It claims that God has ninety-nine names. These will be discussed in a later chapter.[261]

The images of God that the fifteen-century English mystic Julian of Norwich received from God's revelations were personal in the third stage of her awakening as well as transpersonal in the fifth stage of her illumination and union with God. In her summary of her third revelation, she spoke of "the blessed God who always has been, is now, and ever shall be: Almighty, All-wise, All-loving." In her book she repeated these three qualities multiple times: "our Lord, Almighty, All-wisdom, and All-love." Sometime she replaced All-loving with All-good.[262]

Influenced by her Catholic faith, Julian believed in the transpersonal Trinity as well as Jesus as both God and human. She connected her image of God as Almighty, All-wise, and all-loving with her own unique version of the Trinity. "When He made us, God almighty was our kindly Father, and God all-wise our kindly Mother, and the Holy Spirit their love and goodness; all one God, our Lord." She described the second person as Mother as well as Jesus, our Savior. "The great Power of the Trinity is our Father, the deep Wisdom our Mother, and the great Love our Lord," the Holy Spirit. God revealed to her, "it is I who am the Strength and Goodness of Fatherhood; I who am the Wisdom of Motherhood; and I who am Light and Grace and blessed Love" of the Holy Spirit.[263]

Julian also called God our "true Father and Mother" as well as our Maker, our Keeper, and our eternal Lover. God "showed me spiritually how intimately He loves us." Our Maker has for us "the greatness, the sweetness, and the tenderness of the Love." He "keeps us in His blessed Love." We "gaze, eternally marveling at the supreme, surpassing, single-minded, incalculable Love that God, who is Goodness, has for us." It is God's will "that of all the qualities of the blessed Trinity that we should be most sure of, and delighted with, is Love. Love makes Might and Wisdom come down to our level." Not only does God love us, but He also loves everything in existence. He "loves all that He has made." His Love is abundant, many-sided, astonishing, compassionate, and unending. God's first revelation showed Julian a hazelnut and she saw three truths. "The first is that God made it; the second is that God loves it; and the third is that God sustains it." Thus, God is Creator, Lover, and Sustainer. "In short, everything owes its existence to the Love of God." Furthermore, "the whole of life is grounded and rooted in love, and without love we cannot live."[264]

Julian's revelations also showed God as "loving, humble, and gentle" as well as gracious, kind, considerate, compassionate, pitying, and merciful. He is "so holy and awful." Besides helping us by giving us spiritual insight, our Lover "kindles our understanding, He directs our paths, He eases our consciences, He comforts our soul, He lightens our heart. He gives us—partially at least—knowledge and trust in His blessed Godhead." Furthermore, "God rules and upholds both heaven and earth, and all that is, and is supreme in might, wisdom, and goodness." He "was never angry—nor would He be," because He is good, truthful, righteous, loving, and peaceful. When we sin, "it makes no difference at all to His Love." He "forgives our sin when we repent." God "comforts and sympathizes, for He is ever kindly disposed toward our soul, and, loving us, longs to bring us to His bliss."[265]

According to Julian's revelations, "everything opposed to love and peace" does not come from God. We fall because of our own weakness and stupidity. "The remedy is to be aware of our wretchedness, and to fly to our Lord. The greater our need, the more important it is to draw near to Him." When we feel sorrow, anxiety, grief, and depression, God says that "you will experience distress whatever you do. . . . recognize that your whole life is a profitable penance. . . . The remedy is the fact that our Lord is with us, protecting us and leading us into fullest joy." God, "our Protector here, is to be our Bliss there—our way and our heaven is true Love and sure Trust! This is the message of all the revelations."[266]

In the first part of her career, Mother Teresa was a twentieth-century Catholic nun in the religious order of Loreto who taught at a girls' school in Calcutta, India for 18 years. Later she founded the Catholic religious order of Missionaries of Charity that started in India and spread worldwide. She learned her image of God from her parents and from the Catholic Church. As a Loreto nun, she said, "I have been burning with longing to love Him as He has never been loved before." Although she suffered, she was happy. "The heat of India is simply burning. . . . fire is under my feet. . . . The life of a missionary is not strewn with roses, in fact more with thorns; but with it all, it is a life full of happiness and joy." When she thought that she was doing the same work that Jesus did on earth, she felt that she was fulfilling his commandment to "go and teach all nations."[267]

Besides instructing Mother Teresa on its understanding of God, the Catholic Church also taught her about mortal sin, vows, and giving her life to God. As a nun, she said, "I made a vow to God, binding under the pain of mortal sin, to give to God anything that He may ask, not to refuse Him anything." Later Mother Teresa explained her reasons for making this private vow to say yes to Him in all things. "I wanted to give God something very beautiful." Another reason she gave herself fully to Him was "because God has given Himself to us. . . . To give ourselves fully to God is a means of receiving God Himself. I for God and God for me. I live for God and give up my own self."[268]

In Mother Teresa's image, God was loving. "How very wonderful is God in His Infinite Love." She described, "how much is the Love He has for each of you—beyond all that you can imagine. . .. He loves you always, even when you don't feel worthy." Since she believed in the Trinity, she considered Jesus the Son of God. Envisioning herself as Jesus' friend, she said, "Jesus and I have been friends up to now." Seeing herself as Jesus' spouse, she exclaimed, "how happy I am as Jesus' little spouse. . . . I am enjoying my complete happiness, even when I suffer something for my beloved Spouse." In addition, "until you know deep inside that Jesus thirsts for you—you can't begin to know who He wants to be for you. Or who He wants you to be for Him."[269]

According to Lee and associates in their study of images of God, "one gleaming, common thread weaves throughout. For Americans today, God, quite simply, is Love. Christians, Hindus, Jews, and Buddhists alike describe a loving presence who offers a pathway to goodness, peace, and brotherhood. Some imagine Him or Her as limitless Energy; others as a Force of nature." They conclude that "God's Love does appear to be alive and well in America."[270]

Ways to Experience Awakening to the Holy One

We can be awakened to the Divine in many different ways. Institutional religions teach various paths. Many of these contain important truths.

However, numerous people find their roads outside of established religions. An analogy for the many ways to become spiritual is a mountain with multiple paths to the top where the Holy One resides. Some trails that circle around are long and gradual, but less difficult. Other routes are shorter and steeper, but more demanding. There is no right way. All of us must choose the road that best suits who we are as unique individuals. All paths lead to the top and the Sacred Spirit.[271]

As nature lovers, we can experience awe and wonder in the first stage as well as awakening in the third stage while walking in a flowering woods, seeing a gorgeous sunset, sitting on a majestic mountain top, looking at a peaceful lake, studying the unique patterns of beautiful snowflakes, watching magnificent horses race across an open meadow, and listening to the blue waves pound against a sandy shore. Day after day nature paints for us pictures of Infinite Beauty. In his poem "Paradise Lost," John Milton wrote, "in contemplation of created things, by steps we may ascend to God." As art lovers, we can discover the Sacred Spirit through our appreciation of beauty by experiencing gorgeous paintings, the grandeur of spectacular architecture, the taste of gourmet food, the powerful sensations of lovemaking, the emotions aroused by compelling theatre, and the soaring passion of beautiful music. While viewing Michelangelo's marble sculpture of David, I was struck by awe and wonder and awakened by the magnificent splendor of this fifteen-foot statue.[272]

As ritual lovers, we can be awakened to the Holy One by worshipping in a church, synagogue, temple, and mosque as well as by the music, hymns, chants, symbols, art work, sacraments, incense, fasting, ascetic practices, scripture readings, sermons, meditations, and prayers. Intellectuals discover God through spiritual reading, studying, and discussing. Jews and Hindus teach knowledge and wisdom are ways to the Divine. Francis of Assisi, a thirteenth century Italian mystic, said that "the knowledge is knowledge of God. The highest wisdom is that holy wisdom whereby the soul is made One with God." We can also discover the Divine by choosing solitude, silence, simplicity, prayer, meditation, concentration, and contemplation. Solitude and silence lead us to explore the depth within ourselves, our world, and the ONE. A simple way of life helps us keep our mind on the Sacred Spirit and not on material things. Some of us discover the Ultimate Reality through meditation and contemplation. Mother Teresa said, "there is no life of prayer without silence. . . . silence leads to charity."[273]

Caregivers can find the Sacred Spirit by serving others. Caregivers include parents, nurses, doctors, therapists, teachers, day care workers, drug and alcohol counselors, domestic violence workers, rape counselors, and people who help the needy, poor, hungry, homeless, victims, sick, lepers, and the dying. Mother Teresa said, "we show our love for God by putting our love into living action through serving the poorest of the poor." While living among them, she saw God in each of them. "We all should become carriers of God's Love." As activists, we can be awakened to the Divine by fighting prejudice, hatred, discrimination, exploitation, greed, domination, sexism, classism, racism, ecological destruction, abuse, violence, militarism, and war. While trying to transform ourselves and our world, we work to create more respect, liberty, equality, justice, peace, and love for all women and men, all races, classes, and the environment. As Buddha said, "hate is not conquered by hate; hate is conquered by love. This is the law eternal."[274]

In the *Bhagavad Gita*, Hindu sages wrote about ways to experience an awakening. This spiritual classic presented a dialogue between God who was called Krishna and his disciple Arjuna. This dialogue described three yogas as ways that we can become awakened, the yogas of knowledge and wisdom, action and work, and devotion and love. Other ways include renunciation, freedom from attachment, love for all of creation, and making the Holy One our supreme end. The Sacred Krishna said to Arjuna that not by reading the sacred scriptures, or living an austere life, or giving to the poor, or offering rituals, "can I (God) be seen as thou my disciple has seen Me. Only by love can people see Me, and know Me, and come to Me. He who works for Me, who loves Me, whose End Supreme I am, free from attachment to all things, and with love for all creation, he in truth comes to Me."[275]

About the yoga of knowledge and wisdom, the Holy Krishna explained when a person "sees Eternity in the things that pass away and Infinity in finite things," then he has pure knowledge. "He who has faith has wisdom, . . . and he who finds wisdom finds the Peace Supreme." When an individual has a clear vision and "sees Me as the Spirit Supreme, he knows all there is to know, and he adores Me with all his soul." About the yoga of action and work, the Divine Krishna declared, "do thy duty, even if it is humble, rather than another's, even if it be great." The person, who "works on the path of Karma Yoga, the path of consecrated action," is great. The purpose of action is to make the world a better place. The wise individual works unselfishly with no desire for reward, while offering all his actions to the Holy One. The person "whose work is pure attains the Supreme" and "who in all his work sees God, he in truth goes to God."[276]

About the yoga of devotion and love, the Sacred Krishna said that the best yogis are "those who set their hearts on Me and ever in love worship Me, and who have unshakable faith." Those will reach Me "who have all the powers of their soul in harmony, the same loving mind for all, and who find joy in the good of all beings." I will deliver from the cycle of life and death those "for whom I am the End Supreme, who surrender all their works to Me, who with pure love meditate on Me, and set their heart on Me alone." A person becomes "this yogi of union who has good will for all, who is friendly and has compassion, who has no thought of 'I' and 'mine,' whose peace is the same in pleasures and sorrows, who is forgiving, and who loves Me."[277]

The Holy Krishna also said that a yogi of love and union is one "who works for God and not for himself, . . . who complains not and lusts not for things, who has love." This yogi is dear to Me "whose love is the same for his enemies or his friends, whose soul is beyond pleasure or pain, who is free from the chains of attachment, who is happy with whatever he has, whose home is not in this world, and who has love. . . .. But even dearer to Me are those who have faith and love, and who have Me as their End Supreme." A yogi of love and union goes beyond the path of austerity or wisdom or work. "The greatest of all yogis is he who with all his soul has faith, and who with all his soul loves Me."[278]

Tolle describes a number of portals or ways to the Divine. Portals are "pointers to show you how you can bring the dimension of the Unmanifested into your life." One portal is "completely accepting what is." When you are seeking for an answer, you are searching outside yourself. "Don't look for peace. Don't look for any other state than the one you are in now; otherwise, you will set up inner conflict and unconscious resistance. Forgive yourself for not being at peace. The moment you *completely accept* your non-peace, your non-peace becomes transmuted into peace." Enlightenment is "when you accept what is." Another portal is "the cessation of thinking." There are "many way to create a gap in the incessant stream of thought," including meditation, "taking one conscious breath or looking, in a state of intense alertness, at a flower, so that there is no mental commentary running at the same time." Your "continuous mind activity keeps you imprisoned in the world of form and . . . prevents you from becoming conscious of the Unmanifested, conscious of the formless and timeless God-essence in yourself and in all things and all creatures. When you are intensely *present*," your mind stops thinking and become aware of the Source within you.[279]

According to Tolle, to become awakened, you need to be free from the core error, the illusion of the self, "the illusion that you are nothing more than your physical body and your mind." The egoistic mind creates the mental construct of the self. What is missing is the one thing that truly matters, "the awareness of your deeper self—your invisible and indestructible reality." To become aware, "you need to reclaim consciousness from the mind. This is one of the most essential tasks on your spiritual journey." One effective way is "to take the focus of your attention away from thinking and direct it into the body, where Being can be felt in the first instance as the invisible energy field that gives life to . . . the physical body." Thus, "attention is the key to transformation—and full attention also implies acceptance." When you pay deep attention to your energy stream, your spirit, "you may reach this point, this singularity, where the world dissolves into the Unmanifested," the Divine. "This state of connectedness with the Source" is enlightenment.[280]

Tolle claims that "when your consciousness is directed outward, mind and world arise. When it is directed inward, it realizes its own Source and returns home to the Unmanifested," the Ultimate Reality. The Holy One is the Source of the inner energy field of your body that the Chinese call *chi*. My name for your inner energy field is your soul, spirit, inner core of love, and the Divine within you. Your inner energy field or soul is "the bridge between the outer you and the Source. It lies halfway between the manifested, the world of form, and the Unmanifested." When you focus your attention on the inner energy stream, it is like a river and you can follow it back to its Source. Your inner energy field, soul, spirit, chi, and the inner core of love are movement. The Source is "absolute stillness which is nevertheless vibrant with life."[281]

For Tolle, the main portal to the Divine that is "an essential aspect of every other portal" is the NOW, "the intense present-moment awareness," through which you dissolve psychological time and become conscious of the Unmanifested. The timeless NOW and the Unmanifested are "inextricably linked." You feel the Unmanifested directly as "the radiance and power of your conscious presence—no content, just presence. Indirectly, you are aware of the Unmanifested" when "you feel the God-essence in every creature, every flower, every stone, and you realize: 'All that is, is holy.'" Thus, "it is possible to be conscious of the Unmanifested throughout your life. You feel It as a deep sense of peace, . . . a stillness that never leaves you, no matter what happens."[282]

Early Indigenous Tribes Experience Awe and Awakening and Then Produced Their Traditional Religions

Otto says that awe is "a fact of our nature—primary, unique, underivable from anything else." Around the globe, the earliest hunter-gatherer people of indigenous tribes, clans, and ethnic groups lived close to nature and experienced awe and awakening at the beauty, power, magnificence, order, complexity and mystery of the universe. Awe and awakening were aroused by awesome occurrences in humans, animals, and nature. Like children, they were radically amazed people. Unlike children, they realized that their experiences of awe and awakening were spiritual.[283]

For Otto, awe is "the basic factor and the basic impulse underlying the entire process of religious evolution." God and all the products of myth "spring from this root." In awe, "there is something non-natural or supernatural." At the earliest stage of spiritual development, the essential characteristic was an experience of awe "before something 'Wholly Other,'" whether It was called Spirit or God or It was without any name. Awe showed itself in the "first crude, primitive forms" of early religions. Awe is "this feeling which, emerging in the mind of primeval man, forms the starting point for the entire religious development in history." The first images were "later overborne and ousted by more highly developed forms."[284]

Unlike children, the earliest people had not only a spiritual experience of awe, but also an awakening to the Divine, which Otto calls a 'numinous experience,' that has the qualities of being attracting, fascinating, and wonderful. Awe and awakening result in "the profound element of *wonderfulness* and rapture which lies in the mysterious beatific experience of Deity." These spiritual experiences have "the quality of exaltedness and sublimity." In its ennobled form as mystical awe, "the soul, held speechless, trembles inwardly to the farthest fiber of its being." At its highest point, awe and awakening "become an 'overabounding,' 'exuberant,' and 'mystical 'moment.'" These unutterable experiences "may pass into blissful excitement, rapture, and exaltation." The Holy is described as "the highest, strongest, best, loveliest, and dearest" that human can conceive.[285]

Like beautiful music, God is ineffable, indescribable, and inexplicable. Otto calls God the Holy, the 'Wholly Other,' the N*umen*, '*Mysterium Tremendum*,' and "a Mystery inexpressible and above all." The Wholly Other cannot be rationalized or defined. It can only be felt and experienced as well as grasped and glimpsed by inadequate intuitions. The idea of God cannot "be taught, it can only be evoked, awakened in the mind; as everything that comes 'of the spirit' must be awakened." It "can only be induced, incited, and aroused." Nearly everywhere in the arts, "the most effective means of representing the numinous is 'the sublime.'" Architectural examples include the Stonehenge, pyramids, and European cathedrals.[286]

A number of scholars claim that all over the world the earliest people had mystical experiences of awakening that made them believe that the Great Mother Goddess was the Creator of life. Archaeological evidence for this includes myths, customs, and artifacts, such as ancient statues of Goddesses. Possibly as early as 25,000 BCE the Great Mother Goddess was a principal Divinity around the world. Encircling the globe, the Goddess was worshipped under many different names, including Isis, Astarte, Ishtar, Ala, Kali, Venus, Earth Mother, Gaia, and the Sun Goddess. For thousands of years all over the world, the Goddess was supreme, male dominance was not the norm, and there were no signs of war. The evidence shows that during the time when Goddess veneration remained dominant throughout the world, women were active and admired participants in the partnership society and often enjoyed an independent political and economic position.[287]

Archaeologists have documented matricentric, egalitarian, peaceful, partnership, Goddess worshipping cultures in Catal Huyuk in Turkey from 9,000 to 6,000 BCE; southeastern Europe from 7,000 to 3,500 BCE; and India from 4,000 to 2,000 BCE. A Goddess worshipping partnership culture that existed in Minoan Crete from 3,000 to 1,500 BCE was matrilocal, equal, and peaceful. As an urban society with cities numbering as many as a hundred thousand inhabitants, Minoan culture had a centralized government, a nourishing art, joyful play, equitable sharing of wealth, matrilineal inheritance, and egalitarian relationships between the sexes. The women, queens, and priestesses had high status. As changes took place over time, especially the development of agriculture and the domestication of animals, ancient peoples discovered the male role in procreation. Because of this, beliefs that described the creation of the universe by the Goddess alone began to add a male God. At first the male God was secondary and later the two became equals, such as Mother Earth and Sky God. In some religions such as Hinduism, the Goddess was retained alongside the male God, while in others the Goddess was eliminated altogether and the male God became the supreme Creator.[288]

Early African, European, Middle Eastern, Asian, North and South American indigenous peoples' experiences of awe and wonder at nature awakened them to the Sacred Spirit or Creator God or Goddess. Then they believed that the Sacred Spirit placed a spirit within everyone and everything. Thus, they thought that all parts of the universe, including all the land, mountains, rivers, and oceans as well as all the animals and humans, had spirits. Because the Sacred Spirit gave all people and things a spirit, they believed that all were Divine.

Sociologist William Goode says that "this feeling that there is something Sacred, which is powerful, seems to be universal for all primitive religions." This experience of the Divine within people and objects led to the belief that everything and everyone had spirits or souls. Thus, innumerable spirits exist in every flower and tree, in every river and lake, in every hill and mountain, in every breeze and cloud, in every animal and person. "The variation in 'Gods and spirits' and Sacred things is almost infinite." These spirits act as intermediaries between humans and the Supreme Being.[289]

According to Parrinder, from prehistoric times, humans were "conscious of spiritual forces." Thus, they believed that all of creation was Sacred. Not only Africans, Native Americans, and Asians, but also the indigenous peoples of Europe, including the Celtic, Germanic, Slavic, and Baltic peoples viewed everything as Divine. For ancient peoples, spirituality permeated all their life. Evidence included "the remains of their shrines, places of worship, offerings, symbolic figures, representations of Deities, and burial customs."[290]

Early traditional religions had mystics who became their spiritual leaders. Their titles varied, such as priests, shamans, diviners, healers, prophets, ecstatics, ascetics, medicine men and women. Eskimos called their religious leader shaman. These shamans had spiritual experiences called '*anagakoq*' or illumination in which they felt within themselves a luminous fire which gave them the power to see the Unseen Transcendent. These spiritual leaders acted as representatives of the community to the Divine Spirit.[291]

Africans believe in a sky God, earth Goddess, other Deities, a multitude of spirits, ancestors, and evil. For example, the Twi speaking peoples including the Ashanti and Fanti tribes make up the Akan, one of the linguistic groups in Ghana, West Africa. In the Akan religion, God is the Supreme Being named *Nyame*, "the Great One" and "the Most Generous One." *Asase Yaa* is the Earth Mother, the Earth Goddess, and God's consort. Created by the Supreme Being, *abosom* are Divine spirits within everything and everyone. Like everything else, humans are born with a spirit, a soul, a vital force, a Divine spark, a "spark from God," a "breath of God" that is called '*kra*.' It is unique to them and provides them with "a worth above all other creatures of God." Since all humans have within them spirits or sparks of God, they are Divine so it is an abomination to kill them. Some West African tribes have special Sacred trees and animals that they do not abuse or kill, like the royal python.[292]

One Akan creation myth explains why spirits exist. God as Creator first made the sky, the sun, the moon, and the stars. Then He created the land, the rivers, and the plants. Finally, He made humans and the animals. "To protect the human family from elemental evil, Nyame (God) placed spirits" in everything and everyone, in the land, the mountains, the rivers, the trees, the rocks, plants, animals, and the people. "The spirits existed solely for the good of human persons." Africans use rituals, sacrifices, dances, and songs to communicate and develop communion with the spirit world. They not only believe that all people and things have spirits, but they also think that their deceased ancestors have spirits that continue to be involved in human lives. Death is an evil that disrupts a family's harmony. Doing funeral rituals restores that harmony and allows the dead to go to their spiritual abode. Then the spirits of the ancestors help the living. Africans do not worship their ancestors but rather ask them for aid by pouring libations.[293]

The Nuer in the Sudan in Africa worship *Kwoth* or Spirit. The Spirit is both many and one. Although invisible like the air and wind, this supreme

Spirit is present within everything. The Spirit is the unseen, supreme Divine mystery that is revealed in particular natural phenomena, like humans, animals, and tress. Behind everything lies the Spirit that resides in all and raises people's consciousness of Divine mystery. According the Sidney Spencer, a scholar of mysticism, "what is true of Nuer religion is true in substance of primitive religion as a whole." Moreover, "everywhere beneath the forms of religious ceremony or observances, whether it be a cult of ancestors, of animals, of Nature-spirits, of the Sky-God or the Earth-God (or Goddess), there lies the awareness of the Transcendent, which moves men's hearts with awe."[294]

In other parts of Africa, the Supreme Being has many other names, including the "Great Spirit," the "most Merciful," the Creator, the Rainmaker, the "Ruler, Father, Mother, and even the Grandfather, the Originator of the people." One contemporary song title is "God is love!" Most view God as "a Supreme and non-definable Being" who is remote and beyond humans. For the most part, "God is not defined or even described." In one Akan creation myth, God is the Almighty Creator. Another calls Him the "Great Spider." The Akan names for the Supreme Being result in qualities: "confident, a trusted Counselor in time of trouble. . . . the One who listens to our problems, . . . decides wisely, and whose decision gives comfort." Today Ghanaian proverbs that are put as signs on trucks, buses, and buildings express the wisdom of the elders. Many demonstrate a deep-seated belief in God and His traits.

> All people are God's children; not one is a child of the earth.
> All that God created is good.
> God is present.
> If you want to talk to Nyame (God), say it to the winds.
> God never sleeps.
> God will provide.
> It is God who pounds the fufu for the one-armed man.
> It is God who drives the flies from the tailless animal.
> If Nyame has given the sickness, He will provide the medicine.
> Nyame gives you palm wine and someone kicks it over,
> He will fill your cup again.
> No one teaches a child about God.
> God's time is best.[295]

For Native Americans, "spirituality is pervasive throughout all life." They believe in a Supreme Being that gave them their spirit. Creation manifests the Sacred. The natural world is very much alive and "filled with spiritual activity." All the land, the mountains, the rivers, the lakes, animals, trees, plants, and people possess spirits and are Sacred. Thus, the whole universe is Divine. Despite believing that everything and everyone have spirits and are Holy, some tribes pick out certain mountains and other places as special and as sites for their myths and rituals. Other Indian tribes view all animals as mysterious and spiritual, but choose certain ones, like the bear, as more mysterious, special, and spiritual.[296]

The Native American Shoshone tribe lived in the mountainous west for several thousand years, perhaps 10,000. The tribe viewed all life as Sacred and the natural world as rich with spirits. They visited their special Sacred places. One scholar claims that their culture and religion was filled with rules and rituals "every bit as complex as those of the Vatican." Their egalitarian leaders including medicine women and men considered their role as advisory and as an obligation to serve their tribe rather than an opportunity to gain wealth and power. "The highest status act a Shoshone could commit" was "to give others what he had. Generosity was how one achieved social standing." For one thousand years, "they had eliminated war." Their language no longer had a word for it. When others including whites arrived and attack them, they ran and hid.[297]

Native Americans have a worldview that sees the earth as the Great Mother, a living cosmic entity that binds humans into an interrelationship with all other life forms. Thus, they "know the Oneness of all things" and "operate in that knowing." This makes them "take only what they need, live in harmony with the environment, and love the earth." The Supreme Being, Mother Earth, and innumerable spirits influence human life on earth. These forces form a unity, an Oneness, "whole and indivisible." When humans are concerned with problems such as sickness, dangerous lightning, and thunder, they ask for aid from the specific spirits, Gods, and Goddesses connected to their troubles.[298]

One of the features of Native American religions is that they "emphasize a direct experience of spiritual power." Viewing the boundary between animals and spirits as "very vague," they not only think of animals as possessing spirits and as Sacred, but they also consider them as their sisters and brothers. Because they respect them, they try to be in harmony with them. The Ojibway tribe must not hurt or kill their totem animal. After they find it necessary to hunt and kill an animal for food, they do one ritual to ask the animal's forgiveness, another to dispose of the slain animal's unused remains, and another to thank the animal and the Creator for providing food. Tribal religions consider all of the universe as Divine. The Kogi Indians of Columbia who continue to survive today consider the South American mountains as "the Great Mother of All Life." She provides a place for humans to live. The Kogis view the forests, rivers, soil, sky, and ocean as "living and Sacred." They sent representatives to tell the modern world that they are horrified at the "killing of the Mother of All Life."[299]

Crashing Thunder, a Native American mystic of the Winnebago tribe, reported a spiritual experience of awe and wonder. "I prayed to the Earthmaker. And as I prayed, I was aware of Something above me, and there He was. That which is called the Soul . . . that is what one calls Earthmaker. That is what I felt and saw. All of us sitting together, we had all together one spirit or soul."[300]

All over the world there are many examples of traditional peoples who think that animals, trees, and plants "have souls like their own, and they treat them accordingly." The San of the Kalahari desert in northern South Africa, who are also called the !Kung, only kill an animal when food is needed. They thank the animal at the time of the hunt and later when they dance for its soul. The Native American Hidatsa Indians believe that "every natural object has its spirit" and that these spirits deserve consideration and respect. Some tribes believe that since trees have spirits, they are sensitive and feel pain. The Ojibway seldom cut down trees because this causes them pain. Some medicine men claim that they have heard "the wailing of the trees under the axe." In the past in some parts of Austria, peasants believed that trees have souls. They would "not allow an incision to be made in the bark without special cause; they have heard from their fathers that the tree feels the cut not less than a wounded man his hurt. In felling a tree they beg its pardon." In the upper Palatinate in Germany, "old woodmen still secretly ask a fine, sound tree to forgive them before they cut it down."[301]

European Finnish-Ugrian tribes in Siberia have sacred groves of trees "in which nothing might be touched" and "no wood might be hewn and no branch broken." The people of the Fiji islands in the Pacific Ocean "will never eat a coconut without asking leave—'may I eat you, my chief?'" Before the Karo Batek people of New Guinea cut down a tree, they "will offer it betel and apologies." The Kiwai of New Guinea "show great reluctance in felling certain large trees," because they are inhabited by spirits. If it is necessary to cut the tree down, they ask the spirit to move to some other tree. Before the Tagales of the Philippines fell a tree, they make excuses to the spirit in the tree by saying "the priest has ordered us to do it; the fault is not ours, nor the will either." In central India, where the *pipal* tree is Sacred, every child learns to say that "it is better to die a leper than pluck a leaf of the *pipal*."[302]

Some scholars contend that a distinction between the Sacred and the secular, Transcendent and the immanent, the Infinite and the finite, the Holy and the profane, is fundamental to religion. In ancient and contemporary traditional religions, the dividing line between Sacred and secular fades or disappears. Although everything and everyone belongs to the ordinary world, they are also part of the spiritual world. Religion is a pervasive influence and is "never isolated. Thus, nothing within the given society is perceived as non-religious or profane. Every meaningful act is seen as religious or Sacred."[303]

The modern Western opposition between the spiritual and the material world is "foreign to African and most other conceptions of the universe." The difference between Western and traditional African culture is "the sense of Sacredness, of religious mystery, of spiritual powers which pervades every aspect" of life. Thus, there is "no division between the Sacred and profane." Africans have always been very spiritual. Life is religion and religion is life. From the beginning, their culture and religion have been inseparable. "From dance through language and into various aspects of culture, religion manifests itself as primary, permeating every dimension of society." The African Dinka tribe says that "'Divinity is one,' meaning . . . that all power, Divine and human, is interrelated." As the cause of everything, "God is the Unity beyond all . . . that holds everything together." The invisible, infinite Creator is "one but many." Similarly the Western dualism between the Sacred and the secular world "has no counterpart in American Indian thinking." In the Indian worldview, no sharp differentiation exists between humans, spirits, and God. Native American religions have multiple "supernatural powers that govern the world."[304]

Chapter 6

The Awakenings of Mystics of Eastern Religions

The Hindu Sages' Awakenings Produced the Four *Vedas* and the *Upanishads*

Indian sages, mystics, saints, and seers called *rishis* meditated, had mystical experiences of awakening and illumination, and then produced the four *Vedas*, the 3,500-year-old Hindu scriptures. They taught that the Sacred Spirit contains in Himself the seed of the universe and brought it forth. Later He will take it back into Himself. All beings in the universe are involved in this process. Their final goal is to be free of the cycle of birth, death, and rebirth and to be absorbed into the Holy One. The Vedas presented prayers and hymns that sang praises to the Gods, including Indra, Varuna, Mitra, and many others. One theme was "That which exists is One (the One God Brahman), sages call It by various names."[305]

One hymn in the *Rig Veda* has the sages ask the question, "who knows the truth" about creation? What follows, "There was not then what is nor what is not.... The ONE was breathing by its own power, in infinite peace. Only the ONE was: there was nothing beyond. Darkness was hidden in darkness. The All was fluid and formless. Therein, in the void, by the fire of fervor arose the ONE. And in the ONE arose love: Love the first seed of the soul. The truth of this the sages found in their hearts: seeking in their hearts with wisdom, the sages found that bond of union between Being and non-being. Who knows the truth? . . . Only that God who sees in the highest heaven: He only knows whence came this universe, and whether it was made or uncreated. He only knows, or perhaps He knows not." Another translation of the ending of this hymn said, "who in reality knows and who can truly say how this creation came into existence and from what cause? Even the *Devas* (the Gods) were born after the creation came into existence. Hence who can know the cause of the universe? The Source from which the universe sprang, that alone can sustain it, none else. That One, the Lord of the universe, dwelling in Its own Being, undefiled as the sky above, alone knows the truth of Its own creation, none else."[306]

Another important Hindu scripture was the 2,600-years-old *Upanishads*. Considered the final writings of the more ancient Vedas, they were written in India by anonymous sages, visionary philosophers, and seers who had mystical experiences of awakening and illumination. Upanishad is a Sanskrit word that literally means "sitting near devotedly." This brings to mind a Hindu guru with a devoted disciple sitting at his feet learning from him. Another meaning is "secret teachings." Shankara, an eighth century commentator on the Upanishads, called them "the knowledge of Brahman, the knowledge that destroys the bonds of ignorance and leads to the supreme goal of freedom" from reincarnation.

The Upanishads did not describe the actual mystical experiences that the seers had. Instead they presented a multitude of spiritual insights that the sages gained from these experiences. The Upanishads' spiritual teachings that are part of the third stage of awakening will be presented in this chapter. Other teachings that arose in the fifth stage of illumination and union with the Divine will be discussed in a later chapter. In their popular myths and rituals, Hindus worship millions of Goddesses and Gods. Some of them, like the Goddess Kali and the God Vishnu, have a thousand names. However, this polytheistic religion is also a monotheism. All the Goddesses and Gods are manifestations of the One God, "Brahman, the Spirit Supreme," the ONE. As the Upanishads say, Brahman "transforms His One form unto many."[307]

Among the lessons that the Hindu sages learned from their mystical experiences of awakening and then expressed in the Upanishads were descriptions of the Divine. Brahman is the Absolute, the Supreme Spirit, the ONE, the God of life immortal, "the Creator of all, the Guardian of the universe." He "cannot be seen by the eye and words cannot reveal Him." He is "beyond thought and ineffable." Brahman is "not born. He does not die." The "One is unborn, imperishable, eternal." He is "the purest of the pure . . . this Effulgent Being, who is joy and who is beyond joy. Formless is He, though inhabiting forms" in creation. The wise, "the seers, absorbed in contemplation, saw within themselves the Ultimate Reality, the self-luminous Being, the One God, who dwells as the self-conscious power in all creatures. He is One without second. Deep within all beings He dwells, hidden from sight."[308]

Brahman is "immeasurable, inapprehensible, beyond description, never-born, beyond reasoning, beyond thought. His vastness is the vastness of space." Also "greater than all is Brahman, the Supreme, the Infinite." His "Infinity is in all" and He is "ever One beyond time." In addition, "His Infinity is beyond what is great and small, and greater than Him there is nothing." Brahman is "greater than all" and "greater than all greatness." The Immanent and Transcendent Supreme Spirit is "Life and Word and Mind. He is Truth and Life immortal. He is the goal to be aimed at." Brahman is "the foundation of all wisdom. . . .. He is Everlasting and Omnipresent, Infinite in the great and Infinite in the small. He is Eternal, . . . the Source of all creation." Brahman is "the Origin of all" and "the End of all." The truth is that "as from fire aflame thousands of sparks come forth, even so from the Creator an infinity of beings have life and to Him return again." Furthermore, "even as a spider sends forth and draws in its thread, even as plants arise from the earth and hairs from the human body, even so the whole creation arises from the Eternal."[309]

In the Upanishads, Brahman is "the God of Love" who is "loving to all." Thus, "He made a bond of love between his Soul and the soul of all things." He is "the Refugee of all." Furthermore, "in the vision of this God of Love there is everlasting peace" because He is "Peace and Love." As pure Consciousness, Brahman "knows all and sees all." He is "Joy and Light, and Life eternal." As "the radiant Light of all lights," He is "the God of Light" and "the light-giving Sun." Without Him, "the sun shines not, nor the moon, nor the stars; lightning shines not there and much less earthly fire. From His Light all these give light." Thus, "His Radiance illumines all creation" and spreads light in blinding splendor. "The Spirit fills all with His Radiance."[310]

Awakening in the third stage in the Upanishads is a more advanced state, it is also a spiritual consciousness of the presence of Brahman within all people and the whole creation. While traditional religions more than any other faiths taught that everything has a spirit, Hinduism stressed that the Divine is within the soul. It didn't just say that the Sacred Spirit is within the spirit, its *Upanishads* created a concept of the *Atman* that communicated this extremely important insight. The Upanishads presented this advanced mystical awakening repeatedly, especially through two concepts, first, "*Tat Tvam Asi*; That art Thou;" That Atman art Thou Brahman; That my soul is Thou Brahman. Second, "Brahman is all and Atman is Brahman."[311]

Shankara, an eighth-century Hindu mystic and reformer as well as a commentator on the scriptures and the author of a hundred books, explained the meaning of the spiritual ideas of the Atman as well as "Brahman is all and Atman is Brahman." Although Shankara said that the Atman "cannot be defined," he described It. All beings have a soul or spirit called the Atman, dwelling within them. "Man is a pure spirit, free from attachment. The mind deludes him" into the error of identifying his soul, his Atman, with his body. Springing from ignorance, this mistake of thinking the body is the Atman is like considering a piece of rope as a snake. "The acceptance of the unreal as real constitutes the state of bondage. It binds him with chains of lust, anger, and other passions" and "subjects him to a long train of miseries—birth, death, sickness, decrepitude, and so forth." Moreover, "the body is merely a vehicle of experience for the human spirit. He who tries to find the Atman by feeding the cravings of the body, is trying to cross a river by grasping a crocodile, mistaking it for a log." An ignorant person "identifies the Atman with the body." An intelligent one "thinks, 'I am an individual soul united with the body!'" A wise one knows "the Atman as the real I." The Atman is "the Supreme Being," the Divine, "the Ultimate Existence," dwelling within him. Brahman is "the one Atman in all creatures."[312]

According to Shankara, although always present within all of creation, "the Atman remains hidden, as the water of a pond is hidden by a veil of scum." A human with a pure heart "realizes the supreme Atman . . . as God dwelling within; as unending, unalloyed bliss; as the supreme and self-luminous Being." The wise person "can realize the Atman, which is Infinite Being, Infinite Wisdom, and Infinite Love" within him. The Atman hiding within is "a self-existent Reality, which is the basis of the consciousness. . . . It gives intelligence to the mind and intellect. . . . Its nature is Eternal Consciousness. It knows all things. . . . It is the knower of all the activities of the mind and the individual man. It is the witness of all the actions of the body." The Atman is pure Infinite Consciousness, "the Light that shines in the shrine of the heart, the Center of all vital force. It is immutable. . . . By Its nature, the Atman is forever unchanging and perfect" as well as "birthless and deathless. It neither grows nor decays. It is unchangeable, eternal. It does not dissolve when the body dissolves." Within the human body, "in the pure mind, in the secret chamber of intelligence, in the infinite universe within the heart, the Atman shines in its captivating splendor, like a noonday sun."[313]

Shankara claimed that ignorance and bondage "cannot be broken . . . by millions of acts. Nothing but the sharp sword of knowledge can cut through bondage." The perfect knowledge that dispels ignorance and bondage is "the realization of Atman as One with Brahman." A person "whose heart is pure realizes the Supreme Atman. Thereby he destroys his bondage to the world, root and all." By the power of Atman, the wise individual can "rescue his own soul which lies drowned in the vast ocean of worldliness." When you have "a controlled mind and an intellect which is made pure and tranquil, you must recognize the Atman directly within yourself. . . . Thus, you cross the shoreless ocean of worldliness" and "live always in the knowledge of identity with Brahman." Shankara summed up his teaching. "I can tell you the content of a half million verses of spirituality in half a verse: God is real, the world is unreal, the individual soul is none other than God." The Atman that is present in all of creation is none other than Brahman, the Absolute, the Supreme Spirit.[314]

The Upanishads spoke about the Atman. "Concealed in the heart of all beings lies the *Atman*, the spirit, the self." It is "smaller than the smallest atom, greater than the greatest spaces." Atman is the inner spirit within all humans and the cosmos. It is the individual soul, the spiritual core of the identity, of every person and every part of creation. Atman is "the inmost soul of all." Brahman is the Universal Soul within the soul, the Atman. "God is found in the soul when sought with truth and self-sacrifice, as fire is found in wood, water in hidden springs, cream in milk, and oil in the oil-fruit. There is a Spirit who is hidden in all things, as cream is hidden in milk. . . . This is Brahman, the Spirit Supreme." This is "God who is in the fire, who is in the waters, who is in the plants and in the trees." This is "God who is hidden in the heart of all things, . . . the Supreme Soul who dwells forever in the hearts of men." This is "the Universal in all." Not only is Brahman within all beings as their soul, their spirit, their Atman, but also external to them. "He is within all, and He is outside all" and "He is far and He is near." The Spirit of life is far, far away and "yet He is very near, resting in the inmost chamber of the heart." Brahman is "my inmost spirit," my Atman.[315]

The Upanishads outlined the four conditions of the human spirit, the soul, the Atman. First is the waking life that is conscious of external objects and the pleasures of the senses. In the second condition, the Atman is "dreaming, and only conscious of his dreams." The Atman in the third aspect is "in dreamless sleep . . . without desire." In the fourth condition, the Atman is "in his own pure state: the awakened life of supreme Consciousness." This condition is "not the knowledge of the senses. . . . Beyond the senses, beyond the understanding, beyond all expression is the fourth. It is pure unitary Consciousness, wherein awareness of the world and of multiplicity is completely obliterated. It is ineffable Peace. It is the supreme goal. It is One without second. It is the Self. Know It alone!"[316]

Because the individual self is "subject to the law of happiness and misery, it is not free." The Upanishads indicate that in front of humans lie two different paths with two divergent ends. One is the path of the good and the other is the path of pleasure. "Both attract the soul" and "prompt to action." After pondering both and rejecting pleasures and possessions, "the wise prefer the good to the pleasant." In contrast, "the foolish, driven by fleshly desires, prefer the pleasant to the good."[317]

The Upanishads also described the choice between two other paths. One is the path of knowledge and wisdom and the other the path of ignorance. These two "lead to different ends." In the midst of their ignorance, deluded fools think of themselves as wise as they go aimlessly around and around, like "the blind led by the blind." They "who are childish, or careless, or deluded by wealth," and who do not see Brahman shining within all, say that "this is the only world: there is no other." In contrast, "when the wise rests his mind in contemplation on our God beyond time, who invisibly dwells in the mystery of things and in the heart of man, then he rises above pleasure and sorrow." In addition, "when the wise realize the Omnipresent Spirit, who rests Invisible in the visible and Permanent in the impermanent, then they go beyond sorrow." Following the path of meditation, the wise know Brahman and are freed alike from pain and pleasure. "The wise who has seen Him in every being" attain life immortal when they die and leave this life.[318]

Speaking of perceiving Brahman, the Upanishads say that "only the wise who see Him in their souls attain Joy eternal. He is the Eternal among things that pass away, pure Consciousness of conscious beings, the ONE who fulfills the prayers of many. Only the wise who see Him in their souls attain the Peace Eternal." The weak, the careless, and those who practice the wrong austerity do not reach the Spirit, but "the wise who strive the right way lead their soul into the dwelling of Brahman. Having reached the place supreme, the seers find joy in wisdom, their souls have fulfillment, their passions have gone, they have Peace. Filled with devotion, they have found the Spirit in all and go into the All." When we know that Brahman is forever in us, "nothing higher is there to be known."[319]

The Bhagavad Gita's Teachings Were Gained from Other Hindu Sages' Awakenings

Two-thousand-five-hundred-years ago in India, Hindu sages wrote the *Bhagavad Gita* from what they learned from their awakenings. The *Gita* presented a dialogue between God who was called Krishna and his disciple Arjuna. The Divine Krishna described Himself as "the Imperishable, the Infinite, the Transcendent Unmanifested, the Omnipresent, the Beyond all thought, the Immutable, the Never-changing, the Ever One," the Invisible, the Eternal, the ONE, the End Supreme. The Spirit Supreme is "immeasurable, immortal," never-born, everlasting, and beyond all destruction. The Holy Krishna said, "I am the Father of this universe, and . . . I am the Mother of this universe, the Creator of all. . . . I am the Way, and the Master who watches in silence; thy Friend and thy Shelter and thy Abode of peace." As "I am the One Source of all, the evolution of all comes from Me."[320]

The Sacred Krishna said, "listen and I shall reveal to thee some manifestations of My Divine Glory. Only the greatest, Arjuna, for there is no end to My Infinite Greatness. . . . Among creators I am the Creator of Love. . . . I am the Beginning and the Middle and the End of all that is. Of all knowledge I am the Knowledge of the soul. Of the many paths of reason I am the One that leads to Truth. . . . I am Time, Never-ending Time. I am the Creator who sees all. . . . I am the Beauty of all things beautiful. . . . I am the Goodness of those who are good. . . . There is no end of My Divine Greatness, Arjuna. What I have spoken here to thee shows only a small part of My Infinity." In addition, "now I shall tell thee of the end of wisdom. . . . It is Brahman, Beginningless, Supreme, Beyond what is and Beyond what is not. . . . He sees all, He hears all. He is in all and He is. . . . He supports all. . . . He is invisible, He cannot be seen. He is far and He is near, He moves and He moves not. . . . He is the Light of all lights which shines beyond all darkness." Moreover, "the law of righteousness is My Law and My Joy is Infinite Joy." Furthermore, "I come into the earth and with life-giving Love I support all things on earth."[321]

Besides describing Brahman, the Gita produced an advanced awakening by teaching the Divine presence within all things. The Holy Krishna said that "in My Mercy I dwell in their hearts and I dispel their darkness of ignorance by the Light of the lamp of wisdom." When a person "withdraws all his senses from the attractions of pleasures, even as a tortoise withdraws all its limbs, then he has a serene wisdom." When all delusion is gone, we can "reach the Nirvana of Brahman" and "Peace in the Peace of God." The person "who forsakes all desires and abandons all pride of possessions and of self reaches the goal of Peace Supreme. This is the Eternal in man." Moreover, "Brahman is in all. . . . He is within all and He is outside all. . . . He is the Light of all lights . . . dwelling in all. The Spirit Supreme in man is beyond fate. He watches, gives blessing, bears all, feels all," and sustains all.[322]

The Divine Krishna said, "I am the Fire of Life which is in all things that breathe. . . . I am the Heart of all." Thus, "no being that moves or moves not can ever be without Me." Not only "the Eternal in man cannot die," but also "the Spirit that is in all beings is Immortal in them all." When a person sees that "the God in himself is the same God in all that is, he hurts not himself by hurting others, then he goes indeed to the highest path." When a man knows that all people have the Spirit within them and are thus "never-born, everlasting, never-changing, beyond all destruction, how can that man kill a man or cause another to kill?"[323]

The Holy Krishna also said that some of the many ways to God include the three yogas of knowledge and wisdom, action and work, and devotion and love, as well as renunciation, freedom from attachment, love for all of creation and the Divine, and making the Absolute our supreme end. The Divine Krishna also declared that not by reading the sacred scriptures, or living an austere life, or giving to the poor, or offering rituals, "can I (God) be seen as thou my disciple has seen Me. Only by love can people see Me, and know Me, and come to Me. He who works for Me, who loves Me, whose End Supreme I am, free from attachment to all things, and with love for all creation, he in truth comes to Me."[324]

About the yoga of knowledge and wisdom, the Sacred Krishna explained that when a person "sees Eternity in the things that pass away and Infinity in finite things," then he has pure knowledge. "He who has faith has wisdom, . . . and he who finds wisdom finds the Peace Supreme." When an individual has a clear vision and "sees Me as the Spirit Supreme, he knows all there is to know, and he adores Me with all his soul." About the yoga of work and action, the Divine Krishna declared, "do thy duty, even if it is humble, rather than another's, even if it be great." The person, who "works on the path of Karma Yoga, the path of consecrated action," is great. The purpose of action is to make the world a better place. The wise individual works unselfishly with no desire for reward, while offering all his actions to the Divine. The person "whose work is pure attains the Supreme" and "who in all his work sees God, he in truth goes to God."[325]

About the yoga of devotion and love, the Holy Krishna claimed that the best yogis are "those who set their hearts on Me and ever in love worship Me, and who have unshakable faith." Those will reach Me "who have all the powers of their soul in harmony, the same loving mind for all, and who find joy in the good of all beings." I will deliver from the cycle of life and death those "for whom I am the End Supreme, who surrender all their works to Me, who with pure love meditate on Me, and set their heart on Me alone." A person becomes "this yogi of union who has good will for all, who is friendly and has compassion, who has no thoughts of 'I' and 'mine,' whose peace is the same in pleasures and sorrows, who is forgiving, and who loves Me." A yogi of union is one "who works for God and not for himself, . . . who complains not and lusts not for things, who has love." This yogi is dear to Me "whose love is the same for his enemies or his friends, whose soul is beyond pleasure or pain, who is free from the chains of attachment, who is happy with whatever he has, whose home is not in this world, and who has love. . . . But even dearer to Me are those who have faith and love, and who have Me as their End Supreme." A yogi of union goes beyond the path of austerity or wisdom or work. "The greatest of all yogis is he who with all his soul has faith, and he who with all his soul loves Me."[326]

The Awakenings of Later Hindu Mystics

Besides their spiritual classics, Hindu mystics across the centuries produced spiritual writings, including the twelfth-century Hindu mystic Mahadevi who had an honorific title *akka* which meant elder sister. Being "oppressed by her royal surrounding," she gave away all her possessions, abandoned social constraints, and wandered. Describing her mystical experience of awakening in which she saw God, she said, "I have seen Him in His Divine form, . . . Him who illumines the fourteen worlds with the light of His eyes. I have seen Him and the thirst of my eyes is quenched. I have seen the great Lord whom the men serve but as wives. I have seen the Supreme . . . and saved am I." Kabir, a fifteenth-century poor weaver in Benares, India, wrote from the Divine's point of view. "Where do you seek Me, my son? Look—I am right inside you! I am not found in the temple or the mosque, not in Mecca nor the highest heaven. I am not found in prayer nor ritual, not in yoga nor renunciation. If your yearning is pure you will see Me in an instant, you will see Me this moment." Written from his own perspective, "O brother seekers! Only while you are alive is there hope of finding Him. While you are alive, meditate. While you are alive, contemplate. Only while you are alive can liberation be found." Furthermore, "the Lord of all plays His song within you!"[327]

Mira Bai or Mirabai was a sixteenth-century Hindu woman poet and saint. Although she was a princess, she broke a number of social conventions, including *sati* or *suttee*. This custom expected a widow to throw herself on her husband's burning funeral pyre and die so she could serve him in the afterlife. When her father-in-law demanded this, she replied, "I will not become sati! My heart loves only *Hari* (God). The relation of the eldest daughter-in-law exists no more." Her prayer said, "O Bountiful Lord, listen! Can't You hear my prayers? Can't You hear Your name upon my lips? My whole family has turned against me and I am only a burden to them. In all the worlds, I have no one but You to call my own. . . . I cannot find rest until You come to me. . . . The shaft of separation has split open my breasts and the pain will not leave me for even a moment."[328]

Mira prayed, "the fire of the pain of separation is burning in my heart; come and extinguish it. . . . send for me, Lord. Mira has been Your slave in all her lives. Let her be merged in Yourself." In addition, "mine is God, none else. . . . He is my Lord. Father, mother, brother, and kin, none are mine. I have flung aside the pride of family. . . . Pearls and corals I have cast aside. . . . I was born for devotion's sake, but the sight of the world made me captive. . . . save me now." Mira prayed, "You are the refuge of my life and soul. Besides You, there is no shelter for me in the three worlds. I have searched the whole world; none else but You alone pleases me." Praying to Krishna, "in whatever direction I look I find the landscape full of Krishna, the Lord of the Dark Blue." She declared, "making love with the Dark One, fasting, those are my jewels and wealth. . . . I praise the Dark One day and night. My path is ecstasy." Moreover, "You are the omnipotent Lord. Having become Yours, to whom else can I go? You are the Light of my heart. I have none else." Furthermore, "All-pervading One, . . . my Beloved lives in my heart, so I sing happily day and night." And again, "I am true to my Lord. . . . Now the arrow of love has transpierced me and come out, and I have begun singing of knowledge Divine."[329]

The nineteenth-century Hindu mystic Ramakrishna said that at night there are many stars, but not when the sun rises. Are there no stars in the heaven during the day? "Because you behold not God in the days of your ignorance, say not that there is no God." Trying to describe the ocean to a person who hasn't seen it is similar to attempting to picture God who "cannot be explained in words. . . . so one who has realized Brahman can only say, 'Brahman is everywhere.'" God is "beyond mind and speech, beyond concentration and meditation." Many are the different names of water in different languages: *aqua*, *pani*, and *vari*. "Many are the names of God and infinite the forms through which He may be approached." Some call God *Sat-Chit-Ananda*, "Absolute Being-Intelligence-Bliss," others say Allah or Hari or Shakti or Brahman. Some of the names used by Ramakrishna include the Divine Mother, "the Real (i.e. God)," the Absolute, "God, the Unconditioned Spirit," the One, and "the Universal and All-pervading Spirit."[330]

According to Ramakrishna, to ascend to the roof of a house, different means are possible, such as a ladder or a staircase. "Diverse are the ways and means to approach God. Every religion in the world is one of the ways to reach Him. . . . Different creeds are but different paths to reach the Almighty." For Ramakrishna, "God is in all creatures." Brahman is "the One Being manifest as many" as well as "both One and many, and also beyond One and many." He saw that "God is walking in human form and manifesting Himself alike through the sage and the sinner." When he met different people, he saw "God in the form of the saint" or the sinner or the virtuous or vicious or righteous or unrighteous. A holy person who is "a true *Sadhu* finds no distinction between friend and foe, for he sees the same

Spirit present in all." Furthermore, "God dwells in man . . . in the same way as ladies of wealthy families do behind a latticed screen. They can see everybody, but no one can see them. God abides in all in an exactly similar way." When fishes play in a pond covered with scum and reeds, they "cannot be seen from outside, so God plays invisible in the heart of man. . . . So does God see everyone, but no one sees Him until the Lord reveals Himself."[331]

For Ramakrishna, there are four different classes of souls: "(1) the bound, (2) those aspiring to freedom, (3) the freed, and (4) those who are eternally free." The bound are like fishes that are caught in a net. These swim within the net and think that they are safe and free. Such are the worldly-minded who are "immersed in the illusion of the pursuit of pleasure." The aspirants after truth and freedom are the fishes that try to make their escape. "Those that succeed in getting out of the net are freed souls. Some are too careful to fall a victim to the tactics of the fisherman. These are the eternally free." Ramakrishna said that obstacles obstruct the path to God, including egotism, ignorance, and bondage. So long as there is an 'I' and 'mine' in you, "so long as there is egotism, neither Self-knowledge (*Jnana*) nor liberation (*Mukti*) is possible, nor can there be a cessation" of reincarnation, of birth and death. "To reach Him, you have to renounce yourself and the world." You will see Brahman "when the mind is tranquil. When the sea of the mind is agitated by the wind of desires, it cannot reflect God, and then God-vision is impossible." In addition, "so long as God seems to be outside and far away, so long there is ignorance. But when God is realized within, there is true knowledge."[332]

Many ways to experience the Divine were described by Ramakrishna. "There are pearls in the sea; but you must dive again and again, until you find them. So God is in the world, but you will have to persevere to see Him." To achieve God-vision, "effort is necessary." To discover Brahman, "you must offer to Him your body, mind, and riches." In addition, "you get what you seek." You "who seek God get Him," you "who seek wealth or power, get that. . . . You will see God if your love for Him is as strong as the attachment of the worldly-minded person for things of the world." Furthermore, "the less your attachment is to the senses, the more will be your love of God." The more the love for God is deepened in your soul, "the easier it becomes to feel His presence in all beings." Ramakrishna claimed that he prayed to the Divine Mother for "*Bhakti*—pure, sincere love for Thee, unmixed with any worldly desires, such as health, pleasure, money, fame, and so on."[333]

Ramakrishna said, "as the rosy dawn comes before the rising sun, so is a longing and yearning heart the forerunner of the glorious vision of God." Some have already awakened and have certain traits. "They do not care to hear or speak of anything but what relates to God." Before Brahman comes, He sends "sincerity, unselfishness, purity, and righteousness" as well as "yearning, love, reverence, and faith into the heart of the devotee." Several signs of attaining God are the glories of affection, including "discrimination, dispassion, tenderness to all life, service to the good, a love of their company, recounting of God's name and glory, truthfulness—all these."[334]

According to Ramakrishna, a person attains perfection in meditation, when he "becomes surrounded with the Divine atmosphere and his soul communes with God." Thus, "meditate upon Knowledge and Bliss Eternal, and you will have bliss. Bliss indeed is eternal," but "it is covered and obscured by ignorance." *Ananda*, or enjoyment of perfect bliss within, is "one of the signs of God-vision." The person "who has acquired wisdom . . . sees the All-pervading Spirit both within and without." The nearer he approaches God, the more is his "heart flooded with blessed feeling and love for Him. . . . As soon as the love of God begins to blossom in his heart, he finds no pleasure in other things. Instead of this, his happiness now consists only in serving God and doing His will." As his heart turns away from other pursuits, he experiences "the ecstasy of that Holy Communion." Ramakrishna actually saw that "it is the Absolute who has become all things about us; it is He who appears as the finite soul and the phenomenal world! One must have an awakening of the Spirit within to see this Reality." After the Spirit within is awakened, "the next step is the realization of the Universal Spirit." It is "Spirit that can realize Spirit." Unfortunately, "very few understand that the aim of human life is to see God."[335]

An important twentieth-century Hindu mystic is Gandhi who will be discussed later. Another is Swami Muktananda who described his spiritual experience. "As I gazed at the tiny Blue Pearl, I saw it expand, spreading its radiance in all directions so that the whole sky and earth were illuminated by it. It was no longer a Pearl but had become shining, blazing Infinite Light; . . . The Light pervaded everywhere in the form of the universe. I saw the earth being born and expanding from the Light of Consciousness. . . . I could see this radiance of Consciousness, resplendent and utterly beautiful, silently pulsating as supreme ecstasy within me, outside me, above me, below me." Then he explained what he learned from his mystical experience. "All philosophies and scriptures say the same thing: 'God dwells in this human body.' Do not consider your body a mere being of flesh. . . .. It is a noble instrument. . ... God dwells in the body. He is present as fully in you as in the highest Heavens. . . . You should live your normal life, but accord Him the chief place among your daily activities. . . . If you call on Him with love, think about Him with devotion, He will reveal Himself to you. He will grant a vision of the Divine Light of His Love. Then you will know that you are an embodiment of Bliss. You will realize, "I am Shiva (God)! Yes, I am!"[336]

Contemporary scholar Diana Eck writes about how pilgrims travel throughout India to visit Sacred places. These places were written about in Hindu literature and myths: *dhams* are 'homes of God;' *pithas*, 'seats of the Goddess;' and *tirthas*, 'places of spiritual crossing' between earth and heaven. "No place is too small to be counted a *tirtha* by its local visitors. In a sense, each temple is a *tirtha*, especially consecrated as a crossing place between earth and heaven." India's entire land is "a great network of pilgrimage places." Hindu mythology is linked to this Sacred geography. Written over 2,000 years ago, the literature of epics and Puranas "constitute a massive composition and expansion of both Hindu geography and mythic narratives." The Divine presence exists throughout India from its southernmost tip to the Himalayas. "All the ways of speaking of the Divine presence begin to constitute a linked landscape, patterned with Sacred places."[337]

Awakenings of the Mystics of Chinese Religions

Since time immemorial, an indigenous, popular, folk, traditional religion "has been present among the Chinese, interwoven in all the social practices of kinship groups, social and economic groups, and local communities." Elements of this religion that existed for more than three and half thousand years and continues today are local Deities' temples, local ancestral shrines, shrines for local heroes. These are "more frequently, temples of a common pantheon in which elements of all religions are found," not only the folk tradition but also the other Chinese religions of Confucianism, Taoism, and Buddhism. In discussing Chinese religions, different languages may cause confusion. The Chinese written language uses characters, while English uses the Roman alphabet to form words. One of two systems used to represent Chinese into English is the older Wales-Giles that is named after its inventors and is common in the United States. The newer system, Hanyu Pinyin or Pinyin for short, was developed by the Chinese for use in China and it is increasingly used throughout the world. This book uses the Wade-Giles with *Tao* rather than *Dao*, *Lao Tzu* rather than *Laozi*, *Taoism* rather than *Daoism*, *Tao Te Ching* rather than *Dao de Jing*, and *Chuang Tzu* rather than *Zhuangzi*. *Yang* and *yin* are the same in both systems.[338]

The traditional religion included Deities that control the universe, spirits within everything, ancestor veneration, filial piety, and fertility rites. "One of the oldest motifs of Chinese religion is the Earth-God." Another early God was "*Shang-ti*, a term synonymous with *T'ien*," which means Heaven. *T'ien* or Heaven holds the entire cosmos in Its hands and "invests the responsibility for ordering the universe in Its regent upon earth, the Son of Heaven," the Chinese ruler. Besides the major Deities, there are other lesser Gods and Goddesses, "sun, moon, stars, rivers, mountains, the four directions, and localities." The female and male leaders of the Chinese traditional religions include mystics, shamans, healers, diviners, "exorcists, prophets, fortune-tellers, and interpreters of dreams." The shamans acted as intermediaries between humans and Gods and spirits. Interceding for individuals with their personal Deities and spirits, they provided for people's spiritual needs.[339]

Over 2,600-years ago the Chinese developed the concept of Tao. Lao Tzu's *Tao Te Ching* said that "the Tao that can be told is not the eternal Tao." Defining it as the way, the Tao is the Way of Ultimate Reality and the way of the universe. The Tao that is composed of yin and yang is the Unity, the One, in which all things fit together. The Tao and its yin and yang are within everyone and everything. Although all people and all things have the Tao with both yang and yin within them, the yang dominates in some and the yin in others. Yang is active, masculine, strong, hard, light, and heavenly. Yin is passive, feminine, weak, soft, dark, and earthly. The Tao is part of traditional religious beliefs as well as Confucianism and Taoism.[340]

Since the beginning of the twentieth century, revolutionary movements including Communism have attacked the traditional religion, but "the temples and shrines remain. . . . all bearing lively testimony to the omnipresence within living memory of the popular religion." Despite the decline and the absorption of parts of Taoism and Buddhism into the folk religion, "elements of it are present in every Chinese community. . . . Religious beliefs and practices among the people . . . have been present since time immemorial."[341]

Besides the traditional religion, China has two other home-grown religions, Confucianism and Taoism. After Buddhism was imported from India, the three teachings were combined and integrated as one into most people's lives. Thus, none of the three was considered the whole truth. Confucius and his teachings have had a profound influence on the Chinese people for over two thousand years. As the founder of the religion bearing his name, this sixth century BCE philosopher followed the Chinese tradition and believed that the Ultimate Spiritual Reality was the Tao and Heaven (*T'ien*). The operating principle of the Tao is the same principle that operates in humans and the universe. The Way of Heaven is mirrored in the way of the earth. The way of humans corresponds to the Way of Heaven. Confucius said, "the life of the moral person is an exemplification of the Universal Moral Order." Lao Tzu said, "man takes his law from the earth; the earth takes its law from Heaven; Heaven takes its law from the Tao. The law of the Tao is Its being, what It is."[342]

The Analects, *Lun Yu*, was a book of Confucius' sayings that were collected by his disciples. Some of these sayings that called Confucius the master connect Heaven with humans. According to one translation, "the master said, 'Heaven begat the power (*te* or *de*) that is in me.'" Another says, "Sky begat the excellence in me." A different Confucius saying connects the way you treat humans with the way you treat the Divine. "You cannot treat spirits and Divinities properly before you are able to treat your fellow-men properly." While Confucius in the *Analects* stressed the way humans are to behave as individuals and in social relationships, he also thought the way of humans is connected to the Way of Heaven. *Jen* (*ren*) is the key word in Confucius' teachings. To develop *jen* is "to align oneself with the way things are," with the Tao, as well as to embody the Tao. *Jen* means "goodness, man-to-man-ness, benevolence, and love, . . . perhaps best rendered as human-heartedness." In another translation, *jen* is "humanity, love, high principle, and living together in harmony." *Jen* involves respect for oneself and empathy toward others. Jen combines the two Chinese characters, *chung*, conscientiousness, with *shu*, consideration, reciprocity, and being a man of humanity.[343]

Defining *jen* as good and goodness, "the master said, 'in the presence of a good person, think all the time how you may learn to equal her. In the presence of a bad person, turn your gaze within!'" You "who really care for goodness would never let any other consideration come first." In addition, "never for a moment does a noble person quit the way of goodness." The person "whose heart is in the smallest degree set upon goodness will dislike no one." Confucius repeated three times a version of the universal Golden Rule. In one version, Tzu-kung, one of his disciples, asked, "is there any single saying that one can act upon all day and all night?" Confucius repeated what he called "the saying about consideration: 'never do to others what you would not like them to do to you.'"[344]

By developing and practicing *jen*, one becomes Confucius' ideal person, *chun tzu* (*jun zi*). Various translations of *chun tzu* are a gentleman, a morally superior man in character and behavior, a great man, a man of higher type, a sage, a wise man, a scholar, a mature person, a noble person, a person of fully evolved character, a person who manifests human-heartedness, a fully realized human being, and humanity-at-its-best. The aim of all humans is to become *chun tzu*, "a fully realized human being, through expanding one's sympathy and empathy indefinitely" and through spreading them in "concentric circles that begin with oneself" and go out to one's family, community, nation, and finally all humanity. The opposite of *chun tzu* is a small man, "a petty person, a mean person, a small-spirited person."[345]

A human-at-his-best, *chun tzu,* learns the way of Heaven and practices it. In the *Analects,* Confucius made "no claim to be a sage or to be manhood-at-its-best," but his summary of his life by decades indicated that he was. "At 50, I knew what were the biddings of Heaven. At 60, I heard them with a docile ear. At 70, I could follow the dictates of my own heart; for what I desired no longer overstepped the boundaries of right" and the ways of Heaven. "The master said, 'to prefer the Way is better than only to know it. To delight in it is better than merely to prefer it.'" A person of fully evolved character "takes as much trouble to discover what is right as lesser men take to discover what will pay." In addition, "a gentleman can see a question from all sides without bias. The small man is biased and can see a question only from one side." A human-at-his-best "practices what he preaches."[346]

In the *Analects,* Confucius said more about *chun tzu.* A morally superior person in character and behavior "is conscious only of justice; a petty man, only of self-interest." Also "the demands that a gentleman makes are upon himself; those that a small man makes are upon others." A selfless servant "develops the virtues in others, not their vices. A petty man does just the opposite." A mature person "who concentrates upon the task and forgets about the reward may be called man-at-his-best." Confucius advised you to repair your shortcomings, "attack the evil in yourself; do not attack the evil that is in others" as well as to "meet resentment with upright dealing" and to "love your fellow-men." When a noble person "is faultlessly respectful; . . . all are his brothers."[347]

Mencius (*Meng Tzu*) became a follower of Confucius over a hundred years after his death. His book called *Mencius* was probably compiled by his disciples. Mainstream Confucians have adopted his view of human nature. "When left to follow its natural feelings human nature will do good. This is why I say it is good. If it becomes evil, it is not the fault of our original capability. The sense of mercy is found in all people; the sense of shame is found in all people; the sense of respect is found in all people; the sense of right and wrong is found in all people." Asked whether human nature can be likened to a current of water, "Mencius replied, 'it is true that water is neither disposed to east nor west, but is it neither disposed to flowing upward nor downward? The tendency of human nature to do good is like that of water to flow downward. There is no person who does not tend to do good; there is no water that does not flow downward.'" Furthermore, "we see that no person is without a sense of compassion, or a sense of shame, or a sense of courtesy, or a sense of right and wrong. The sense of compassion is the beginning of humanity, the sense of shame is the beginning of righteousness, the sense of courtesy is the beginning of decorum (*li*), the sense of right and wrong is the beginning of wisdom. Every person has within himself these four beginnings; just as he has four limbs."[348]

The legendary founder of Taoism is Lao Tzu who was said to live in the sixth century BCE. His name is translated as the old master, the old teacher. Stories assert that he instructed Confucius or at least met with him once. At which time Confucius said, "today I have seen Lao Tzu and he is like a dragon!" Taoism reveres and follows *Tao Te Ching*, which is attributed to Lao Tzu and is considered one of its most sacred texts. The title is translated as the *Classic of the Way and Its Power*. Although Lao Tzu is often said to be the author of this book of 81 sayings or poems, scholars think that it was not written by a single person and it did not attain its final form until the third century BCE. The translations of the *Tao Te Ching* vary drastically perhaps because it is written so concisely with so few Chinese characters. What people in the West think of as Taoism, the Chinese people still understand to be Teaching about the Tao (*Tao-chiao*).[349]

While Confucianism is humanistic, emphasizing ethics and social relationships, Taoism is mystical. As Huston Smith says, "Confucius' focus is on the human, Lao Tzu's on what transcends the human. . . . Confucius roams within society, Lao Tzu wanders beyond." Taoism is spirituality balanced; Confucianism is concerned with humanity-at-its-best and social responsibility. Contemporary Taoist Mantak Chia and William Wei explain that "in the West, we think with our minds and feel with our hearts. In the Tao, we learn to think with our hearts and feel with our minds." When we see reality for what it really is, "the direction on what to do comes from the heart." Taoists refer to the mind as the monkey mind because it always gets into a great deal of mischief and it is always active. To think and feel with the heart, we need to slow down the mind. Meditation slows the mind so there is stillness within and we feel the Oneness, "the Infinity, which is the Tao."[350]

In the *Tao Te Ching*, Lao Tzu expressed one of the most important ideas about the Tao, the Divine. "The Tao that can be told is not the eternal Tao. The name that can be named is not the eternal Name. The Unnamable is the eternally Real. . . .. Free from desire, you realize the Mystery. Caught in desire, you see only the manifestations." The Tao is "like the eternal Void, filled with infinite possibilities. It is hidden but always present." Added to this, "the Tao is called the Great Mother, empty yet inexhaustible; It gives birth to infinite worlds. It is always present within you. You can use It any way you want." Before Heaven and earth, the Tao is the One "reaching everywhere" with "its primordial simplicity." Furthermore, "there was something formless and perfect before the universe was born. It was Serene. Empty. Solitary. Unchanging. Infinite. Eternally present. It was the Mother of the universe.

For lack of a better name, I call it the Tao. The Tao is great. The universe is great. Earth is great. Man is great. These are the four great powers."[351]

Lao Tzu also said, "the great Tao flows everywhere. All things are born from It. . . . Since It is merged with all things and hidden in their hearts, It can be called humble. Since all things vanish into It and It alone endures, It can be called great." Moreover, "every being in the universe is an expression of the Tao. It springs into existence, unconscious, perfect, free, . . . The Tao gives birth to all beings, nourishes them, maintains them, cares for them, comforts them, protects them, takes them back to Itself, creating without possessing, acting without expecting, guiding without interfering. That is why love of the Tao is the nature of things." Besides, "eyes look but cannot see It. Ears listen but cannot hear It. Hands grasp but cannot touch It. Beyond the senses lies this Unity—Invisible, Inaudible, Intangible. . . . Know That Which is beyond all beginnings and you will know everything right here and now. Know everything in this moment and you will know the eternal Tao."[352]

The first part of the *Tao Te Ching* attempts to describe the indescribable Tao, the Divine, while the second part explains how to use Its power. Lao Tzu writes about the sage, *shen-jen*, also called the master, the ideal person who is in tune with the Tao. "The master by residing in the Tao sets an example for all beings." The sage is also called the skillful master of the Tao, the person of superior ability, the great man, those "different from ordinary men," the sanest person, the scholar of the highest class, a man of humanity, and man-at-his-best. The sage practices the paradoxical Chinese concept of *wei wu wei*. The translation of *wei* is action or doing, while *wu wei* is lack of action or non-doing. Possible translations of *wei wu wei* are creative letting be; actionless activity; creative quietude; natural, spontaneous, selfless action; and cutting with the grain. My preference is going with the flow. This means that when we are in tune with the Tao, we start going which is doing, while we also yield, we let go, and we let the natural process of the river take us wherever it goes, which is non-doing. As Lao Tzu said, because he is in harmony with the Tao, "the master gives himself up to whatever the moment brings. . . . He doesn't think about his actions; they flow from the core of his being. He holds nothing back from life."[353]

Lao Tzu also said, "true mastery can be gained by letting things go their own way. It can't be gained by interfering." Furthermore, "the journey of a thousand miles starts beneath your feet. Rushing into action, you fail. Trying to grasp things, you lose them. . . . Therefore, the master takes action by letting things take their course. . . . He simply reminds people of who they have always been. He cares about nothing but the Tao. Thus, he can care for all things." Moreover, "man-at-his-best, like water, serves as he goes along;

like water he seeks his own level, the common level of life, loves living close to the earth, living clear down in his heart, loves kinship with his neighbors." In addition, "if you open yourself to the Tao, you are at One with the Tao and you can embody It completely. . . . Open yourself to the Tao, then trust your natural processes; and everything will fall into place."[354]

According to Lao Tzu, "the world is the Tao's own vessel. It is perfection manifest. It cannot be changed. It cannot be improved. . . . Allow your life to unfold naturally. Know that it too is a vessel of perfection. Just as you breathe in and breathe out, so sometimes you're ahead and other times you're behind. . . . To the sage all of life is but a movement toward perfection." To unfold, "the Tao never does anything, yet through It, all things are done. If powerful men and women could center themselves in It, the whole world would be transformed by Itself, in Its natural rhythms. People would be content with their simple, everyday lives, in harmony, and free of desire. When there is no desire, all things are at peace." To amplify, "abide at the center of your being; for the more you leave it, the less you learn. Search your heart and see if he is wise who takes each turn. The way to do is to be." Similarly, "the way to use life is to do nothing through acting, the way to use life is to do everything through being." Furthermore, "practice not doing . . . when action is pure and selfless, everything settles into perfect place."[355]

Lao Tzu's sage is a person who through balancing feels "at endless ease with everything." As he said, "be utterly humble and you shall hold to the foundation of peace. Be at one with all these living things which, having arisen and flourished, return to the Quiet whence they came." Lao Tzu compares the sage who is in tune with the Tao with those who are not. "Chase after money and security and your heart will never unclench. Care about people's approval and you will be their prisoner. Do your work, then step back." This is "the only path to serenity." Furthermore, "he who rushes ahead doesn't go far. He who tries to shine dims his own light. . . . He who has power over others can't empower himself. . . . If you want to accord with the Tao, just do your job, then let go." In addition, "the surest test if a man be sane is if he accepts life whole, as it is, without needing by measure or touch to understand the measureless untouchable Source. . . . The Source, which, while it appears dark emptiness, brims with a quick force farthest away and yet nearest at hand."[356]

According to Lao Tzu, "the sage embraces the One (the Tao) and comes to know the whole world. Not displaying himself, he shines forth. Not promoting himself, he is distinguished. Not claiming reward, he gains endless merit. Not wanting glory, his glory endures. . . . The ancient saying, 'surrender brings perfection,' is not just empty words. Truly, to the yielding comes the perfect, to the perfect comes the whole universe." Besides surrendering and yielding, "empty your mind of all thoughts. Let your heart be at peace. Watch the turmoil of beings, but contemplate their return. Each separate being in the universe returns to the common Source. Returning to the Source is serenity. If you don't realize the Source, you stumble in confusion and sorrow. When you realize where you come from, you naturally become tolerant, disinterested, amused, kindhearted . . . Immersed in the wonder of the Tao, you can deal with whatever life brings you." Furthermore, "when a superior man hears of the Tao, he immediately begins to embody It. When an average man hears of the Tao, he half believes It, half doubts It. When a foolish man hears of the Tao, he laughs out loud." Moreover, "one who lives by his inner truth . . . walks without making footprints in the world. Going about, he does not fear the rhinoceros or tiger."[357]

Another important mystic of Taoism besides Lao Tzu is Chuang Tzu (Zhuangzi), who lived in the fourth century BCE. His book, *Chuang Tzu*, is one of the backbones of Taoism. Scholars consider him the author of only the first seven of the 33 chapters. Chuang Tzu taught about the Tao by describing his conversation with a master named Tung-kuo who asked, "this thing called the Way—where does it exist?" Chuang Tzu answered, "there is no place it doesn't exist. . . . It is in the ant. . . . It is in the tiles. . . . It is in the piss and dung." However, he also said that since there are many ways of thinking, we humans cannot be sure that we have the right perspective. "The standard of human virtue, and of positive and negative, is so obscured that it is impossible to actually know it." Chuang Tzu also said, "joy and anger, sorrow and happiness, caution and remorse, come upon us by turns, with ever-changing moods. They come like music from hollowness, like mushrooms from damp. Daily and nightly they alternate within us, but we cannot tell whence they spring." An old maxim says, we humans are in the Tao as fish are in water. Our participation in the Tao is beyond our understanding, so we must simply act and go with the flow. We are not the measure of all things, only the Tao is.[358]

Chuang Tzu said, "the true sage pays no heed in mundane affairs. . . . He adheres, without questioning, to the Tao. . . . he roams beyond the limits of this dusty world." In addition, "the perfect man is a spiritual being, not bound by flesh. Were the oceans to boil up around him, he would not feel hot. . . . Neither life nor death can touch him—how much less so the concern of gain or loss?" Describing the sage's uniqueness, he said, "the repose of the sage is not what the world calls repose. . . . When water is still, it is like a mirror, . . . The mind of a sage being in repose becomes the mirror of the universe, the speculum of all creation. Repose, tranquility, stillness, inaction—these were the levels of the universe, the ultimate perfection of the Tao. . . . Repose, tranquility, stillness, inaction—these were the source of all things. Keep to this when coming forward to pacify a troubled world, . . . In your repose you will be wise; in your movements powerful."[359]

Chuang Tzu offers several stories similar to the following that explain going with the flow, including one about cutting up an ox. When the Prince of Lu saw the wood bell stand that Master Carpenter Ch'ing carved, he asked, "what is the secret of your art?" Ch'ing replied, one thing is that "before I set about carving the wood, I guard against anything that will diminish my vital force. I keep all distractions at a distance and my mind becomes still. After three days in this state, I lose all thought of reward or personal benefit. After five days, I no longer care about praise or blame, or what it takes to make a good or bad stand. After seven days I lose all notion that these hands or this body belongs to me. I don't even know why I am making this stand or for whom. My skill is focused on but one thing; all disturbance of the outer world is gone. It is only then that I enter the forest in search of the right tree. I find one of exquisite form. Seeing the bell stand within the folds of the grain, I set my hand to the chisel to free it. . . . it is very simple, I just bring my own nature in harmony with that of the wood. What people suspect is the work of some supernatural force is no more than this."[360]

Confucius helped preserve and possibly edit ancient traditional Chinese texts that existed in his time. These are now often called the Confucian classics. One of these, the *I Ching: The Book of Changes* (*Yijing* or *Zhouyi*) is viewed as an ancient divination manual. Besides its practical and philosophical side, Taoism has a religious side that includes divination or foretelling the future using I Ching methods of eight trigrams and 64 hexagrams. *I Ching* said, "man has received from Heaven a nature innately good, to guide him in all his movements. By devotion to this Divine Spirit within himself, he attains an unsullied innocence that leads him to do right with instinctive sureness and without any ulterior thought of reward and personal advantage."[361]

Awakenings of Shinto Mystics of Japan

Indigenous Shinto developed from a Japanese traditional religion and retained its elements. Since earliest times down the centuries through the development of Shinto and the arrival of Buddhism in the sixth century CE and into the present, the Japanese people have maintained a sense of wonder and awe as well as "that primary sense of the Numinous in all things" which is often lost with the creation of civilization. Long before the development of Shinto, sometime after 10,000 BCE, the semi-nomadic fishing, hunting, and planting Ainus lived in the northern and main islands of Japan. Later the

Yamato clan, which became dominant and from which the current imperial family descended, infiltrated from Korea into southern Japan. Besides doing sacrifices and ceremonial burials, the Ainus practiced a traditional religion of the mountain bear cult that included rituals for a fire-Goddess, the Goddess of the hearth. The bear was "a visiting mountain God, the owl a village God, the dolphin a God of the sea." Fish, birds, insects, and animals were also visiting Gods. "Mount Fuji, the Sacred mountain of Japan," which is now an extinct volcano, was "almost certainly . . . a reference to the Goddess Fire."[362]

When Buddhism arrived in Japan in the sixth century CE, the name Shinto was coined to describe the older indigenous, traditional religion. Shinto means the way of the *kami*, the way of the Gods. Although the word kami is undefinable; it is often translated as spirits or Gods. Kami are "superior and extraordinary beings," spirits, and Deities that are in humans, the ancestors, animals, birds, plants, trees, mountains, seas, wind, storms, and other natural phenomena. "All beings are endowed with kami (Sacred) nature." The early Japanese thought that the cosmos was "a gigantic organism permeated by the kami (Sacred) nature." They believed that "no tree could be marked for felling . . . and no forge fire lit without appeal to the kami residing in each." An eighteenth-century Shinto, Motoori Noringao, said that kami was "anything whatsoever which is outside of the ordinary, which possessed superior power, or which was awe-inspiring." Kami was anything, human or animal or plant or mountain or sea. There was a "conviction in Shinto that . . . there should be no sharp lines of distinction between the Sacred and the secular." Nature, humans, society, kami, and Buddha were "all parts of a greater cosmic unity." The purpose of rituals was to love and give thanks to the kami and thus ensure that they were helpful to humans.[363]

The 712 CE *Kojiki*, the Record of Ancient Masters, and the 720 CE *Nihongi*, the Chronicles of Japan, were handed down orally and then they became Shinto's earliest written records. Until after World War II, they were used as textbooks by every teacher who taught Japan's early history. The Nihongi mentioned "eight hundred myriad spirits," while both the Kojiki and Nihongi spoke of "eight million kami." The Japanese prayed to both kami and Buddha because "at the popular level Shinto and Buddhist ideas were intermingled." Filled with religious feeling, their prayers were emotional and not rational. "Shinto, at root, is a religion not of sermons but of awe." It does "not produce words but . . . goes beyond them." Its emphasis is on intuitiveness and religious experience rather than reason. The Japanese tried to "feel the reality of the kami, for a direct experience of Divinity and a sensitive recognition of mystery" rather than believe intellectual doctrines.

Shinto rituals are a "recognition and evocation of an awe that inspires gratitude to the Source . . . of Being."[364]

Amaterasu was and is the Sun Goddess or "Heavenly Illuminating Great Kami." In the past and present, Shinto taught that the Japanese Emperors were "literally descendants of the Sun Goddess." Amaterasu was "the Divine ancestress of the imperial family" which still exists today. The sun was and is the symbol on the Japanese flag. Japan was and is "a Divine nation, a land permeated by numerous kami" that was "ruled by an unbroken line of Sun-born Emperors in perfect harmony of thought and feeling with the Sun Goddess."[365]

Chapter 7

Jewish and Christian Mystics' Awakenings

Biblical Prophets' Awakenings

The founders and prophets of Judaism had mystical experiences of awakening. Around 1800 BCE, God called Abram and later named him Abraham. In this spiritual awakening, he experienced God speaking to him. The Hebrew *Bible*, that can also be called the Jewish scriptures that Christians call the Old Testament, described God telling him, "go from your country and your kindred and your father's house to the land that I will show you. I will make of you a great nation, and I will bless you, and make your name great, so that you will be a blessing." Abram left his country, because God instructed him. With his wife Sarah, he went to Canaan, Egypt, and other places. Abram had another mystical experience of enlightenment in which God spoke to him. "The word of the Lord came to Abram in a vision. 'Do not be afraid. Abram, I am your shield; your reward shall be very great.'" Abram answered God that "you have given me no offspring, and so a slave born in my house is to be my heir." God took him outside and said, "'count the stars, . . . so shall your descendants be.' . . . On that day the Lord made a covenant with Abram, saying, 'to your descendants I give this land, from the river of Egypt to the great river, the river Eurphrates.'"[366]

When Abram was 99 years old, "the Lord appeared to Abram," and said, "I am God Almighty, walk before me, and be blameless. And I will make my covenant between Me and you, and will make you exceedingly numerous." After Abram fell on his face, God told him, "as for Me, this is my covenant with you: you shall be the ancestor of a multitude of nations." Then the Lord changed his name from Abram to Abraham. God gave "an everlasting covenant, to be God to you and to your offering after you." The Lord also said that he gave them "all the land of Canaan, for perpetual holding: and I will be their God." As a sign of the covenant, every male at eight days old shall be circumcised.[367]

Around 1200 BCE, when Moses was watching his father-in-law's flock on Sinai, the mountain of God, he had a mystical experience of awakening. "There the angel of the Lord appeared to him in a flame of fire out of a bush. . . . When the Lord saw that he had turned aside to see, God called to him out of the bush. . . . 'come no closer! Remove the sandals from your feet, for the place where you are standing is holy ground. . . . I am the God of your father, the God of Abraham, the God of Isaac, and the God of Jacob.' And Moses hid his face, for he was afraid to look at God." Then the Lord said, "I have observed the misery of My people . . . and I have come down to deliver them from the Egyptians, and to bring them up out of that land to a good and broad land, a land flowing with milk and honey, to the country of the Canaanite." When Moses wanted to know the Lord's name, God answered him, "I AM WHO I AM . . . I AM has sent Me to you," the Israelites.[368]

God gave Moses the ten commandments. "God spoke all these words: "I am the Lord your God, . . . You shall have no other gods before Me. You shall not make for yourself an idol, . . . You shall not make wrongful use of the name of the Lord your God, . . . Remember the Sabbath day, and keep it holy.. . . Honor your father and your mother, . . . You shall not murder. You shall not commit adultery. You shall not steal. You shall not bear false witness against your neighbor. You shall not covet your neighbor's house; you shall not covet your neighbor's wife, or male or female slave, or ox, or donkey, or anything that belongs to your neighbor." When Moses convened all of Israel, he spoke about God giving the covenant and the ten commandments, "Hear, O Israel, the statues and ordinances that I am addressing to you today; you shall learn them and observe them diligently. The Lord our God made a covenant with us at Horeb," another word for Sinai. God spoke to the Jews, "I the Lord your God am a jealous God, punishing children for the inequity of their parents to the third and fourth generation of those who reject Me, but showing steadfast love to the thousandth generation of those who love Me and keep My commandments."[369]

Other major Jewish prophets also had mystical experiences of awakening and taught the spiritual insights that they gained from them. Biblical scholars claim that the writings of Isaiah are the work of three prophets, not one, but they were put in one scroll that was attributed to Isaiah. First Isaiah, also called Proto-Isaiah, mainly included chapters 1 to 38, Second Isaiah, also referred to as Deutero-Isaiah, went from chapter 39 to 55, and Third Isaiah, Trito-Isaiah, covered chapters 56 to 66. In the eighth century BCE before the Jewish exile to Babylon, First Isaiah of Jerusalem preached about his mystical vision and experience of awakening. When God spoke to him, he did not feel worthy. "I saw the Lord sitting on a throne, high and lofty; and the hem of his robe filled the temple." Each of the seraphs that were in attendance had six wings. Two wings were used to cover their faces, two to cover their feet, and two to fly. One seraph said to another, "Holy, holy, holy is the Lord of hosts; the whole earth is full of His glory." The voices caused the house to shake and to fill with smoke. Isaiah said, "woe is me! I am lost, for I am a man of unclean lips, and I live among a people of unclean lips; yet my eyes have seen the King, the Lord of hosts." One of the seraphs lifted a burning coal from the altar with tongs, flew to him, touched his lips with it, and said, "now that this has touched your lips, your guilt has departed and your sin is blotted out."[370]

Then the voice of the Lord said, "whom shall I send, and who will go for us?" Isaiah answered, "here I am; send me!" Referring to the people's rebellion against Him, God replied, "go and say to this people: 'keep listening, but you do not comprehend; keep looking, but you do not understand.'" Isaiah asked how long before the people would listen, see, comprehend, and understand. The Holy One answered, "until cities lie waste without inhabitants, and houses without people, and the land is utterly desolate; until the Lord sends everyone far away." Describing another vision, First Isaiah gave God's description of His people. "The Lord has spoken: I reared children and brought them up, but they have rebelled against Me. The ox knows its owner, and the donkey its master's crib; but Israel does not know, my people do not understand. Ah, sinful nation, people laden with iniquity, offspring who do evil, children who deal corruptly, who have forsaken the Lord, who have despised the Holy One of Israel, who are utterly estranged." First Isaiah gave God's description of Himself and said some of the people will return to Him. "The Lord of hosts is exalted by justice, the Holy God shows Himself holy by righteousness. . . . let the plan of the Holy One of Israel hasten to fulfillment."[371]

First Isaiah predicted the coming of the *Messiah*. In Hebrew, Messiah meant the Anointed One. It was *Christos* in Greek and Christ in English. Jews waited throughout the biblical times and are still waiting today for the coming of the Messiah. Describing the Messiah, Isaiah said, "the Lord Himself will give you a sign. Look, a young woman is with child and shall bear a son, and shall name him Immanuel." In addition, "for a child has been born for us; a son given to us; authority rests upon his shoulders; and he is named Wonderful Counselor, Mighty God, Everlasting Father, Prince of Peace. His authority shall grow continually, and there shall be endless peace from the throne of David and his kingdom. He will establish and uphold it with justice and with righteousness from this time onward and forevermore." Furthermore, "the Spirit of the Lord shall rest on him, the Spirit of wisdom and understanding, the Spirit of counsel and might, the Spirit of knowledge and the fear of the Lord. . . . with righteousness he shall judge the poor, and decide with equity for the meek of the earth." First Isaiah said that for Israel "God is my strength and my might; He has become my salvation." Moreover, "the Lord will have compassion on Jacob and will again choose Israel, and will set them in their own land."[372]

Second Isaiah was an anonymous prophet of the Jewish exiles in Babylon who lived about 150 years after First Isaiah. Like First Isaiah, Second Isaiah described his people as rebellious and faithless. The Holy One said to Israel, "do not fear, for I am with you, do not be afraid, for I am your God; I will strengthen you, I will help you." In addition, "I am the Lord, I have called you in righteousness, . . . I have given you as a covenant to the people, a light to the nations, to open the eyes that are blind, to bring out the prisoners from the dungeon. . . . I will lead the blind . . . by paths they have not known, I will guide them. I will turn darkness before them into light, the rough places into level ground. . . . I will not forsake them." Furthermore, "I love you. . . . Do not fear, for I am with you." Comforting His people, God "will have compassion on His suffering ones." Calling them to awaken, the Lord declared, "with everlasting love I will have compassion on you. . . . I will make with you an everlasting covenant, my steadfast, sure love."[373]

Preaching after the return of the Jewish exiles to Jerusalem from Babylon early in the sixth century BCE, Third Isaiah, who was probably a disciple of Second Isaiah, said, "maintain justice, do what is right. . . . You shall call, and the Lord will answer; you shall cry for help, and He will say, 'here I am.' The Lord will guide you continually, and satisfy your needs." Third Isaiah described the Messiah speaking about himself. "The Spirit of the Lord God is upon me, because the Lord has anointed me, He has sent me to bring good news to the oppressed, to bind up the brokenhearted, to proclaim liberty to the captives, and release to the prisoners, . . . to comfort all who mourn in Zion." God said to the Jews, "you shall be called priests of the Lord, you shall be named ministers of our God. . . . For I the Lord love justice, I hate robbery and wrongdoing . . . and I will make an everlasting covenant with them." Third Isaiah said that the Lord "has shown them according to His Mercy, according to the abundance of His steadfast Love. For He said, 'surely they are My people.' . . . It was no messenger or angel but His presence that saved them; in His love and in His pity, He redeemed them." Remembering the olden days, the people asked, "where is the One who put within them His Holy Spirit?" and said, "you, O Lord, are our Father; our Redeemer." God declared, "I am about to create new heavens and a new earth" and "as a mother comforts her child, so I will comfort you."[374]

God spoke to another prophet, Jeremiah, "son of Hilkiah, of the priests who were in Anathoth in the land of Benjamin." Preaching between the years 626–580 BCE, Jeremiah said, "now the word of the Lord came to me saying, . . . I appointed you a prophet to the nations." When he complained that he was a boy who did not know how to speak, the Holy One answered, "you shall go to all to whom I send you, and you shall speak whatever I command you, do not be afraid of them for I am with you." Jeremiah spoke God's message, "My people have committed two evils: they have forsaken Me, the Foundation of living water, and dug out cisterns for themselves, cracked cisterns that can hold no water."[375]

The Holy One told Jeremiah to say, "if you return to Me, if you remove your abominations from My presence, and do not waver, and if you swear, 'as the Lord lives!' in truth, in justice, and in righteousness, then nations shall be blessed." Furthermore, "if you truly amend your ways and your doings, if you truly act justly one with another, if you do not oppress the alien, the orphan, and the widow, or shed innocent blood . . . then I will dwell with you in this place." Jeremiah told how God spoke about His Love for Israel and relationship with it. "Know Me, that I am the Lord, I act with steadfast love, justice, and righteousness." Describing the Lord as the true "living God and everlasting King," he reported the Holy One saying, "I will give them a heart to know that I am the Lord; and they shall be My people and I will be their God, for they shall return to Me with their whole heart."[376]

Jeremiah was persecuted for bringing God's messages to the people. After he spoke "all that the Lord had commanded him to speak," then "the priests and the prophets and all the people laid hold of him saying, 'you shall die!'" Nevertheless, he continued preaching and quoted the Holy One as saying, "I will be the God of all the families of Israel, and they shall be My people. . . . I have loved you with an everlasting love; therefore, I have continued My faithfulness to you." In addition, Jeremiah said, "the days are surely coming, says the Lord, when I will make a new covenant with the house of Israel and the house of Judah. . . . I will put My law within them and I will write it on their hearts; and I will be their God, and they shall be My people."[377]

More minor Jewish prophets also had mystical experiences of awakening and taught the spiritual insights that they gained from them. Amos, a shepherd from Tekoa in the eighth century BCE, said, "I am no prophet, nor a prophet's son; but I am a herdsman, and a dresser of sycamore trees, and the Lord took me from following the flock, and the Lord said to me, 'go prophesy to My people Israel . . . You say, . . . you that trample on the needy, and bring to ruin the poor of the land, . . . Surely, I will never forget any of their deeds.'" The Holy One offered a better way. "Seek good and not evil, that you may live; and so the Lord, the God of hosts, will be with you, . . . Hate evil and love good, and establish justice." In addition, "let justice roll down like waters, and righteousness like an ever-flowing stream."[378]

Hosea, another eighth-century BCE Jewish prophet, described the Lord as a loving husband and Israel as an unfaithful wife. The Holy One said through Hosea, "you will call Me, my husband, . . . I will make for you a covenant . . . I will take you for My wife forever; I will take you for My wife in righteousness and in justice, in steadfast love, and in mercy. I will take you for My wife in faithfulness; and you shall know the Lord. . . . I will say . . . 'you are My people;' and he shall say, 'You are my God.'" The Holy One explained to Israel that earlier He led them out of Egypt with "cords of human kindness, with bands of love." Now "there is no faithfulness or loyalty, and no knowledge of God in the land. Swearing, lying, and murder, and stealing and adultery break out; bloodshed follows bloodshed. . . . For a spirit of whoredom has led them astray, and they have played the whore, forsaking their God." They make sacrifices and offerings to false idols. The Lord proclaimed, "I desire steadfast love and not sacrifice, the knowledge of God rather than burnt offerings."[379]

Micah, a later eighth-century BCE rural Jewish prophet, said, "as for me, I will look to the Lord, I will wait for the God of my salvation; my God will hear me." Furthermore, "I am filled with power, with the Spirit of the Lord and with justice and might, to declare to Jacob his transgression and to Israel his sin." Speaking to the rulers of Israel, he said, "should you not know justice?—you who hate the good and love the evil, who tear the skin off my people." The Holy One has informed people "what is good; and what does the Lord require of you but to do justice, and to love kindness, and to walk humbly with your God." Then the Lord "will again have compassion upon us; He will tread our iniquities under foot" and "will show faithfulness to Jacob and unswerving loyalty to Abraham."[380]

Over many centuries, the Bible's psalms were written by different authors who had experiences of awakening. A psalmist talked to the Holy One, "I, through the abundance of Your steadfast Love, will enter Your house. . . . Lead me, O Lord, in Your righteousness because of my enemies;

make Your way straight before me." Another spoke about God, "the Lord is my shepherd, I shall not want. . . . Even though I walk through the darkest valley, I fear no evil; for You are with me." Yet another conversed with the Divine, "make me to know Your ways, O Lord; teach me Your paths. Lead me in Your truth, and teach me, for You are the God of my salvation. . . . All the paths of the Lord are steadfast love and faithfulness, for those who keep His covenant and His decrees."[381]

A psalmist spoke to the Holy One, "You have multiplied, O Lord my God, Your wondrous deeds and Your thoughts toward us. . . . Sacrifice and offering You do not desire, . . . I delight to do Your will, O my God, Your law is within my heart. . . . Do not, O Lord, withhold Your Mercy from me; let Your steadfast Love and Your Faithfulness keep me safe forever." Another said, "God is our refuge and strength, a very present help in trouble. Therefore, we will not fear, . . . The Lord of hosts is with us; the God of Jacob is our refuge. Come, behold the works of the Lord." Yet another conversed with the Holy One, "have mercy on me, O God, according to Your steadfast Love; according to Your abundant Mercy blot out my transgressions. . . . Create in me a clean heart, O God, and put a new and right spirit within me. Do not cast me away from Your presence, . . . You have no delight in sacrifice; . . . The sacrifice acceptable to God is a broken spirit; a broken and contrite heart."[382]

Describing the Lord, a psalmist said, "Father of orphans and Protector of widows is God in His holy habitation. God gives the desolate a home to live in; He leads out the prisoners to prosperity, . . . O God, when You went out before Your people, . . . the earth quaked . . . at the presence of God, . . . in Your Goodness, O God, You provided for the needy." Another described the Holy One, "You, O Lord, are good and forgiving, abounding in steadfast Love to all who call upon You. . . . You, O Lord, are a God merciful and gracious, slow to anger and abounding in steadfast Love and Faithfulness." Yet another said about the Divine, "I declare that Your steadfast Love is established forever; Your Faithfulness is as firm as the heavens. . . . Righteousness and Justice are the foundations of Your throne; steadfast Love and Faithfulness go before You." Then the Lord spoke, "I will not remove from him My steadfast Love or be false to My Faithfulness, I will not violate My covenant. . . . Once and for all I have sworn by My Holiness." The first verse of psalm 136 contained the line, "for His steadfast Love endures forever." That line was repeated in every one of the psalm's 26 verses. Very obviously the repetition emphasized the author's view of the importance of God's steadfast Love that other authors also mentioned in many different psalms.[383]

In the book with her name, Judith prayed, "Your strength does not lie in numbers, nor Your might in violent men; since You are the God of the humble, the help of the oppressed, the support of the weak, the refuge of the forsaken, the savior of the despairing. Please, please, God of my father, God of the heritage of Israel, Master of heaven and earth, Creator of the waters, King of your whole creation, hear my prayer."[384]

Awakenings of Later Jewish Mystics

The Talmud is composed of 63 tractates or treatises of the literature of the Rabbis, including the Mishnah and Gemara. Written over a number of centuries, it was not formally closed until about 600 CE. Not translated into English until the first half of the twentieth century, the Talmud is called the Oral Torah, while the Bible is the Written Torah. According to contemporary Jewish scholar Jacob Neusner, the Talmud is not only "an encyclopedia of information," but also a protracted, sustained, and uniform inquiry into the Hebrew scripture. In both the Bible and the Talmud, "the existence of God is regarded as an axiomatic truth" so no proofs are presented. In the Talmud, "one may know, make known, and have the knowledge" that God is the Holy One, the King of Kings, the Designer, Creator, Discerner, Witness, and Judge. "He will summon to judgment; Blessed be He, in whose presence is neither iniquity, or forgetfulness, nor disrespect of persons, nor taking of bribes—for everything is His."[385]

In the Talmud, Rabbi Jacob said, "better a single moment of awakening in this world than eternity in the world to come. . . . Why? A single moment of awakening in this world is eternity in the world to come." Another Rabbi taught that "everything that God, the Source and Substance of all, created in this world flows naturally from the essence of God's Divine nature. . . . Creation is the extension of God. Creation is God encountered in time and space. Creation is the Infinite in the garb of the finite. To attend to creation is to attend to God."[386]

Kabbalah is a Hebrew word literally means 'receiving' or 'that which is received.' It is a mystical tradition that interprets Judaism's ancient wisdom including the Jewish scriptures, as it attempts to understand God. In the Kabbalah, God's name is the Hebrew word, *Ein Sof*. Despite the teaching that Ein Sof cannot be defined because It exceeds all description, It means without end, Endless, without boundaries, Boundless, the Infinite, and "the Unnamable One." The *Zohar, The Book of Splendor*, the thirteenth-century canonical book of the Kabbalah, said that Ein Sof is the Blessed Holy One, the Holy of Holies, the Holy Spark, "the High Spark, Hidden of all Hidden," the King, "the Ineffable One, the Unrevealed," and "the Holy Ancient One." Ein Sof manifested Itself in this world through ten *Sefirot* which are emanations, attributes, or powers of God. According to the sixteenth-century Spanish kabbalist Moses Cordovero and others, the ten Sefirot are (1) *Keter* is Crown, (2) *Hokhmah* is Wisdom, (3) *Binah* is Understanding, Intelligence, (4) *Hesed* is Love, (5) *Gevurah* is Power or *Din* Judgment, (6) *Tif'eret* is Beauty, (7) *Netzah* is Eternity, Lasting Endurance, (8) *Hod* is Majesty, (9) *Yesod* is Foundation or *Zaddik* Righteous One, and (10) *Shekhinah* is Divine Presence or *Malkhut* Kingdom.[387]

First appearing from the third to the sixth centuries CE in Palestine, an early Kabbalah book named *Sefer Yetzirah, the Book of Creation or the Book of Formation*, said that God is "the Lord of Hosts, the God of Israel, the Living *Elohim*, the King of the Universe, the Almighty, Merciful, and Gracious God; He is great and exalted and eternally dwelling in the Height, His name is holy." The One Living God is "eternal and forever; Voice, Spirit, and Word" as well as "the only Creator and the only Formator, and no one exists but He." This book mentioned that the cosmos is composed of Divine forces including "the ten mysterious emanations of God called *Sefirot*." God's "ten ineffable Sefirot, ten and not nine, ten and not eleven, understand with wisdom and apprehend with care; examine by means of them and search them out." His ten attributes are "without limits: the Infinity of the Beginning and the Infinity of the End, the Infinity of Good and the Infinity of Evil, . . . and only One Lord God, the trusty King rules them all from His holy dwelling in all eternity. . . . their goal is infinite. His word is in them when they emanate and when they return."[388]

Azriel of Gerona, a thirteenth-century Spanish kabbalist, experienced awakening and said that "anything visible, and anything that can be grasped by thought, is bounded. Anything bounded is finite. Anything finite is not undifferentiated. Conversely, the Boundless is called Ein Sof, the Infinite. It is absolutely undifferentiation in perfect changeless Oneness. Since It is Boundless, there is nothing outside of It. . . . Emanating from Ein Sof are the ten Sefirot. They constitute the process by which all things come into being and pass away. They energize every existent thing that can be quantified. . . . Everything is from Ein Sof; there is nothing outside of It. . . . Ein Sof cannot be conceived, certainly not expressed, though It is intimated in everything." Another thirteenth-century Spanish kabbalist Abraham Abulafia had a mystical experience. "God woke me from sleep and I studied *Sefer Yetzirah* . . . and the hand of God was upon me, . . . and my spirit was quickened within me, and the Spirit of God came into my mouth, and a Spirit of holiness moved about me, and I saw many awesome sights and wonders." Abulafia also said, "the main thing is to apprehend His Reality" and "make thyself ready to direct thy heart to God alone. . . . Be careful to abstract all thy thought from the vanities of the world."[389]

A thirteenth-century German El'azar of Worms experienced God and said, "when you contemplate the Creator, realize that His encampment extends beyond, infinitely beyond, and . . . infinitely everywhere. . . . God . . . is within everything." Moses Cordovero, the sixteenth-century Spanish kabbalist, explained that "a person should have two aspects: The first aspect should be in communion in solitude with his Creator in order to increase and perfect his *chochmah* (wisdom); the second should be to teach others the chochmah with which the Holy One, Blessed be He, has endowed him." Moses Hayyim Luzzatto, an eighteenth-century kabbalist, said, "you are walking in the presence of God while being right here in this world."[390]

An eighteenth-century German Gluckel of Hameln, who was married at age 14, wrote her memoirs as her way of offering advice for her 12 children. "We sinful men are in the world as if swimming in the sea and in danger of being drowned. But our great, merciful, and kind God, in His great Mercy, has thrown ropes into the sea that we may take hold and be saved. These are our holy Torah. . . . whatever you lose, have patience, for nothing is our own, everything is only a loan. . . . We men have been created for nothing else, but to serve God and to keep His commandments and to obey the Torah, for He is thy life."[391]

Israel ben Eliezer, called the *Baal Shem Tov* or the Bearer of the Good Name, an eighteenth-century Ukrainian, founded and led Hasidism, a Jewish revivalist movement. Since he wrote no books, scholars study a single letter he wrote that discussed his mystical experience. "I engaged in an ascent of the soul, . . . and I saw wondrous things in a vision. . . . That which I saw and learned in my ascent it is impossible to describe or to relate . . . . But as I returned to the Lower Garden of Eden, I saw many souls—both of the living and the dead. . . .. They were all in such a state of great rapture. . . . Many of the wicked had done *teshuvah* (repentance) for their sins and were pardoned. . . . I went higher, step by step, until I entered the palace of the Messiah . . . There I witnessed great rejoicing."[392]

Rabbi Abraham Isaac Kook, a twentieth-century Palestinian, said, "God lavishes according the Divine force. The one receiving, however, is bounded. . . . God lavishes the good immeasurably according to the Divine gauge. Thus, the Good is Divine, limitless, although the created receiver cannot receive it—unless he is . . . repaired through his desire to return to the limitless Source, to become One with the Divinity." In addition, Kook claimed that "in the flow of the Holy Spirit, one feels the Divine Life Force coursing the pathways of existence, through all desires, all worlds, all thoughts, all nations, all creatures." The twentieth-century Jewish theologian Martin Buber wrote that in Hasidism "all that is necessary is to have a soul united with itself and indivisibly directed to its Divine goal. . . . your own character, the very qualities which make you what you are, constitutes your special approach to God, your special potential use for Him. Do not be vexed at your delight in creatures and things! But do not let it shackle itself to creatures and things; through these, press on to God."[393]

As described earlier, Buber explained how humans have two kinds of relations, *I-Thou* and *I-It*. He also claimed that they can have a relation with God that he called *I-Eternal Thou*. "Every particular Thou is a glimpse through to the Eternal Thou." Some are "moved to think of and to address their Eternal Thou as an It." When a person "gives his whole being to addressing the Thou of his life, . . . he addresses God." To be in a pure absolute relation with God is "to see everything in the Thou, . . . he who sees the world in Him stands in His presence. . . . He who goes out with his whole being to meet his Thou . . ., finds Him. . . . God is the 'wholly Other'; but He is also the wholly Same, the wholly Present. Of course, He is the *Mysterium Tremendum* . . . but He is also the Mystery of the self-evident, nearer to me than my I." A person's sense of Thou "cannot be satiated till he finds the Endless Thou. . . . God is the Being that is directly, most nearly, and lastingly over against us."[394]

Buber continued, only "God, the Eternal Presence," can be "in one, all-embracing relation . . . Only One Thou never ceases by its nature to be Thou for us." In other words, "the Eternal Thou can by its nature not become It." The person "who knows God knows also very well remoteness from God, and the anguish of barrenness in the tormented heart, but he does not know the absence of God: it is we only who are not always there." When I heard the twentieth-century Jewish theologian Abraham Heschel speak years ago, his thought that stayed with me was his passionate cry, 'don't hate.' His book, *Man's Quest for God*, claimed that "to live without prayer is to live without God, to live without a soul." A person is "aware of His presence long before he thinks of His essence. And to pray is to sense His presence." Prayer is "an act that happens between man and God—in the presence of God" and involves "the decision to enter and face the presence of God." To pray is "to expand the presence of God in the world. God is Transcendent, but our worship makes him Immanent." Moreover, "unless the outer life expresses the inner world," spiritual life stagnates and decays. "Prayer is the quintessence of the spiritual life." Above all, "life is a partnership of God and man."[395]

The twentieth-century Italian Natalia Ginzburg wrote about what to teach children. "I think they should be taught not the little virtues but the great ones. Not thrift but generosity and an indifference to money; not caution but courage and a contempt for danger; not shrewdness but frankness and a love for truth; not tact but love for one's neighbor and self-denial; not desire for success but a desire to be and to know." Contemporary feminist theologian Judith Plaskow said that "as feminists, we are committed to the notion that 'the personal is political,' that many of women's seemingly personal problems are a function of fundamental social inequities, and can be resolved only as those inequities are addressed." Furthermore, as Jewish women, "'the spiritual is political,' because of the ways in which Judaism as a religious tradition diminished us as women, and the demands and priorities of the larger social system constituted impediments to our relationship with the Sacred. In this situation, politics is the necessary work we do to make the world safe for our spirituality."[396]

Jesus' Awakenings

Jesus was a mystic who had spiritual experiences of awakening. Then he taught what he learned from his mystical experiences. What was his central teaching? Most contemporary biblical scholars assert that Jesus' principal message was the kingdom of God. Some refer to it as God's reign or rule to remove the gender bias. According to the Jesus Seminar, "God's imperial rule is the theme of Jesus' teaching" in the synoptic gospels. John Reumann, a biblical scholar, claims that when one hundred New Testament scholars around the world, whether Catholic, Protestant, or non-Christian, are asked, what is Jesus' central teaching, "the vast majority of them—perhaps every single expert—would agree that his message centered in the kingdom of God." Biblical scholar Marcus Borg contends that "the phrase the 'kingdom of God' is perhaps the best shorthand summary of the message and passion of Jesus." Again Borg claims, "what is the story of Jesus most centrally about? The kingdom of God."[397]

What did Jesus mean by the kingdom of God? Scholars debate the meaning of this phrase. In my opinion, Jesus' clearest, most essential, and mystical message was in Luke's gospel. "The kingdom of God is within you." Some translate this as "the kingdom of God is among you." The Jesus Seminar translates this as "God's imperial rule is right there in your midst." In my book, *The Heart of Jesus' Teaching: The Key to Transforming Christianity and Our World*, I explain that the best, most helpful, and fundamental meaning for the kingdom of God is the presence of the God. One way to demonstrate the meaning of the kingdom of God is by replacing it with the presence of God in Jesus' sayings. First, let's replace the word kingdom with presence in the various translations of Luke's important proclamation. The presence of God is within you. The presence of the Holy One is among you. The presence of the Divine is right there in your midst.[398]

Now let's replace the word kingdom with presence in other parts of the gospels. Jesus proclaimed the good news of the presence of God. The presence of the Holy One is at hand. The presence of the Sacred Spirit is near and has come near. The presence of the Divine has come to us. Jesus sent his disciples to proclaim the good news of the presence of the Holy One. This meaning also fits in the beatitude. "Blessed are you who are poor, for yours is the kingdom of God," for yours is the presence of the Spirit. It also works in Jesus' prayer to our Father. "Your kingdom come. Your will be done on earth as it is in heaven." Your presence come. Your will be done on earth as it is in heaven.[399]

After Jesus said that you are not to worry about what you will eat or drink, he taught, "strive first for the kingdom of God and His righteousness, and all these things will be given to you as well." This can be restated as, strive first for the presence of God and His righteousness. Luke's gospel had a parallel saying to the one in Matthew, but added "Do not be afraid, little flock, for it is your Father's good pleasure to give you the kingdom," to give you the Divine presence. Jesus said, "not everyone who says to me, 'Lord, Lord,' will enter the kingdom of heaven, but only the one who does the will of my Father in heaven." Not everyone who says to me, 'Lord, Lord,' will enter the presence of God. In Mark, with parallels in Matthew and Luke, Jesus said, "let the little children come to me; . . . for it is to such as these that the kingdom of God belongs," that the presence of God belongs. Whoever does not receive the kingdom of God, the presence of God, as a little child will never enter it.[400]

Using stories and parables that rural people would understand, Jesus said, "the kingdom of heaven is like a treasure hidden in a field, which someone found and hid." The presence of God is like a hidden treasure. When people experience the hidden presence of the Divine, they will be joyful and be willing to give all they have to maintain that presence. Jesus said, "the kingdom of God is like a mustard seed that someone took and sowed in his field; it is the smallest of all the seeds, but when it has grown it is the greatest of shrubs and becomes a tree." The presence of God is like a mustard seed that starts extremely small, but grows until it is extremely large. Jesus also said, "the kingdom of heaven is like yeast that a woman took and mixed in with three measures of flour until all of it was leavened." The presence of God is like yeast. When a woman experiences the presence of the Holy One, she mixes it in with her daily life until all of it is raised up.[401]

Jesus experienced the Divine presence within him. The Father "dwells in me." He also felt he was within God and united with Him. "Believe me that I am in the Father and the Father is in me." Thus, "the Father and I are one." A number of times he repeated, "the Father is in me, and I am in the

Father." God "is with me; He has not left me alone." And again, "I am not alone because the Father is with me." Jesus often prayed because he loved the Father deeply. Besides going to the synagogue to pray and teach, he went off alone to pray and he even spent entire nights praying. As he prayed to the Holy One for his followers, he asked that "they may be one, as we are one, I in them and You in me, that they may be completely one." Thus, he acknowledged again that the Father and he were one. Speaking to the Father, Jesus asked that people know that You "have loved them even as You loved me." Further, Jesus requested from God that "the love with which You have loved me may be in them, and I in them." In Nazareth, Jesus went to the synagogue on the Sabbath, as was his custom, and read the prophet Isaiah's words. "The Spirit of the Lord is upon me, because He has anointed me to bring the good news to the poor." Afterwards he said, "today this scripture has been fulfilled in your hearing."[402]

Thus, Jesus' first essential teaching was that the presence of the God is within us. His second fundamental message was *love*. Jesus experienced the Father as loving and he declared the first and greatest commandment was to love God. "You shall love the Lord your God with all your heart, with all your soul, and with all your mind, and with all your strength. This is the greatest and first commandment. And a second is like it: You shall love your neighbor as yourself." Besides borrowing these two commandments from the Hebrew scriptures, he taught a more radical love. "You have heard that it was said, 'you shall love your neighbor and hate your enemy.' But I say to you, love your enemies and pray for those who persecute you." These essential messages are the heart of Jesus' teaching.[403]

Because Jesus was a mystic who loved the Father, he moved into action to do His work which was to reveal the Divine message as he understood it. A number of times in John's gospel, he said, "I came from God" and the Father sent me. "My teaching is not mine but His who sent me." Similarly, "the word that you hear is not mine, but is from the Father who sent me." Furthermore, "I have not spoken on my own, but the Father who sent me has Himself given me a commandment about what to say and what to speak. . . . What I speak, therefore, I speak just as the Father has told me." At the last supper, Jesus said, "the One who sent me is with me; He has not left me alone, for I always do what is pleasing to Him." Jesus declared that he did not speak and act on his own, but "the Father, who dwells in me, does His work." In addition, "I do as the Father has commanded me, so that the world may know that I love the Father." Moreover, "I have made known to you everything that I have heard from my Father." Praying to God, he said, "I have made Your name known . . . the words that You gave me I have given to them." Just before his arrest, he prayed, "I have glorified You on earth by finishing the work You gave me to do." Furthermore, "I have kept my Father's commandments and abide in His Love."[404]

Jesus taught about God whom he called *Abba*, the Aramaic word for Father. He said, "pray then in this way: Our Father in heaven." He also said, "God is Spirit, and those who worship Him must worship in spirit and truth." In addition, "whoever blasphemes against the Holy Spirit can never be forgiven." Distinguishing himself from God, he asked a man, "why do you call me good? No one is good but God alone." After asking his disciples to consider the birds of the air and the lilies of the field, he said, "if God so clothes the grass of the field which is alive today and tomorrow is thrown into the oven, how much more will He clothe you—you of little faith!" Quoting the Hebrew Bible, he said, "hear, O Israel, the Lord our God, the Lord is One" and "worship the Lord your God, and serve only Him." He asked, "have you not read in the book of Moses, in the story about the bush, how God said to him, 'I am the God of Abraham, the God of Isaac, and the God of Jacob?' He is God not of the dead, but of the living." In John's gospel, Jesus presented an image of the relationship among God, his disciples, and himself, "I am the true vine, and my Father is the vine grower. . . . I am the vine, you are the branches. Those who abide in me and I in them bear much fruit. . . . My Father is glorified by this, that you bear much fruit and become my disciples. As the Father loved me, so I have loved you; abide in my love."[405]

Christian Mystics' Awakenings

Throughout the centuries, Christian mystics wrote glowingly about the Holy One, including the Divine as Love. In a sermon in the Acts of the Apostles, Paul described the Sacred Spirit. "The God who made the world and everything in it, He who is Lord of heaven and earth, does not live in shrines made by human hands, nor is He served by human hands, as though He needed anything, since He Himself gives all mortals life and breath and all things. From one ancestor He made all nations to inhabit the whole earth, . . . so that they would search for God . . . though indeed He is not far from each one of us. For 'in Him we live and move and have our being.'" In his epistles, Paul depicted God in many different ways. Besides His wrath, severity, and righteous judgment, he described God's truthfulness, steadfastness, wisdom, kindness, mercy, compassion, and love. "God is faithful, and He will not let you be tested beyond your strength." The immortal, eternal God is "All in All." Like Jesus, Paul repeatedly referred to God as "*Abba*! Father!" Reiterating "God is One," he said, "there is no God but One," and "there is One God, the Father, from whom are all things." The Divine is the Creator and "the Source of your life." Besides being "the God of Hope," the Sacred Spirit is "the God of steadfastness and encouragement" and "the God of Love and Peace." In addition, "God's Love has been poured out into our hearts."[406]

In his first epistle, John said that "God is Love" and He loves us. He also declared that the Divine is within us and we are within Him. "Let us love on another, because love is from God; everyone who loves is born of God and knows God. Whoever does not love does not know God, for God is Love. . . . if we love one another, God lives in us, and His Love is perfected in us. By this we know that we abide in Him and He in us, because He has given us of His Spirit. . . . So we have known and believe the Love that God has for us. God is Love, and those who abide in love abide in God, and God abides in them."[407]

A fifth-century African bishop Augustine of Hippo became one of Catholicism's leading theologians. In his book *Confessions*, he described his sins and mystical experiences of awakening. His description of God is elaborate and spread throughout his book. "Great art Thou, O Lord, . . . great is Thy Power, and Thy Wisdom is infinite." God is "the highest and best, most all-powerful, most merciful and most just, most deeply hidden and most nearly present, most beautiful and most strong, constant and yet incomprehensible, changeless yet changing all things, never new, never old, making all things new, . . . always acting and always at rest, . . . upholding, filling, and protecting, creating, nourishing, and bringing to perfection, . . . You love, but with no storm of passion; You are jealous, but with no anxious fear; You repent, but do not grieve." Augustine exclaimed, "my Father and highest God, O Beauty of all things beautiful, O Truth." You are a Spirit who is everywhere. You are "not only good but Goodness" as well as "whole, true, supreme, and infinite." God is "the permanent and abiding Light" and "the Truth presiding over everything." Not only did Augustine believe that God "cares for us," but he also called Him Mercy and Love. He spoke to God, "O eternal Truth and true Love and beloved Eternity!" and "O, Love, ever burning, and never extinguished, Charity, my God, set me on fire!"[408]

In Augustine's advanced awakening, he said, "I was seeking You, my God. . . .. But You were inside me, deeper than the deepest recesses of my heart." In addition, "You Yourself are all my good, You, Almighty, who are with me even before I am with you." Moreover, "late it was that I loved you, . . . You were with me and I was not with You. . . . You called, . . . You shone, . . . You touched me, and I burned for Your Peace." Furthermore, "You are everywhere, . . . You alone are always present even to those who have put themselves furthest from you. . . . You have not deserted Your creation in the same way as they have deserted their Creator. . . . You are in their hearts." The Truth that is within says, "your God is . . . the Life in your life." In addition, "You fill the heaven and the earth . . . You who fill everything are wholly present in everything which You fill . . . Everywhere You are present in Your entirety."[409]

In the sixth century, Denys the Areopagite said "the most important name" for the Divine is the Good. The Cause of all things is "the transcendently Good, the transcendently Divine, the transcendently Existing, the transcendently Living, the transcendently Wise." God who is life-giving is "overflowing with love for mankind, . . . calls us back to Itself after we have strayed, . . . and will bring us to perfect life and immortality." Besides awakening to God and His Love for humanity, Denys experienced the Divine within all people and things. The Good is "the supra-Divine transcendentally One God who dwells indivisibly in every individual and who is . . . undifferentiated Unity." In all of us, "He is in our minds, in our souls, and in our bodies." Not only is He in all people, but God is also "present in all things" and is everywhere. "He penetrates all things" and He is "the Being pervading all being." The One is "the underlying element of all things." It is "at the center of everything and everything has It for a destiny."[410]

Francis of Assisi, the thirteenth-century Italian founder of the Franciscan religious order, had mystical experiences of awakening that led him to expand the Lord's Prayer. "Our Father, most Holy, Creator, Redeemer, Savior, Comforter, Who art in heaven, with the angels and saints enlightening them to knowledge of Thee, inflaming them to love of Thee, for Thou, Lord, art Love; dwelling in them . . . Thy will be done in earth as it is in heaven that we may love Thee with all our hearts, . . . with all our strength devoting every power and faculty of mind and body to the service of Thy Love and to no other end." The thirteenth-century Italian Clare of Assisi worked with Francis. "Go forward . . . on wisdom's path. Believing nothing, agreeing with nothing, which would dissuade you from your resolution. Or which would place a stumbling block for you on your way. So that you may offer your promises to the Most High God, in the pursuit of the Sacred goals to which the Spirit has summoned you." Furthermore, "place your mind before the mind of Eternity! Place your soul in the brilliance of God! Place your heart in the heart of the Divine! And transform your entire being into the image of the Godhead Itself through contemplation."[411]

One of the purposes of the fourteenth-century English mystic Richard Rolle's book, *The Fire of Love*, was to show God's supreme indescribable Love. Divine Love is "a fire which sets our hearts aflame so that they glow and burn, and it purges from them all the foulness of sin." True lovers say, "my God, my Love, surge over me, pierce me by your Love, . . . reveal your healing medicine to your poor lover." Our souls cannot know "the fire of eternal Love," unless they stop worldly vanity of every kind. What we do shows the strength of our love. If we really love the Holy One, our actions will demonstrate it. The purer our love, the closer is the Divine presence to us. "Our worth before God accords with the degree of love in our hearts."[412]

In the fourteenth century, Catherine of Siena wrote about her dialogues with the Divine who is Love. This Italian mystic and reformer described God as eternal, ineffable, immeasurable, unimaginable, unspeakable Love. The Holy One was also joyous Love, infinite Love, and "fiery abyss of Charity." God said to Catherine, "I ask you to love Me with the same love with which I love you." In addition, "all I want is love. In loving Me, you will realize love for your neighbors. . . . service proves your love for Me." Once the soul loses her selfishness, sheds her body, and comes to Me her final goal, "I am One thing with you . . . those who love Me live in Me and I live in them." People whose will has "become One with Me in love" are "made One with Me and I with them."[413]

Meister Eckhart, the fourteenth-century German Dominican, said that God "is nearer to me than I am to myself; He is just as near to wood and stone, but they don't know it." Hence, "thou need not seek Him here or there. He is no farther off than the door of the heart. There He stands and waits and waits until He finds thee ready to open and let Him in." Teresa of Avila, the sixteenth-century Spanish Carmelite nun, said that she understood "how our Lord was in all things, and how He was in the soul, and the illustration of a sponge filled with water was suggested to me." Jacob Boehme, the seventeenth-century German Lutheran shoemaker, said that if "thou conceive a small minute circle, as small as a grain of mustard seed, yet the Heart of God is wholly and perfectly therein; and if thou art born in God, then there is in thy self (in the circle of thy life) the whole Heart of God undivided."[414]

The sixteenth-century Italian mystic Catherine of Genoa experienced union with God and felt the fires of Divine Love. The Divine acts "with pure Love. . . . He loves us and will not ever leave off doing us good." God shows us pure Love that never ceases. This flaming merciful Love "penetrates as deep as hell. . . . In this world, the rays of God's Love . . . encircle man all about, hungrily seeking to penetrate him." God binds the person "to Himself with a fiery Love that by itself could annihilate the immortal soul. In so acting, God so transforms the soul in Him that it knows nothing other than God; and He continues to draw it up into His fiery Love." Catherine saw "rays of lightning darting from that Divine Love to the creature, so intense and fiery." The soul is purified in "the fire of God's Love." Once all its imperfections are cast off, "the soul rests in God. . . . Our being is then God."[415]

Ignatius of Loyola, the sixteenth-century Spanish founder of the Jesuit religious order, said in his *Spiritual Diary* that he felt "deeply within myself . . . the presence of the Father." In his *Spiritual Exercises*, he wanted people to "consider how God dwells in creatures; in the elements, giving them existence; in the plants, giving them life; in the animals, giving them sensations; in human beings, giving them intelligence; and finally, how in this way He dwells also in myself, giving me existence, life, sensation, and intelligence; and even further, making me His temple, since I am created as a likeness and image of His Divinity Majesty."[416]

In the sixteenth century, Teresa of Avila, the Spanish founder of reformed Carmelite convents, described seven dwelling places in her book *The Interior Castle*. The sixth was spiritual betrothal to God. "Often when a person is distracted and forgetful of God, His Majesty will awaken it. His action is as quick as a falling comet." The individual's soul "knows that He is present, . . . it thinks that God is with it." In addition, "God has another way of awakening the soul." He speaks to the soul in many ways. "Some seem to come from outside oneself; others, from deep within the interior part of the soul." Indeed, "the surest signs that they are from God . . . are these: the first and truest is . . . the locutions from God effect what they say. . . . The second sign is the quiet left in the soul . . . the readiness to engage in the praises of God. . . . The third sign is that these words remain in the memory for a very long time."[417]

Brother Lawrence, a seventeenth-century French Carmelite, had experiences of the Divine presence within him. "The holiest, most universal, and most necessary practice in the spiritual life is the presence of God." For more than thirty years, "I occupy myself solely in keeping myself in God's holy presence. I do this simply by keeping my attention on God and by being . . . lovingly aware of Him." Besides calling this "practicing the presence of God moment by moment," Brother Lawrence referred to it as "a silent, secret, and nearly unbroken conversation of the soul with God." He claimed that "we should continue our love relationship with Him, remaining in His holy presence at times by acts of adoration, or praise, or request, and at other times by acts of self-offering, or thanksgiving, or by other means." He recommended that we renounce "everything that was not Himself."[418]

When Brother Lawrence kept himself at rest with God in the center and depth of his soul, he was not afraid of anything. "The more I see my weakness and wretchedness, the more I am caressed by God." The thing that consoled him was that by faith he saw God. "I no longer believe, but I *see* and *experience* what faith teaches." He claimed that "by practicing the presence of God, we have reached our goal of being with Him." He closed many of his letters, "I am in our Lord." Consistently advocating this message, he was always saying the same thing. "If I were a preacher, I would not preach anything else than the practice of the presence of God."[419]

William Blake, the eighteenth-century English poet, described an experience of awakening. "To see the world in a grain of sand and heaven in a wild flower, hold Infinity in the palm of your hand and Eternity in an hour." Rufus Jones, a twentieth-century Quaker, wrote of awakening. "In these highest mystical moments of contact with the real presence of God, there is a sense of having arrived at the goal of life." During the last months of his life, Chardin wrote a friend, "I now live permanently in the presence of God." A contemporary American S.G. McKeever promotes a message in his book, *Paths Are Many, Truth Is One*, about the unity of all religions. "The essence of everyone's spiritual journey" is the trip to God. "The penultimate goal of all spiritual seekers is the experience of direct communion with God." Thus, "the ultimate goal of life is a conscious union with God and Truth." McKeever repeatedly stresses the advanced experience of awakening. "God resides within each of our hearts" as well as "God does exist in everything." Moreover, "the essence of the spiritual journey" is "to become conscious of the living presence of the Infinite and Eternal within our consciousness" at this very moment. "This simple truth, that God exists within man, has been the core of spiritual teachings for thousands of years." His book provides multiple examples from many different religions.[420]

Desmond Tutu, a contemporary South African Anglican Archbishop who fought to end apartheid, says that "God loves us perfectly and infinitely already" as well as "prodigally and without limit." The one central truth is that "God loves me." All of creation is "the consequence of God's Love, the result of the outpouring of this Divine Love and Life that has no beginning and no end. . . . Everything exists because it is loved." In addition, "all can be transformed by the Divine, . . . Everything can communicate the Holy," even everyday things and people. "All can become translucent, a manifestation of God." We are "God-carriers."[421]

Chapter 8

Muhammad and Islamic Mystics' Awakenings

Muhammad's Awakenings

Muhammad ibn Abdallah, the prophet and founder of Islam, had multiple mystical experiences of awakening over more than twenty years. This Arab merchant was a member of the Quraysh tribe, which was a Bedouin tribe that settle in Mecca in Arabia. For many years before his first experience, he retired for a short time to a cave on Mount Hira. There he fasted, prayed, meditated, and gave alms to the poor. In 610 at the age of 40 when he was on one of his spiritual retreats, Muhammad had a mystical experience of the presence of the angel Gabriel who spoke for *Allah*, the Arabic word for God. This mystical experience of awakening made him aware of Allah as the One and only God in contrast to his Arab tribe that worshipped Allah as the High God among many Gods and Goddesses.[422]

Gabriel's first revelation to Muhammad was recorded in the 96th *surah* or chapter of the Islamic Arabic sacred scripture, translated as the *Koran* into English, or to use a more exact transliteration, *Qur'an*, that means recitation. According to the Qur'an, Gabriel told Muhammad to speak for and recite about Allah. "In the name of Allah, the Compassionate, the Merciful. Recite in the name of your Lord, the Creator, who created man from clots of blood! Recite! Your Lord is the Most Bountiful One, who by the pen has taught mankind things they did not know." When he came out of the cave, he heard the same voice say, "O Mohammad! Thou art Allah's messenger, and I am Gabriel!" The Qur'an says that the Night of Power is the night Muhammad received this first message from Allah. "The Night of Power is better than a thousand months."[423]

For over twenty years, Muhammad had mystical experiences of awakening and he received messages from the angel Gabriel that brought him a new consciousness of Allah. For the first few years that he heard these revelations, he thought that despite his own doubts they came from God. When he confided in his wife Khadija, she supported him in that belief that they came from Allah and thus she was his first convert. By 612 after two years of revelations, he began to preach and slowly he gained converts. During Muhammad's spiritual experiences, Gabriel recited revelations to him verse by verse, surah by surah, that later became the Qur'an. He remembered them, but he did not write them down because as the Qur'an says, he could not read or write. "Never have you read a book before this, nor have you ever transcribed one." Receiving these messages was painful for Muhammad. "Never once did I receive a revelation, without thinking that my soul had been torn away from me." These messages taught him that Allah sent apostles and scriptures to the Jews and Christians. He came to believe that he and the Qur'an were Allah's messenger and scripture for the Arabs.[424]

The revelations that Muhammad received from his mystical experiences were memorized, written down, collected during his life, and finally compiled by his disciples into the Qur'an some twenty years after his death. Then and today Muslims consider the Qur'an the verbatim, infallible word of God revealed and dictated to the prophet Muhammad by the angel Gabriel. They read the Qur'an literally. Many Muslims say the Qur'an cannot be translated, because it loses too much. In the Qur'an, Allah repeated a number of times His messenger's purpose and His scripture's content. "Mankind were once one nation. Then Allah sent forth prophets to give them good news and to warn them." The Qur'an covers many subjects including multiple decrees about Allah and about how humans need to believe in Him, relate to Him, and treat others. The opening words give the flavor of the Qur'an. "In the name of Allah, the Compassionate, the Merciful. Praise be to Allah, the Lord of Creation, the Compassionate, the Merciful, the King of Judgment-day!" It continues, "You alone we worship, to You alone we pray for help. Guide us to the straight path, the path of those whom You have favored, not of those who have incurred Your wrath, nor of those who have gone astray."[425]

This theme of two paths is repeated many times in the Qur'an. True believers follow the straight path, the right path, the path of salvation, the path of Allah, by having faith in Him, submitting to Him, putting trust in Him, making a covenant with Him, praying, doing good works, avoiding evil, and giving alms to the poor. As the Qur'an says, "they have done good works, ... praying ..., and sharing their goods with the beggars and the destitute." On the Day of Judgment, this path leads to "the Gardens of Delight," to Paradise. "Those who do good works shall be rewarded with abundant blessings" and "shall dwell in bliss" in heaven. Those unbelievers, wrongdoers, and sinners who follow the other path of affliction and Hell "say one thing and do another," amass worldly riches, fill their life with pleasure, oppose good works, do evil, renounce faith in Allah, invent falsehoods about Him, and believe in other Gods and Goddesses. On the Day of Judgment, "every hardened unbeliever, every opponent of good works, and every doubting transgressor who has set up another God besides Allah" will be "cast into the fierce, tormenting flames" of Hell and drink boiling water.[426]

Ninety-nine Names of Allah and the Five Pillars of Islam

Muhammad's many mystical experiences resulted in multiple different names for Allah in the Qur'an. Different translations of the Qur'an provide different descriptions of those names, such as "to God belong the most beautiful names" or "the fairest names" or "the most excellent names." Two of those names are recorded in the phrase, "in the name of Allah, the Compassionate, the Merciful," that appears at the beginning of every one of the 114 surahs of the Qur'an except one, surah nine. An alternative translation of this phrase is "in the name of Allah, the Beneficent, the Merciful." In addition, Allah is "All-Merciful and All-Love" and "the Mighty, the Praised One, the Sovereign of the heavens and the earth, the Witness of all things." In addition, "Allah is One, the Eternal God. He begot none, nor was He begotten. None is equal to Him." His "Mercy and Compassion embraces all things." Furthermore, "neither on earth nor in heaven shall you escape His reach, nor have you any besides Allah to protect and help you."[427]

The contemporary Islamic scholar Seyyed Hossein Nasr says that "at the heart of Islam stands the reality of God, the One, the Absolute and Infinite, the Infinitely Good and All-Merciful, the One who is at once Transcendent and Immanent, greater than all we can conceive or imagine, yet ... closer to us than our jugular vein. The One God, known by his Arabic name, Allah, is the central reality of Islam." Testifying to Allah's Oneness "lies at the heart of the credo of Islam."[428]

The thirteenth-century Spanish Sufi Muslim mystic Muid ad-Din ibn al-Arabi, hereafter called al-Arabi, said of Allah's most beautiful names, their "number is immeasurable." Traditional Islamic accounts say that the 99 most beautiful names of Allah are derived from the Qur'an, even though the lists in various texts differ. Muslims have a rosary consisting of 99 beads or 33 beads with a tassel that in the past and present they run through their fingers three times to say the 99 names of Allah. Today calligraphic depictions of Allah's 99 names frequently decorate Muslim houses.[429]

In 1904 in Damascus, Muhammad al-Madani presented "the ninety-nine most beautiful names of Allah" from the Qur'an. To provide the flavor, here are the first two of his 99 names, "1. Allah, the Name that is above every name. 2. *al-Awwal*, the First, who was before the beginning." The list of Allah's 99 names of John Baldock, a contemporary scholar of Sufism, the Islamic mystical tradition, claims to include several standard variations. His first two names are "1. *Ar-Rahman* The Compassionate; the Beneficent; the Gracious; the Infinitely Good; the All-Merciful. 2. *Ar-Rahim* The Merciful; the All-Beneficent." Shortening al-Madani's list to only the key English words, it includes Allah, the First, the Last, the Contriver, the Maker, the Beneficent, the Observant, the Spreader, the Inner, the Raiser, the Enduring, the Relenting, the Mighty One, the Majestic, the Gatherer, the Accounter, the Guardian, the Truth, the Judge, the Wise, the Kindly, the Praiseworthy, the Living, the Well-Informed, the Humbler, the Creator, Lord of Majesty and Honor, the Gentle, the Merciful, the Compassionate, the Provider, the Guide who leads believers in the right-minded way, the Exalter, the Watcher, the Peace-Maker, the Hearer, the Grateful, the Witness, the Forbearing, and the Eternal. Those are al-Madani's first forty names of Allah.[430]

Al-Madani's last fifty-nine "most beautiful names of Allah" are the Afflicter, the Outer, the Just, the Sublime, the Mighty, the Pardoner, the Knowing One, the High One, the Forgiving, the Pardoning, the Rich, the Opener, the Seizer, the Able, the Most Holy One, the All-Victorious, the Strong, the Self-Subsistent, the Great One, the Munificent, the Gracious, the Deferrer, the Faithful, the Self-Exalted, the Proud, the Firm, the Originator, the Answerer, the Glorious, the Computer, the Quickener, the Abaser, the Separator, the Fashioner, the Restorer, the Honorer, the Giver, the Enricher, the Well-Furnished, the Prevailer, the Bringer-Forward, the Observer of Justice, the King, the Possessor of the Kingdom, the Causer of Death and Life, the Avenger, the Preserver, the Helper, the Light, the Guide who leads believers in the straight path, the Unique, the Loving, the Inheritor, the Wide-Reaching, the Administrator, the Patron, the Safeguard, the Liberal Giver. The nineteenth-century author Johann Wolfgang von Goethe remarked that if he called God by the Muslim's 99 names, "I shall yet fall short and have said nothing in comparison to the boundlessness of His attributes." In his 1880 article in the *Journal of the Royal Asiatic Society*, Redhouse collected from various lists 552 different names for Allah.[431]

Most descriptions in the Qur'an present Allah's Oneness and other attributes. Some portray His presence. "He is God in heaven and God on earth." Truthful people who believe in Allah and His apostle "shall testify in their Lord's presence." Allah warns them, "do not dispute My presence," and advises, "when My servants question you about Me, tell them that I am near." When they call to Him, He answers their prayers and wants them to answer His call. Sinners "seek to hide themselves from men, but they cannot hide themselves from Allah. He is with them when they utter in secret what does not please Him."[432]

A *hadith* or saying of Muhammad has Allah say, "I was a hidden treasure, I wanted to be known. Hence, I created the world so that I might be known." The world is an epiphany of Allah. As the Qur'an says, "to those whose faith is firm We have already revealed Our signs." Muslims need to see signs of Allah in the natural world. "In the creation of the heavens and of the earth and the succession of night and day and in the ships that speed through the sea with what is useful to men; and in the waters which God sends down from the sky, giving life thereby to the earth after it has been lifeless, and causing all manner of living creatures to multiply thereon; and in the change of the winds, and the clouds that run their appointed courses between sky and earth: in all this there are signs (*ayat*) indeed for a people who use their reason."[433]

Muhammad became awakened to Allah's presence everywhere as well as to the Divine presence within all people and things. As the Qur'an says, "to Allah belongs the east and west. Whichever way you turn, there is the Face of Allah. He is omnipresent and all-knowing." In addition, "to Allah belongs all that the heavens and the earth contain." Furthermore, "we will show them Our signs in all the regions of the earth and in their own souls, until they clearly see that this is the truth." Two of the 99 names of Allah also reflect this. Al-Madani's ninth name is "the Inner, who is immanent within all things" and his forty-second name is "the Outer, who is without as well as within."[434]

Muhammad learned a number of lessons from his mystical experiences, including what beliefs and practices that Allah wants. Belief in the One God, Allah, was his first and foremost teaching. Contemporary Islamic author I.A. Ibrahim says that "the Arabic word Allah occurs in the Qur'an more than 2,150 times." The Qur'an says, "we are God's and unto Him we shall return" and "there is no refuge from God but in Him." A hadith says, "whoever loves to meet God, God loves to meet him." Muhammad and His followers were also to believe in angels, the books that Allah revealed to

His messengers, all his prophets and messengers, the Last Day of Judgment, Divine predestination, and human free will. As the Qur'an says, "believers, have faith in Allah and His apostle, in the Book He has revealed to His apostle, and in the Scriptures He formerly revealed. He that denies Allah, His angels, His Scriptures, His apostle, and the Last Day, has strayed far from the truth."[435]

From his mystical experiences, Muhammad learned the five pillars as the framework for the practices for a Muslim's life. The Qur'an teaches these pillars: the testimony of faith; prayer five times a day at dawn, midday, afternoon, evening, and night; almsgiving to the needy; fasting during the month of Ramadan; and a pilgrimage to Mecca once in a lifetime if possible. The first and most important pillar is the testimony of faith called *Shahadah*. "There is no God but Allah and Muhammad is His prophet." To convert to Islam, this creed must be said with conviction. The Qur'an has many proclamations about prayer, the second pillar, including "when you have performed prayer, remember God. . . . Surely the prayer is a timed prescription for the believers." In addition, "remember your Lord deep in your soul with humility and reverence, and without ostentation."[436]

The third pillar is almsgiving, charitable contributions to kin, the needy, orphans, beggars, travelers, and to free slaves. The following statement from the Qur'an describes true piety. This is also translated as righteousness and being upright. It also summarizes a number of the beliefs and pillars. "True piety is this: to believe in God, and the Last Day, the angels, the Book, and the prophets; to give of one's substance, however cherished, to kinsmen, and orphans, the needy, the traveler, beggars; to ransom the slave; to perform the prayer; and to pay the alms." It continues, "And they who fulfill their covenant, . . . and endure with fortitude misfortune, hardship and peril, these are they who are true in their faith, these are truly God-fearing." Fasting is the fourth pillar. "The month of Ramadam was the time in which the Qur'an was sent down as guidance for mankind. . ., let him take up the fast throughout it." The fifth is the pilgrimage to Mecca, if possible. "Make the pilgrimage and visit the Sacred House for His sake" and "proclaim among men the pilgrimage."[437]

Awakenings of Islamic Mystics Called Sufis

Sufism is "the mystical heart of Islam," according to Baldock. Sufi mystics wanted to have spiritual experiences of Allah like Muhammad did. Not content with only outward conformity to Islamic law and practices, they quest for mystical consciousness of Allah. Sufis are Muslims who work to master themselves so that they are not governed by their egos and 'lower selves.' Travelling the Sufi path and transforming their awareness, they are guided by their 'higher self.' Attaining mystical experiences of awakening, they abandon themselves to the Divine Unity.[438]

Baldock says that the Arabic word *jihad* is often translated as holy war. It derives from a root word meaning to 'struggle,' 'strive,' or 'exert.' In its outer meaning, "jihad refers to the defense of Islam and the Islamic community." In its inner sense, it means "self-purification and the 'war' against the ego or lower self." For Muhammad, the lesser holy war was the conflict with external enemies. The greater holy war was facing the conflicts within the self. A Sufi sees his inner world according to a hadith or saying of Muhammad. "Whoever knows himself knows his Lord." A thirteen century Persian named Mahmud Shabistari described a Sufi as "a seeker of Unity, a soul freed from the shackles of himself." Sufis "have renounced good and evil. . . . They have cast away all thoughts of name and fame, . . . They fall, and rise again, between union and separation. Now shedding tears of blood, now rising up to a world of bliss . . . Now a mystic whirl, dancing in the arms of their Beloved. . . . they are blind to this world, indifference to great and small, . . . Who are these guys?—They are Sufis."[439]

One of the aims of Sufis is to replace their own qualities with Allah's 99 most beautiful names. One of Muhammad's hadith said, "pattern yourselves on God's characteristics." Another said, "God has 99 characteristics; whosoever patterns himself on one of them, enters Paradise." One Sufi method is to immerse themselves in Allah's attributes by using the Islamic rosary to recite His 99 names. Another practice is for a Sufi spiritual master called *shaykh* to prescribe for his disciple one of Allah's names as well as the number of times he is to repeat the name. Sufi writers employ powerful symbols to explain the Divine Unity. One symbol is the human as lover and Allah as the Beloved. Another symbol is the individual human as a drop of water and the ocean as the Divine Unity. An Islamic writer Bustan of Sa'di said, "a single drop of rain fell from a cloud in the sky, but was filled with shame when it saw the sea so wide. 'Next to the sea then, who am I?'"[440]

According to Baldock, the Sufi way is "a practical path of transformation and fulfillment which enables us to free ourselves from the veils of ego, to unite the inner and outer worlds, and to discover the unified self within." The *raison d' etre* of the Sufi path is to transform our consciousness, awaken us to the inner world, and apprehend the Divine Reality. The goal of the Sufi way is "for the drop (the individual self) to merge with the Ocean of Being from whence it came." Everyone experiences this at death. Sufis try to make this transition consciously before death. "Die before you die" is a Sufi saying. Thus, Sufis attempt to die to whom they have been conditioned to think they are, so that they might become who they are capable of becoming. "The path is crowned by that illuminating knowledge … which in Sufism is never separated from love."[441]

Rabi'a al-Adawiyah, hereafter called Rabi'a, was "one of the most famous woman saints of Islam and a prominent figure in the Sufi tradition." This saint or friend of Allah was an ascetic Sufi, a flute player, and a former slave from Basra, Iraq, who died in 801. The theme of her writings was love. Approaching Allah as her Lover, she wrote, "O my Lord, the stars are shining and the eyes of men are closed, and kings have shut their doors, and every lover is alone with his beloved, and here am I alone with Thee." In addition, "my love for God so possessed me that no place remains for loving or hating any save Him."[442]

In a poem that is still recited today, Rabi'a wrote, "I love Thee in two ways: one selfishly, the other a love that is worthy of Thee. It is selfish love when I spend all my time thinking exclusively of Thee and no other. The other love is when the veil is raised by Thee, thus revealing Thyself to me. Neither way am I praiseworthy. In both the praise is all Thine." One of her famous prayers is: "O God! If I worship Thee from fear of Hell, burn me in Hell; and if I worship Thee from hope of Paradise, exclude me from Paradise; but if I worship Thee for Thy own sake, then withhold not Thy eternal Beauty." Another prayer is, "O Lord! Whatever share of this world You could give to me, give it to Your enemies; and whatever share of the next world You want to give to me, give it on Your friends. You are enough for me."[443]

Many stories about Rabi'a show her speaking with a striking directness to those who came to her because of her piety and renown. Asked, "where do you come from?" Rabi'a answered, "from the other world." To the follow up question, "and where are you going?" she replied, "to the other world." Speaking with a thirty-year-old man who was wearing a bandage around his head, she asked, "why are you wearing that bandage?" After he answered that his head hurt, she asked if his life involved much pain and suffering, to which he answered no. Then she said, "for thirty years you have enjoyed good health and yet you never once wrapped yourself in the bandage of gratefulness. But as soon as your head hurts you put on the bandage of complaint!" When Rabi'a was ill, a leading scholar visited her. Her response to his continually vilifying the world was, "if you weren't so attached to the world you would have nothing to say about it, good or bad. … if you really love something you never stop talking about it." After Salih of Qazwin told his followers, "knock, and the door will be opened," Rabi'a responded to him. "It has never been shut." Since she thought your actions should not be motivated by desire for reward, she said, "conceal your good deeds, as you conceal your evil deeds."[444]

In the eighth century, Shaqiq of Balkh was a successful Persian merchant until he gave away all his possessions. Then he became a Sufi mystic and lived an ascetic life. As a living example of the spiritual state, he taught what he learned from his awakening. Stressing trusting Allah, Shaqiq explained three things you need to practice. First, "with your mind and your tongue and your actions you declare God to be One" and "you devote all your actions to Him alone." Second, "you should trust Him more than the world or money or uncle or father or mother or anyone on the face of the earth." Third, after you do the two above things, "it behooves you to be satisfied with Him and not to be angry on account of anything that vexes you. . . . Let your heart be with Him always."[445]

Dhu 'I-Nun al-Mesri, a ninth-century Egyptian Sufi, prayed about the Divine presence in nature. "O God, I never hearten to the voices of the beasts or the rustle of the trees, the splashing of the waters or the song of the birds, the whistling of the wind or the rumble of thunder, but I sense in them a testimony to Thy Unity and a proof of Thy Incomparableness: that Thou art the All-prevailing, the All-knowing, the All-wise, the All-just, the All-true, . . . O God, I acknowledge Thee in the proof of Thy handiwork and the evidence of Thy acts." After trying to find God by praying and fasting and getting nowhere, a ninth-century Persian Sufi named Bayazid al-Bistami asked, "O God, what is the way to Thee?" The reply came, "leave yourself behind, and come to Me." Baba Kubi of Shiraz, an eleventh-century Persian, described his mystical experience. "In the market, in the cloister—only God I saw. In the valley and on the mountain—only God I saw. Him I have seen beside me oft in tribulation; in favor and in fortune—only God I saw. In prayer and fasting, in praise and contemplation, in the religion of the Prophet—only God I saw."[446]

Abu Hamid Muhammad al-Ghazali, an eleventh-century Persian Sufi theologian and philosopher, said, "what is distinctive of mysticism is something which cannot be apprehended by study, but only by immediate experience . . ., by ecstasy and by moral change." There is a difference "between knowing the definition of health and satiety, together with their causes and presuppositions, and being healthy and satisfied! . . . Similarly, there is a difference between knowing the true nature and causes of the ascetic life and actually leading such a life and forsaking the world." What he desired was not attained by study "but only by immediate experience and by walking the mystic way." Through his experience he saw that "all things are a ray of the essential Light of God. . . . The one real Light is God."[447]

Earlier when he was a teacher, Al-Ghazali taught worldly success. Now "I am calling men to the knowledge whereby worldly success is given up and its low point in the scale of real worth is recognized." We need "to clean the well of the psyche of the polluted rubbish which constantly flows into it by the social currents." Learning from the Sufis, he said that "if you do not put yourself to work for the good," you will be preoccupied with evil. Speaking about his own death, he said that my brethren think I am this corpse that you bury. "I swear by God, this dead one is not I. When I had formal shape, then this, my body, served as my garment. I wore it a while. . . .. A bird I am: this body was my cage but I have flown, leaving it as a token."[448]

Shihab al-Din Yahya al-Suhrawardi, a twelfth-century Iranian Sufi, described his mystical experience of awakening. "Suddenly I was wrapped in gentleness; there was a blinding flash, then a diaphanous light in the likeness of a human being. I watched attentively and there He was." Continuing, "He came towards me, greeting me so kindly that my bewilderment faded and my alarm gave way to the feeling of familiarity. And then I began to complain to Him of the trouble I had with this problem of knowledge. 'Awaken to yourself,' He said to me, 'and your problem will be solved.'"[449]

The thirteenth-century Spanish Sufi mystic al-Arabi was called the Great Master. This author of more than 250 books had a vision of a young girl named Nizam, who was surrounded by a heavenly aura. His interpretation of his vision was that she was an incarnation of *Sophia* or Divine Wisdom. This epiphany had a long lasting, profound effect on him. Nizam became "the object of my quest and my hope, the Virgin Most Pure." Realizing that you cannot love God if you only use philosophy's rational arguments, he said, "if you love a being for his beauty, you love none other than God, for He *is* the Beautiful Being." Therefore, when you love humans and other parts of creation in all their aspects, "the object of love is God alone." In a collection of his poems, the *Diwan*, he said, "I never cease to allude to the Divine inspirations, the spiritual visitations, the correspondences [of our world] with the world of Angelic Intelligences. In this I conformed to my usual manner of thinking in symbols; because the things of the invisible world attract me more than those of actual life."[450]

"The Oneness of Being," . . . also referred to as the "Unity of Being" was one of al-Arabi's themes. God said, "listen! I am the Reality of the world, the Center of the circle. I am the Parts and the Whole. . . . I call again and again but you do not hear Me, I appear again and again but you do not see Me." God continued, "Love Me, love yourself in Me. No one is deeper within you than I. Others may love you for their own sake, but I love you for yourself. If you take one step toward Me, it is only because I have taken a hundred toward you. I am closer to you than yourself. . . . I want you to see Me—and no one else."[451]

According to al-Arabi, "knowledge of mystical states can only be had by actual experience, nor can the reason of man define it, . . . as is also the case with knowledge of the taste of honey, the bitterness of patience, the bliss of sexual union, love, passion, or desire, all of which cannot possibly be known unless one experiences them directly." The person "who unites in his knowledge of Deity both Transcendence and Immanence in a universal way, even though it is not possible to know such a thing in detail because of the infinitude of cosmic forms, nevertheless knows Him in a general way, just as he may know himself." Another theme of al-Arabi's was the 'Perfect Man' who is a male or female and who is "a pure, clean, absolute mirror" of God who is Absolute Beauty. "Having realized his/her full potential as a human being, the Perfect Man embodies the Real and thus serves as a bridge . . . between the two worlds: heaven and earth, or Divine and human."[452]

Seeing the Divine in all of creation, al-Arabi said, "God made the creatures like veils, . . . he who knows them as such is led back to Him, but he who takes them as real is barred from His presence." Calling the Holy One 'the Cloud' or 'the Blindness,' he said, "the whole reality of God is unknowable." It follows from this that since no one can know the whole truth about God, no one religion can either. As al-Arabi said, "do not attach yourself to any particular creed, so that you may disbelieve all the rest, otherwise you will lose much good, nay, you will fail to recognize the real truth of the matter. God, the Omnipresent and Omnipotent, is not limited by any one creed, for . . . 'wherever you turn, there is the face of Allah,'" as the Quran says. Being open to all faiths, he said, "my heart is capable of every form. It is a pasture for gazelles, a monastery for Christian monks, . . . I follow the religion of Love. Whatever way Love's camel takes, that is my religion and my faith."[453]

Jalal-al-Din Rumi, hereafter called Rumi, was a Persian who lived most of his thirteenth- century life in Turkey. Known to his disciples as Master, he was a Sufi mystic, poet, teacher, theologian, who is frequently read today. His poem named the *Masnawi* was and is called the Sufi Bible. In addition, he was the founder of the most famous of the Sufi orders called *Mawlawiyyah*. Its members were known as the 'whirling dervishes' because they used dance as a method of concentration. As the Sufis spun around continuously, they felt the boundaries of selfhood dissolve as they melted into their dance. This gave them a foretaste of *fana*, the annihilation of the self, and "the ecstatic absorption in God." Rumi described being awake with both the eyes and the heart. "There are many whose eyes are awake and whose hearts are asleep; . . . But he who keeps his heart awake will know and live this Mystery; . . . his heart will open hundreds of eyes. . . . Be awake always, be a seeker of the heart, be at war continually with your carnal soul." In addition, "foment a restlessness in the heart of the one who thinks only of bread! . . . Close those eyes that see only faults, open those that contemplate the Invisible, so no mosques or temples or idols remain, so 'this' or 'that' is drowned in His fire."[454]

According to Rumi, "infinite mercy flows continually," but people are asleep and can't see it. When an individual awakens, he frantically "runs continually here and there," thinking the goal is further on. "It's this false thinking that blocks him from the path that leads to himself" and the Ultimate Reality. "The paths are many, but the goal is one." The variety of roads is immense and the differences between them are infinite. "However, they are all in harmony and are one." Once travelers arrive at their goal which is God, "all quarreling and vicious squabbling about the different paths" and saying, 'you're wrong,' vanishes. "They realize that what they were fighting about was the road only, and that the goal was one." Rumi said, "I will hunt for the Beloved with all my power and all my strength and passion. . . . God has told us, He is with us." He is always so extremely close to me. Unfortunately, my heart "cannot understand this except slowly and indirectly, after I have "accomplished many journeys and fulfilled the path's duties."[455]

Rumi claimed, "nearness to God is common to us all, because we're all created and sustained by God, but only the authentically noble possess and live that nearness that's a constant upswelling passion of love." In addition, "a true seeker must transcend those joys and delights that are just the ray and reflection of the glory of God. He must not let himself grow content with such things, even though they are of God, come from God's grace, and are of the radiance of God's beauty, for they are not eternal." A person needs to know that "the world of created things is like pure and limpid water in which shines the attributes of the Omnipotent One." While the water in the river changes innumerable times, the Divine attributes of Consciousness, Mercy, and Justice are "changeless and eternal."[456]

God said to Rumi, "I brought you, your time, your breath, your possessions, your lives. If you dedicate these things to Me, their value is eternal Paradise. This is what I think you are worth." Do not sell yourself at a small price. "You are more precious than both heaven and earth." Rumi prayed, "O my Beloved! Take me, liberate my soul, fill me with Your Love, and release me from both worlds. When I set my heart on anything but You, a fire burns me from inside. . . . Take away everything that takes me from You." Allah said, "for Indians, the language of India's admirable. . . . I do not consider the tongue and its words; I look at the spirit and character. I look into the heart to see if it's evil; the heart's the essence, . . . the essence is what matters. . . . Fire your soul with the passion of adoration: destroy with this fire all thought and expression. . . . The religion of love differs from all other religions; for lovers God is their religion and their faith."[457]

Rumi said, "last night I learned how to be a lover of God, to live in this world and call nothing my own. I looked inward. . . . Heaven calls me . . . a hundred thousand cries, yet I cannot hear. . . . All I hear is the call of my Beloved." His advice was that "there is a force within that gives you life—seek that. O wandering Sufi, if you are in search of the greatest treasure, don't look outside, look inside, and seek that." His other advice was to "rejoice in Him and nothing else but Him. He is spring; all other things are winter. Everything other than Him drags you slowly to damnation." When children and youth go the carefree way, they find only traps. "Set out now, while you're strong, on the heart's vast plain: you'll never discover joy on the plain of the body. The heart's the only house of safety, . . . There's where you'll find trees and streams of Living Water."[458]

One of Rumi's insights was that your yearning for the Divine is actually God's message to you. A prophet Khidra said, God told me to say to you, "Wasn't it I . . . who made you busy with My Name? Your calling out, 'Allah, Allah!' was My 'Here I am!' Your longing for Me was My messenger to you." Rumi offered the extremely important insight that life is NOW, in this present moment. The carnal self "has stolen every life and mirrors for you a theater of false tomorrows. The whole of life is now, is today, is this eternal moment. Never listen . . . to the promises of this trickster. Untie the knot of existence and reign in your fantasies so you can at last escape the tyrannical false self." Rumi said, "how can I—or anyone else—ever cease being astonished that He whom nothing can contain is contained in the heart?" Furthermore, "the root of the entire matter is love. So when you feel love hot within you, . . . when you feel the goal of all things—the quest for God—to be alive in you," search passionately further and deeper. Moreover, "I see the world radiant and brimming with magnificence, . . . my mind and consciousness reel with bliss."[459]

A fifteenth-century Muslim Persian named Jami said about Allah, "various grades of created things are theaters of His revealed beauty, and all things that exist are mirrors of His perfections." Thus, "all through eternity God unveils His exquisite form. . . . Wherever God looks, Love is always there; . . . God and Love are as body and soul. God is the mine, Love is the diamond."[460]

Malcolm Little, who was later called Malcolm X, was a twentieth-century thief and drug pusher who went to prison where he learned about and later joined the Nation of Islam, an African American Muslim group. After becoming one of its leaders and serving it for years, he became disillusioned with its top leader but not with Islam. Before his assassination, he made an Islamic pilgrimage to Mecca in 1964 where he had an awakening that he described in a letter. "Never have I witnessed such sincere hospitality and overwhelming spirit of true brotherhood. . . . For the past week, I have been utterly speechless and spellbound by the graciousness I see displayed all round me by people of *all colors*. I have been blessed.. . . . We are all participating in the same ritual, displaying a spirit of unity and brotherhood. . ... We were *truly* all the same—because their belief in one God has removed the 'white' from their *minds*, . . . from their *behavior*, and . . . from their *attitude*."[461] Malcolm X continued, "each hour here in the Holy Land enables me to have greater spiritual insight. . . . as racism leads America up the suicide path, I do believe, . . . the whites of the younger generation . . . will turn to the spiritual path of *truth*—the *only* way left to America to ward off the disaster that racism inevitably must lead to."[462]

Chapter 9

Love for Our Neighbors and Ourselves Is the Fourth Stage

Awakening Leads to Love for Our Neighbors and Ourselves

The key to awakening is to develop our consciousness of the Holy One. An advanced step is an awareness that Infinite Love is within me as my inner core of love, that the Divine is within all people, and that the Holy One is within all of reality. Awakening produces love, because when we realize that we are all Sacred, we want to love our neighbors and ourselves. This love is the fourth stage on the mystical way to the Divine.

Awakening produces love. Then our love opens us up to a new awakening. This causes a back and forth movement, an oscillation, between awakening and love.

> Our awakening produces love for our neighbors and ourselves.
> Our love creates to a new awakening.

Spirituality produces love. Our glimpse of Infinite Love within us as our inner core of love makes us want to express love for our neighbors and ourselves. Once we are better able to love people, we love the Holy One more deeply and experience a more profound awakening. Contemporary religious expert Karen Armstrong says that "all faiths insist that compassion is the test of true spirituality." Compassion "brings us into relationship with the Transcendence," that we call God, Brahman, Tao, Nirvana, Trinity, and Allah.[463]

Spirituality produces a genuine morality that is a way of life that promotes life and love. The source of our moral conscience is our loving inner core. We are to act only out of love because that is what we are, because that is our human nature. Since mystical experiences makes us aware of our loving inner core, they help deepen our moral conscience. An ethical life affirms, preserves, fosters, and creates more life and love in our everyday lives and in the future. To decide the morality of actions, business practices, political choices, and careers, the ultimate criterion is whether they create or harm love and life. Ethical people are co-creators of love with the Sacred Spirit. The twentieth century scientist Albert Einstein said that "morality is of the highest importance—but for us, not for God." It is "a purely human matter, albeit the most important" for people. The contemporary Buddhist leader, the Dalai Lama, says, "whether a person is a religious believer does not matter much. Far more important is that they are a good human being." In the Hindu scripture *Bhagavad Gita*, the Divine Krishna said, the Spirit Supreme, Brahman, is "attained by an ever-living love. In Him all things have their life, and from Him all things have come."[464]

Whatever denies, diminishes, distorts, injures, or destroys love and life is unethical. To be immoral is not to be loving and to harm ourselves, other people, and nature. To be unethical is to act contrary to our human nature, to our loving inner core, to our spirit, to the Divine within us.

Spirituality produces a minimum of ethical actions and a maximum of a lifelong vocation of love. It assists us in nurturing loving individuals and creating communities of love. Our ultimate mission is to help make the world a better, more loving place. Thus, we are called to work for a cause larger than ourselves. Through our vocation that is precious to us, we devote ourselves to the cause of serving humanity by spreading respect, caring, equality, liberty, justice, and love for everyone. Thinking locally and globally, we act locally and globally. Our vocation is not to remain ignorant about existing injustices or to be unaware of them or to stand by and do nothing. Our mission is to take nonviolent action to prevent and eliminate inequality and injustice. We are the bearer of Divine Love.

According to Armstrong, compassion is "an attitude of principled, consistent altruism" that is "summed up in the Golden Rule." Each faith has "formulated its own version of what is called the Golden Rule, 'do not treat others as you would not like them to treat you,' or in its positive form, 'always treat others as you would wish to be treated yourself.'" In addition, these faiths insist that "you cannot confine your benevolence to your own group; you must have concern for everybody—even your enemies."

Unfortunately, some religious leaders "rarely speak of compassion but focus instead on such secondary matters" as doctrines and rules for sexual behavior, "implying that a correct stance on these issues—rather than the Golden Rule—is the criterion of true faith." Many have scant regard for compassion even though our world is threatened by an enormous imbalance of a few elite who are fabulously wealthy, while billions of people suffer in cruel poverty, with widespread violence, and with environmental catastrophes, such as tremendous hurricanes, flooding, and wild fires. Armstrong recommends that we support and act on the 2009 Charter for Compassion that says, "the principle of compassion lies at the heart of all religious, ethical, and spiritual traditions, calling us to always treat all others as we wish to be treated ourselves."[465]

The world's spiritual traditions have versions of the Golden Rule. In the seventh century BCE, Zoroaster, a Persian prophet, founded Zoroastrianism. This religion asserted that "whatever is disagreeable to yourself, do not do unto others." The Buddhist scriptures said, "hurt not others with that which pains yourself." In addition, "hate is not conquered by hate, hate is conquered by love. That is a law eternal." After its founding in the fifth century BCE, Indian Jainism's scripture said, "a man should wander about treating all creatures as he himself would be treated."[466]

When Jan Yung asked about how to become a human-at-his-best, also called a superior person or a gentleman or a great person, Confucius answered, "do not do to others what you would not desire yourself. Then you will have no enemies either in the state or in your home." Another time a disciple asked, "is there one word that will keep us on the path to the end of our days?" Confucius responded, "yes. Reciprocity! What you do not wish yourself, do not unto others." A similar idea was expressed by one of Confucius' disciples. "If a great man is faultlessly respectful, if he is humble within the rites to his fellow men, then in the whole, wide world, all are his brothers."[467]

In the Hindu *Gita*, the Divine Krishna spoke to his disciple Arjuna about the connection between awakening and love. "God is in all, . . . He is within all and He is outside of all. He is the ONE in all. . . . And when a man sees that the God in himself is the same God in all that is, he hurts not himself by hurting others; then he goes indeed to the highest path." Be a yogi, "because the yogi goes beyond those who follow the path of the austere [the ascetics], or of wisdom, or of work. And the greatest of all yogis is he who with all his soul has faith, and he who with his soul loves Me." As "men love Me in the same way, they find My Love; for many are the paths of men, but they all in the end come to Me." Those who have "the same loving mind for all . . . reach in truth My very Self." Another Hindu scripture said, "this is the sum of duty: do naught unto others what you would not have them do unto you."[468]

In Deuteronomy in the Jewish Bible, God had Moses teach, "hear, O Israel: The Lord our God, The Lord is One. You shall love the Lord your God with all your heart, and with all your soul, and with all your might." In Leviticus, the Lord spoke to Moses saying, "you shall not hate in your heart anyone of your kin; you shall not reprove your neighbor; you shall not take vengeance or bear a grudge against any of your people, but you shall love your neighbor as yourself." The first century Jewish Rabbi Hillel said, "what is hateful to yourself do not do to your fellow man. This is the whole Torah. All the rest is commentary."[469]

The Jewish teacher Jesus who founded Christianity called two of the Hebrew Bible's commandments the greatest and he taught them. In all three of the synoptic gospels, Jesus said, "'you shall love the Lord your God with all your heart, and with all your soul, and with all your mind.' This is the greatest and first commandment. And a second is like it: 'you shall love your neighbor as yourself.' On these two commandments hang all the law and the prophets." In John's gospel, Jesus said, "I give you a new commandment, that you love one another. Just as I have loved you, you also should love one another. By this everyone will know that you are my disciples, if you have love for one another." Later he repeated this, "this is my commandment, that you love one another as I have loved you. No one has greater love than this, to lay down one's life for one's friends." Besides these commandments, Jesus taught the Golden Rule. "In *everything* do to others as you would have them do to you; for this is the law and the prophets." Notice that he said, do this in everything you do.[470]

Muhammad had spiritual experiences of Allah who taught him to express love. The Quran said that "by the light of day, and by the fall of night, your Lord has not forsaken you, nor does He abhor you. . . . You shall be gratified with what your Lord will give you. Did He not find you an orphan and give you shelter? Did He not find you in error and guide you? Did He not find you poor and enrich you?" Furthermore, "therefore do not wrong the orphan, nor chide away the beggar. But proclaim the goodness of your Lord." The Quran also explained the consequences of goodness and love. "For him that gives in charity and guards himself against evil and believes in goodness, We shall smooth the path of salvation; but for him that neither gives nor takes and disbelieves in goodness, We shall smooth the path of affliction." The Islamic *Traditions of Mohammed* said, "no one of you is a believer until he loves for his neighbor what he loves for himself."[471]

An eighteenth-century Bahai writing observed, "if thine eyes be turned to justice, choose thou for thy neighbor that which thou choose for thyself." A proverb of the Yoruba tribe in Nigeria said, "one going to take a pointed stick to pinch a baby bird should first try it on himself to feel how it hurts."

Albert Schweitzer, the twentieth-century Christian scholar, theologian, and medical missionary in Africa, said that "in religion there are two different currents: one free from dogma and one that is dogmatic. That which is free from dogma bases itself on the preaching of Jesus; the dogmatic bases itself on creeds of the early church and the reformation. . . . The religion of love taught by Jesus is non-dogmatic, so that it can be adopted in any age."[472]

Learning Self-love

Underhill claimed that the stage between awakening and illumination is not love but purification or purgation, although she claimed that it could be referred to "under one symbol or another." In my mystical way, the fourth stage between awakening and illumination is love for our neighbors and ourselves. In my mind, her stage of purifying is part of learning to love ourselves. In order to love ourselves, we need to purge our egotism and other negative traits. As Underhill said, the newly awakened self needs the "long slow process of transcendence, of character building," and learning to love, in order to reach higher stages on the mystical way. "Activity is now to be her watchword, pilgrimage the business of her life." Our spiritual existence is "an endless becoming" and a series of purifications to get rid of our selfishness and to help the finite self slowly approach the nature of the Infinite Source.[473]

Learning to love is a perpetual process that involves first purifying ourselves by "getting rid of all those elements" of our old life "which are not in harmony with Reality" and not in sync with our inner core of love, including "illusion, evil, imperfection of every kind" as well as a self-centered life, wrong values, materialistic desires, negative thoughts, critical words, mean actions, prejudice, hatred, exploitation, dominating behaviors, abuse, cruelty, violence, and "those superfluous, unreal, and harmful things which dissipate" our precious energies. "It is not love but lust . . . the very food of selfhood—which poisons the relation between the self and the external world."[474]

Once we awaken to the Divine Goodness and Perfection, we become more conscious of the wrongdoings, imperfections, mistakes, and the shortcomings of our thoughts, feelings, words, values, and deeds. Most of us crave finite material goods, even though we are born for the Infinite. We act selfishly, even though we are basically loving. We behave as rugged individualists who are only concerned with ourselves as number one, even though we are essentially interconnected with all people and nature. When we become aware of the Sacred Spirit, our wrong, immoral activities cause us to experience sadness and distress. We alternate between ecstatic consciousness of the Holy One and the sorrow and pain about our imperfect behavior and actions. We oscillate between our happiness about experiencing Infinite Love and our grief over the limits of our own love.

A recurrent theme in Mother Teresa's private writings and speaking was the "mystery of God's Greatness and her nothingness," the Divine Goodness and her selfishness. "In my meditations and prayer, . . . there stands one thing very clear—my weakness and His Greatness." She felt, "God is calling me—unworthy and sinful that I am." Referring to "all my many great sins," she said, "I am really unworthy of all He is doing for me and in me." Feeling "so terribly helpless," she said, "I am a little nothing," but I long to take away all His suffering.[475]

Seeing herself as selfish and proud, Mother Teresa said, "I want to be all for Jesus. . . . Many times this goes upside—down—so my most reverend 'I' gets the most important place." I am always the same proud person. "By nature, I am sensitive, love beautiful and nice things, and all that comfort can give—to love and be loved—I know that the life of a Missionary of Charity will be minus all these. The complete poverty, the Indian life, the life of the poorest will mean a hard toil against my great self-love." Mother Teresa felt inadequate. "I feel sometimes afraid, for I have nothing, no brains, no learning, no qualities required for such a work, and yet I tell Him that my heart . . . belongs completely to Him and Him alone." She did not want her ignorance and inadequacies to prevent her from doing God's will perfectly. When she was trying to get church approval for her new order of nuns, the Missionaries of Charity, she told the archbishop to "think not of me—for I am very sinful and most unworthy of His love—but just only to think of Him and the love He would receive from the sisters and the souls under their care."[476]

Answering Jesus, Mother Teresa said, "I am so afraid.—This fear shows me how much I love myself.—I am afraid of the suffering that will come—through leading that Indian life . . . living with them and never having anything my way." Feeling that material comforts had taken possession of her heart, she told Jesus, "I am so stupid—I do not know what to say—but do with me whatever You wish—as You wish—as long as You wish." Ten years after founding the Missionaries of Charity, she said, "my greatest humiliation and daily sacrifice I have to make continually is meeting people, priests. How horrible I feel inside when I have to speak to people. With the sisters and the poor, I don't feel like that." Speaking of God, she said, "it is His work, and not my work. I am only at His disposal. Without Him I can do nothing." Often she felt "like a little pencil in God's hands. He does the writing. He does the thinking. He does the movement, I have only to be the pencil." That made her "realize His tender concern for me and my nothingness—His fullness and my emptiness—His infinite love and my childlike love." In addition, "it is only when we realize our nothingness, our emptiness, that God can fill us with Himself. When we become full of God, then we can give God to others."[477]

After becoming conscious of our imperfections, we need not only to work to stop our wrong thinking and behaviors but also to transform ourselves. We need to do this by getting in touch with our inner core of love and by learning to love ourselves. An honest appraisal of our positive and negative traits is a place to begin. Constantly criticizing our negatives is counter-productive and only produces sadness and depression. No human is perfect. We all have faults.

The first step to become loving toward ourselves is to accept ourselves as we are with all our shortcomings and excellent qualities. After that, we can work to improve and transform ourselves.

As Underhill said, changing ourselves is "a process, an education directed toward the production of . . . a new life." Transforming ourselves is a lifelong process. An image that helps explain our transformation is to picture our soul as a mirror covered with dirt. We need to clean the mirror so that we can see the Divine within ourselves. Transformation helps us see Infinite Love within us as our inner core. After awakening, our immoral actions and sins causes us to feel sorry and repent. We want to remove all that stands between ourselves and goodness. Gradually we try to get rid of all that is not in harmony with our progress toward illumination and union with the Divine by shedding our selfishness, materialistic desires, egotistical feelings, unsupportive words, negative thoughts, critical judgments, wrong values, hostile actions, prejudice, contempt, hatred, manipulation, exploitation, controlling behaviors, abuse, cruelty, and violence. Some of the many ways to strip away our harmful behavior that causes suffering are confession, contrition, repenting, doing penance, making amends, and forgiving ourselves.[478]

Underhill said that "it is in this torment of contrition, this acute consciousness of unworthiness, that we have the first swing back of the oscillating self from the initial state of mystic pleasure to the complementary state of pain." In the fourteenth century, German Dominican Henry Suso said, "come, my soul, depart from outward things and gather thyself together into a true interior silence that thou may set out with all thy courage and bury and lose thyself in the desert of deep contrition." In the sixteen century, the Spanish Carmelite nun Teresa of Avila said that the "burning of love into the soul" purges all vices.[479]

In the sixteenth century, an Italian mystic Catherine of Genoa was totally dedicated to charity work, including helping the poor and hospitalized. As an author, she said that she "experienced the fiery Love of God, a Love that consumed her, cleansing and purifying all, so that once quitted this life she could appear forthwith in God's presence." Seeing sin as "the source of all suffering" and being concerned about barriers to love, she wrote, "this impediment is the rust of sin. As it is consumed, the soul is more and more open to God's love. Just as a covered object left out in the sun cannot be penetrated by the sun's rays, in the same way, once the covering of the soul is removed, the soul opens itself fully to the rays of the sun. The more rust of sin is consumed by fire, the more the soul responds to that love, and its joy increases. Not that all suffering disappears, but the duration of that suffering diminishes."[480]

Mahatma Gandhi, the twentieth-century liberator of India from British colonialism, said, "the purer I try to become, the nearer to God I feel myself to be." Furthermore, "my imperfections and failures are as much a blessing from God as my successes and talents, and I lay them both at His feet." We need to be transformed because "God can never be realized by one who is not pure of heart." To purify ourselves, we need to rid ourselves of our negative traits and behaviors. To realize God, we need to be "completely free from anger and lust, greed and attachment, pride and fear" as well as "to remain untouched by immorality, untruth, . . . political gain." We must practice no egotism, no lying, no deceiving, no hatred, no evil-thoughts, no ill will, no bitterness, no fraud, no finding-fault, "no malice, no anger, no distrust, no fear of death or physical hurt." While "we know that both good and evil exist, . . . we must choose the one and shun the other." God is "the only Reality."[481]

Detachment

Another way to transform ourselves is practicing detachment, a misunderstood spiritual concept. For some, detachment is a way of purifying ourselves, while for others, it is a way of love. Possessiveness and viewing things as "mine" poison the relationship between ourselves and the world, because our attachments can distract our attention, create conflicts in our minds, clutter up our hearts, burden our spirit, and divert us from the path to the Holy One. We need to detach from our selfishness. Some ways to do this include living in the present moment NOW, being a force for good, and acting only out of love. In the fourteenth century, the German Dominican Meister Eckhart said, "detachment is the best of all, for it cleanses the soul, clarifies the mind, kindles the heart, and wakes the spirit." Practicing detachment allow us to form healthy, loving attachments. In the *Gita*, the Divine Krishna said, the individual "who is free of the chains of attachments; who is balanced in blame and in praise, whose soul is silent, who is happy with whatever he has, whose home is not in this world, and who has love—this man is dear to Me."[482]

Mystics advocate two different versions of detachment, one moderate and the other extreme. In the fourteenth century, Catherine of Siena, an Italian mystic who dialogued with the Divine, said that God distinguished between "the way of ordinary love" and "the way of perfect love." Describing moderate detachment and the way of ordinary love, God said to Catherine that it is not sinful to have material things. "After all, everything is good and perfect, created by Me, Goodness itself." Worldly things were made to serve humans. My intention was not that people would make themselves slaves to earthly pleasures. "They owe their first love to Me. Everything else they should love . . . not as if they owned it but as something lent them." In extreme detachment and the way of perfect love that all are *not* obligated to follow, people rise above desiring material things and "they let go of the world and all its pleasures." They sell all they have and give it to the poor.[483]

As Underhill said, detachment for many mystics is "a more moderate abandonment of outward things." Our five senses are not opposed to the Divine unless they become the total focus of all our energy. The true rule is "giving up those things which enchain the spirit, divide its interests, and deflect it on its road to God," whatever those things may be. "It is attitude, not acts that matter." The moderate detached attitude allows us to love people, worldly things, and all of creation, because they are vessels of the Sacred Spirit, but not to lust after them. We practice selfless use of material things, but not selfish possession. Plato said, "the true order is to use the beauties of the earth as steps along which one mounts upward for the sake of that other Beauty," the Divine. Besides talking to animals and flowers, the Italian mystic Francis of Assisi in the thirteenth century wanted every convent to have a garden "in order that all who saw the flowers might remember the Eternal Sweetness." In the sixteenth century, the Spanish mystic Teresa of Avila in her early contemplative life said, looking on "trees, water, and flowers . . . helped her to recollect the presence of God."[484]

In the sixteenth century, John of the Cross, a Spanish mystic, offered extensive descriptions of the dark night of the soul. In one he said, "we call this detachment the night of the soul." By this he did not mean the absence of things, "for absence is not detachment, if the desire remains." Rather detachment means "suppressing desire and avoiding pleasure." This sets the soul free even if possessions are retained. "It is not things of this world that occupy or injure the soul, . . . it is rather the wish and desire for them." Our soul is not empty as long as we desire worldly things. "But the absence of this desire for things produces emptiness and liberty of the soul, even when there is an abundance of possessions." Radhakrishnan, a twentieth-century

Hindu sage, said that "detachment of the spirit and not renunciation of the world is what is demanded from us . . . What matters is not possession or non-possession of things, but our attitude toward them. . . . It is what a man is, not what he has, that matters. It is his frame of mind that matters." Mother Teresa said that renouncing means offering our lives to God in an attitude of faith. "Renunciation also means love. The more we renounce, the more we love God and humanity."[485]

According to Underhill, some mystics think that "desires and attachments affect the soul." Thus, they practice extreme detachment because they think that we need to strip ourselves of "all those interests which nourish selfhood, however innocent and useful. . . . The only rule is the ruthless abandonment of everything which is in the way" of reaching God. This extreme detachment means the death of all our desires, except our yearning for the Divine. We do not want or crave or covet anything, except union with the Holy One. We do not claim anything as our own. In the eleventh century, Abr Hamid al Ghazzali, a Persian Islamic Sufi mystic, who like the early Franciscans practiced complete renunciation of worldly goods, said that we need to uproot from the soul all our "violent passions, . . . vicious desires and evil qualities, so that the heart may become detached from all that is not God, and give itself for its only occupation meditation upon the Divine Being." In the seventeenth century, Frances de Sales, a French mystic, said that we all have "the Sacred inclination to love God above all things." Antoinette Bourignan, a seventeenth-century Flemish woman, asked God to speak to her soul. She heard, "forsake all earthly things. Separate thyself from the love of creatures. Deny thyself."[486]

As Gandhi said, "we treat trivialities as realities." We must renounce all worldly attachments, "discard all wealth, and all possessions." To see God face to face, we need restraint in thought, word, and deed because "this freedom from all attachments is the realization of God as Truth."[487]

Eight Steps to Become More Loving

Our selfish selves live in the material world. Our mystical experiences of awakening can help produce our new loving selves that live in both the material and spiritual world. After abandoning our old ways, we follow a different path with new goals. We mystics want to express love for our neighbors and ourselves. To transform ourselves and remake our character, we need not only to purge ourselves of our negative words and deeds that cause suffering, but also to cultivate our positive actions that create love for others.

But what is love? How do I love myself? How do I love people and creation? How do I love the Holy One? These are extremely difficult questions. Talking about the weather, without being able to do anything about it, is often to kill time. Discussing love, without suggesting we can do something about it, is often to kill hope. But there is hope. Infinite Love is within us as our inner core of love. Because of this, we are all born lovers. We need to love and be loved to find out who we are. The more we express our love, the deeper our discovery of our true self. When we fail to spread our love, we diminish ourselves.

Even though vocalists sing about love; novelists describe it; movies and TV portray it; poets write about it; psychologists, philosophers, and theologians try to define it, we need to attempt to define it for ourselves, because there are so many misunderstandings about it. Definitions range from Plato's insights to minimalist statements, like the novel *Love Story*'s assertion that "love is never having to say you are sorry." In his *Symposium*, Plato, speaking through Aristophanes' myth, said that people's intense yearning is for "meeting and melting into one another, thus becoming one instead of two." As a longing for reunion, love is "the desire and pursuit of the whole."[488]

In my definition, love is our creative life force, dynamic power, vital energy, passionate soul, and vibrant spirit. Thus, our inner core of love is our spirit, our soul, our energy, our power, our life force, our heart, our essence, and our fundamental human nature. Love is not only the spirit of all people, but also the spirit of all reality. It is more than desire, attraction, and emotion. It is an intense power that moves us. Love is our creative life force that drives us toward communion with others in spirit, while also driving us as individuals to achieve our fullest personal development. We need to balance these two drives, the first toward self-love and the second toward love for other people. The reason love is the most important reality in life is because it unites our striving for personal development with our drive toward social connectedness. Thus, love is the answer to both our individual and social needs.[489]

Many experts have written accounts of what is love and how to become more loving. In the sixteenth century, the Spanish mystic Teresa of Avila said that in order to ascend on the path to the Divine, "the important thing is not to think much but to love much, and so do that which best stirs you to love." She wondered how many people know what love is. Love "doesn't consist in great delight but in desiring to please God in everything, in striving, insofar as possible, not to offend Him. . . .. These are the signs of love."[490]

The twelfth-century French mystic Bernard of Clairvaux described four stages in the growth of love. The sixteenth-century Spanish mystic John of the Cross explained ten stages of love. Erich Fromm's 1956 *The Art of Loving* said the four "basic elements, common to all forms of love, . . . are *care, responsibility, respect, and knowledge*." Contemporary Deepak Chopra writes about the *Path to Love*. Armstrong's 2010 book explains that "we have a natural capacity for compassion as well as cruelty" and presents her *Twelve Steps to a Compassionate Life*. All her twelve steps are meant to educate as well as "to bring forth the compassion that . . . exists potentially within every human being so that it can become a healing force in our own lives and in the world."[491]

In my book, *Feminism and Love: Transforming Ourselves and Our World*, my eight steps to become more loving are offered to help us develop and express fully our inner core of love and to make our world a more compassionate place that nurtures loving individuals and creates communities of love. After reading critically as many authors you can, decide for yourself which steps are accurate and eliminate those that are inaccurate. Then create your own steps. To learn to love, we need to begin with our love for our family and friends. Personal love is the starting point. While I say there are eight steps, most of these steps incorporate several concepts. None of these steps is beyond any of us. In fact, we are familiar with them and already possess most, if not, all of them. We need to practice the steps not only toward others, but also toward ourselves. If we don't love ourselves, it is much more difficult to love others. While reading, studying, learning, knowing, and creating the steps is extremely important, that is not the end of the process. We can't learn to play tennis by reading a book. We have to go out on the court to practice and play. If we yearn to be more spiritual, we need to focus on the stages, like awakening, and perform them. If we want to be more loving, we need to learn the steps and do them. Love is too important to take for granted.

The eight steps on the path to becoming more loving are:

1. Accepting, respecting, and listening that lead to
2. Responding, caring, helping, and being supportive which produce
3. Understanding, knowing, and empathizing that grow into
4. Sharing and giving which create
5. Appreciating, thanking, and celebrating that breed
6. Apologizing and making amends which bring about
7. Forgiving that culminates in
8. Trusting.[492]

The first step to become more loving is accepting myself and others as we are. It is accepting my own and others' shortcomings as well as our goodness and loving inner core. Accepting involves respecting, affirming, and listening to myself and others. Those who think that women, minorities, the poor, or anyone else is inferior and who discriminate against them lack respect, cripple love, and deny the Divine presence within them. Responding to my own and others' needs is the second step on love's path. Some shout about their troubles, while others whisper. No one's problems remain completely unexpressed because total silence is itself a cry for help. Responding incorporates being responsible, being concerned, caring, helping, being supportive, and honoring the value and worth of myself and others as well as treating people with respect, equality, freedom, justice, and love. Genuine concern always involves helping. Where there is no help, there is no love. Love produces action. It lives and grows through expressing itself. However, it is better to teach people to fish than to give them fish to eat.[493]

Step three is understanding myself and others with both my head and heart, my knowing and feeling, my rational thinking and insightful intuition, my reason and my compassion. Understanding includes knowing and empathizing. To empathize is to feel others' feelings, to think their thoughts, and to understand their values and actions. Empathy is the process of putting myself in their moccasins, walking with them, and seeing the world from their point of view. Sharing myself with others is the fourth step in becoming more loving. It involves being honest and giving as well as expressing and communicating my heart and soul. Sharing is the heart of the loving process. The most important thing that we have to give is our deepest self, our loving inner core, our spirit, the Divine within us. Sharing ourselves with other people is important, but it is just as important to dedicate ourselves to making the world a more loving place. Our work is the way we express our love to the larger community. As Kahlil Gibran said, "work is love made manifest."

Appreciating, celebrating, and being thankful for myself and others is the fifth step. My initial reaction when I appreciate your inner beauty, goodness, and spirit is to stand in awe. Hindus go a step further because they realize that the Divine is within all of us. When they greet each other, they join their hands together and bow to acknowledge the Sacred Spirit within each of us. The twentieth century novelist Antoine de Saint-Exupery's *Little Prince* exhibits appreciation. After going through the first four steps of loving his rose, he said that it is not a common rose, like a hundred thousand roses. It is "unique in all the world." The sixth step is apologizing after making a mistake, quarreling, or having a conflict. An authentic apology includes expressing genuine sorrow by words and actions, making amends, trying to heal any injury done, working not to repeat the same harmful acts again, and changing myself.

Forgiving myself and others is the seventh step. It is not loving the unlovable, but focusing on the good within myself and others, while understanding and empathizing with the unacceptable. To forgive is to love the sinner, while hating the sin. Not to forgive is to refuse to love. Contemporary spiritual leader Marianne Williamson says that "not forgiving, then, is granting victory to those who wronged us, in that we allow them to shape our reality. . . . Forgiveness is the most powerful key to new beginnings." It re-establishes our relationship with others even though they harm us. It does not forget the damage because psychological injuries leave scars that may later be torn open. To forgive is to accept and love others in spite of the damage they do to us. Trusting myself and others is the eighth step. Trust helps us attempt the impossible, but deeply desired task of giving ourselves totally. Genuine trust means there is completely open, honest communication, and participation in each other's lives.[494]

When love exists, there is a lifelong bond created that may change forms as well as increase and decrease in intensity, but it never ceases to exist. In the Bible, Paul said, "love never gives up; and its faith, hope, and patience never fail. Love is eternal. . . . These three things remain: faith, hope, and love; and the greatest of these is love." Twentieth-century Protestant theologian Paul Tillich said, "love lasts, love alone endures, and nothing else besides love, nothing independent of love." When we love deeply, we become committed. Commitment encompasses all eight qualities of love. We accept, respect, respond, care, understand, empathize, share, give, appreciate, thank, apologize, make amends, forgive, and trust our loved ones.[495]

How Do We Love the Holy One?

We learn to love the Divine by following the eight steps to becoming more loving. In the first step, we need to accept that the Holy One is infinite, incomprehensible, and ineffable. We need to respect that because Infinite Love is so far beyond our finite understanding, we can only catch tiny, brief glimpses of the Sacred Spirit in the goodness and spirit of other humans and creation. We also need to accept that because the Ultimate Reality is an infinitely incomprehensible Mystery, we cannot fully understand the way that the ONE relates to all of creation. We need to face the fact that the reasons for natural disasters and humans' evil actions are beyond our finite minds. We need to listen to the Holy One Who speaks to us through creation, humans, and all religious traditions. Second, we need to show our love for the

Divine by responding and caring for the needs of people and creation. The universe with all its people is a magnificent gift from the Sacred Spirit and we need to care for, help, and protect everyone and everything.

In the third step, we need to try to know and understand the Holy One, even though the Ultimate Reality is Infinite and thus is totally beyond our comprehension. Despite Infinite Love being beyond the reach of our finite minds, we need to attempt to learn as much as possible through as many mediums as possible, such as listening to religious leaders, reading and studying spiritual writers and sacred scriptures, attending rituals, exploring nature, and many other ways. Fourth, we need to listen to the best of our ability and with the depth of our being in order to hear the Holy One share, communicate, and reveal Its Infinite Self to us through people and nature. We can also share our deepest self with the Divine.

Fifth, we appreciate all the Divine gifts of people and creation. Then we are thankful for Infinite Love and show it by expressing our love from the depth of our inner core. We also have celebrations and ceremonies to show our thankfulness and appreciation. In the sixth step, we apologize for all our wrongdoings and work to improve ourselves. We make amends wherever possible. Seventh, we need to beg forgiveness of the Holy One for all our misdeeds. In the eighth step, we need to trust the Sacred Spirit, no matter how difficult it is to do.

A number of mystics write about how to love God, such as Bernard of Clairvaux's four degrees of love. In his *Confessions*, Augustine of Hippo, the fifth-century African bishop and theologian, said that without a doubt he loved God, but asked, "what do I love when I love You? . . . And what is this God?" In his Christian handbook entitled *Enchiridion of Faith, Hope, and Love*, he asked, what is "the proper mode of worshipping God?" His answer was that "God is to be worshipped with faith, hope, and love." Moreover, "these must be the chief, nay, the exclusive objects of religion." He unfolded "each of these three graces, viz, what are we to believe, what are we to hope for, and what are we to love?" His answer about believing was many times longer, although he gave a short summary. "It is enough for the Christian to believe that the only cause of all created things, whether heavenly or earthly, whether visible or invisible, is the goodness of the Creator, the one true God, and that nothing exists but Him." In speaking of hope, he said that "everything that pertains to hope is embraced in the Lord's Prayer."[496]

For Augustine, love is "greater than the other graces, . . . the greater the measure in which it dwells in a man, the better is the man in which it dwells." When inquiring whether a person is good, do not ask what he believes or hopes, "but what he loves. For the man who loves aright no doubt believes and hopes aright. . . .It is not possible to hope without love." Given by God, "every commandment has love as its aim." As Paul said in the New Testament, "the aim of such instruction is love that comes from a pure heart, a good conscience, and sincere faith." In addition, "'God is Love.' Wherefore, all God's commandments . . . are rightly carried out only when the motive principle of action is the love of God and the love of our neighbor."[497]

Awakened Mystics Advocated Love for Our Neighbors and Ourselves

Many awakened mystics advocated love for our neighbors and ourselves, because awakening produces love. In the Hindu spiritual classic *Bhagavad Gita*, the Divine Krishna said to his disciple Arjuna, "hear now how a person reaches Brahman, the highest vision of Light. When . . . the soul is in harmony . . . and his selfishness and violence and pride are gone; when lust and anger and greediness are no more, and he is free from the thought 'this is mine'; then this man has risen on the mountain of the Highest: he is worthy to be One with Brahman, with God. . . . beyond grief and desire his soul is in peace. His love is one with all creation, and he has supreme love for Me. By love he knows Me in truth, Who I am, What I am." The person "who has good will for all, who is friendly and has compassion; who has no thoughts of 'I' or 'mine,' whose peace is the same in pleasures and sorrows, and who is forgiving, this yogi of union, ever full of joy, . . . this man loves Me."[498]

Moses taught the Jews to love themselves, their neighbors, and God. "Hear, O Israel: The Lord is our God, the Lord alone. You shall love the Lord your God with all your heart and with all your soul, and with all your might." In addition, "you shall love your neighbor as yourself." His ten commandments show what not to do in order to be loving.[499]

Being a good Jew, Jesus taught the commandment to love God as well as to love your neighbor and yourselves by quoting the Hebrew scripture, "you shall love your neighbor as yourself." Teaching how to be loving, Jesus explained what the King who represents God said to the blessed. You will inherit the kingdom of God, the presence of the Divine, because "I was hungry and you gave me food, I was thirsty and you gave me something to drink, I was a stranger and you welcomed me, I was naked and you gave me clothing, I was sick and you took care of me, I was in prison and you visited me." Then the righteous asked when did we do these things? The King said, "truly I tell you, just as you did it to one of the least of these who are members of my family, you did it to me." Then he said to those who are not blessed, "you that are accursed, depart from me into the eternal fire." They asked why and he answered, "truly I tell you, just as you did not do it to the one of the least of these, you did not do it to me." Another time a young man who had kept God's commandments asked Jesus, "what do I still lack?" Jesus answered, "if you wish to be perfect, go, sell your possessions and give the money to the poor, and you will have treasure in heaven; then come, follow me."[500]

In the fifth century, Augustine said that Christians are to practice mercy and love, such as "the man who gives food to the hungry, drink to the thirsty, clothing to the naked, hospitality to the stranger, shelter to the fugitive," as well as "visits the sick and imprisoned, ransoms the captive, assists the weak, leads the blind, comforts the sorrowful, heals the sick, puts the wanderer on the right path, gives advice to the perplexed, supplies the wants of the needy," and pardons the sinner. They are not to "return evil for good" and not "to return evil even for evil." There are many ways to show love but none is "greater than to forgive from the heart a sin" committed against you. While it is "a comparatively small thing to wish well" or to do good to a person who has not harmed you. "It is a much higher thing, and is the result of the most exalted goodness, to love your enemy, and always to wish well," and to do good to the person who wishes you ill and wants to hurt you. You need to begin your works of mercy with yourself. "'To have mercy on thy soul is pleasing to God.'" You must ask God to forgive your debts, as you from your heart forgive your debtors. Also you need to practice "loving God with the love which He has Himself bestowed."[501]

The Islamic scriptures, the Quran, repeatedly urges the believer to have "faith and do what is right" and "do good works" and "love your kindred. He that does a good deed shall be repaid many times over." Pray to the Lord in fear and hope; "give in charity of that which We have bestowed" on you. "Be charitable; Allah loves the charitable." Moreover, "the righteous man is he who believes in Allah . . . and the Scriptures and the prophets; who for the love of Allah gives his wealth to the orphans, to the needy, to the wayfarers, and to the beggars, and for the redemption of captives, who attends to his prayers and pays the alms-tax." The duty incumbent on all is to "be steadfast in prayer, enjoin justice, and forbid evil. Endure with fortitude whatever befalls you." For "Allah loves those who act in justice." Moreover, "Allah enjoins justice, kindness, and charity to one's kindred, and forbids indecency, wickedness, and oppression."[502]

Allah urges people to help the needy by asking, "did He (Allah) not find you an orphan and give you shelter? Did He not find you in error and guide you? Did He not find you poor and enrich you? Therefore, do not wrong the orphan, nor chide away the beggar. But proclaim the goodness of your Lord." Moreover, "do your slaves share with you on equal terms the riches which We have given to you?" In addition, "requite evil with good, and he who is your enemy will become your dearest friend." Furthermore, "do not treat men with scorn, nor walk proudly on the earth. Allah does not love the arrogant and vainglorious." Allah blesses the believers "who give alms to the destitute; who restrain their carnal desires (except with their wives and slave-girls, for these are lawful to them) and do not transgress through lusting after other women." For the person who "gives in charity and guards himself against evil and believes in goodness, We shall smooth the path of salvation." In addition, "serve no other gods besides Allah. . . . Give to the near of kin their due, and also to the destitute and the wayfarers. . . . You shall not kill your children for fear of want. . . . You shall not commit adultery. . . . You shall not kill any man whom Allah has forbidden you to kill, except for a just cause."[503]

In the thirteenth century, Francis of Assisi, the Italian founder of the Franciscan religious order, was called "an apostle of love." His whole life "radiated an active and limitless love" for God, his neighbors, and all of creation. In his famous prayer, he said, "Lord, make me an instrument of your peace; where there is hatred, let me sow love; where there is injury, pardon; where there is doubt, faith; where there is despair, hope; where there is darkness, light; where there is sadness, joy. O Divine Master, grant that I may not so much seek to be consoled as to console; . . . to be loved as to love. For it is in giving that we receive." In his *Last Will and Testament*, Francis called himself God's "little servant." When he was young, "it seemed a very bitter thing to look at lepers." Once he helped them, what "had seemed so horrible to me was transformed into happiness of body and soul for me." After this experience, he "renounced the world." Then "the Lord gave me such faith in His Church." After God gave him brothers, "the Most High Himself revealed to me how I must live in accordance with the precepts of the Holy Gospel." The simple Franciscan rule outlined a way of life that included living a life of absolute poverty and giving "all we had to the poor."[504]

Francis expressed his love for all of God's creation throughout his life. When he was gravely ill, he composed "the Song of Brother Sun" that illumined this love. "Most High, Almighty, Good Lord, to Thine be the praise, the glory, the honor, and all blessing. To Thee alone, Most High, are they due. . . . Praise to Thee, my Lord, for all Thy creatures, above all Brother Sun who brings us the day and lends us his light. . . . Lovely is he, radiant with splendor, and he speaks to us of Thee. . . . Praise to Thee, my Lord, for Sister Water, who is so useful and humble, precious and pure. . . . Praise to Thee, My Lord, for our sister Mother Earth who sustains and directs us, and brings forth varied fruits, and colored flowers, and plants."[505]

In the thirteenth century, Hadewijch urged all of us to serve God who is Love. At the end of a long vision, she said, "the heart . . . symbolizes the fruition of Love through feeling. My beloved, help all persons in their affliction impartially, whether they do you good or evil. Love will make you capable of it. Give all, for All is yours!" In the fourth stanza of a poem, she wrote that "he who wishes to become Love performs excellent work, . . . he is unconquered, and equal in strength to the task of winning the love of Love, whether he serves the sick or the well, the blind, the crippled or the wounded—he will accept this as his debt to Love." Continuing in the fifth stanza, she called on him "to serve strangers, to give to the poor, to comfort the sorrowful as best he can, to live in the faithful service of God's friends . . . with all his might.. . . If he thinks his strength will fail, let him trust henceforth in reliance on Love." Furthermore, "I gave full trust to Love, . . . friends and strangers, young and old, whom I served in every way—giving them my heart's affection—and favored their success in Love."[506]

Hadewijch's advice for a person who began to make progress was that he "must see that he does not lose zeal for good works, but serve for the honor of Love and live in high hope of what his heart has chosen." She knew brave knights. "They ever serve in the chains of Love, and they fear no pain" or grief. They wish to travel through all the land which the loving soul ever found with Love in Love; their noble heart is of lordly turn; they know what Love teaches with love, and how Love honors the loyal lover with love." The lover of Love says, "the servant's law is fear, but love is the law of sons." Seeing clearly, the person "who loves must live with full truth; when he understands with truth that he does too little for Love; . . . he learns fully how Love shall practice love; and this judgment . . . makes him give all for All, in order to content Love."[507]

In the thirteenth century, the Islamic mystic Rumi used an image to explain how awakening leads to love. "Winter is the season of gathering-in, summer the season of giving. . . . In mystical life, gathering-in is prayer and silent contemplation, adoration and thanksgiving; giving is the performing of acts of love and justice in the world. Breathe in through worship the majestic peace, bliss, and strength of the Most High; breathe out in loving and just action the power that has been bestowed on you by the Beloved." For the suffering of afflicted hearts, "there's no cure, except the retreat into Love. . . . See the Friend directly, or burn in longing for Him—what does the whole world matter apart from that?" In addition, "Love has made her (the soul) turn away from all worldly attachments; . . . look for the happiness of a supreme lover of God—all joys of this world are nothing to it." In the school of Divine Love, if "you don't even know the alphabet, don't worry; you'll be filled like Mohammed. . . . The Love of God is a fire that consumes all difficulties; . . . you are loved by Him.[508]

Rumi also said, "serve God, if you want to be a lover, service is the way of winning love, and it works. . . . All the robe of honor the lover desires is the vision of the Beloved. Love is not contained in speaking or hearing; Love is an Ocean whose depth is invisible, there are innumerable drops in this boundless Sea." Rumi repeated the phrase, "Through love," twenty times. "Through love bitter things seem sweet. . . . Through love agonies are healing balms. Through love thorns become roses. Through love a prison becomes a rose garden. Through love sickness is health." Elsewhere, "love is the astrolabe of the mysteries of God. Whether love comes from the earth or from heaven, in the end it draws us to the Beloved. . . . In speaking of Love, the intellect is impotent, . . . only Love Itself can explain Love." In addition, "if destiny comes to help you, Love will come to meet you. A life without love isn't a life—God doesn't take it into account. Every second that unravels far from love is a source of shame before the Lord." Furthermore, "Love is all that exists; without love, no one has the right to enter His house. They ask, 'what is love?' Reply: 'Giving up your self-will.' . . . It is Love and the lover that live eternally—don't lend your heart to anything else."[509]

Female and male Catholic religious orders, like the Franciscans and Carmelites, have been giving service and expressing love for centuries. In the seventeenth century, a French priest Vincent de Paul was called an "apostle of charity" and had a gospel of love. He founded the Catholic religious order of the Congregation of the Mission that still exists today. Its mission is to serve the poor and needy. A French widow Louise de Marillac with Vincent de Paul founded the female Catholic religious order of the Daughters of Charity that still exists today. In 1647, Louise wrote instructions to the sisters on how to be effective servants of the poor. "As for your conduct toward the sick, may you never take the attitude of merely getting the task done. You must show them affection; serving them from the heart—inquiring of them what they might need; speaking to them gently and compassionately; procuring the necessary help for them."[510]

Fighting injustice is a way to express love. John Woolman, an eighteenth-century American Quaker, led a life of traveling, preaching, and championing the freedom of slaves, working for better treatment of the Indians, fighting poverty and other social evils. In his *Journal*, he wrote that slaves are "the people by whose labor the other inhabitants are in great measure supported, and many of them in the luxuries of life. These are the people who have made no agreement to serve us." Hearing their cries to the Most High, he asked, "should we . . . neglect to do our duty" to fight this oppression? Woolman also wrote about the injustices to the Native Americans since the Europeans came. For a pittance, they sold their land, their inheritance that gave them their livelihood, and "have been driven back by superior force" to unfamiliar places that lack their form of subsistence. Europeans "for the sake of gain, induced them to waste their furs in purchasing liquor which tended to the ruin of them and their families." Woolman fought to stop these injustices.[511]

One way to love and serve people and the Holy One is to work for respect, equality, freedom, and justice for all. In 1995, the Jesuit religious order founded in the sixteenth-century had their General Congregation that issued a statement. It said that an earlier congregation "made a brief mention of the 'unjust treatment and exploitation of women' as part of a list of injustices" that Jesuits were called to address. The 1995 document went into depth to describe the situation of "the dominance of men" and "the discrimination against women in family life, education, employment, public life, media, sex trafficking" as well as "too frequently, outright violence against women." This is "a universal reality." Because of race, poverty, migration, and war, many women "suffer a double disadvantage." Changes have begun "chiefly because of the critical awakening and courageous protest of women."[512]

As Jesuits, we accept our responsibility "to do what we can to change this regrettable situation" by speaking about what we learn from women. Thus, "we are being faithful... to our mission," including "the promotion of justice." First, we Jesuits "ask God for the grace of conversion. We have been part of a civil and ecclesial tradition that has offended women." Concretely, "we invite all Jesuits, as individuals and through their institutions, to align themselves in solidarity with women." Some examples include "explicit teaching of the essential equality of women and men," supporting "liberation movements which oppose the exploitation of women," using inclusive language, promoting the education of women, and genuinely involving women in Jesuit ministries and institutions, including decision making.[513]

Contemporary American Margaret Wheatley who tries to utilize the new science in changing businesses and other organizations stresses the importance of relationships, connection, participation, and love. "Love in organizations, then, is the most potent source of power we have available. And all because we inhabit a quantum universe that knows nothing of itself, independent of its relationships. This web of relationships is so dominant." In organizational theory, attention is shifting from external reward to intrinsic work motivators such as our deep longings for "community, meaning, dignity, and love." No longer are we keeping love isolated in the home. Moreover, "in the new science, the underlying currents are a movement toward... giving primary value to the relationships and connections in the constant flux of dynamic processes." In this world, "relationship is a key determiner." Thus, "what is critical is the relationship."[514]

For quantum physicists, as Wheatly says, relationships are "all there is to reality. . . . In organizations, we are at the edge of this new world of relationships." Furthermore, "if nothing exists independent of relationship, . . . we can move away from . . . polar opposites" and either-or thinking. "The quantum world has demolished the concept of the unconnected individual. More and more relationships are in store for us, out there in the vast web of universal connections." We can no longer "study anything as separate from ourselves." Connections are "the fundamental elements of all creation." While quantum physicists discuss "cosmic interconnectivity," businesses and organizations talk about connections, relationships, and participation. "As physicists describe this participatory universe," organizations are involved in "the current and growing shift toward participative management." Wheatley believes that "the movement toward participation is rooted . . . in our changing perceptions of the organizing principles of the universe."[515]

Contemporary American McKeever has a living Indian Hindu teacher, Sri Chinmoy, the author of over 1,300 books. His teacher says that self-giving is one of the essential components of the spiritual life. One hour of unconditional self-giving is equal to one hour of the highest meditation. The opposite of selfishness is self-giving by which he means serving others. McKeever say that "in a moment of pure self-giving we put our self, or ego, the little 'I,' in a place of secondary importance and apply our awareness to the needs of those we are acting for." Moreover, "if our actions are stemming from humility and love, then our self-giving will be unconditional, free of any expectation regarding result or outcome." McKeever explains that awakening leads to love and self-giving. Humility is "based on a profound awareness of the God and spirit that moves through and sustains all of existence. True self-giving is founded upon this feeling." Self-giving also results in awakening. "When we serve others—self-giving—we expand our awareness of God in all." Thus, "to see God in the depths of our meditation is indeed a powerful experience. To see God in all that exists is a still higher experience. To serve God in all is the highest experience."[516]

Marianne Williamson, a contemporary author, an interpreter of the *Course in Miracles*, and a 2020 presidential candidate, wants us all to become more loving. In her approach, "God is Love." Moreover, "Love is the all-encompassing Reality of God and thus can have no opposite. . . . Love is the only eternal Truth." Furthermore, "Love is ultimately Real, nothing else has ultimate effect." Love is "the heart of all things." Besides Love, God has many names, such as the Internal Teacher, the Comforter, Jesus, and the Holy Spirit. One key in any situation is "to be clear about two things: who am I, really? And why am I here?" In describing humans, she says that since God is Love and we are children of God, we are "made for love." Love is what we are. "In fact, love is our natural state of being." We need to know that God lives within us and has Infinite Love for us. God dwells in our mind and we have the "perfection of God, potential in all of us whether manifest or not, yet always available for full expression. Each of us is pregnant with the manifestation of that perfection, for that is who we are."[517]

Our purpose is to love, according to Williamson. "Each of us has a unique part to play in the healing of the world. Each of us is assigned by God a function that only we can fill." We need to realize that we are "here to serve a greater plan than our own, as vessels through which the love that is the heart of all things flows through us to bless the world." We are "created for the purpose of extending His Love into the world." Our assignment in every relationship is "the enlightenment of all concerned." In our family, work, and everywhere, "the purpose of every relationship is the healing of the world." Our entire life becomes our calling, our ministry, a way to fulfill our "divine purpose," and "a way to serve God and to serve the world." Moreover, "we experience who we really are, what it is we're meant to do, in any moment when we pour our love into the universe." Enlightenment is "the power to think in ways that reflect and attract all the love in the world" and it is "the answer to every problem."[518]

According to Williamson, we need to remember that we are unlimited spiritual beings and not merely material beings. When we have negative thoughts about not being good enough, we need to realize that in God's Mind, we are never inadequate. We are "blessed eternally." Our mortal self can be damaged, but not our spiritual self. On the material plane, "none of us are perfect all the time. But on the spiritual plane, all of us are perfect all the time. Who we really are—perfect creatures, unchangeable and unlimited." Enlightenment is to identify with our spiritual rather than our material reality. We need to put love first. This means knowing who we are and knowing that the universe supports us in creating the good, the true, the holy, and the beautiful. It means knowing that we are on earth for a purpose. We need to make love our bottom line. "Love leads us to act with impeccability, integrity, and excellence. Love leads us to serve, to forgive, and to hope." In sharing God's Love, we share His Power and we need to align with His Infinite Love. His Perfection is our eternal home, to which we are programmed to return.[519]

Williamson explains how to become more loving. In her metaphysical perspective, "every experience begins with a thought, and our experience changes when we change the thought. . . . Every thought is a cause that produces an effect." Thus, "the most powerful, liberating thing that we can do is to break from fear-based thinking that dominates our world" and shift our thinking to love. Our loving thought has one effect and our fearful thought has a different one. Her goal is for us to relinquish fear and accept love in our hearts to replace it. "Love is real and fear is not; love comes from God, fear does not." The rule is that "love casts out fear." Williamson has seen "miraculous transformations occur when we change the nature of our thinking from fear and limitation to faith and love." In her definition, "a miracle is a shift in perception from fear to love—from a belief in what is not real, to faith in that which is." We need to realize that even extremely entrenched illusions "cannot stand in the presence of love." We need to start "by identifying our own lovelessness and being willing to let it go." God as an Internal Teacher helps us "cross the bridge from fear to love." Whatever our problems, we need to realize that "miracles are summoned by conviction" and "an infinite field of miraculous possibility awaits our open-mindedness and love."[520]

People ask Williamson, will love solve the starvation of children in Africa or other serious world problems? Her answer is that the "starving children in Africa are not poor because their consciousness is unaligned with love; they're poor because ours is. A billion people on earth live in 'deep poverty'—that is, on less than a dollar a day. A billion more live on less than two dollars a day.... It is a collective lovelessness on the part of the advanced nations of the world that allows us to accept the reality of deep poverty.... When we collectively make love our bottom line—making humanitarian values rather than short-term economics the organizing principle of human civilization—then the situation will indeed miraculously change." An economist Jeffery Sachs says that "one hundred billion dollars (one-seventh of the annual military budget in the United States) could eradicate poverty within ten years."[521]

A practical addition to Williamson's statement that Africans are poor because our consciousness is not aligned with love is that the earlier colonialism and the later imperialism of developed countries were examples of the lovelessness that caused most of the problems that continue to fester in the third world, including severe poverty, poor governments, environmental destruction, and violence. The colonialists thrived at the expense of the indigenous people; extracted their raw minerals; exploited, humiliated, oppressed, and brutalized them; communicated their contempt, hatred, and belief that they were inferior; and destroyed the tribal, cultural, and religious traditions that provided for their health and well-being. These practices left long-term consequences, including psychological scars, social damage, economic and political problems, and spiritual destruction. Moreover, the colonialists created nations with artificial boundaries that separated tribes into two different countries and joined those that didn't belong together.

These artificial boundaries continue to cause problems, for example in Iraq and the Middle East as well as in Africa.

The Five Steps of Personal Empowerment and Community Transformation

First, we need to learn how to become personally more loving toward our neighbors and ourselves. Then we need to learn how to change our local, national, and global communities so that they nurture loving individuals and create communities of love. The following five steps can help us achieve personal empowerment and community transformation.

Unawareness and Denial Are the First Step.

The point of departure is the status quo where most of us are unaware that we aren't empowered to be our true selves but rather we are encouraged to conform to our culture's sexist and racist rules and customs. Every young American is socialized into and expected to conform to a white male dominating social structure that treats women, minorities, the poor, and foreigners as inferior and discriminates against them daily. We are taught to ignore and deny that people in our community, nation, and world, including ourselves, are suffering. Poverty is widespread in the US and around the world. US practices damage and destroy our environment. Many of us ignore and deny that others suffer because of poverty, sexism, racism and ecological destruction. Denial is mechanism that we use to avoid seeing truths that are too painful. We fear becoming conscious of the fact that our society mistreats many while rewarding only a few. Our lack of self-love and sense of personal worth make us conform in order to gain approval and advantages as well as to avoid being punished and losing the little safety and security we have.[522]

We all have a socially assigned identity that teaches us to conform to cultural rules, such as girls are to be beautiful and get married while boys are to be tough and run society. We also have a loving inner core identity. When females accept their socially assigned identity and act out submissive femininity, they are alienated from their creative life force, vibrant spirit, and loving inner core. The imposed image makes them feel like a sex object, instead of a talented self-determining person. When males accept the cultural identity of being tough and dominating, they deny their loving inner core. Our dual consciousness is a vehicle for our oppression, but also for our liberation. No one can live without a socially assigned identity, but our loving inner core can help us find our authentic self. When we have mystical experiences, we become aware of our loving inner core and we want to be true to ourselves.

The Second Step Is the Beginning of Awareness, But Remaining Silent.

Before we can be free, we must be conscious of our bondage. Awareness is the starting point for empowerment and transformation. Consciousness is the beginning of freedom. When we have a mystical experience of awakening, we get in touch with our loving inner core that conflicts with our socially assigned identity and our awareness begins. We realize that by conforming to the cultural rules, we are not being true to ourselves. Two courses of action open up. On one hand, we can deny our awareness and affirm our socially assigned identity of being a submissive female or a tough, dominating male as well as conform to cultural rules of ignoring or denying people's suffering. On the other hand, we can take the first step toward overcoming our conformity by welcoming our new consciousness and getting in touch with our loving inner core and our true self. Then we have the courage to stop ignoring or denying the problems in our society, but we still remain silent.

Anger and Saying No to Abuse Are the Third Step.

Our mystical experience of the Sacredness of all of us makes us aware that every kind of suffering and abuse is wrong. Awareness breeds anger. Once our consciousness is raised, we feel tremendous, pent-up anger and sometimes rage. Anger is a righteous, appropriate response to every type of disrespect, unfairness, injustice, and lack of freedom as well as to domination, abuse, cruelty, and violence. As the African American poet Audre Lorde said, "anger is an appropriate reaction to racist attitudes, as is fury when the actions arising from those attitudes do not change." Anger can be destructive or constructive. Destructive anger that should be avoided is the anger expressed by people who have not dealt with their feelings. It attempts to retaliate against those who harm them. Constructive anger is the anger expressed by people who deal with their feelings. It tries to stop suffering and abuse. Constructive anger is a creative, passionate energy that empowers us to say no to abuse. As Lorde said, it is not anger that destroys us, but "our refusals to stand still, to listen to its rhythms, to learn from it, to move beyond the manner of presentation to the substance, to tap that anger as an important source of empowerment."

The beginning of empowering and liberating ourselves is awareness of the problems that block our freedom. However, when we are conscious but remain silent, our bondage continues. After becoming aware, we need to speak out publicly and say no. At first, we only share our new consciousness with our family and friends. Later we get the courage to join groups that are speaking out publicly against abuse. We need to speak because we only become fully conscious when we share with someone else. Lorde urges us to transform our silence into speech and action. We need to speak about "the poisonous seepage of hatred," discrimination, and abuse that we eat like daily bread. Then we need to act.

The Fourth Step Is Finding Our Voice, Affirming Ourselves, and Learning to Love.

After becoming aware of mistreatment, getting angry, and saying no, we need to find our own voice and say yes to ourselves by affirming our own value, goodness, spirit, and inner core of love. The more we find our own voice, the more we affirm our own loving inner core, the more we love ourselves. When we affirm our own identity, we become actors instead of conformers. Once we learn to say I'm OK, we need to learn to affirm that you're OK. Then we can say that suffering and abuse are not OK. It is important to condemn the sin but not the sinner, to halt the violence but not destroy the batterer. Mistreating the abuser does not affirm myself. After removing the dominator's foot from my neck, I need to stand up straight and affirm myself. However, I also need to love my enemy, the batterer. Thus, I should not knock him into the dirt and put my foot on his neck. When we are in touch with our loving inner core, we love ourselves and others. Having a clear perception of reality, we resist conforming to cultural rules. Our love radiates outward to others and our world.

Stopping Abuse, Loving All, and Transforming Our World Are the Fifth Step.

When we have a mystical experience of awakening, we experience the Divine within everyone and everything. We realize that all suffering and abuse are wrong. Thus, we become aware, feel anger at any mistreatment of people and the environment, say no, find our voice, say yes to ourselves, and learn to love ourselves. Then we want to spread our love beyond our family and friends into the wider world. We work to create sisterhood and brotherhood for all. This makes us aspire to become Divine instruments who try to fulfill the Sacred Spirit's aim of changing our world to reduce or even stop all types of the hatred, prejudice, discrimination, injustice, inequality, abuse, and violence that cause suffering and replace them with love. As Divine ambassadors, we yearn to change our world by promoting personal empowerment and community transformation. We try to build a new world where respect, liberty, equality, justice and love are the guiding principles. This new world will work to nurture loving individuals and create communities of love.

As Divine messengers, we join organizations that have similar purposes, because we recognize that the world's problems are collective so we need to work for collective solutions. When we work together, we briefly experience respect, equality, justice, freedom and love that will be persistent realities in the new world. This small glimpse of loving individuals in a community of love gives us the courage and steadfastness to devote our lives to the cause of transforming the world.

As the Sacred Spirit's representatives, we do not believe what many in our culture affirm that the end justifies the means. In contrast, we say that our methods need to be consistent with our goals. Since our aim is peace, our actions need to be peaceful. Since our purpose is equality for women and minorities, we need to treat all people as equals. We need to be concerned with both our means and our results. Since our goal is to create loving individuals and communities, we need to act only out of love. Since our aim is to promote personal empowerment and community transformation, our methods must be democratic and not dominating and controlling. One way to determine whether we are controlling or loving is to discover whether we are inhibiting or empowering others to be free, to be true to themselves, and to be more loving.

We need to examine every aspect of our culture to distinguish the constructive from the destructive, the loving from the harmful. From small items such as sexist, racist, and ethnic slurs to the largest institutions such as the Catholic Church that has discriminated against women for 2,000 years, we need to speak out to make them less destructive and more loving. Targets for transformation included everyone and everything. Not only do we need to affirm, empower, and free individuals, organizations, and social structures from their particular forms of discrimination and subordination, but we also need to nurture loving individuals and create communities of love.[523]

Love Leads to the Next Mystical Stage of Illumination and Union with the Divine

Awakening leads to love. Our love produces more awakenings. After we swing back and forth between the stages of awakening and love, our love opens us up to the next mystical stage of illumination. As the sixteenth-century Italian Catherine of Genoa was "plunged in the Divine furnace of purifying love, she was united to the Object of her love," the Holy One. Fighting our selfishness and wrong acts as well as developing our love leads to illumination. As the seventeenth-century German mystic Jacob Boehme said, "I began to fight a hard battle against my corrupted nature, and with the aid of God I made up my mind to overcome the inherited evil will, to break it, and enter wholly into the love of God." He did not succeed in his striving to change himself, but as he wrestled, he experienced illumination. "A wonderful light arose within my soul. . ... In it I recognized the true nature of God and men, and the relation existing between them." As Underhill said, mystics' consciousness alternates between "the bitter struggle of pure purgation and the peace and radiance of the illuminative life." Trying to transform their multiple imperfections and working to learn how to love themselves and others lead to "the most bitter physical and moral sufferings," but this state fluctuates with their "Divine glimpse and beam of joy arising in the soul" and sometimes their "delirious joy" of experiencing illumination and union with God.[524]

The work to learn to love, to transform the world, to live in time but encounter Eternity that leads to the next spiritual stage of experiencing illumination and union with the Holy One is a lifelong process and struggle. As we labor to be better people, we continually fail. The important thing is to start again and continue our efforts. Slowly our old selfish self loses the battle with our new loving self. But even our new self continues to fail, but hopefully less often. As our mystical experiences help us to express our love, our compassion shows us the way to the Sacred Spirit. Thus, we oscillate back and forth between radiating love and experiencing illumination and union with Infinite Love.

Chapter 10

Illumination and Union with the Holy One Are the Fifth Stage

Illumination Is a Deeper Spiritual Experience than Awakening

In the third stage on the mystical way, our consciousness awakens to the Divine within everyone and everything. This awareness causes us to love ourselves and our neighbors which is the fourth stage. Thus, our awakening is followed by love. We swing back and forth between the joy of awakening and the open-heart of love. When we first experience the oscillation between these new experiences of awakening and love, it seems as though they are the complete and final stages on the spiritual path. Then love leads us to an even deeper spiritual experience of the fifth stage of illumination. When we develop an illuminated consciousness, we realize that we are still on the mystical way. Our quest is not fulfilled. Like awakening, illumination has other names, such as enlightenment, spiritual experience, cosmic consciousness, transcendent encounter, conversion, religious encounter, and mystical experience of the Sacred Spirit. To distinguish between them in this book, stage three is called awakening and enlightenment, while stage five is illumination and union. However, distinctions are also made between illumination and union, but not between awakening and enlightenment.[525]

Radically different from our normal perception, illumination is deeper, clearer, a more intense, and more enhanced mystical consciousness than awakening of the Divine presence within us and all of creation. It is awakening on steroids. Every blade of grass and every flower, every insect and every animal, every river and every ocean, every hill and every mountain, every planet and every star, every female and every male person, is filled with the Sacred spirit. They are on fire with the Holy One.

Underhill said that "the mark of the illuminated consciousness" is "closely connected to the sense of the 'presence of God' or the power of perceiving the Absolute." Thus, illumination "at its best balances and completes the experience of the presence of God at its best. . . . It entails the expansion rather than the concentration of consciousness; the discovery of the Perfect One self-revealed in the many." Its characteristic expression is that "the world is charged with the grandeur of God; it will flame out" unless we turn our thoughts into our own soul, where the Divine is hidden. Illumination raises our consciousness to the Transcendent Ultimate Reality. It is "a lifting of consciousness from a self-centered to a God-centered world." It results in the perception of "essential goodness, truth, and beauty—Light, Life, and Love . . . by the heart" and "the apprehension of Infinite Life immanent in all living things."

According to Underhill, in illumination, a person "sees, feels, and knows in one piercing act of loving comprehension" that the Divine is within all of creation. Illumination is "this loving vision" that, as Erigena said, "every visible and invisible creature is a theophany or appearance of God." For thousands of years, mystics experienced illumination. In the twelfth century, Bernard of Clairvaux, a French mystic, said that "I have felt that He was present, I remember He has been with me." In the fourteen century, Walter Hilton, an English mystic, said that the Divine presence can be felt and can be known better by experience than by words. That Sacred presence is "the life and the love, the might and the light, the joy and the rest of a chosen soul." Once we have felt the Holy presence, we may not stop desiring it, because "it is so good in itself and so comfortable." The sixteenth century Spanish mystic, Teresa of Avila, admitted that in the beginning "I did not know that God was in all things." Later, "I felt His very presence."[526]

Jacob Boehme was a seventeenth-century German shoemaker and also a Lutheran mystic who had illuminations. When he was young, a biographer said that "he was surrounded by Divine Light seven days and stood in the highest contemplation and kingdom of joy." Years later when he gazed into a pewter dish which reflected sunlight, he "fell into an inward ecstasy, and it seemed to him as if he could look into the principles and deepest foundations of things." Then when he stepped outdoors, "he gazed into the very heart of things, the very herbs and grass, and that actual nature harmonized with what he had inwardly seen." From this time on, he had a frequent, growing consciousness of the Divine as well as some times of darkness. Ten years after his vivid illumination, it was repeated in an enhanced form. After his earnest yearning and seeking, "the gate opened to me, so that in one quarter of an hour I saw and knew more than if I had been many years at a university. . . . For I saw and knew the Being of all beings, the Byss and the Abyss, and the Eternal Generation of the *Holy Trinity*, the Descent and Origin of the world, and of all creatures through the Divine Wisdom."[527]

After his illumination, George Fox, a seventeenth-century English mystic who founded the Society of Friends, also called the Quakers, said, "now was I come up in spirit through the flaming sword into the Paradise of God. All things were new. . . . The creation was opened to me. . . . Great things did the Lord lead me unto, and wonderful depths were opened unto me beyond what can by words be declared; but as people come into subjection to the Spirit of God, and grow up in the image and power of the Almighty, they may receive the world of wisdom that opens all things, and come to know the *hidden Unity in the Eternal Being*." William Law, an eighteenth-century English Anglican mystic, said that "everything in temporal nature . . . is descended out of that which is Eternal, . . . so when we know how to separate the grossness, death, and darkness of time from it, we will find what it is in its Eternal state." He stressed dedicating our whole life to God, not just part. We have a responsibility to love God "at all times" and "in all places."[528]

Gandhi offered an interesting insight. "If we are all sons of the same God and partake of the same Divine essence, we must partake of the sin of every person whether he belongs to us or to another race." Mother Teresa experienced the Divine presence within all people. She saw "Christ in the distressing disguise" of the poor, the sick, the lepers, and the dying. Going into the slums of Calcutta, India for the first time in 1948 was "my first meeting with Christ in his distressing disguise." Jesus made himself "the Hungry One, the Thirsty One, the Naked One, the Homeless, and kept calling—I was hungry, naked, homeless." When you cared for them, "you did it to Me.—The Bread of Life and the Hungry One." After founding the Missionaries of Charity, she wanted them "to love God for His sake and the poor for Him, in Him, with Him."[529]

Illumination Is the Deep, More Advanced Mystical Experience That We Are within the ONE

When we become more illuminated, we experience ever more deeply that the Sacred Spirit is within all people and the entire cosmos. This deeper awareness of the Holy One within everyone and everything leads to the more profound mystical experience that we are within the ONE. All of us are within the Divine Depth, within the Ultimate Reality. The Divine is the Sacred Ocean of Infinite Love. We are all drops of love within the Sacred Ocean. When we experience our awakening and our early illuminations, we become aware that Infinite Love is within us as our inner core of love. When we have a more advanced illumination, we have the deeper spiritual consciousness that we are within Infinite Love. Our heart, our essence, our substance, and our nature are within Infinite Love. Thus, Infinite Love embraces, envelopes, surrounds, penetrates, and permeates us.

Awakening and illumination have similarities. In both of them, we experience the Divine presence within us. Infinite Love is within us as our inner core of love. However, we realize it much more deeply in illumination. These two are also different. In awakening, we feel separate from God. We know that we are physical bodies with a spiritual dimension. We are two separate individual beings, a human and a Divine Being. In contrast, in illumination, we realize that since our birth, we have always been within the ONE. We have never been separate from the Holy One. Many view us as physical bodies with mystical abilities and with a spiritual nature. Rather than that, we are all spirits with physical bodies. We are spirits within the Eternal, Universal Spirit. All of us are living within the Ultimate Reality, within the Tao, Allah, God, and Brahman. We are within Infinite Love and composed of the same substance. Our human nature is both a physical body and the Divine presence, both a human and Sacred Spirit, both finite and Infinite Love.

Underhill briefly mentioned that the illuminated life involves experiencing "all creatures in God and God in all creatures." Illumination is "dwelling within the substance of Goodness, Truth, and Beauty" and "an entrance here and now into that Absolute Life within the Divine Being." In addition, "the whole world is seen and known in God and God is seen and known in the whole world." The Chinese Tao with its dynamic yin and yang forces is within all of us and all of creation. Since we are all composed of yang and yin that make up the Tao, we are also within the Tao.[530]

To illustrate this, let's view our spirits within the Sacred Spirit as individual members of a chorus working within the Wisdom and Vision of the Sacred Conductor. Sometimes we do not realize our place within the

Wisdom of the Conductor. When this happens, we think we are our own separate self. We do not sing in harmony. Instead of our singing being united with our Conductor, we are distracted by our desire to enhance our own status, fame, wealth, possessions, and power. In contrast, illumination helps us recognize our place within the Wisdom of the Sacred Conductor, so that we work with and sing in sync with Her. Thus, we transform ourselves from a self-centered, selfish, self-seeking way of thinking and living to a Divine-centered consciousness and way of being.

Although the mystic way and Infinite Love are always the same, we all experience them differently because of who we are. Our experiences of illumination, our images of the Divine, and our success in traveling to the end of the mystic way differ depending on our traits, abilities, and efforts; our acceptance, revision, and rejection of our religious training; our capacity for self-discipline, self-renewal and self-transcendence; our steadfastness, passion, and our courage; our mystical experiences and spiritual insights; our caring, compassion, and love for all people; and the duration, durability, and intensity of our love for the Holy One.[531]

For Over 2,600 Years, Mystics Have Written about Illumination

Throughout the centuries, many mystics wrote about their spiritual experiences of illumination that we are within the Divine. Some of the oldest are in the 2,600-year-old Hindu *Upanishads*. One of the *Upanishads'* most important insights that rose out of mystics' experiences of illumination was that *"Brahman is All and Atman is Brahman."* Atman can be translated as my individual spirit or soul. Brahman is another word for God, the Supreme Spirit, the Universal Soul, the Absolute. Thus, the interpretation is that the Absolute is All and my individual spirit is the Supreme Spirit. My own soul is the Universal Soul. My understanding of illumination revises this because words are important. The word 'within' is crucial. Instead of my individual spirit is the Supreme Spirit, I stress that my soul is *within* the Universal Soul. Instead of Atman is Brahman, I say that Atman is *within* Brahman. The individual spirit of everything is *within* the Supreme Spirit. All people's souls are *within* the Universal Soul. As the Upanishads say, "The whole universe is in Him and He dwells within our heart." It is important to emphasize that my spirit is not equal to the Supreme Spirit. I am only a drop of love in the Sacred Ocean of Infinite Love.[532]

When we delve deeply into the first part of the Upanishads' statement that "Brahman is All and Atman is Brahman," we realize that since the individual soul, Atman, is part of the All, it is "One with Brahman," One with the Universal Soul, and "One with the ONE." When we see the Absolute, the soul, and the world, we perceive them as three, but we really see Brahman, the ONE, "the Universal in all." Thus, "the Spirit that is in all things" is "the essence of all." Brahman is "the supreme abode wherein dwells all that moves and breathes and sees." His "radiance illumines all creation. Far spreading before and behind, right and left, above and below, is Brahman, the Spirit eternal. In truth Brahman is All." Moreover, "all beings in our universe are parts of His infinite splendor. . . . From Him comes the universe and unto Him it returns."[533]

The Upanishads expressed the teaching of the identity of Atman and Brahman another way. "TAT TVAM ASI, Thou art That," which means "Thou art God." Thou, my spirit, is That, God, the Spirit Supreme. Thou, this loving inner core of mine, is That, God, Brahman. "An invisible and subtle essence is the Spirit of the whole universe." Thou, this person, is That, the Absolute Brahman. "Thou this man and Thou this woman art . . . God who appears in forms infinite. Thou the blue bird and . . . Thou the cloud" are God. "As fire, though one, takes new forms in all things that burn; the Spirit, though one, takes new forms in all things that live. He is within all and is also outside. As the wind, though one, takes new forms in whatever it enters; the Spirit, though one, takes new forms in all things that live." Brahman is "God hidden in all beings, their inmost soul who is in all. He watches the works of creation, lives in all things." He is "the Soul of all the universe."[534]

The Upanishads said that humans "feel sad in their unwisdom." When they behold the Spirit within all creation, they "become free from sorrow" and "leave good and evil behind. . . . In silent wonder the wise see Him as the Life flaming in all creation. This is the great seer of Brahman, who, doing all his work as Holy work, in God, in Atman, in the Self, finds all his peace and joy." Having realized that everything is within Brahman, "the seers find joy in wisdom, their souls have fulfillment, their passions have gone, they have peace. Filled with devotion, they have found the Spirit in all and go into the All."[535]

In the beginning of the Hindu *Bhagavad Gita*, an interpreter named Sanjaya explained to a King the setting for this book of dialogues between the Holy Krishna, another name for God, and his disciple Arjuna. Although Sanjaya rarely interjected his own comments, he presented a powerful image of the Infinite Divinity as the light of a thousand suns. "If the light of a thousand suns suddenly arose in the sky, that splendor might be compared to the radiance of the Supreme Spirit." Then he said that "Arjuna saw in that radiance the whole universe in its variety, standing in a vast Unity in the body of the God of the Gods. Trembling with awe and wonder, he . . . spoke to his God. 'I see in Thee all the Gods, O my God, and the infinity of the beings in Thy creation.'"[536]

The Holy Krishna described God called Brahman and Spirit to his disciple. "The Spirit is everlasting, omnipresent, never-changing, never-moving, ever ONE. Invisible is He to mortal eyes, beyond thought and beyond change. Know that He is, and cease from sorrow." For those who have no vision even though they follow the letter of the scriptures, "their soul is warped with selfish desires." Furthermore, "those who love pleasure and power . . . have not the determination ever to be One with the ONE." In contrast are those who realize all creation is within the Spirit. "All this visible universe comes from My Invisible Being. All beings have their rest in Me." In addition, "they worship Me as One and as many, because they see that all is in Me."[537]

The Holy Krishna said that "Joy supreme comes to the yogi whose heart is still, whose passions are peace, who is pure from sin, who is One with Brahman, with God." This yogi "soon feels the joy of Eternity, the infinite joy of union with God. . . . When he sees Me in all and he sees all in Me, then I never leave him and he never leaves Me. He who is this Oneness of Love, loves Me in whatever he sees, wherever this man lives, in truth this man lives in Me." When he sees the whole universe, he realizes "all is One in Me." When he knows that all is ONE in Me, "he enters into My Being." In addition, "when a man sees that the infinity of various beings is abiding in the ONE, and is an evolution from the ONE, then he becomes One with Brahman." Moreover, "by love he knows Me in truth, who I am and what I am. And when he knows Me in truth he enters into My Being." Furthermore, "I am the same to all beings, and My Love is ever the same; but those who worship Me with devotion, they are in Me and I am in them."[538]

Many mystics described illumination in their own words. In the sixth century BCE, Pythagoras, a Greek philosopher, said, "take courage, for the human race is Divine." The sixth-century BCE Chinese mystic Lao Tzu said, the Tao is "this Unity—Invisible, Inaudible, Intangible." In addition, "the great Tao flows everywhere. All things are born from It. . .. It is merged with all things and is hidden in their hearts. . . . all things vanish into It and It alone endures." The fourth-century BCE Chinese Taoist Chuang Tzu (Zhuangzi) referred to an old maxim that we humans are in the Tao as fish are in water. Our participation in the Tao is beyond our understanding, so we must simply act and go with the flow.[539]

In his first letter in the New Testament, John said, "let us love one another, because love is from God; everyone who loves is born of God and knows God. Whoever does not love does not know God, for God is Love. . . . Since God loved us so much, we also ought to love one another. No one has ever seen God; if we love one another, God lives in us, and his love is perfected in us. By this we know that *we abide in Him and He in us*, because He has given us His spirit. . . . God is Love, and those who abide in love abide in God and God abides in them."[540]

In the fourth century, Augustine wrote about the fifth stage of illumination and union. All things "owe their existence to You, not in a spatial sense, but because Your Being contains everything." It is by self-restraint that "we are brought together and brought back to the One after having dissipated ourselves among the many." When "I cleave to Thee with all my being, then . . . my life shall be a real life, being wholly full of Thee." With my whole self, "I shall cling to You united, . . . wholly alive will my life be all full of You. Those whom You fill, You raise up."[541]

Augustine thought about all God's creation. Then, "I thought of You, Lord, as surrounding it on every side and penetrating it, but being in all directions Infinite. It was as though there were a sea, which everywhere and on all sides through immensity was just one infinite sea, but which had inside it a sponge which, though very big, was still bounded. This sponge, of course, would in all its parts be completely filled with the immeasurable sea. So I thought of Your creation as finite and as filled with You, who are Infinite. And I said, 'here is God, and here is what God has created; and God is good and is most mightily and incomparably better than all of these. Yet He, being good, created them good, and see how He surrounds them and fills them.'"[542]

In the sixth century, Denys the Areopagite said that "everything, every part of everything, participates in the One." The Cause of all "infinitely transcends everything and yet gathers everything within It." However, he went even further. Since God is 'Being Itself,' all "being is contained in Him." Moreover, "It is by Him and in Him and for Him that all things exist." The Cause of all "uniquely contains all" and "all things are contained beforehand in and are embraced by the One in its capacity as an inherent Unity." Furthermore, "all being derives from, exists in, and is returned toward the Beautiful and the Good." In the thirteenth century, Mechthild of Magdeburg said, "the day of my spiritual awakening was the day I saw and knew all things in God and God in all things." The same century, Eliziezar ben Judah, a German Jewish rabbi, said that "everything is in Thee and Thou are in everything; Thou fills everything and does encompass it."[543]

In the fifteenth century, Julian of Norwich had illuminations that she called Divine Revelations. She saw that "our essential being is in God" and "with absolute certainty that our substance is in God." She realized "quite clearly that our eternal friendship, our continuing life and existence is in God." Because of "the eternal and unchanging nature of His Love, . . . there will be no separation between His Love and our souls." Our Lord "made us One in His Charity" and "One in blessedness." Furthermore, "our soul is so deeply set in God . . . that we cannot come to know it until we first know God, its Creator, to whom it is joined." For "God is nearer to us than our own soul, for He is the ground in which it stands, . . . Our soul reposes in God, its true rest, and stands in God, its true strength, and is fundamentally rooted in God, its eternal Love."[544]

Julian's Divine revelations showed her that God is "the Foundation of our nature" and "the Ground of our life and existence." In addition, "the Foundation of our reason is in God, who is the substance of everything natural." Besides being our Foundation, "He is going to be our fullest Bliss." Because of this, "we ought to love our God in whom we have our own being." Julian not only revealed the third stage of awakening that the Holy One is within us, but she also showed the fifth stage of illumination that we are within the ONE. "We are all enfolded in Him and He is in us." Thus, "our Lord God lives in us, and is here with us; notwithstanding that He clasps and enfolds us in His tender Love, never to leave us; notwithstanding that He is nearer to us than tongue and heart can think or tell." Again, "our Lord and Maker is so near us; He is in us and we are in Him, completely safe through His great Goodness." Our faith is "a right understanding, and true belief, and sure trust, that with regard to our essential being we are in God, and God in us."[545]

The sixteenth-century Islamic mystic from India, Mirabai who called God Krishna, sang, "O Krishna, You are the tree, I am the bird that rests in Your branches, You are the ocean, I am the fish that swims in Your depths, You are the hill, I am the peacock that dances on Your top, You are the full moon, I am the chakor bird that never turns its gaze from Your Light. . . . You are the Lord of the three worlds, I am Mirabai, the one who sings Your song, hoping You will hear me."[546]

Over the centuries, Judaism had a mystical tradition called Kabbalah that called God *Ein Sof*. A sixteenth-century Spanish kabbalist Moses Codovero said that "the Creator, Ein Sof, is the Cause of causes, One without second." Ein Sof has ten emanations or attributes that are referred to as *sefirot*. "Before anything emanated, there was only Ein Sof." After Its emanations, "Ein Sof is present in all things in actuality, while all things are present in It." Furthermore, "there is nothing that is not pervaded by the power of Divinity. . . . God is everything that exists, though everything that exists is not God. It is present in everything, and everything comes into being from It. Nothing is devoid of Its Divinity. Everything is within It; It is within everything and outside of everything. There is nothing but It."[547]

The contemporary Jewish theologian Buber said, "how foolish and hopeless would be the man who turned aside from the course of his life in order to seek God." In fact, "there is no such thing as seeking God, for there is nothing in which He could not be found." Moreover, "every particular Thou is a glimpse through to the Eternal Thou." Even more, "in each Thou we address the Eternal Thou." To say "'here world, there God' is the language of It," but "to include the whole world in the Thou, . . . to include nothing beside God but everything in Him—this is the full and complete relation" with the Eternal Thou. "God is the 'wholly Other;' but He is also . . . the wholly Present . . . nearer to me than my I." We know remoteness from God as well as anguish and barrenness in our hearts. We do "not know the absence of God; it is we who are not always there." Contemporary mystic Fox says that "a healthy mysticism is panentheistic." It is not dualistic. The Divinity is not 'out there' separate from creation. "Panentheism means that 'all things are in God and God is in all things.' . . . Panentheism melts the dualism . . . creation is in God and God is in creation."[548]

Illumination transforms us and brings us experiences of deep happiness, peace, and ecstasy. In the twelfth century, Hugh of St. Victor, a German mystic, said that "I am suddenly renewed. I am changed. I am plunged into an ineffable peace. My mind is full of gladness, all my past wretchedness and pain are forgotten. My soul exults, my intellect is illuminated, my heart is afire, and my desires are satisfied. I know not where I am, because my Love has embraced me." My soul desires nothing, but to rest in my Beloved.[549]

Throughout this book, I have been hesitant to include the more sensational mystical experiences, because these might cause people to fail to recognize their own incidents as spiritual experiences. However, Robert Browning, the English poet, helped answer this hesitation. "Truth is within ourselves" and "to know, consists in opening out a way whence the imprisoned splendor may escape." Rabindranath Tagore, a twentieth-century Nobel Prize winning Hindu poet, described his experience of illumination to his friend, C.F. Andrews. While Tagore was watching a sun rise, "suddenly, in a moment, a veil seemed to be lifted from my eyes. I found the world wrapt in an inexpressible glory with its waves of joy and beauty bursting and breaking on all sides. The thick shroud of sorrow that lay on my heart in many folds was pierced through and through by the light of the world, which was everywhere radiant."[550]

H.P. Shepland wrote in a letter that "I know nothing of the ecstasy of the mystics except for one illuminating personal experience. A flash of insight . . . unsought, surprising—a split-second of Time containing all Time, not so much a vision of beauty and harmony, but a certain knowledge that they existed." This was "the briefest moment, yet so illuminating and life-giving that it still seems more vivid than all the days and years of my life. The best description I can find is that it was a marriage of mind with the Universal Mind." Another mystic had an illumination that "I have never forgotten." Sitting on the seashore, only half-listening to a friend, and picking up some sand, "I suddenly saw the exquisite beauty of every little grain, . . . from each of which a brilliant shaft of light was reflected, which each tiny crystal shone like a rainbow." Next "suddenly, my consciousness was lighted up from within and I saw in a vivid way how the whole universe was . . . no matter how dull and lifeless . . . nevertheless filled with this intense and vital beauty. For a second or two, the whole world appeared as a blaze of glory." After it quieted down, "it left with me something I have never forgotten and which constantly reminds me of the beauty locked up in every minute speck of material around me."[551]

Meditation and Contemplation Are Ways to Illumination

Besides Underhill's five stages on the mystical way, she claimed that the three states or degrees of mystical prayer and contemplation are ways to illumination. The mystic life is a "process of organic development, . . . a movement of consciousness toward higher levels," a striving for the goal of illumination and a growth in love for God as well as for all people and creation. To develop their spiritual life, people use mysticism and its methods: "the steps of the ladder, the substances of the progressive exercises undertaken by the developing self, its education in the art of contemplation," the "steep stairs of love," and "the three 'degrees of prayer or orison.'" Mystics' descriptions of their progress in mystical prayer and contemplation are "bewildering in their variety" of states, degrees, phases, steps, stairs, divisions, and stages. Mystics' stages are based on their individual experience. The sixteenth century Spanish nun Teresa of Avila's description of her own states varies in her three principal works. The divisions into parts is an attempt to help spiritual seekers. Like life, the mystical process is "one and continuous—not a stairway but a slope." The divisions among the steps and multitude of terms make it difficult to compare different mystics' processes.[552]

Underhill proposed three states of mystical prayer and contemplation, "the gradual process of change, by which the mystical consciousness matures, and develops its apprehension of God." These three are meditation, quiet, and contemplation, or "concentration, silence, and the new perception which results." These states have nothing in common with petitioning God for the things that we need and want. They are nothing but yearning for God. Meditation, Underhill's first state, involves withdrawing from the external world by "concentrating our whole attention on one act of loving sight," on our breathing, on one scripture reading, on one attribute of the Divine, on one name of God, on one idea or one image of the Holy One, on one thought or one word or one aspect of the life of our religious leader. Whatever we choose to focus on, we need to meditate and dwell on it more than think about it. As we ignore the world and meditate, we are illumined.[553]

Her first state of meditation develops into the second state of the prayer of 'inward silence or simplicity' or quiet. Unlike some others who discuss silence, Underhill said that "true 'quiet' is a means, not an end; . . . It is a phase in the self-growth in contemplation, a bridge," a transition, which leads from our old life to contemplation and union with God. From the meditative practice of loving attention, we glide into the half-way house of silence where there are no words and "an almost complete suspension of the reflective powers. The strange silence which is the outstanding quality of this state . . . is not describable." Silence helps us not to twist our experience into our own concepts. It assists us to stop analyzing, and "to let things be as they are, to receive and be content." The watchword is "humble receptivity." It is like the soaring of an eagle that has great swiftness without waving its wings. This passing into the quiet is "the turning from doing to being." With the door shut tight on the external world, the soul becomes aware that "it is immersed in a more real world." Silence results in ineffable peace, bliss, and an "utter speechless resting in the Absolute Life."[554]

Thus, Underhill's first state of meditation "trained the self in spiritual attention; and at the same time lifted it to a new level of perception where . . . it received a new inflow of life." In her second phase of silence, the self "passed on to a state characterized by a tense stillness in which it rested." As the true quiet becomes deeper, it passes into the third state of contemplation, where a person's "knowledge of the external world is lost, all the messages of the senses are utterly ignored." Contemplation is "a supreme manifestation of that indivisible power of knowing," where a person's "thought, love, and will become a unity, and feeling and perception are fused." It is a mental "attitude of the whole personality, a self-forgetting attentiveness, a profound concentration, a self-merging, which operates a real communion between the seer and the seen." The aim of "the mystic's contemplation is always some aspect of the Infinite Life." Contemplation "establishes communion between the soul and the Absolute." Thus, in the first of Underhill's two marks of true contemplation, the mystic has an "experience of the All," the Totality. Second, "this revealed Reality is apprehended by way of participation," by way of active outgoing self-giving, by way of expressing love for all.[555]

When the soul contemplates, it becomes consciousness of two levels of the Ultimate Reality, time which is the world of becoming and Eternity which is the world of Being. Eckhart, the fourteenth century German mystic, said that the soul is "in a place between time and Eternity; with its highest powers it touches Eternity;" and with its lower powers it is in time. Boehme, the seventeenth century mystic, said to a beginner, "when both thy intellect and will are quiet and passive to the expressions of the Eternal Word and Spirit, and when thy soul is winged up above that which is temporal, the outward senses and the imagination being locked up by Holy abstraction, *then* the Eternal Hearing, Seeing, and Speaking will be revealed in thee." Then "the soul, leaving all things and forgetting herself, is immersed in the Ocean of Divine Splendor, and illuminated by the Sublime Abyss of Unfathomable Wisdom."[556]

During contemplation, we experience the Divine presence within us and communion within the Holy One. Although the presence and communion are brief, the memory remains forever. Teresa of Avila said that in the contemplative act, "God visits the soul in a way that prevents it doubting, when it comes to itself, that *it has been in God and God in it.* . . . though years may pass before the state recurs, the soul can never forget it nor doubt its reality." The fourteenth-century English classic, *The Cloud of Unknowing*, claimed that contemplation is striving "to fix your love on God, forgetting all else." Then "your spirit is purified and strengthened by this contemplative work more than by all others put together." In addition, other humans are "marvelously enriched by this work of yours." Nicolas Berdyaev, a twentieth-century Russian mystic, said that "contemplation can only be interpreted as love, as the ecstasy of love." We "contemplate in love" about ourselves, other people, nature, and "God who is Love." In the fourteenth-century, Richard Rolle, an English mystic, said that "contemplation is the joyful song of God's Love." It is not reached without great labor and without forsaking "all the world's vanity." The "contemplation of Love Everlasting" results in jubilation and joy untold.[557]

Union with the Holy One

In awakening, the third stage on the mystical way, our consciousness of the Divine within everyone and everything begins to develop. This awareness of the Sacred Spirit within us creates love for ourselves and our neighbors in the fourth stage. Then we move back and forth between awakening and love. This spiritual experience of love results not only in illumination, but also in union with the Ultimate Reality in the fifth stage. This makes us feel that the fire of Divine Love surrounds and permeates us. This is a beautiful and joyful experience.[558]

For many mystics, their spiritual journey is not only the act of knowing but also the act of love and union with the Divine. It is not only to *go to* the Holy One but also to be *united* to the ONE. As Underhill said, the unitive life is "essentially a state of free and filial participation in Eternal Life." It is being "One with the rhythm of the Universal Life," a "consummation of love," and "an intense and continuous communion" with the Sacred Spirit. Union is "the final triumph of the spirit, the flower of mysticism, humanity's top note, the consummation toward which the contemplative life . . . has moved from the first." Mystics who experience union reach the Transcendent Reality. Their "full consciousness of Reality completes the circle of Being." Furthermore, "the simplest expression of the unitive life . . . is that it is the complete and conscious fulfillment here and now of Perfect Love."[559]

Underhill says that one of the marks of the unitive life is "a complete absorption in the interests of the Infinite." As an example, the sixteenth century Hindu Mira Bai spoke to God, "You are the ocean, I am the fish that swims in your depth." Another mark is a consciousness of sharing the Divine strength "which results in a complete sense of freedom, an invulnerable serenity," and the urge to do creative activity. When we unite with the Sacred Spirit, our consciousness is widened to encompass Universal Life. Our view of our surface selves becomes a realization of our "real, Eternal self." When we reach our long-sought communion with the Transcendent Reality, we are intact but "wholly penetrated—as a sponge by the sea—by the Ocean of Life and Love."[560]

Awakening has similarities and differences with union. Both awakening and union have differences with illumination. In awakening as well as before we experience union, our souls feel separate from the Holy One, even though we have a spiritual consciousness of the Divine within us. We think that we are our body, our individual self, and our unique identity. We are physical bodies with a spiritual dimension. We realize that we are two separate individual beings, a human and a Divine Being. We are aware that we are children of God. The Holy One is our Father, our Mother, our Beloved, who is separate from us.

In union, we become conscious that our soul is not separate and apart from the Ultimate Reality, but rather we are united to the Divine. We are spirits with physical bodies who are united to the Sacred Spirit. When we experience union, we still feel that we are two separate individuals, a human spirit and the Sacred Spirit, uniting. However, we humans are not equal to the Divine, since we are only a drop of love in the Sacred Ocean of Infinite Love.[561]

Awakening and union have differences with illumination. In illumination, we realize that since birth, we have always been within the ONE. We have never been separated from the Holy One. Rather than being physical bodies with a spiritual dimension, we are spirits with physical bodies who are now and have always been within the Universal, Eternal Spirit. We are drops of love within the Sacred Ocean of Infinite Love. Thus, we are surrounded, engulfed, saturated, and penetrated by Infinite Love.

What happens to the surface selves of the mystics who renounce all selfhood, who merge their wills with Eternal Truth, who are united with the Holy One, and who are "dwelling within the Ocean of Divine Love?" Does their 'self-naughting' result in them becoming nothing? Underhill explains one view that says "the total annihilation of the personality" is the goal of the mystical way. This view is that "the stripping off of the I, the me, the mine, utter renunciation, or 'self-naughting'—self-abandonment to the direction of a larger Will—is an imperative condition of the attainment of the unitive life." The discarding of the mind to make space for the vision of the Divine needs to be applied to the whole life. "There is a final swallowing up of that willful selfhood, that surface individuality." Then "something new is established." The self is made part of the Holy One, "humbly taking its place in the corporate life of Reality." The self is "devoured, immersed in the Abyss, sinks into God, Who is the Deep of the Deeps."[562]

Henry Suso, the fourteenth-century German Dominican priest, provides an example of this view. "When the good and faithful servant enters into the joy of his Lord, . . . he forgets himself, he is no longer conscious of his selfhood; he disappears and loses himself in God and becomes One Spirit with Him, as a drop of water which is drowned in a great quantity of wine. For even as such a drop disappears, taking the color and taste of wine," so it is with the servants of the Sacred Spirit. "All human desires are taken from them . . . and they are immersed in the Divine Will. . . . His being remains, but in another form, in another glory, and in another power." What is this form, "if it be not the Divine Nature and the Divine Being" that they pour themselves into and which pours Itself into them, and becomes One thing with them?"[563]

Therese of Lisieux, the nineteenth-century French Carmelite nun, claimed that she disappeared when she was united with Jesus. "I knew that I was loved and I declared, 'I love You and I give myself to You forever!' . . . For a long time, Jesus and little Therese had gazed at each other and they understood each other. On that day it was no longer a matter of gazing: it was union. There were no longer two of us. Therese had disappeared like a drop of water lost in the depth of the ocean. Only Jesus remained."[564]

There is a second view. After the soul was drawn into the Divine Unity, Jan van Ruysbroeck, a fourteenth-century Flemish priest, said that "the creature in its inward contemplation feels a distinction and an otherness between itself and God." Even though "the spirit feels itself to be One Truth, One Richness, and One Unity with God," yet there is "an essential distinction between the being of the soul and the Being of God." In the seventeenth century, Boehme claimed that "the soul is set in the Deity; the Deity penetrates through the soul, and dwells in the soul, . . . but does not alter it . . . but only gives it the Divine Source." In nineteenth century, the Hindu holy man Ramakrishna reported a Hindu sage saying that "enlightenment is not the loss of individuality, but the enlargement of individuality," because you realize that you are Divine.[565]

In the twentieth century, Buber described our experience of the Divine as the relation between an I and the Eternal Thou. When we as finite, natural, spiritual beings are in relation with the Eternal Thou, we do not give up our I. "The I is indispensable" in our relation with the Eternal Thou, "since a relation is only possible between I and Thou. It is not the I, then, that is given up, but the false self-asserting that makes a man flee to the possessing of things." Disagreeing with mystics who say that we cease to exist when we are merged or are united with the Sacred Spirit, he says that we are not one. We are not swallowed up by Eternal Thou into a unity, so that there is no longer an I. We do not become the Ultimate Reality; we are not deified; and we are not a single Being. He also disagrees with mystics who say that we are absorbed in the Eternal Thou or entered into "the Divine One." In this absorption, "the Thou does not in truth exist at all, for there is in truth no twofold being," because of "the identification of the human with the Divine." Buber claims instead that "what the ecstatic man calls union is the enrapturing dynamic of relation, not a unity."[566]

My answer to whether our spirits disappear when we are united with the Divine is speculation. I do not know for sure. However, my best thinking and spiritual experiences tell me that while we are alive, we work to transform rather than renounce ourselves. When we experience the fifth stage, we realize that the Holy One is within us and we are within the ONE. Our spirits, that are also called our souls, our inner cores of love, and the Divine presence within us, are never annihilated because they are always within the ONE. Since birth, we are never separate from the Ultimate Reality. When we die, our bodies decay in their graves. From our birth to our death and beyond, our souls continue to live forever within the Holy One. A way of understanding this is to look at the relationship of our arm to our body. Our arm is within our body and is the same nature and substance as our body. It is not equal to the body. Though it is part of the body, it does not lose its own identity and function. It does not disappear, but rather participates as part of the whole. One drop of love in the Sacred Ocean of Infinite Love is not equal to the Ocean, but it has its own identity and work.

Underhill describes illumination as her stage three and union as her stage five, unlike my illumination and union together as my stage five. In my opinion, the reason Underhill is able to separate them into two different stages is because her description of illumination is so vague that is not clear what she means by this stage. Her fifth stage of union is clear. My description of illumination is that we are within the Holy One. Being within the ONE is union. Although I use both illumination and union to describe the fifth stage, my preference would be to call the fifth stage by only one name, illumination, because that includes union. One reason is that those who name the fifth stage union often explain it as though when we were born, we were completely separate from the Ultimate Reality and then later in life we experience being united. Those who write about spiritual marriage and divinization often view it this way. In contrast, it is my belief that all of us were always, are always, and will always be within the Sacred Spirit. When we reached this stage, we realized that although we thought from birth on that we were separate from the Holy One, we never actually were. We were always within Infinite Love, always in union with the Holy One. We did NOT change from being separate from the Ultimate Reality to being in union. We only changed our consciousness from thinking that we were separate to realizing that we were always within the ONE.

Another reason I favor illumination is that union implies that when the Divine and I form a union, we are equals, as the words spiritual marriage indicates. In contrast, I believe that when my individual soul is within the Universal Soul, it is not equal to It. I am only a drop of love within the Sacred Ocean of Infinite Love. Even though creation is within the Creator, it is not equal to It. However, my name for this fifth stage is both illumination and union, because so many mystics portray their experiences as union, spiritual marriage, and divinization.

Mystics throughout the Centuries Experienced Union with the Divine

Throughout history, mystics wrote about union with the Divine. The Hindu *Upanishads* called Brahman the "great Unity." Everything is within this Unity. An image that shows the great Unity between Atman and Brahman is rivers flowing into the ocean where they find their final peace. In the ocean, the names and forms of the individual spirits that flow into Brahman disappear.[567]

In the *Upanishads*, the Supreme Spirit is "the essence of all" means that the Spirit is not only the essence of Buddha, but also the essence of an amoeba, a rock, the wind, a duck, and a whale. The Spirit is "the ear of the ear, the eye of the eye, . . . the mind of the mind, the life of life." Brahman pervades all. However, Buddha expresses his essence more clearly and fully than other things. Although a cup, a bucket, and a water tower all contain the same water, there are differences between them in the amount of water they hold. Nevertheless, what is more important is the essential Unity of all life and the essential Divinity of all life. Brahman is "the ONE, the only God," who is "the root and flower of all things." There is no other reality except the Supreme Spirit, the ONE, Infinite Love.[568]

In the Hindu *Bhagavad Gita*, the Holy Krishna said, "I am in the heart of all." All are in Me and I am in them. On the highest path, "a man sees that the God in himself is the same God in all that is." Thus, "when a man sees that the infinity of various beings is abiding in the ONE, and is an evolution from the ONE, then he becomes One with Brahman."[569]

Nirvana is the ultimate goal of all Buddhists. It is impossible to explain because it is a mystical concept that is ineffable and beyond words. Some define it as "the extinction of craving" and others as the annihilation of our separate selfhood. Still others say it is a life beyond death. As a word, Nirvana means 'to blow out' or 'to extinguish.' Some say Nirvana means the total extinction of the self. My interpretation is that when we live by Buddha's Four Noble Truths and Eightfold Path, we reach Nirvana. Nirvana is the state we reach when we extinguish all our desires. It is also the extinction of the boundaries between you and me so that when I look at you, I see myself. When our boundaries are annihilated, we experience Nirvana, the Boundless Life, and Oneness with all. Contemporary religious experts Robert Ellwood and Barbara McGraw claim that Nirvana is not annihilation, but rather the universalization of the self, "the falling away of all barriers so that the mind becomes undifferentiated from horizonless Infinity" and the self "lives purely on the level of universal compassion and Oneness with the joy of all beings."[570]

Nirvana is the state in which everything that restricts us and keeps us from experiencing the Boundless Life and Oneness is removed. When we stop seeing other people and the natural world as separate from ourselves, we will experience them as One with ourselves and reach Nirvana. Although it is the state of being beyond our body, our mind, our thoughts, our feelings, and our actions, we do not have to go anywhere to reach Nirvana. Although most of us do not realize it, experiencing Nirvana, the Boundless Life, and Oneness are available all the time, right here and now. Nirvanic vision is to see all people and things including ourselves as interrelated and as

One. Contemporary religious scholars Denise and John Carmody say that when we reach Nirvana, "we sense the Oneness of all beings . . . by being in the midst of the moving, interconnected field." More succinctly, Nirvana is experiencing the Boundless Life, Oneness with all. According to Huston Smith, "some say, 'the dewdrop slips into the shining sea.'" Others prefer to think of the dewdrop as opening to receive the sea itself." The fifteen-century Islamic Sufi Kabir said, "all know that the drop merges into the ocean but few know the ocean merges into the drop." Buddha said, "bliss, yes bliss, my friends, is Nirvana."[571]

Our current thoughts about Nirvana are small compared to when we will experience full illumination and bliss. "As an inconsequential dream vanishes completely on awakening, as the stars go out in deference to the morning sun, so the individual awareness will be eclipsed in the blazing Light of total awareness." Buddhism teaches the transitoriness, the perpetual perishing, of everything finite. "The waves follow one another in an eternal pursuit." Thus, there is a "sense of radical impermanence of all things finite." Accepting continual change frees us from clutching for permanence. Accepting perpetual change can also free us from clinging to our desires and thus assist us in living the Four Noble Truths and Eightfold Path. Accepting our fleetingness can help us experience Nirvana, the Boundless Life.[572]

Buddhism's teaching of impermanence is connected to its contention that humans have *anatta*, no soul, no atman, no spiritual substance, no permanent identity. According to Huston Smith, "this denial of spiritual substance was only an aspect of Buddha's wider denial of substance of every sort," of his denial of permanence. Buddha gave this advice, "regard this phantom world as a star at dawn, a bubble in a stream, a flash of lightning in a summer cloud." This teaching of *anatta* or no soul or no atman can be compared to the Hindu teaching of atman is Brahman, the individual soul is the Universal, Absolute Soul. This teaching of no soul can be interpreted as disagreeing with our conventional way of seeing ourselves as separate from other people and things. When our boundaries are extinguished, we no longer perceive ourselves as separate selves, as individual souls. We experience Nirvana, the Boundless Life, and Oneness. This teaching of no soul also helps us live the Four Noble Truths and the Eightfold Path. From birth, we humans assert our selfhood, our individuality. When we think that we are a separate individual with our own soul, we suffer because we crave things and cling to them. When we no longer think of ourselves as separate, we can stop having desires and being attached as well as begin to overcome our suffering, to live the Four Noble Truths, and to follow Eightfold Path to Nirvana.[573]

A wandering ascetic asked Buddha if an *Arhat*, a holy person who extinguishes all desires and lived the Four Noble Truths and Eightfold Path, would continue to exist after death? Despite the fact that Buddhists believed in reincarnation, he answered that "the word reborn does not apply to him. . . . The term not-reborn does not apply to him." The ascetic was bewildered. Then Buddha explained that "this doctrine is profound, recondite, hard to comprehend, rare, excellent, beyond dialectic, subtle, only to be understood by the wise. Let me question you. If there were a fire blazing in front of you, would you know it?" Yes said the ascetic. "If the fire went out, would you know it?" Again came yes. "If now you were asked in what direction the fire had gone, . . . could you give an answer?"[574]

Then Buddha said, in death, consciousness, feelings, perceptions, and everything by which the Arhat might be known is gone. "Profound, measureless, unfathomable, is the Arhat even as the mighty ocean; reborn does not apply to him nor not-reborn, nor any combination of such terms." During life on earth, an Arhat is "increasingly free" from the world's happenings, desires, worries, and passions. Progress continues with "every growth of inwardness, peace, and freedom." As long as the spirit is tied to the body, its freedom from desires is not complete. Increased freedom brings a larger life and being. In death, total freedom brings Being Itself, Oneness, Nirvana.[575]

In the fourth century BCE, the Confucian Chuang Tzu said that the sage "discards the confused and obscure; honors the meek and humble; and blends everything into a Universal Whole. As men toil on to obtain some reward, . . . he has merged all things into complete Unity. . . . On and on goes his delight." In addition, "only the truly intelligent understand this principle of the Identity of all things." In fact, "all things are One."[576]

In John's gospel, Jesus clearly said that he was united with God. In answering one of his disciples, he asked, "do you not believe that I am in the Father and the Father is in me? The words that I say to you I do not speak on my own, but the Father Who dwells in me does His works. Believe me that I am in the Father and the Father is in me." Using a metaphor to explain their connection, he said, "I am the vine, and my Father is the Vine Grower." Then Jesus described his union with his followers. "I am the true vine, you are the branches. . . . As the Father loved me, so I have loved you; abide in my love. If you keep my commandments, you will abide in my love, just as I have kept my Father's commandments and abide in His Love." Later "I am not alone because the Father is with me." Jesus repeated several times that the Father and he are One. "We are One." Asking God on behalf of those who believe in him, Jesus said "that they may be One, as You, Father, are in me and I am in You, may they also be in us, so that the world may believe that You have sent me. . . . They may be One, as we are One. I in them and You in me, that they may become completely One, so that the world may know that You have sent me and have loved them even as You loved me." He also said, "this is Eternal life, that they may know You, the only true God."[577]

Jesus' strong connection with God was shown when he said, "the word that you hear is not mine, but is from the Father who sent me." He repeated this. "I have not spoken on my own, but the Father who sent me has Himself given me a commandment about what to say and what to speak. . . . What I speak, therefore, I speak just as the Father has told me." Besides telling what the Father wanted him to say, "I do as the Father has commanded me." Again, "I seek to do not my own will, but the will of Him who sent me." Not only did Jesus say that the Father told him what to say and how to say it, but he also told his disciples that the Spirit of God would speak through them when they got into trouble for preaching that the kingdom of God is near, the presence of the Divine is near. "Do not worry about how you are to speak or what you are to say; for what you are to say will be given to you at that time; for it is not you who speak, but the Spirit of your Father speaking through you."[578]

At the beginning of the sixth century, Denys the Areopagite presented three stages that still have influence today. His threefold mystical way to the Divine was first purification, second illumination, and third union and complete perfection. In his third stage, mystics are "supremely united to" and belong completely to God who is beyond everything. Those who reach union and total perfection are "truly and supernaturally enlightened."[579]

In the Talmud, Rabbi Gamliel said, "as a river empties into the ocean, empty yourself into Reality. When you are emptied into Reality, you are filled with compassion, desiring only justice. When you desire only justice, the will of Reality becomes your will. When you are filled with compassion, there is no self to oppose another and no other to stand against oneself." Speaking about himself and Allah in the tenth century, al Hallaj, an Islamic Iraqi mystic, said that "I am He whom I love, and He whom I love is I. We are two Spirits dwelling in one body. If thou see me, thou see Him, and if thou see Him, thou see us both."[580]

The thirteenth-century Jewish kabbalist Moses de Leon said that "God is unified Oneness—One without second, inestimable. Genuine Divine existence engenders the existence of all creation. The sublime, inner essences secretly constitute a chain linking everything from the highest to the lowest. . . . There is nothing—not even the tiniest thing—that is not fastened to the links of this chain. Everything is . . . caught in Its Oneness. God is One, God's secret is One, all the worlds below and above are all mysteriously One. Divine existence is Indivisible. The entire chain is One. Down to the last link, everything is linked with everything else; so the Divine essence is below as well as above, in heaven and one earth. There is nothing else."[581]

In the thirteenth century, the Islamic Sufi mystic Rumi said, "if you can detach yourself from all worldly worries, . . . if you can separate yourself from the house of desires, you will come into the sanctuary of Divine Majesty, in the heart of the Ocean of Unity." Since the spirit of prayer is "more virtuous than the form," it helps us "arrive at union with God in a way that only God knows." Moreover, "may the inhabitants of the earth become One in their hearts, unite their plans and designs with the dwellers in heaven! All separation and polytheism and duality will vanish for there's only Unity in Real Existence." Furthermore, "dying to yourself is the fundamental principle and you haven't adhered to it. Your suffering cannot end before this death is complete. You cannot reach the roof before climbing the ladder. . . . You cannot come to know God but by denying what opposes Him. You want Reality unmasked? Choose death! Not death that drags you to the tomb—but the death that is a transmutation so you at last change into the Light." In addition, "when you are truly and finally lost in Love, when the soul has truly been united to God, to speak of God is to speak of the soul and to speak of the soul is to speak of God."[582]

In the thirteenth century, Hadewijch, a Flemish Beguine, whose writing had the word love on almost every page, called God Totality, Love, and Almighty Love. "God, who created all things and who, above all, is Love, . . . that Love now draws the loving soul to Herself in the closest union." Love is "an unconceivable Wonder which has thus filled my heart." Furthermore, "Love, Your Being is so far from me—whereas all my delight comes from You. . .. All that gives light to my heart, searches for You in Your Totality. . . . Alas, how should anything content me, Love, save You in Your Totality? It is my lot that I do not possess You fully, and that I cannot fully content You with veritable, high-minded, and lavish love." Moreover, "Love gives counsel to the sorrowful and comforts those who are sorrowing."[583]

Hadewijch recorded some of her visions and spoke about her union with God. One Easter Sunday, I "had gone to God and He embraced me in my interior senses and took me away in spirit." A voice said to her, "with regard to all things, know what I, Love, am in them! And when you fully bring Me yourself, as pure humanity in Myself, through all the ways of perfect love, you shall have fruition of Me as the Love who I am. Until that day, you shall love what, I, Love, am. And then you will be Love, as I am Love. . . . In My Unity, you have received Me and I have received you." In one of her many poems, she wrote, "the loving soul wants Love wholly, without delay; . . . liberty wishes to lead it instantly where it will become One with the Beloved."[584]

In one of her letters, Hadewijch said that God will teach you "with what wondrous sweetness the loved one and the Beloved dwell in the other, and how they penetrate each other in such a way that neither of the two distinguishes himself from the other. But they abide in one another in fruition, . . . while one sweet Divine Nature flows through them both, and they are both One thing through each other, but at the same time remain two different selves—yes, and remain so forever." How is this indwelling and penetrating achieved? In her poems, she wrote "if he loved Love with the power of love, he would speedily become Love with Love." For Hadewijch, "the loved soul attains to the Beloved so closely that it cannot be parted from the dear Beloved, . . . that it lives for the Beloved." In addition, "to those who give themselves thus to content Love, . . . with love they shall cleave in Oneness to Love, . . . where Love gives all love. . . . To all those who desire Love, . . . after themselves becoming Love, they draw Love into themselves" and "cry: I am all Love's, and Love is all mine!" And again, "we can indeed make bold to say: 'You are mine, Beloved, and I am Yours!'"[585]

The fourteenth-century *Theologica Germanica* saw "God as the Eternal only Perfect One." Then "if the best has to be loved," the Eternal, the only Good, the Perfect One "should be loved above all." To "want, desire, or strive after anything except God, . . . the Eternal, only perfect Good," is wicked. In the fourteenth century, Eckhart said, "if I am to know God directly, I become completely He and He I, so that this He and this I become and are One I." Catherine of Siena experienced God as saying to her that the souls "thrown into the furnace of My Charity, no part of their will remaining outside but the whole of them being inflamed in Me. . . . No one can seize these souls, or draw them outside of Me, because they are made *one thing* with Me, through grace, and I never withdraw Myself from them."[586]

In the fourteenth century, Ruysbroeck said that mystics hear "the invitation of Love" which "draws interior souls toward the One and says 'come home.'" Enlightened souls have "the Love of God as something drawing or urging them into the Unity. . . . Thus the Unity is ever drawing to Itself and inviting to Itself everything that has been born of It." These illuminated people with free spirits are "lifted up above reason into . . . the Eternal indrawing summons of the Divine Unity . . . until they reach the summit of their spirits. There their bare understanding is drenched through by the Eternal Brightness, even as the air is drenched through by the sunshine. And the bare, uplifted will is transformed and drenched through by abyssal Love."[587]

Ruysbroeck continued, "yet the creature does not become God, for the union takes place in God through grace and our homeward-turning love, and therefore the creature in its inward contemplation feels a distinction and an otherness between itself and God. . . . All is full and overflowing, for the spirit feels itself to be One Truth and One Richness and One Unity with God. Yet even here there is an essential tending forward, and therein an essential distinction between the being of the soul and the Being of God; and this is the highest and finest distinction which we are able to feel." In other writings, Ruysbroeck said, "when Love has carried us above and beyond all things, . . . above the Light, into the Divine Dark, there we are wrought and transformed by the Eternal, . . . and as the air is penetrated by the sun, thus we receive . . . the Incomprehensible Light, enfolding us and penetrating us. . . . our thought, life, and being are uplifted in simplicity and made One with the Truth which is God."[588]

According to Ruybroeck, there are three ways a person enters the God-seeing life. "The inward lover of God, who possess God in fruitive love; and himself in adhering and active love; and his whole life in virtues according to righteousness; through these three things, and by the mysterious revelation of God, such an inward man enters into the God-seeing life. . . . Only he with whom it pleases God to be united in His Spirit, and whom it pleases Him to enlighten by Himself, can see God, and no one else. The mysterious Divine Nature is eternally and actively beholding and loving . . . in the essential Unity of God; all inward spirits are One with God in the immersion of love." Furthermore, "the super-essential contemplation" is "the source of all holiness and of all perfection of life."[589]

The fourteenth-century anonymous English author of *The Cloud of Unknowing* said that a cloud of unknowing lies between us and the hidden God. We "may know completely and ponder thoroughly every created thing and its works, yes, and God's works, too, but not God Himself. Thought cannot comprehend God. And so, I prefer to love Him Whom I cannot know. Though we cannot know Him, we can love Him. By love He may be touched and embraced, never by thought." We need to see "that nothing lives in thy working mind but a naked intent stretching unto God, not clothed in any special thought of God, . . . but only that He is as He is. . . . Think no further of thyself than I bid thee do of thy God, so that thou be One with Him in spirit and in thought, . . . for He is thy being and in Him thou art that thou art: . . . He is in thee both as thy cause and thy being. And therefore, think on God . . . that He is as He is, and thou art as thou art." He is "Him that is All." Underhill said of Teresa of Avila that she thinks that the true prayer of quiet is "a sort of peace, . . . All her powers are at rest. She understands, but otherwise than by the sense, that she is already near her God, and that if she draws a little nearer, she will become by union One with Him."[590]

In the fifteenth century, Julian of Norwich made a summary of the first of her sixteen revelations in which God spoke of the union of our soul and God. "When He made us, He joined and united us to Himself." Our soul was "at its creation united to its Creator." Furthermore, "we are eternally united to Him in love." Moreover, "our soul is united to Him who is unchangeable Goodness, . . . For the soul is completely united to God by His own Goodness, and nothing whatever can come between God and the soul." Human nature is "so joined and united to Him that it must have some substance that has never been and never can be separated from Him." Julian's description of the way to union was that "the soul, when it is really at peace with itself, is at once is united to God." He "has made everything, and also works in and through everything." Julian hoped that "His grace will continue . . . to unite us all with Him and with one another in the true and lasting Joy" that is God. Our Lord "made us One in His Charity" and "One in blessedness." He revealed Himself as "I whom am Unity" and "I who am All." The sixteen-century Italian Catherin of Genoa said, "I do not see or feel myself to have either soul, body, heart, will, or taste, or any other thing except Pure Love."[591]

Marie of the Incarnation, a seventeenth-century French mystic and missionary nun, explained that "one morning as I was at prayer God absorbed my spirit in Himself. . . . Once again I was granted a vision" of the Holy One. "Through love my soul found itself in a state of extreme familiarity with and fruition of the God of Love." Then she was "engulfed in the presence of this most adorable Majesty." The Divine "took possession of my soul and, embracing it with an inexplicable love, united it to Himself. . . . No longer being myself, I abided in Him through the intimacy of love and union, so that I lost myself and no longer aware of myself, having become Him by participation." Thus, "the soul constantly experiences the presence of this gracious Being who has taken possession of her in spiritual marriage and who inflames and consumes her with a fire so agreeable and pleasant that it is impossible to describe."[592]

Ramakrishna, a nineteenth-century Hindu holy man, said that mystical consciousness reaches union with the Holy One when it becomes aware that "all that is, has been, or ever will be" is Divine. "The Absolute is the only Reality, all else is unreal." We become merged in God consciousness when we realize that "all is Thine." Humans and all of creation are seen as different faces of the One Ultimate Reality. Everything that exists is Divine and "whatever is, is God." Picture a drop of water once it falls into the ocean. It is still an individual drop, but it is also One with the ocean. Its substance is the same as the ocean. A Hindu story, that Ramakrishna told, has a guru say that "everything that exists is God." A disciple takes this teaching literally. When an elephant-driver shouts to the disciple to move away from his elephant, he does not. He thinks, why move? I am Divine and so is the elephant, so why fear? Then the elephant dashes him aside, hurting him severely. When he asks about this, the guru says that it is true that you and the elephant are God, but why didn't you listen to the elephant-driver who is also Divine?[593]

Ramakrishna described two kinds of consciousness, a worldly and a mystical one. A selfish ego creates a worldly consciousness that is possessive of its personal belongings. A worldly consciousness says, "this is my body, my money, my status, my power, my fame, my spouse, my child, and my house." Its main concern is 'I' and 'mine.' A worldly consciousness comes between the Holy One and me, so that I feel separated from the Divine. An image of this is when a log is thrown across a stream, the water appears to be divided into two. When the log is removed, the water appears to be a single undivided reality.[594]

A worldly consciousness creates an illusion of 'I' and 'mine' that forgets that there is nothing that I can call my own. In contrast, a Divine-centered soul creates a mystical consciousness that says "nothing is mine," neither my home, nor my possessions, nor my spouse, nor my child. "Whatever I see, feel, or hear, even my body, is not mine." All is God's. A worldly awareness says that I am the driver of my chariot. A mystical consciousness says that "I am the chariot, Thou are the driver; I do as Thou make me to do; I speak as Thou will me to speak; I behave as Thou, within me, behave; not I, but Thou." A worldly awareness feels that all physical things and people are separate from each other and from the Divine. This creates an illusion of separateness. When mystics with a spiritual consciousness look at people and the world, they are convinced that the ultimate substance of all is Divine. Thus, when they give up the illusion of separateness, they merge into the Holy One. This is similar to salt dissolving in water. The salt does not cease to exist. The water shows the effects of the dissolved salt; it tastes salty. Liberation from a worldly consciousness is possible when mystics realize that the Holy One is within everyone and they are within the ONE. "When egoism vanishes, Divinity manifests Itself."[595]

Mother Teresa experienced union with the Holy One before she founded the Missionaries of Charity. "Before the work started there was so much union—love—faith—trust—prayer—sacrifice." Seeing Jesus as God, she remembered that Jesus "just gave Himself to me—to the full. The sweetness and consolation and union of those six months passed but too soon." When Mother Teresa was terribly afraid to found the Missionaries of Charity, Jesus spoke to her. "*Even if the whole world is against you, laughs at you, . . . fear not—it is I in you, with you, for you. You will suffer—suffer very much—but remember I am with you.—Even if the whole world rejects you—remember you are my own—and I am yours only. Fear not. It is I . . . I shall never leave you.*" Mother Teresa said, "as for myself—there is but one desire—to love God as He has never been loved before—with deep personal love.—In my heart there seems to be no other thing but He—no other love but His." Mother Teresa wanted to grow in "deep personal union of the human heart with the heart of Christ." In addition, "once you have got God within you, that's for life. . . . That's the most beautiful part of God, being Almighty and yet not forcing Himself on anyone."[596]

Writing to her Missionaries of Charity, Mother Teresa said that she wanted them to live in union with Jesus. We need to "see only Jesus in us." We need to be "so given to him—that we find his eyes looking through ours, his tongue speaking, his hands working, his feet walking, his heart loving." The first Rule for the Missionaries of Charity said that their particular purpose is "to carry Christ into the homes and streets of the slums, among the sick, dying, the beggars, and the little street children." However, in order to be able to do all this, "the sisters must first learn to live real interior lives of close union with God—and seek and see Him in all they do for the poor."[597]

Mother Teresa's spiritual life exemplified darkness and Divine absence co-existing with union with the Holy One. Acknowledging this, she said, "how this thing must sound foolish to you because of its contradiction." She experienced multiple experiences of both being in darkness and being habitually with God. When she was on the verge of saying no to God, she said, "I feel as if something will break in me." Then will come "that darkness, that loneliness, that feeling of terrible aloneness. Heaven from every side is closed. . . . Gone is the love for anything and anybody.—and yet—I long for God. I long to love Him with every drop of life in me—I want to love Him with a deep personal love. . . . My mind and heart are habitually with God." Fifteen years after Jesus spoke to her, Mother Teresa said, "I know I have Jesus—in that unbroken union—for my mind is fixed on him and in him alone, in my will." A few years later she said, "there is in my heart a very deep union with the will of God. I accept not in my feeling—but with my will, the will of God.—I accept His will—not only for a time but for eternity."[598]

Radhakrishnan, a twentieth-century Hindu sage, said that humans are first aware of their separateness from the Sacred. The normal condition of humanity is a conscious separation of ourselves from the Divine. Then they experience union. When a sudden flame of supreme mystical consciousness results in a vision and intimately felt presence of union with the Holy One, our whole being is "ablaze with purpose." Realizing our union with the Sacred brings "a rapture beyond joy, a knowledge beyond reason, a sensation more intense than that of life itself, infinite in peace and harmony."[599]

Fox claims that mystical union with the Holy One is not the loss of ourselves or our soul, but a unity in diversity. Our soul is within God and the Divine is within our soul. All of creation is within the ONE and the Holy One is within all creation. McKeever not only stresses the advanced awakening in the third stage that "God exists in everyone," but he also writes about the fifth stage of union. "God created existence out of Himself. Therefore, existence is part and parcel of God. From a single flame, countless other flames can be lit. So too, from God can come infinite becomings, all having the essence of God." Moreover, "the ultimate goal of life is a conscious union with God and Truth."[600]

Union Can Be Experienced as Deification and Spiritual Marriage

Underhill described two of the ways that mystics experience union. Her first way is 'deification' which is also called 'divinization.' "The mystics of the impersonal and metaphysical type—the seekers of a Transcendent Absolute" view the end of the quest as 'deification.' They become "partakers of the Divine Nature" and 'God-like' people. In the fourth century, Athanasius of Alexandia said that Christ "became man that we might be made God." In the fourth century, the western Augustine said, "just as Christ was made a sharer in your mortality through his humanity, so he makes you a sharer in his immortality." In the fourteenth century, Eckhart said, "our Lord says to every living soul, 'I became man for you. If you do not become God for me, you do me wrong.'"[601]

While deification is present in the West, it is dominant in Eastern Orthodox Christianity. *Philokalia*, an anthology of older texts that was edited by two Greek Orthodox monks, is Eastern Orthodox Christianity's principal spiritual book after the Bible. The Orthodox Christian tradition sees God as utterly Transcendent but "insists on His total and ineradicable presence in man and in every form of created existence." It teaches that deification means "a sharing in God's life, a participation in the Divine," and a partaking in the Sacred nature. Irenaeus of Lyons in the second century said that Jesus as God "became what we are in order to make us what He is." In the fourth century, Athanasius of Alexandria often repeated that Jesus "assumed humanity that we might become God." Mark the Ascetic said that Jesus humbled himself and took on our human nature. "He became like us in all things except that he was without sin. . . . He took upon himself, becoming what we are, so that we might become what He is."[602]

In the seventh century, Maximus the Confessor was a monk and abbot from Constantinople, who lived for years in Rome and collaborated with western Christians. "When God brought into being natures endowed with intelligence and intellect, He communicated to them, in His supreme Goodness, four of the Divine attributes by which He sustains, protects, and preserves created things. These attributes are Being, Eternal Being, Goodness, and Wisdom.... What He is in His essence the creature may become by participation. This is why man is said to have been created in the image and likeness of God." He also said that "love makes man God,... If we are made, as we are, in the image of God, let us become the image of both ourselves and of God; or rather let us become the image of the whole God, bearing nothing earthly in ourselves, so that we may consort with God and become Gods." The Holy One "intended for God (Christ) to become human" and He "tended for humanity to become Divine."[603]

In the fourteenth century, Gregory Palamas, who was born in Constantinople, a monk at Mount Athos, and archbishop in Greece, said that "God's nature is everywhere." In addition, "this resplendence and deifying energy of God... deifies those who participate in it" and "constitutes Divine grace." Besides writing about deification, he discussed union. "All the virtue we can attain and such imitation of God as lies in our power does no more than fit us for union with the Deity, but it is through grace that this ineffable union is actually accomplished. Through grace, God in His entirety penetrates the saints in their entirety, and the saints in their entirety penetrate God's entirely, exchanging the whole of Him for themselves, and acquiring Him alone." Eastern Orthodox Matthew the Poor said that "union with God is not a subsidiary issue of faith and doctrine. It is the basis of all faith and doctrine. It is the ultimate aim of God for sending His only Son to the world to become man."[604]

Underhill explains a second way that mystics experience union. "The mystics of the personal and intimate type" describe their loving communion as 'a spiritual marriage' of their soul with the Divine. This marriage is the perfect and lifelong union of the Lover and beloved. It is not self-loss but "self-fulfillment in the union of heart and will." The unknown author of the "Epistle of Prayer" said that the soul is knit to the Sacred Spirit and "that makes it One with Him in love." In the New Testament, Paul said that he who draws near to the Divine "is One Spirit with God." In addition, "in Him we live and move and have our being." Although the Holy One and the soul are two, "in grace they are so knit together that they are but one in spirit." The marriage made between the Divine and the soul "shall never be broken." In the thirteenth century, Islamic Sufi Rumi said, "with Thy Sweet Soul, this soul of mine has mixed as water does with wine." Who can separate the wine and water or Thee and me? "Thou has become my greater self;... Thou has my being taken on, and shall I not now take on Thine?... Thy Love has pierced me through and through."[605]

Teresa of Avila, a sixteenth-century Spanish nun, used an image to describe the union of spiritual marriage that seems to make the soul and the Divine not only merge into one, but also makes them seem like they are equal. "The union is like the joining of two wax candles to such an extent that the flame coming from them is but one, or the wick, the flame, and the wax are all one." Then she utilized different images to portray this union in which the soul and the Sacred Spirit did not seem to be equal. "In spiritual marriage the union is like what we have when rain falls from the sky into a river or fount; all is water, for the rain that fell from heaven cannot be divided or separated from the water of the river. Or it is like what we have when a little stream enters the sea, there is no separating the two. Or, like the bright light entering a room through two windows; although the streams of light are separate when entering the room, they become one."[606]

In Teresa of Avila's *Interior Castle*, the sixth dwelling place is spiritual betrothal. The soul and the Divine can be "separated and each remains by itself." In her seventh dwelling place of spiritual marriage, the two "can no longer be separated" and are united. Her union of spiritual marriage "takes place in the very interior center of the soul, which must be where God Himself is. . . . The Lord appears in this center of the soul. . . . the soul, I mean the spirit, is made One with God. . . . The soul always remains with its God in that center." Again, "the Lord puts the soul in this dwelling of His, which is the center of the soul itself." How does this union occur? "In emptying ourselves of all that is creature and detaching ourselves from it for the love of God, the same Lord will fill us with Himself."[607]

Another mystic who discussed union as a spiritual marriage is John of the Cross, a sixteenth-century Spanish Carmelite monk. "The soul advances until it reaches spiritual marriage, which is the very highest" stage. "In the consummation of spiritual marriage between God and the soul, there are two natures in One Spirit and Love. . . . Then the two natures are so united, what is Divine is so communicated to what is human, that, without undergoing any essential change, each seems to be God." In this marriage, "she (the soul) finds a much greater abundance and fullness of God, a more secure and lasting peace, and a sweetness incomparably more perfect" than in earlier stages. Now "the soul lives a life so happy and so glorious, as it is the life of God."[608]

According to John of the Cross, the soul as the bride addresses God who is the Bridegroom as my Brother and thus "she shows the equality between them in the betrothal of love, before she entered the state of spiritual marriage." In contrast, the seventeenth-century French mystic Frances de Sales makes a distinction between first "uniting or joining one thing and another" and second clasping or pressing one thing against or upon another." While the mother clasps her baby and presses it to her, similarly "our Lord, showing His Divine Love to the devout soul, draws her wholly to Him. . . .

Then with burning love, He clasps the soul, joins with it, and presses her" to Him. While the baby throws itself into the mother's arms, the soul "not only consents and gives herself to the union that God makes, but also cooperates with all her power, forcing herself to join and press more and more to the Divine Goodness. . . . Her union and connection to the Sovereign Sweetness depends wholly on the Divine operation."[609]

The Insights of Mechthild of Magdeburg about Illumination and Union

Mechthild of Magdeburg, a thirteenth-century German Beguine, wrote a book, *The Flowing Light of the Godhead*, that provides insights about illumination and union with the Holy One. Her book was a message to "all religious people, both the bad and the good." Her claim was that all who want to understand "should read it nine times." When she asked, "Lord God, who made this book?" God answered her, "I made it" and gave it its title. The Lord greeted her with knowledge and with the Divine presence at age twelve and for many decades afterwards. This greeting "pours forth from the flowing God into the poor, parched soul unceasingly with new knowledge, in new contemplation, and in special enjoyment of the new Presence. O sweet God, inwardly on fire, outwardly blossoming, . . . You have given this to the least." When "You, Lord, shall infuse me with your grace, then I can flow from Your Love."[610]

Mechthild spoke to the Lord, "greetings to You, living God, You are mine before all things. . . . When my enemies pursue me, I flee to Your arms. . . . I am a low-born bride; and You are my lawful Husband. I shall ever rejoice about this. . . . Even though I am not worthy of You. Ah, Lord, draw me up to You. Then I shall be pure and radiant. If You abandon me to myself, I shall remain dark and sluggish." God answered her. "I respond to your greeting with such a heavenly flood: were I to give Myself to you in all My Power, you would not preserve your human life, you well know I must hold back My Might and hide My Splendor to let you remain in earthly misery until all My Sweetness rises up to the heights of Eternal glory." Her soul requested, "Lord, love me passionately, love me often, and love me long." God answered "that I love you passionately comes from My nature, for I am Love Itself. That I love you often comes from My desire, for I desire to be loved passionately. That I love you long comes from My being Eternal, for I am without an end and without a beginning."[611]

Nine qualities of the Lord that Mechthild praised were humility, mercy, humiliation, generosity, wisdom, might, nobility, intimacy, and love. The soul also praised the "flowing God in Your Love." The Lord described the soul, "you are an enhancement of My most sublime Love." Mechthild described what the soul said about its nature. "A fish in water does not drown, a bird in the air does not plummet.... God has created all creatures to live according to their nature. How then am I to resist my nature? I must go from all things to God, who is my Father by nature, my Brother by his humanity, my Bridegroom by love, and I His bride from all eternity." In addition, she explained 17 kinds of sin that "drive a person so far from God that he can never come back unless great force is exerted on him by the Trinity. Vanity is the first sin that begins to chase a person away from God, and if we don't leave it, then lust arises up." Then she repeated the same phrase fifteen more times, "If we don't leave it," followed by each of the other fifteen sins: greed, sloth, lying, perjury, anger, slander, pride, hatred, vengeance, despair, insolence, shamelessness, perverted wisdom, unbelief, and distrust.[612]

Describing her mystical experiences, Mechthild said that God "reveals to her His Divine heart.... He places her into His glowing heart. When the exalted Sovereign and the little waif thus embrace and are united as water and wine,... she says: 'Lord, You are my Lover, my desire, my flowing Fount, my sun; and I am Your reflection.'" Moreover, "my body is in great torment, my soul is in sublime bliss;... When He draws her up, she flows. She cannot hold herself in check until He brings her within Himself. She would like to speak but cannot, so utterly has she been enmeshed in sublime union with the awe-inspiring Trinity."[613]

Mechthild said that three things make a person worthy of the path to the Lord. First, "one submits to God relinquishing all human control" and "one piously holds on to God's grace and willingly keeps it by being forgiving in all things as far as is possible for a human will." Second, "one welcomes all things except sin." Third, "one does all things equally to God's honor.... Relieving my most basic need counts as much in God's sight as if I were in the highest state of contemplation that a human being can attain. Why? If I do it out of love in order to give honor to God, it is all one and the same. But when I sin, I am not on this path."[614]

Mechthild said that "the elevation of the soul comes about in love.... There is no elevation beyond that of love." God said, "to love freely must always be the highest value for people." In her view, "true love of God has seven approaches. Cheerful love leads the way. Fearing love takes on the task. Strong love can accomplish much. Loving love receives no honor. Wise love has knowledge. Free love lives without heartache. Powerful love is forever happy." God said to the soul, "when you love, we two become One Being. And when we two are One Being, then we can never be parted. Rather a blissful abiding prevails between us."[615]

Chapter 11

Transpersonal Images of the Divine during Illumination and Union

Transpersonal Images of the Divine
during Illumination and Union

In the third stage of awakening, we seek a personal God. We picture the Holy One with personal, human qualities, like our own. We have a humanized, and thus minimized, image of the Sacred Spirit. For example, we yearn for the Father's Love and we fear His harsh punishment for our sins. We worship a human Jesus as God who suffered and died on the cross. Mechthild of Magdeburg described a personal loving Divine. "O God, so generous in the outpouring of Thy gifts, so flowing in Thy Love, so burning in Thy desire; so fervent in union! O Thou who does rest on my heart and without whom I could no longer live!" Hindus worship 330 million personal Goddesses and Gods like Kali and Shiva who have human attributes. Although Buddha was originally a Hindu, he eliminated all its personal Goddesses and Gods and taught the heart of his new religion, his Four Noble Truths and Eightfold Path that leads to Nirvana, a transpersonal concept. After his death, some in the Buddhist tradition resurrected Goddesses and Gods and even turned Buddha himself into a God, a personal image.[616]

During the fifth stage of illumination and union, we have a deeper and more intense awareness of the Holy One within us. We also have mystical experiences that we are within the ONE. Because of this, we develop different images of the Ultimate Reality. Illuminated mystics in the fifth stage prefer transpersonal concepts of the Divine and less often use personal images. A transpersonal concept of the Divine is not impersonal. It is not less than personal. It is beyond the personal. For example, in the third stage of awakening, we say God is loving, a personal image. In the fifth stage of illumination and union, we realize that the Divine is Infinite Love, a transpersonal concept. Other transpersonal concepts include the Ultimate Reality, the Absolute, the Spirit, Goodness, Truth, Wisdom, Power, Light, Life, Being, the Holy One, and the ONE.[617]

One of the reasons why illuminated mystics favor transpersonal images is that they are more helpful in understanding that the Holy One is within us and we are within the ONE, that Infinite Love is within us as our inner core of love and we are within Infinite Love. In the fifth stage, illuminated mystics do not picture the Sacred Spirit as the God who rewards those who keep His commandments, who punishes sinners, who is jealous and wrathful, who interferes in our life on earth, who rules the universe, or who wants to be adored, glorified, and worshipped. However, the personal images in the third stage serve as s bridge to the fifth phase of transpersonal concepts, where the Holy One is beyond these limited personal human traits and actions.[618]

Hindu scholars use different names for the personal and transpersonal. What is referred to as the personal God, Hindus call Brahman with attributes and a form. The transpersonal Divine is Brahman without attributes and a form. Some refer to a personal God and the Godhead. Otto used personal and supra-personal. Griffins, an expert on world religions, offers a choice different from a personal or impersonal or transpersonal image of God. "The mystery of the Godhead, of ultimate Truth and Reality, is not found in a personal God nor in an impersonal Absolute but in an interpersonal relationship, or a communion of love."[619]

As Armstrong says, "Judaism, Christianity, and—to a lesser extent—Islam have all developed the idea of a personal God" that has helped them "to value the Sacred and inalienable rights of the individual." However, "a personal God can be dangerous" because we "assume that He loves what we love and hates what we hate." It seems that "the idea of a personal God can only be a stage in our religious development. The world religions all seem to have recognized this danger and have sought to transcend the personal conception of Supreme Reality. . . . All three of the monotheistic religions developed a mystical tradition, which made their God transcend the personal category" and created transpersonal concepts, such as the Buddhist Nirvana and the Hindu Brahman.[620]

On the popular level, Hinduism is a polytheistic religion with millions of personal Goddesses and Gods, like Kali and Shiva. Hindu B.R. Kishore says that "Hinduism is monotheistic and polytheistic." Besides all the polytheistic, personal Goddesses and Gods, it also teaches the One God, Brahman, the Absolute, the Spirit Supreme, a monotheistic, transpersonal image. Ramakrishna, a nineteenth century holy man taught that "all the Gods and Goddesses are but various aspects of the One Absolute Brahman." Thus, Brahman is One and Hinduism is also a monotheism. This sage also said that a personal Goddess or God is called *Saguna* Brahman, the Divine with attributes and a form. The *Nirguna* Brahman is the Impersonal Absolute without attributes and a form. "God the Absolute and God the Personal are one and the same."[621]

The transpersonal Holy One is linked to the personal God as water is connected to ice. When formless water freezes, it takes on the solid form of ice. Later the ice melts back into formless water. Similarly, a formless transpersonal image of the Divine called Brahman can be represented by concrete personal forms, such as Kali and Shiva. In Ramakrishna's words, "as water when congealed becomes ice, so the visible form of the Almighty is the materialized manifestation of the all-pervading, formless Brahman. . . . As ice is essentially water, remains in water, and afterwards melts into it, so the Personal God is part and parcel of the Impersonal, remains there, and ultimately merges into It and disappears." To think of God as formless is right, but "meditating upon Him as a Being with a form is equally right." Do not say my description of God is "the only correct, rational, and tenable one and those who believe in a personal God are wrong."[622]

Both personal and transpersonal images are useful as long as they continue to provide life-promoting meaning for individuals and religions. In the third stage, many believers prefer and exclusively use personal images, while in the fifth stage they choose transpersonal images. A number of believers use both images. Our preference depends on our personality, religion, culture, spirituality, and our stage on the mystical way. As Ramakrishna said, a personal God is not a statue of an individual dying on the cross in a church and "not the clay image" in a Hindu temple. In our early years, we may need to fix our minds on a personal God with a form, like Jesus or Kali. "When we have attained success therein, we can easily fix it upon the Formless," Impersonal Absolute. "The more you advance in spirituality, the less you will see the attributes of God."[623]

When we view God as a Person, we think that She has a gender, is like us, and acts as we do. Since we are Her children, we picture Her punishing us when we are bad and rewarding us when we are good. We think She loves us as we love Her. Since we are human, we think She acts like humans. Because God bestowed multiple benefits on us, many of us thank Her, love Her, and try to serve Her. Of course, God is *not* a human being, *not* a person. The transpersonal Divine as Infinite Love, the Holy One, or the Ultimate Reality, does not love us as we love It. In fact, we don't know for sure how Infinite Love thinks, feels, speaks, acts, and loves, or even if It does any of these things. We can only speculate about Infinite Love, as we speculate about what love is. There are as many definitions of love as there are people. My understanding of love is our creative life force, dynamic power, vital energy, passionate soul, and vibrant spirit. Thus, I think that Infinite Love is the Infinite Creative Life Force, Dynamic Power, Vital Energy, Passionate Soul, and Vibrant Spirit as well as the Ultimate Reality, Being, the Holy One, and the ONE. With our illuminated consciousness, we realize that Infinite Love is within us as our inner core and we are within It and have Its nature. We are a drop of love within the Sacred Ocean of Infinite Love.

Illumination helps us experience the transpersonal Divine who is everywhere and surrounds, penetrates, and permeates all people and nature with Infinite Love. This Transcendent, yet Immanent, Holy One fills all reality with Love. With our enhanced illuminated consciousness, we realize that we are within the forward-moving Divine Life. Our mystical experiences of illumination make us aware that the Infinite Love is always present here and now shining throughout the cosmos and energizing it. We are also conscious that all of us are always within the ONE. We have never been separate from the Ultimate Reality.

In the fifth stage of illumination, some mystics use both personal and transpersonal images of God. The concept of the Divine that they learned in their childhood religion is still part of their thinking. For example, Catholicism and its theology use a transpersonal concept of the Trinity which is considered a Mystery. The Trinity is God the Father, God the Son who is Jesus, and God the Holy Spirit, three Persons in one God. The Trinity and Holy Spirit are transpersonal concepts, while God the Father and Jesus His Son are personal images. As a Catholic, when Mother Teresa used the word God, she probably meant God the Father. But she also thought that "Jesus is God; therefore, his love, his thirst is infinite. Our aim is to quench this infinite thirst of a God made man." By "using the four vows of Absolute Poverty, Chastity, Obedience, and Charity towards the poor," the Missionaries of Charity, the religious order she founded, tried ceaselessly to "quench the thirsting of God by their love for the souls they bring to Him."[624]

Mystics' images of the Divine encompass the widest possible latitude. At their best, these concepts are symbolic, because mystics' experiences of the Holy One go beyond the words they employ. Underhill claimed that "in the highest experiences of the greatest mystics, the personal category appears to be transcended" and replaced by transpersonal images because the All-inclusive Infinite ONE is beyond finite descriptions. Even though mystics use transpersonal concepts of the Divine, their "communion with God is always personal, . . . It is communion with a living Reality, an object of love, capable of response." Mystics believe that "the spirit of man, itself essentially Divine, is capable of immediate communion with God, the One Reality." While the Absolute of the philosophers is "impersonal and unattainable, the Absolute of the mystics is lovable, attainable, alive." The relationship between mystics and the Sacred Spirit is "a double movement," a self-giving on the human side answering the self-giving on the Divine side. This double movement is "found in all great mysticism."[625]

Scholars and Illuminated Mystics View the Divine as Love

Bede Griffins, a contemporary Catholic priest, an expert on world religions, and the editor of *Universal Wisdom*, says that "the Spirit in all religion is the Reality. . . . But there is one expression of the Spirit which is more meaningful than all others and that is Love. Love is invisible, but it is the most powerful force in human nature." The love that Jesus spoke of is Buddha's compassion (*karuna*), love as the *prema* and *bhakti* which the *Bhagavad Gita* proclaimed, and the rapturous love of the Sufi saints. "Ultimately a religion is tested by its capacity to awaken love in its followers, and, what is perhaps more difficult, to extend that love to all humanity. In the past religions have tended to confine their love to their own followers, but always there has been a movement to break through these barriers and attain universal love. The Universal Wisdom is necessarily a message of universal love."[626]

Armstrong, a contemporary expert on world religions, says that throughout religious history, there was "a striking similarity in Jewish, Christian, and Muslim ideas of the Divine." Not only these three but most other world religions had a God of Compassion and taught the principles of compassion and love for all. Christian mystics of the Middle Ages "preached a God of Love." In looking for a meaningful concept that will work today, Armstrong suggests the mystics' God of Love might be a possible alternative.[627]

Illuminated Christian Mystics Used Transpersonal Images, including the Divine as Love

Throughout the centuries, Christian mystics wrote glowingly of the Divine as Love as well as other transpersonal images. Paul referred to the "God of Love." John's first letter said, "God is Love." John Cassian, a fourth-century monk, said that "as God loves us with a Love that is true and pure, a Love that never breaks, we will be joined to Him in never-ending unshakeable love, and it will be such a union that our breathing, thinking and talking will be God."[628]

In his book, *Mystical Theology*, Denys the Areopagite explained a three-step process for naming God. All three of his steps describe transpersonal concepts, such as "the Cause of all things." His first step provided affirmative images, his second step denied his affirmative concepts, and his third went beyond both affirmative and negative images.

Denys' first step starts with the most exalted God and go on a downward path through creation affirming an ever-increasing number of names for God. "Since It is the Cause of all beings, we should posit and ascribe to It all the affirmations we make in regard to beings." In this first affirmative stage, Denys' transpersonal names for God in his book *The Divine Names* included the Good, Being, Life, Wisdom, Power, Perfection, the One, and the Unity. "The most important name" is Good, "the Divine Goodness, which surpasses every name and every splendor." This "inexpressible Good" is "the transcendently overwhelming Goodness" and "the supra-excellent Goodness." Moreover, "the essential Good . . . extends goodness into all things." In addition, "the Cause of all loves all things in the superabundance of His Goodness, that because of this Goodness, He makes all things, brings all things to perfection."[629]

In Denys' first affirmative step, other names for the Divine include "the absolutely transcendent Goodness, Being, Life, and Wisdom." However, "the name 'Being' extends to all beings which are, and It is beyond them. The name 'Life' extends to all living things, and yet is beyond them. The name 'Wisdom' reaches out to everything . . . and surpasses them all." God is 'He Who is,' 'Being Itself,' the 'Supra-Being,' the 'Superabundant Life,' and the 'Superabundant Wisdom.' The Cause of all things "has a foreknowledge of everything" and "He knows everything else." In addition, "God is Power" and "His Power is infinite." For Denys, "the most enduring" names are the Perfect and the One. The Cause of all beings is "absolute Perfection." It is the One, "All in All," and "absolute Unity." The One is "overwhelming indivisibility" and "utterly comprehensive Unity." Despite all these affirmative names for God, we "can neither discuss nor understand the One, the Super-Unknowable, the Transcendent, Goodness itself."[630]

In Denys' second step of naming the Divine, we begin from the lowest category in nature and rise upward through creation to humans. As we climb to the Transcendent Cause of all things, we deny all our affirmations. "More appropriately, we should negate all affirmations, since It surpasses all being." This second stage of negation in naming God is necessary because when "we measure the Divine by our human standards," we "are led astray." Therefore, Denys' second step denies all the affirmations about God. The Cause of all is "not soul or mind, nor does It possess imagination, conviction, speech, or understanding. . . . It has no power, It is not Power, nor is It Light. It does not live nor is It Life. . . . It is not Wisdom. It is neither One nor Oneness, Divinity nor Goodness. Nor is It Spirit."[631]

Denys' third stage begins as our language falters because God is beyond all affirmations and denials. "Now we should not conclude that the negations are simply the opposites of the affirmations, but rather that the Cause of all is considerably prior to this, beyond privations, beyond every denial, beyond every assertion." Denys asked, "is it not closer to reality to say that God is Life and Goodness rather than that He is air or stone?" The more we rise, "the more language falters, and . . . it will turn silent completely, since it will finally be at One with Him who is Indescribable." We become "speechless and unknowing."[632]

In the thirteenth-century, Angela de Filigno, an Italian mystic, utilized many transpersonal images of the Holy One, including Love, to describe what she learned in her mystical experiences of illumination. The Sacred Spirit is Wisdom, Goodness, Power, Justice, Beauty, Love, and the All. "I beheld the ineffable fullness of God, but I can relate nothing of it, save that I have seen the fullness of Divine Wisdom, wherein is all Goodness." Further she said, "so greatly does the Good exceed all my words that my speech seems to be blasphemy." Opening the eyes of my soul, "I beheld nothing save the Divine Power, in a way that is utterly indescribable, so that through the greatness of its wonder, the soul cried . . . 'the whole world is full of God.'" She comprehended that "the Power of God exceeds and fills all." Understanding that the world is a little thing compared to God's Power and Justice, she said that "I was lifted higher still. . . . I beheld a Thing, as fixed and stable as It was indescribable, and more than this I cannot say, save that . . . It was all Good." My soul was "filled with indescribable joy, so that it was . . . placed in this great and ineffable state."[633]

Another time Angela de Filigno said, "I beheld a Beauty so great that I can say nothing, save that I saw the Supreme Beauty which contains in Itself all Goodness." Perceiving the Divine, "I saw Love advancing gently toward me, and I saw the beginning but not the end. There seemed to me only a continuation and an eternity, but directly this Love reached me, I beheld all these things more clearly. . ... Then I was filled with Love . . . and my soul fainted with longing to attain to the All." Francis of Assisi, a thirteenth century Italian mystic, wrote to God, "You are Love, Charity," Wisdom, Hope, Justice, and all riches. Jacopone da Todi, a thirteenth-century Italian Franciscan, said to God, "Love, Love, I am One with You, let me embrace You alone. . . . Love, You are my life; my soul cannot live without You."[634]

In the thirteenth century, Mechthild of Magdeburg wrote that the Divine's "loving greeting came every day and caused me both love and sorrow; the sweetness and glory increased daily" and continued for decades. "God never left me. He brought me such sweetness of love, such heavenly knowledge, such inconceivable wonders, that I had little use for earthly things." God said to Mechthild that "I love you passionately comes from my nature, for I am Love Itself." In addition, "I shall never reject you." Speaking to God, Mechthild said, "Love, Your Light is broad in the soul. Your Gleam is radiant, Your Glory inconceivable, Your Wisdom infinite." Divine Love flows into the soul "without effort, as a bird glides through the air without moving its wings." It penetrates, engulfs, and saturates the soul. God's Love is "a thousand times more powerful than creatures can ever receive." We are "bathed in Love as bright as the sun." The loving soul and God "mingle as the air is infused with sunshine." Between us, "there shall be love forever." However, the soul cannot love the Holy One alone, but "must love God also in other creatures." Being enlightened, the soul "loves all that God loves." Thus, "the soul reaches its heights in Love, . . . There is nothing higher than Love." In addition, "Love leads to all good" and "Love rules over all." Thus, "there is nothing so wise, nor so holy, . . . nor so perfect as Love."[635]

In the fourteenth century, an English mystic Richard Rolle explained in his book *The Fire of Love* that true lovers say, "my God, my Love, surge over me, pierce me by your Love, . . . reveal your healing medicine to your poor lover." Souls cannot know "the fire of Eternal Love," unless they stop worldly vanity of every kind. "If it is for God's sake that we love everything," then we love the Divine within all things. "Since the human soul is capable of receiving God alone, nothing else than God can fill it; which explains why lovers of earthly things are never satisfied." Rolle claimed that God's Love is "a fire which sets our hearts aflame so that they glow and burn, and it purges them from all the foulness of sin." What we do demonstrates the strength of our love. If we really love God, our actions will show it. Our love for our neighbor comes from our love of God. The purer our love, the closer is the Divine presence. We who love much are truly great, while those who love little are less, "for our worth before God accords with the degree of love in our hearts." Therefore, Love is "the sweetest and most useful thing a rational creature can ever acquire.... Love unites my love and me and makes of two one."[636]

In her dialogue with God, Catherine of Siena, a fourteenth-century Italian mystic, reformer, and author, called the Holy One ineffable, immeasurable, unimaginable, unspeakable, and eternal Love. God said to Catherine, "all I want is love. In loving Me, you will realize love for your neighbors. If you are bound by this love you will do everything you can to be of service wherever you are.... service proves your love for Me." Being inseparable, "love of Me and love of neighbor are one and the same thing. Since love of neighbor has its source in Me, the more the soul loves Me, the more she loves her neighbor." In addition, God said, "what I ask of you is nothing other than love and affection for Me and for your neighbor."[637]

God also said to Catherine, besides doing "your duty to love your neighbors as your own self," souls that are grounded in love reach for the Infinite and try to "love Me above all things." These souls always feel God's presence within them and never lose it. "Knowing Me they love Me. And in loving Me, their selfish will is swallowed up and lost." The soul goes from imperfection to perfection "by living virtuously with a sincere heart free to love Me without self-interest." Once the soul loses her selfishness, sheds her body, and comes to Me her final goal, "she knows the truth. Seeing Me, the eternal Father, she loves; loving, she is satisfied." In addition, "those who love Me live in Me and I live in them."[638]

In the fourteenth century, Walter Hilton, an English mystic, said that "perfect love makes God and the soul to be as if they both together were but One thing." Thomas a Kempis, the author of the fourteenth century spiritual classic *Imitation of Christ*, said that the burning love of my soul cries, "my God and my Love, You are all mine and I am Yours." In addition, "nothing is sweeter than love, nothing stronger,... nothing fuller or better in heaven or earth; for love is born of God and can rest only in God, above all created things.... Love knows no limits, but ardently transcends all bounds.... love sees nothing as impossible, for it is able to achieve all things."[639]

Meister Eckhart, the fourteenth-century German Dominican, said that the soul "is created in a place between time and Eternity; with its highest powers it touches Eternity, with its lower time." The two worlds of becoming and Being are the two stages of reality where the human spirit meets the Divine. Eckhart claimed, "I am sure... that if a soul knew the very least of all that Being means, it would never turn away from it."[640]

In the fifteenth century, Julian of Norwich, an English anchoress, experienced the Divine revelations of a transpersonal Ultimate Reality. "God is Love" and "our Love, Joy, and Bliss." God is "eternal sovereign Truth, eternal sovereign Wisdom, eternal sovereign Love uncreated" as well as "Almighty, All-Wisdom, and All-Love." Furthermore, "in His Love, He clothes us, enfolds us, and embraces us, this tender Love completely surrounds us, never to leave us." His "same single Love pervades all." It is "altogether the most tremendous Love and marvelous Joy. In addition, "Charity keeps us in faith and hope, and hope leads us on in Charity. In the end it will be all Charity." Julian understood "this Light of Charity in three ways. . . . 'Uncreated Charity' is God; 'created charity' is our soul in God; 'given charity' is virtue. . . . It works in us so that we love God for Himself, and love ourselves in God, and love what God loves for His sake."[641]

In her Divine revelations Julian saw that God has innate, essential, fundamental, superlative Goodness. "God is All that is good; . . . He is the Goodness in all good things." He is "unchangeable Goodness" and "nothing but Goodness." Moreover, "His Goodness enfolds every one of His creatures." God is also Righteousness, Power, "Life, Truth, Love, Peace" and "the Being of all that is." The Trinity is "everlasting Being. Just as He is eternal, without beginning," so also His purpose is eternal. Our Father who is "God Almighty, who is Being, knew and loved us from eternity." God revealed Himself to Julian. "I who am Light and Grace and blessed Love; I who am Trinity; I who am Unity; I who am the sovereign Goodness of every single thing;" and "I who am All."[642]

Julian's Divine revelations said that "three of God's attributes" are "Life, Love, and Light. In 'Life' there is this marvelous intimacy, and in 'Love' that gentle courtesy, and in 'Light' our everlasting nature. These three exist in one Goodness." While for me the most meaningful names for the Ultimate Reality are the Holy One and Infinite Love, my niece Abby preferred the Light. Julian's revelations help me understanding It. "Our light is none other than God." By this Light, God leads us. "Because of the Light we live" and go forward. When we are enlightened, "in the shining brightness of the Light, we shall see perfectly." Our "faith is our Light in darkness and our Light is God, the everlasting Day." Furthermore, "this Light is Charity" and "the greatest Light that shines most brightly" is "the glorious Love of our Lord." It is a Light that "we can live in profitably, and in which we may strive to deserve" to be with God everlastingly.[643]

Like Julian, other illuminated mystics, according to Underhill, "experience a kind of radiance, a flooding of the personality with new Light." Their world is transfigured. "They report an actual and overpowering consciousness of radiant Light, ineffable in its splendor." The Spirit's radiance is "the Light of a thousand suns." They gaze deeply into "the Infinite Light Divine," they bask in "the sunbeams of the Uncreated Light," and they are lit up by the Indwelling Light. Augustine said, "I entered into the secret closet of my soul, led by Thee; and this I could do because Thou was my Helper. I entered, and beheld with the mysterious eye of my soul the Light that never changes." It was not like the normal light that all see, but altogether different. "He who knows the truth knows that Light; and he who knows It, knows Eternity. Love knows It."[644]

The revelations of the twelfth-century German Hildegarde of Bingen described "a special Light, more brilliant than the brightness round the sun." Mechthild of Magdelburg experienced illumination as "the flowing Light of the Godhead" and as "the rippling tide of Love which flows secretly from God into the soul and draws it mightily back to its Source." Teresa of Avila called it "a Light which knows no night; but rather, as it is always light, nothing ever disturbs it." These experiences led mystics to describe God as "a Divine Light" and "Undifferentiated Light." Not being distracted by worldly anxieties, their heightened enlightened consciousness of the Divine Light brightens their whole life.[645]

Catherine of Genoa, a sixteenth-century Italian mystic, felt the fires of Divine Love and said that the all good God acts "with Pure Love. . . . He loves us and will not ever leave off doing us good." The Divine Merciful Love never ceases and "penetrates as deep as hell. . . . In this world, the rays of God's Love . . . encircle man all about, hungrily seeking to penetrate him." God "binds the soul to Himself with a fiery Love." With His Love, "God so transforms the soul in Him that it knows nothing other than God; and He continues to draw it up into His fiery Love." Catherine saw that "man by love makes himself one single thing with God and finds there every good." The soul is purified in "the fire of God's Love." The last stage of love is the burning away of the soul's flaws and "transforming itself into God." This stage is not the action of humans, but it is "the workings of God, of that flaming Love," and of "the pure and intense Love of God alone."[646]

Jacob Boehme, a seventeenth-century German mystic, said, "O highest Love, You have appeared to me. Remain in me. Embrace me in Yourself. Keep me in You so I cannot bend from You. Fill my hunger with Your Love." John Tauler, a fourteenth century German mystic, said that "the well of life is Love, and he who dwells not in love is dead." In the seventeenth century, an English nun Dame Gertrude More said something similar to Tauler. "Let me love, or not live!" In addition, "my God, let me walk in the way of Love . . . Let this Love wholly possess my soul and heart, which may live and move only in . . . pure and sincere love for Thee. . . . once to have seen Thee is to have learned all things! Nothing can bring us to this sight but love. But what love must it be? . . . it must be an ardent love, a pure love, a courageous love, a love of charity, a humble love, and a constant love. . . .. Let me love nothing instead of Thee, for to give all for love is a most sweet bargain." Furthermore,

"O Love, Love, even by naming Thee, my soul loses itself in Thee . . . nothing can satiate a reasonable soul, but only Thou." Thou art "that One thing which is only necessary and which alone can satisfy our souls."[647]

H. Emilie Cady, a Unity mystic who lived in the first part of twentieth century, called God "the indwelling One who is Love" as well as "All-Wisdom, All-Love." Abiding at the center of all of us, the One manifests "more and more of Himself, pure Intelligence, perfect Love," until we become conscious that we are One within the Holy. After becoming aware that we are One within God, we realize that we are "surrounded and filled with Divine Love." A flood of God's Love permeates and saturates our entire being healing us morally and physically. When we assert our Oneness with God, "there is instantly set in motion all the power of Omnipotent Love" to rescue us. "There is nothing to fear; . . . Perfect Love reigns and all is good." Losing sight of our differences, we "become conscious of our oneness with one another and our Oneness with God. We are One always and forever." Furthermore, "God flows through us to others." The current of unlimited Divine Love and Life always goes through us to help others. "It is God's words spoken through our lips." We are "co-workers with God." Even though we cannot see love, "all the Love in the universe is God."[648]

The twentieth-century Protestant theologian Paul Tillich criticized personal images of God and utilized transpersonal concepts. "The concept of a 'Personal God,' interfering with natural events, or being 'an independent cause of natural events,' makes God a natural object besides others, an object among others, a being among beings, maybe the highest, but nevertheless, *a being*. This indeed is . . . the destruction of any meaningful idea of God." To call God the Supreme Being still makes Him just another being. "God does not exist. He is Being Itself beyond essence and existence." Besides referring to God as Being Itself, Tillich used other transpersonal names, Spirit, Divine Life, the Infinite Power of Being, the Depth of Existence, the Ground of Being, Ultimate Concern, and Love.[649]

Chardin believed in a personal God, but he also called God by transpersonal names such as Spirit, Ultimate Spirit, Soul, the All, the Universal Whole, Universal Reality, Power, Light, Omnipresent, Being, Supreme Center, Center of centers, Omega, the Prime Mover, the First Cause, and "a blazing Fire whose flames spread out like rays all around It." Not only is some of his writing scientific, but some is also poetic and mystical. "In the beginning was *Power*, intelligent, loving, energizing. . . . In the beginning there were not coldness and darkness: there was *Fire*. . . . So, far from light emerging gradually out of the womb of darkness, it is the Light, existing before all else was made, which patiently, surely, eliminates our darkness. . . . You, my God, are the inmost depths, the stability of that Eternal milieu, . . .

in which the cosmos emerges gradually into being.... Everything is Being; everywhere there is Being and nothing but Being."[650]

Chardin used ideas, such as monism and paganism that were criticized by Catholic authorities. However, he avoided their pitfalls by stressing God's Infinity. "Like the monist I plunge into the all-inclusive One; but the One is so perfect that as It receives me and I lose myself in It, I can find in It the ultimate perfection of my own individuality. Like the pagan I worship a God Who can be touched; and I do indeed touch Him—this God—over the whole surface and into the depths of that world of matter which confines me: but to take hold of Him, ... I must go always on and on through and beyond each undertaking, unable to rest in anything, borne onward at each moment by creatures, ... in a continuing welcoming them and in a continuing detachment from them.... Being lost in what is greater than oneself, ... I rise up toward the Spirit Whose vesture is the magnificence of the material universe but Who smiles at me from far beyond all."[651]

A contemporary Catholic Benedictine nun Joan Chittister says that "God as cosmic Unity and everlasting Light" moves her heart. Free of legalism and maleness, "my God is the fullness of Life, the consummation of Hope, the Light on the way, and the Light at the end." She lives her life in "consciousness of God and of goodness everywhere." The Divine has many faces and names. "In the new world I must allow no one to draw too small a God for me." Desmond Tutu, a contemporary South African Anglican Archbishop, says that the only central truth is that "God loves me." God loves everything, including "the rabble of slaves." All of creation is "the consequence of God's Love, the result of the outpouring of this Divine Love and Life that has no beginning and no end.... Everything exists because it is loved." We don't have "to do anything except be there," because "God loves us perfectly and infinitely already." In addition, "all can be transformed by the Divine," even the normal, everyday things and people. The Holy One sends us to help "realize God's dream of a new kind of society—gentle, caring, compassionate, sharing."[652]

The World's Religions Use Transpersonal Images

Illuminated mystics of most religions use transpersonal concepts of the Holy One. Both the *Upanishads* and *Bhagavad Gita* include transpersonal images of God called Brahman. In the Upanishads, He is the Absolute, the Supreme Spirit, Life Immortal, Truth, Joy, Existence, Eternal, Infinite, Peace, Love, the ONE, and *Sat-Chit-Ananda* which translates Infinite Being, Consciousness, and Bliss. "Brahman is All." In the Gita, the Holy Krishna said, behold "by hundreds and then thousands, My manifold celestial forms of innumerable shapes and colors . . . See the whole universe with all things as One in Me." The visionary narrator added that "the Infinite Divinity was facing all sides, containing all marvels. If the Light of a thousand suns suddenly arose in the sky, the splendor might be compared to the radiance of the Supreme Spirit." The Sacred Krishna described God as the Supreme End, "the Imperishable, the Infinite, the Transcendent Unmanifested; the Omnipresent, the Beyond all thought, the Immutable, the Never Changing, the Ever One."[653]

The disciple Arjuna said in the Gita that "all around I behold Thy Infinity. . . . Nowhere do I see a beginning or middle or end of Thee, O God of all, Form Infinite! I see the splendor of an Infinite Beauty which illumines the whole universe. It is Thee! How difficult Thou art to see! But I see Thee: as Fire, as Sun, blinding, incomprehensible. Thou art Imperishable, the highest End of knowledge, the Support of this vast universe. Thou, the Everlasting Ruler of the law of righteousness, the Spirit . . . I behold Thy Infinite Power . . . Heaven and earth and all the infinite spaces are filled with Thy Spirit. How could people not bow down in love before Thee, God, Spirit Supreme? Thou, the God of creation, Thou Infinite, Eternal Refuge of the world! Thou who art All that is, and All that is not, and All that is Beyond . . . Thou Infinite presence in whom all things are . . . God of all. All powerful God of immeasurable might. Thou art the End of all: Thou art All."[654]

Over 2,500 years ago, the Chinese developed a transpersonal concept of the Divine called the Tao that underlies and unifies all things. The Tao is the indefinable Reality that is difficult to translate and explain. Perhaps the best English translation of the Tao is the Way. Lao Tzu, the legendary founder of Taoism, began his spiritual classic, *Tao Te Ching*, with the assertion, "the Tao, the Way that can be trodden, is not the enduring and unchanging Tao. The name that can be named is not the enduring and unchanging Tao." The Tao is the cosmic Way, the transcendent Origin, the guiding Force, and the Ultimate Reality of the universe. As the fundamental law of life, the Tao is the primal Energy that unifies all life processes and governs everything. The Tao is composed of the dynamic interplay of the yin and yang life forces that make up everything in existence. While everything includes both life processes, one tends to prevail. The Tao with its yin and yang life forces creates the interdependent, harmonious Unity of life.[655]

The ultimate goal of all Buddhists is Nirvana, a transpersonal image that is mentioned in the Hindu scriptures. Some say Buddhism is atheistic, because it has no concept of a *personal* God. Others say Nirvana is a transpersonal concept of the Divine. Buddha insisted that Nirvana is indescribable, unutterable, incomprehensible, inconceivable, and ineffable. Nagasena, an heir of Buddha, said that Nirvana is like the wind. "Nirvana exists, but it is not possible to show It." Buddha said, "bliss, yes bliss, my friends, is Nirvana." Edward Conze, a Buddhist scholar, said that Nirvana is not a personal God. However, it is a transpersonal image or what Huston Smith and some mystics refer to as the Godhead in order to distinguish It from a personal God. Conze compares the attributes of the transpersonal Divine with Nirvana and finds "almost no difference at all." Although it is not a personal image, "Nirvana is permanent, stable, imperishable, immovable, ageless, deathless, unborn, and unbecome." Furthermore, Nirvana is "power, bliss, and happiness, the secure refuge, the shelter, and the place of unassailable safety." It is "the real Truth and supreme Reality." In addition, Nirvana is "the Good, the supreme goal and the one and only consummation of our life, the eternal, hidden and incomprehensible Peace."[656]

The Jewish scriptures, the Bible and the Talmud, present both personal and transpersonal images. The Divine is Lord, King, Father, Liberator, and Savior, as well as steadfast Love and the One God. The *Kabbalah*, a Jewish mystical tradition, attempts to understand God. This Hebrew word literally means 'receiving' or 'that which is received.' In the Kabbalah, God's name is the Hebrew word, *Ein Sof*. Despite the teaching that Ein Sof cannot be defined because It exceeds all description, It means without end, the Endless, without boundaries, the Boundless, the Infinite, and "the Unnamable One." The *Zohar, The Book of Splendor*, the thirteenth-century canonical book of the Kabbalah, said that Ein Sof is the Blessed Holy One, the Holy of Holies, the Holy Spark, 'the High Spark, Hidden of all Hidden,' the King, 'the Ineffable One, the Unrevealed,' and 'the Holy Ancient One.' Ein Sof manifested Itself in this world through ten *Sefirot* which are emanations, attributes, or powers of God. According to the sixteenth-century Spanish kabbalist Moses Cordovero and others, the ten Sefirot are (1) *Keter* is Crown, (2) *Hokhmah* is Wisdom, (3) *Binah* is Understanding, Intelligence, (4) *Hesed* is Love, (5) *Gevurah* is Power or *Din* Judgment, (6) *Tif'eret* is Beauty, (7) *Netzah* is Eternity, Lasting Endurance, (8) *Hod* is Majesty, (9) *Yesod* is Foundation or *Zaddik* Righteous One, and (10) *Shekhinah* is Divine Presence or *Malkhut* Kingdom.[657]

Aristotle, the fourth-century BCE Greek philosopher, had a transpersonal image of God as the Unmoved Mover. "Life also belongs to God; for the actuality of thought is life, and God is that Actuality. . . . God is a living Being, eternal, most good, so that life and duration continuous and eternal belong to God; for this *is* God."[658]

Muhammad's many mystical experiences of Allah resulted in the Quran which uses multiple personal and transpersonal names that are recorded in His 99 names. Different translations of the Quran provide different descriptions of those names. Two of those personal names are repeated more than 113 times in the Quran, "Allah, the Compassionate, the Merciful," that are also translated as "the Beneficent, the Merciful." Other transpersonal names in the Quran say that Allah is "All-Merciful and All-Love." In addition, "Allah is One, the Eternal God. He begot none, nor was He begotten. None is equal to Him." His "Mercy and Compassion embraces all things." Furthermore, "neither on earth nor in heaven shall you escape His reach, nor have you any besides Allah to protect and help you." The contemporary Islamic scholar Nasr says that "at the heart of Islam stands the reality of God, the One, the Absolute and Infinite, the Infinitely Good and All-Merciful, the One who is at once Transcendent and Immanent, greater than all we can conceive or imagine, yet . . . closer to us than our jugular vein. The One God, known by his Arabic name, Allah, is the central reality of Islam." Testifying to Allah's Oneness "lies at the heart of the credo of Islam."[659]

The thirteenth-century Sufi Muslim mystic al-Arabi said of Allah's most beautiful names, their "number is immeasurable." Traditional Islamic accounts say that the 99 most beautiful names of Allah are derived from the Quran, even though the lists in various texts differ. Despite the fact that deciding whether the names are personal or transpersonal is open to interpretation, most of the 99 beautiful names are personal. Some of the 99 names are transpersonal: the First, the Last, the Inner, the Outer, the Mighty One, the Truth, the Eternal, the Knowing One, the High One, the Most Holy One, the Great One, and the Light.[660]

The nineteenth-century English poet William Wordsworth had a sense of an 'unseen Power' or 'Spirit' that was within nature. This Spirit, this transpersonal image, has:

> A presence that disturbs me with the joy
> Of elevated thoughts, a sense sublime
> Of something far more deeply infused
> Whose dwelling is the light of setting suns,
> And the round ocean and the living air,
> And the blue sky, and in the mind of man:
> A motion and a Spirit, that impels
> All thinking things, all objects of thought
> And rolls through all things.[661]

Gandhi was the Hindu mystic who was also an activist for the freedom of India from British colonialism. "God is Life, Truth, Light. He is Love." In addition, "God is not a person. . . . God is the Force. He is the essence of Life. He is pure and undefiled Consciousness. He is eternal and . . . the all-pervading living presence. The living Force which we call God can be found if we know and follow His law leading to the discovery of Him in us." His law is the law of love. "God is Truth and Love; God is ethics and morality;

God is fearlessness. God is the Source of Light and Life and yet He is above and beyond all these. God is conscience. . . . He transcends speech and reason. . . . He is a personal God to those who need His personal presence. . . . He is the purest Essence. He simply is to those who have faith. . . . He is in us and yet above and beyond us." Moreover, "there is an indefinable mysterious Power that pervades everything. . . . there is underlying all that changes an unseen Living Power that is changeless, that hold all together, that creates, dissolves, and re-creates. That informing Power or Spirit is God. He alone is. . . . The search for Truth is the search for God. Truth is God. God is, because Truth is. . . . His names are legion. Truth is the crown of them all."[662]

Tolle use transpersonal images of God. The One is "pure Consciousness: the Unmanifested." We are the manifested. The Unmanifested is not separate from the manifested. The Divine is also "the Life within every form, the inner Essence of all that exists," and "the formless and timeless God-essence in yourself and in all things." For Tolle, "space and time are ultimately illusory, but they contain a core of truth. They are two essential attributes of God, Infinity and Eternity. . . . Whereas space is the still, infinitely deep realm of no-mind, the inner equivalent of time is presence, awareness of the eternal Now. . . . When space and time are realized within as the Unmanifested—no-mind and presence—external space and time continue to exist for you," but they are less important.[663]

Underhill used many transpersonal names for God. Sometimes she was speaking for herself and other times quoting other mystics. Here are some Sacred names in her classic *Mysticism*. The Divine is the One, All, Absolute, Infinite, Spirit, Spirit of Life, Beauty, Truth, Source, Creator, Reality, Eternity, Love Divine, Beloved, Pure Love, Light, Inward Light, Indwelling Light, Uncreated Light, Transcendence, Immanence, Being, Divine Dark, secret Silence, "Flaming Heart of things," Plotinus' "Foundation of Life, Foundation of Intellect, Principle of Being, Cause of good, Root of the soul." Underhill's two modes of God led to her "almost perfect definition of the Godhead." In the first mode, many mystics perceive "His utter Transcendence." Names for this mode include the One; "the strange, dark, Unfathomable Abyss of Pure Being;" the Tree of Life; the Divine Dark; "the Wholly Other for whom we have no words;" the Transcendent Light; and "the uncreated, unconditional Source." Never forget, said John of the Cross, a sixteenth-century Spanish monk, "God is inaccessible." The way to see the Divine is "to enter the Darkness, the Cloud of Unknowing." Such a way of conceiving the Holy One accords with a mind and "temperament which leans to pessimism" and utter humility.[664]

Many other mystics utilize Underhill's second mode of seeing the Divine as Immanence. These lean toward optimism and the realization that the Holy One is within their soul. Plotinus, a third century Egyptian mystic, said, God "is not external to anyone, but is present within all things, though they are ignorant that He is so." Names for this mode are "the Divine and loved Companion of the soul;" Inward Light; He Who is in all; "the indwelling Spirit; and Inward Love." Both modes of the Transcendence and Immanence are helpful. Some, including Underhill, try to reconcile them. The first mode's "Transcendent Light" and the second's "Inward Love" complete each other and form "an almost perfect definition of the Godhead which is the object of the mystic's desire: the Divine Love which, Immanent in the soul, spurs on that soul to union with the Transcendent and Absolute Light—at once the Source, the Goal, the Life of created things."[665]

Finding the Divine through Silence, Unknowing, and Darkness

In her book, *The Case for God*, Armstrong describes the history of mystics and theologians in all religions throughout the centuries saying that God is unknowable, ineffable, indefinable, inexplicable, indescribable, and completely incomprehensible. Many also stress the importance of silence and unknowing in speaking about God. Some contend that "silence is the only medium in which it is possible to apprehend the Divine." In her Epilogue, she says that "it is perhaps time to return to a theology that asserts less and is more open to silence and unknowing."[666]

In contrast, Underhill described silence as the second state between meditation and contemplation on the way to illumination and union. Silence is "a state of preparation" and "the necessary prerequisite of all contemplation." The prayer of silence melts into contemplation. "Its stillness is ruffled by its joy. The quiet reveals itself as an essentially transitional state" that introduces the self into contemplation, illumination, and union. Silence has two aspects. First is "the aspect of deprivation, of emptiness which begins it" and the second is "the aspect of acquisition, of Something found, in which it is complete." All mystics "lean to one side or the other, to the affirmative or negative element." When the negative aspect dominates a mystic's consciousness, he "describes it as a Nothingness, a pure Passivity, an Emptiness. . . . Presently, however, he becomes aware that Something fills this emptiness, Something omnipresent, intangible, . . . he begins to notice That which has always been within. . . . It permeates his consciousness." Underhill described as examples of the negative aspect the mysticisms of Denys the Areopagite, Eckhart, and others "as above all things an Emptiness, a Divine Dark, an ecstatic Deprivation." As examples of the affirmative aspect, Teresa of Avila and others felt that an element of "joy seems better than none. To them it was a sweet calm, a gentle silence, in which the lover apprehends the presence of the Beloved, a God-given state."[667]

According to Underhill, for those negative mystics who view the Divine as utter Transcendence, God only seems to be "a Nothing, a Dark, a Self-loss." The transitory phase of silence seems to be permanent, even though it is a means, not an end. "The Divine Dark, the Nothing," is a halfway house to contemplation. For those who are negative, the true goal of contemplation is "an inarticulate communion, a wordless rapture, a silent gazing upon God." In contrast, for those who are affirmative and view the Divine as Immanence, the true end of the spiritual life is "a free mutual act of love" between the soul and the Divine, "the supreme meeting between the lover and the Beloved," their loving union, and the self's entering "more and more into the Heart of Reality." Thus, "the measure of the mystic's real progress is and must always be his progress in love." His consciousness of the Divine is "an apprehension of the heart."[668]

In the first of Denys the Areopagite's three step process for naming God, we begin with God and go downward giving affirmative names for the Divine. In his second phase, we start from below in nature. As we climb, we deny our affirmations. Denys' third step begins as our language falters because God is beyond affirmations and denials. "The Cause of all is considerably prior to this, beyond privations, beyond every denial, beyond every assertion." The more we rise, "the more language falters, and . . . it will turn silent completely, since it will finally be at One with Him who is Indescribable." We become "speechless and unknowing." Denys' third and last step of naming God is also his third and final stage of union with the One. In this step after affirming the Divine names and then denying them, we realize that the Cause of all is "beyond every assertion" and "It is also beyond every denial." Thus, "the good Cause of all is both eloquent and taciturn, indeed wordless." His three steps lead to the One that is "neither word nor act of understanding, since It is on a plane above all this."[669]

In Denys' third step, we reach the Divine "Who has made the shadows His hiding place" and Who dwells in the darkness. We leave behind us everything we understood and strive upward as much as we can toward "union with Him Who is beyond all being and knowledge. By an undivided and absolute abandonment" of ourselves and everything, "shedding all and freed from all," we "will be uplifted to the ray of the Divine shadow which is above everything that is." In addition, "the more we take flight upward, the more our words are confined to ideas" that our finite minds can form. Now "we plunge into that Darkness which is beyond intellect" and "find ourselves not simply running short of words but actually speechless and unknowing." God is "unknowable and is beyond the reach of mind or of reason," but "we know him" because He is "the Cause of all things. God is therefore known in all things and as distinct from all things. He is known through knowledge and through unknowing." We create images of Him, but "He cannot be understood, words cannot contain Him."[670]

According to Denys, when we "push ahead to the summit of the Divine ascents," we contemplate "the holiest and highest of the things" that lie "below the Transcendent One." Through them, "His unimaginable presence is shown" and we "plunge into the truly mysterious Darkness of unknowing." Here we "renounce all that the mind may conceive" and we "belong completely to Him Who is beyond everything." Here we are "supremely united to the completely Unknown by an inactivity of all knowledge, and know beyond the mind by knowing nothing." Denys prayed that "we could come to this Darkness so far above light." He wanted us "to lack sight and knowledge so as to see, so as to know, unseeing and unknowing" which lie "beyond all vision and knowledge." By unseeing and unknowing, we really see and know "the Transcendent One in a transcending way." Denys provided the example of sculptors who see a beautiful image inside the stone before they even start carving. "They remove every obstacle to the pure view of the hidden image, and simply by the act of clearing aside, they show the beauty which is hidden." Thus, we realize that "the Cause of all is above all and is not inexistent, lifeless, speechless, mindless. . . . It is not in any place and can neither be seen nor be touched. . . . It passes through no change, decay, division, loss, no ebb and flow."[671]

Denys said that the Cause of all "cannot be grasped by understanding. . . . It is nothing known to us. . . . There is no speaking of It, nor name nor knowledge of It. Darkness and light, error and truth—It is none of these. . . . It is both beyond every assertion, . . . it is beyond every denial." Furthermore, "just as the senses can neither grasp nor perceive the things of the mind, . . . by the same standard of truth, beings are surpassed by the Infinity beyond being, intelligences by that Oneness which is beyond intelligence. Indeed the Inscrutable One is out of reach of every rational process. Nor can any words come up to the Inexpressible Good, the One, this Source of all unity, this Supra-existent Being. . . . It is and It is as no other being is. The Cause of all existence . . . alone could give an authoritative account of what It really is." This hidden Transcendent God is "ineffable and nameless." The Super-Unknowable is "rightly nameless and yet has the names of everything that is." Thus, "with a wise silence we do honor to the Inexpressible." Denys' writings, including his three stages to union and three processes of naming God, have influenced Christian thinking throughout the centuries until today.[672]

In the fourteenth century, Eckhart said, "if you love God as He is God, as He is Spirit, as He is Person, and as He is Image—all this must go! Then how should I love Him? You should love Him as He is NonGod, a Nonspirit, a Nonperson, a Nonimage, but as He is—pure, unmixed, bright 'One' separated from all duality; and in that One we should sink eternally down, out of 'something' into 'nothing.'" Eckhart raised the question, "it must be asked whether this (new) birth is best accomplished in man when he does the work and *forms and thinks himself into God*, or when he keeps himself in silence, stillness, and peace, so that God may speak and work in him; . . . the best and noblest way in which thou may come into this work and life is by keeping silence, and letting God work and speak. When all the powers are withdrawn from their work and images, there is this word spoken." By saying that silence is "the best and noblest way," Eckhart was recommending this way rather than "thinking himself into God."[673]

Why must one way be better than another? Why can't it be both/and rather than either/or? Why can't people use many ways or choose the most appropriate and meaningful for themselves?

Little is known about the English author of the fourteenth-century *Cloud of Unknowing*, except that he may have translated and been influenced by Denys the Areopagite. A beginner asked, "who am I to think about God Himself and what is He?" The author responded, "I cannot answer you, except to say, 'I don't know.' For with this question you have brought me into the same darkness, the same cloud of unknowing, where I want you to be!" Although we can ponder many things, no one can think of God. If we persevere with our prayers, liturgy, and Divine reading, "I will leave on one side everything I can think, and choose for my love that which I cannot think! . . . Why? Because God may well be loved but not thought. By love He may be caught and held but by thinking never."[674]

Miguel de Molinos, a seventeenth-century Spanish priest, said in his *Spiritual Guide* that "by not speaking nor desiring, and not thinking, . . . the soul arrives at the true and perfect mystical silence wherein God speaks with the soul, communicates Himself to it, and in the abyss of Its own depth teaches it the most perfect and exalted wisdom. He calls and guides it to this inward solitude and mystical silence, when He says that He will speak to it alone in the most secret and hidden part of the heart." Furthermore, "the true contemplative, coming to this plane of utter stillness, does not desire 'extraordinary favors and visitations,' but the privilege of breathing . . . the atmosphere of love."[675]

Carolyn Stephen who died at the beginning to the twentieth century, wrote that Quakers, who are also called the Society of Friends, believe in the importance of silence and the inner light. The founder George Fox and the early Friends were mystics who had "a vivid consciousness of the inwardness of the Light of Truth." Underlying their teaching was this fundamental truth: "God, who spoke of old. . ., still speaks; and we may every one of us, if we will, hear that Divine voice in the secret of our hearts." When Stephen was invited to her first Friends' meeting one Sunday, "I found myself one of a small company of silent worshippers, who were content to sit down together without words, that each might feel and draw near to the Divine presence, unhindered at least, if not helped, by any human utterance . . . My whole soul was filled with the unutterable peace of the undisturbed opportunity for communion with God." Here with the Friends she might "join with others in simply seeking His presence. To sit in silence . . . might open to me (as it did that morning) the very gate of heaven." For more than seventeen years Quaker meetings have been "the place of the most soul-subduing, faith-restoring, strengthening, and peaceful communion."[676]

For Stephen, "one corner-stone belief upon which the Society of Friends is built is the conviction that God does indeed communicate with each one of the spirits that he has made, . . . and that in order to hear the Divine voice thus speaking to us we need to be still; to be alone with Him in the secret place of His presence; that all flesh should keep silent before Him." Moreover, "the silence we value is . . . the deep quietness of heart and mind." This silence is "the essential preparation for any act of true worship" and "the essential condition at all times of inward illumination." To the silent, listening heart, "God does speak intelligibly."[677]

According to Stephen, we all have an inner light that was described by Fox in many ways: "the Light, Life, Spirit, and grace of Christ; the Seed, the new birth, the power of God unto salvation;" the hope of glory; and Christ within. This light was "the power which would heal sin." Fox's daily business was to "turn people to the light within.'" A cardinal doctrine of the Quakers is that if we will attend "to the Divine influence in our own hearts," we will have personal experiences of the meaning of God's inspiration. "A true mystic believes that all men have, as he himself is conscious of having, an inward life, into which as into a secret chamber, he can retreat at will. . . . He finds there, first repose, then an awful guidance; a light which burns and purifies; a voice which subdues; he finds himself in the presence of God. . . . The Divine guidance is away from self-indulgence, often away from outward success. . . . Its evidence of success is in the inmost, deepest, most spiritual part of our existence."[678]

In his sermon, "Jacob's Wrestling" with the Divine, F.W. Robertson described God as dwelling in darkness. "God is approached more nearly in that which is indefinite than in that which is definite and distinct. He is felt in awe and wonder and worship rather than in clear conception. There is a sense in which darkness has more of God than light. He dwells in the thick darkness. Moments of tender, vague mystery often bring distinctly the feeling of His presence." Moreover, "in sorrow, haunted by uncertain presentiments, the gloom disperses, the world's joy comes again, and . . . the Being who has touched us . . . and wrestled with us, yet whose presence, even when most terrible, was more blessed than His absence. It is true, even literally, that darkness reveals God: every morning God draws the curtain of the garish light across His eternity, and we lose the Infinite. We look down on earth instead of up to heaven. . . . In the pettiness of life we seem to cease to behold Him: then at night . . . in the solitary, silent, vague darkness, the Awful One is near."[679]

Robertson also preached that "names have a power, a strange power in hiding God. Who does not know how we satisfy ourselves with the name of some strange bird or plant? . . . It is a mystery perplexing us before. We get the name and fancy we understand . . . but in truth we are more hopelessly ignorant." Before naming it, we "searched—now we fancy we possess it" because we named it. The name "covers the abyss of our ignorance. . . . God's plan was not to give names and words, but *truths of feeling*." When Jacob felt a religious awe, he was not to develop "formal expressions, which would have satisfied . . . the craving of the intellect and shut up the soul: Jacob felt the Infinite, Who is more truly *felt* when least *named*."[680]

Ramakrishna used personal and transpersonal concepts, but he also recommended silence. "Nothing can be predicated of the Absolute and Unconditioned. No sooner do you talk of It than you state the Infinite in terms of the finite, the Absolute in terms of the relative, the Unconditioned in terms of the conditioned. Your silence is more eloquent than the shouting forth of a 100-sacred-verses and the quoting of 100 authorities."[681]

Tolle describes silence as another portal or way to God that "opens up every moment." Do you hear a car passing or a dog barking? Look for God in the silence. "Paying attention to the outer silence creates inner silence: the mind becomes still." Thus, a portal opens. "Every sound is born out of silence, . . . and during its life is surrounded by silence. . . . The Unmanifested is present in this world as silence. . . . Nothing in this world is so like God as silence. All you have to do is pay attention to it. . . . As you do that the dimension of silence grows within you. You cannot pay attention to silence without simultaneously becoming still within. Silence without, stillness within. You have entered the Unmanifested." In addition, "when you are utterly and totally present, you encounter It (God) as the still inner space."[682]

For some people, God is unknowable and totally incomprehensible. His hiding place is in the darkness. The only way to know Him is by silence. This understanding of the Holy One is most helpful to them. Others of us agree that the Divine is Infinite and we are finite. We cannot comprehend Infinity. The Infinite One is so far beyond our finite capacities we cannot even begin to grasp It. The Sacred Spirit is either a totally incomprehensible or an infinitely comprehensible Mystery. However, the Divine gave us our minds to try to learn about the truth and reality. Although we can never know and understand Infinite Love, we have some ideas about what love is. To know the creator of this book, study this book. To know the Creator, study creation. Even though we will never totally comprehend the Creator, we can know something. The Ultimate Reality gave us the universe with its galaxies, stars, planets, mountains, oceans, trees, plants, animals, and humans. When we study all of this, we learn something about the Ultimate Reality that is helpful to us, but we are still infinitely far from learning everything. We learn something about the Sacred Ocean of Infinite Love because we are drops of love within It.

The Dark Night of the Soul and the Divine Absence

Underhill claimed that "the Dark Night of the Soul" is the fourth stage on the mystical way. It is located between Underhill's third stage of illumination and her fifth stage of union. Its name comes from the phrase used by sixteenth-century Spanish Carmelite monk, John of the Cross, who wrote *The Dark Night of the Soul*. Disagreeing with Underhill, I contend that the dark night of the soul is NOT a stage on the mystical way. My reasons will be explained later.[683]

John of the Cross claimed that the dark night is a form of contemplation. "The dark night is an inflowing of God into the soul, which cleanses it." By this inflowing, "God secretly teaches the soul and instructs it in the perfection of love." This "produces two special effects in the soul, for by both purifying and enlightening it, this contemplation prepares the soul for union with God in love." The dark night "produces two sorts of darkness or purgations" because of "the two divisions of man's nature into sensual and spiritual. Thus, the first night or purgation will be sensual, in which the soul is purified according to the senses, subjecting them to the spirit." The second night or purgation will be "spiritual, in which the soul is purified and stripped in the spirit, and which subdues and disposes it for union with God in love." Thus, "the dark night is an inflowing of God into the soul, which cleanses it of its ignorance and imperfections, habitual, natural, and spiritual." Furthermore, "because the light and wisdom of contemplation is most pure and bright, and because the soul on which it beats is in the dark and impure, the soul that received it must suffer greatly." Another way "the soul suffers pain comes from its natural, moral, and spiritual weakness."[684]

Underhill described what Catherine of Siena, the fourteenth-century Italian mystic, said about how God withdrew from her, so that her soul would "see and know her defects" and rise from imperfection to perfection. God said to her, "in order to raise from imperfection . . . I withdraw Myself from her, . . . which I do in order to . . . cause her to seek Me in truth. . . . Then, if she loves Me without thought of self, and with a lively faith, . . . she rejoices in the time of trouble." Thus, "the end and purpose of all her self-knowledge" is "to rise above herself, . . . digging up the root" of selfishness with the love of virtue. Selfishness is replaced with loving all and with serving God.[685]

In the sixteenth century, Jeanne Marie Guyon, a French spiritual seeker, described the swing back and forth between illumination and the dark night of the soul. In illumination, "the presence of God never left me for an instant. But how dear I suffered pain for this time of happiness! For this possession, which seemed to me entire and perfect, . . . was but the preparation for a total deprivation, lasting many years, without any support or hope of its return." During the long periods of almost continuous privation, it seemed that "I had utterly lost Thee." Even then, "I had from time to time inflowings of Thy Divinity so deep and intimate, so vivid and so penetrating," that it was possible for me to think that Thou were "hidden from me and not lost." When "Thou did return with more goodness and strength, Thou did return also with greater splendor, so that in a few hours Thou did rebuild all the ruins of my unfaithfulness and did make good to me with profusion all my loss."[686]

All that William Law, an eighteenth-century English author, would say of inward spiritual delights and the dark night is that they are not holiness, piety, or perfection, but they are God's "call to seek after holiness and spiritual perfection. . . . This alone is the true kingdom of God opened in the soul when, stripped of all selfishness, it has only one love and one will in it; when it has no motion or desire but what branches from the Love of God, and resigns itself wholly to the Will of God." His conclusion is that "nothing has separated us from God but our own will." All the disorder and sickness of our nature "lies in a certain fixedness of our own will" where we live and act wholly for ourselves. Any evil in us "arises from this selfishness." In the purification of the dark night, we need to tear out of us "the deepest root of all selfishness." Tearing up the root of egotism results in active love.[687]

Mother Teresa, a twentieth-century Catholic nun who spent her life serving the poorest of the poor, experienced darkness. In her private writings, the first mention of darkness appeared about ten years before Jesus spoke to her. "Do not think that my spiritual life is strewn with roses. . . . Quite the contrary, I have more often as my companion 'darkness.' And when the night becomes very thick—and it seems to me as if I will end up in hell—then I offer myself to Jesus. If he wants me to go there—I am ready—but only under the condition that it really makes him happy."[688]

Jesus spoke to Mother Teresa. "*I want Missionaries of Charity—who would be my fire of love among the very poor, the sick, the dying, the little street children. . . . Wilt thou refuse?*" His request frightened her. Although she was afraid, she accepted Jesus' call. She said that these nuns were "to become so united to God so as to radiate Him" in the slums. "Love should be the fire that will make them live life to the full. If the nuns are very poor, they will be free to love only God—to serve Him only—to be only His." The sisters are to "act the charity of Christ among the poor." In addition, "in the work there will be surrender of all I have and all I am—there will be absolutely nothing left.—Now I am His, only His—I have given Him everything—I have not been seeking anything for myself for some time now." Only one year later she said that "though there has been plenty of suffering and tears, there has not been one moment of regret. I am happy to do God's will."[689]

After Jesus stopped speaking to her, Divine absence and darkness descended on her and continued for almost four decades until her death, except for one month interruption. She experienced "this terrible sense of loss—this untold darkness—this loneliness, this continual longing for God—which gives me that pain deep in my heart.—Darkness is such that I really do not see—neither with my mind nor with my reason—the place of God in my soul is blank.—There is no God in me—when the pain of longing is so great—I just long and long for God—and then it is that I feel—He does not want me—He is not there. . . . Sometimes—I just hear my own heart cry out—'my God' and nothing else comes.—The torture and pain I can't explain."[690]

Mother Teresa felt that God had "taken even the power of speech. . . . I keep up the joy exteriorly. I deceive people with this weapon—even my sisters." After eleven years of Divine absence, "I have come to love the darkness.—For I believe now that it is a part, a very, very small part of Jesus' darkness and pain on earth. You have taught me to accept it." She believed that "He wants . . . to drain out of me every drop of self." She felt that she had nothing to say, because "the darkness is so dark, the pain is so painful. Sometimes the grip of pain is so great. . . . When I help my sisters, . . . when I teach them to love Him with a deep—devoted—personal love—I long to be able to do the same." She felt that "I am just alone—empty—excluded—just not wanted. . . . The greater the pain and the darker the darkness, the sweeter will be my smile at God." Despite her feelings of darkness both before and after Jesus spoke to her, Mother Teresa gave herself continually and totally to serving God by helping the poor.[691]

The dark night of the soul, according to Underhill, is a period of spiritual darkness. After experiencing the brilliance of the Holy Light in the stage of illumination, some of us experience an intense darkness. After becoming conscious of the Sacred presence, we experience the Divine absence. After realizing how pure and perfect the Holy One is, we become more aware of how impure and imperfect we are. Then we can totally lose our consciousness of the Divine and experience the absence of the Sacred Spirit. The dark night is "an overwhelming sense of darkness and deprivation" and "a period of utter blankness and stagnation." It is also "a period of fatigue" and exhaustion. The darkness and Divine absence are so strong and deep that they overpower our consciousness and plunge us into a "state of negativity and misery" whose essence is the loss of the illumination and union. We feel completely separated from and abandoned by the Holy One. This negative consciousness causes us to feel helplessness, pain, anguish, disharmony, distress, deprivation, stagnation, miseries, and torments. Some mystics have a "motto: *I am nothing, I have nothing, I desire nothing.*"[692]

Underhill explained that after we experience the transcendent illumination of the Holy One, then we oscillate to face "impotence, blankness, solitude," as well as "the dark fire of purification." Thus, "progress in contemplation, for instance, is marked by . . . an alternation of light and shade," of intuitions of Reality and aridity or the drying up of spirituality, of joyous and painful consciousness, and of illumination and the dark night of purification. These oscillations "occur most often at the beginning of a new period." Once we feel so strongly our shortcomings and selfishness, we "lose the power to do and learn to surrender our will" to the Holy One. "The path of light lies through the surrender to the confusion and ignorance of the dark" and to the Divine will. The dark night is a process of purification and cure of our soul; a development of responsibility and character; a giving up of egotism; a renouncing of I, me, and mine; a growth in love for all people; and a doing away with the separateness from the Divine. Some mystics refer to the dark night as "an education in selfless constancy, a 'school of suffering love,'" and "a mystic death."[693]

There are several reasons why I disagree with Underhill and say that the Dark Night of the Soul is NOT a separate stage. The first reason is that most mystics do not mention the dark night of the soul. Those who did not recorded it probably did not have that experience. If they did experience it, they did not think it was worthy of being reported.

The second reason is that it is true that when we realize the magnificence and greatness of Infinite Love, we understand more deeply and clearly our own insignificance, inconsequentiality, and unworthiness as well as our own shortcomings, limited abilities, defects, mistakes, faults, and wrong actions. Some mystics may connect these two realizations of the grandeur of the Sacred Spirit and the unworthiness of humans. This may lead to the dark night and Divine absence for some mystics, like Mother Teresa. However, they may not lead to the dark night and Divine Absence for most mystics. Think of our own lives. Remember all those nights when we could not sleep, because we were agonizing over our own faults and wrong actions of the day or week before. Most of us probably do not think of the Holy One at all during these sleepless nights. If we do think of the Sacred Spirit, we may pray for help. However, most of us are busy punishing ourselves for our own mistakes and limited abilities. We do not compare ourselves to the Divine. We realize that we are finite and cannot be compared with Infinite Love in any way. There is no comparison. When we have a sleepless night, it is not a dark night of the soul, but rather it is a night when we are strongly critical of ourselves, upset, angry, and depressed because of our faults, limited abilities, and terribly wrong actions. No thoughts of the Divine are involved, because we know the Sacred Spirit loves us no matter what we do. Is it a lack of self-love or a lack of faith in Infinite Love or something else that make some mystics experience the dark night of the soul and feel the Divine absence?

Third, what is described as the dark night of purification is not a separate stage, but rather it is one of the many experiences of purification that happens as mystics oscillate between the fifth stage of illumination and the sixth stage of love. For those who experience them, darkness and Divine absence lead to the defeat of our egotism and our deep transformation. The difference between the self-transformation in the fourth and sixth stages of love is the difference between cutting off a branch and pulling the tree out by its roots. The agony of being immersed in darkness and Divine absence causes us to feel powerless, deprived, and lonely. This ignites a painful fire that leads to spiritual purification. All the many kinds of purification and transformation purge our habitual selfishness, false desires, materialistic yearnings, negative thoughts, critical words, egotistical feelings, wrong values, hostile behaviors, and our cruel, violent actions. All transformations help us achieve detachment, root out egotism, cleanse the very core of our being, remake our character, learn self-love, and express love for all people and creation.[694]

Describing the dark night, contemporary mystic William Johnson says that "love is like a fire." The Divine loving fire purges the soul of all its contrary qualities before it transforms the person. "The great suffering of the dark night is caused by love. . . . mystical love is a devouring fire that consumes everything that might oppose it." The dark night is "a journey of love" in which the mystic freely goes away from all things to be united with the Holy One.[695]

Chapter 12

Love for All People and All of Creation Is the Sixth Stage on the Mystical Way

Mystical Experiences of Illumination Result in Love for All, the Sixth Stage

Our spiritual experiences flow naturally into acts of love. Love flows naturally into mystical experiences. Awakening is the spiritual experience of the Divine presence within everyone. It generates love for our neighbors and ourselves. This love results in the mystical experience of illumination that the Holy One is within us and we are within the ONE. This makes us feel and want to express love for all people and all of creation. As Underhill said, illuminated consciousness is "produced by love, of necessity, it produces love in turn." This love for all people and all of creation is the sixth stage on the mystic way to the Divine.

> Illumination and union create love for all people and all of creation
> Love for all people and all of creation generate illumination and union

The natural expression of a mystical experience of illumination and union with the Sacred Spirit is love for everyone and everything.[696]

Authentic spirituality creates love in all areas of our life, in our caring for our family and friends, in our passionate longing to learn, in our desire to do work that helps others, in our yearning to stop injustice, in our search for the meaning of life, and in our longing for the Ultimate Reality. In the New Testament, Peter's second letter said, through spiritual experiences, "you may escape from the corruption that is in the world because of lust, and may become participants of the Divine nature. For this very reason, you must make every effort to support your faith with goodness, and goodness with knowledge, and knowledge with self-control, and self-control with endurance, and endurance with Godliness, and Godliness with mutual affection, and mutual affection with love."[697]

What we consider Divine affects our behavior. The deeper our commitment to the Holy One, the stronger our course of action. The more fervent our Ultimate Concern, the more passionate our desire to work for It. The deeper our illumination, the more extensively we spread our love. Spirituality without any action flowing from it is lacking. A mystical experience demands a response and is not complete without one. The genuineness of faith is gauged by what it produces in loving actions. The Jewish scriptures teach people to love God by keeping the commandments. The Christian scriptures say "faith without works is dead" and "by their fruits you shall know them." Separating spirituality from action leads to a deterioration of spirituality and a decrease of action. The ultimate activity that flows from our mystical experiences is to express love for all, personally, locally, nationally, and internationally. Expressing love includes working to take suffering, injustice, inequality, lack of freedom, abuse, cruelty, and violence out of our families, communities, nations, and our world.

After we mystics experience the Ultimate Reality, one of the ways we express our love is to communicate our life-giving spiritual wisdom in order to teach and enlighten others. Union with the Holy One endows us with a new vision that we want to share with the world to open new paths for the human race. Brushing aside everything that veils the ONE, we try to help the Divine break into the world. Wanting to enlarge people's horizons, we bear witness to the Eternal within the temporal, the Holy within the secular, the Sacred within the profane, the Infinite within the finite, and the Transcendent within the immanent.[698]

When Jesus visited, Martha was doing all the work and complained to him about her sister Mary who sat and listened to him. "Tell her to help me." Jesus answered Martha, "you are worried and distracted by many things, there is need of only one thing. Mary has chosen the better part." Jesus' mystical experiences led him to express his love by communicating spiritual wisdom. Some early mystics used this story to conclude that the contemplative life is superior to the active life. Augustine, the fifth century African bishop, outlined three principles. First, both ways are good. Second, contemplation is better than the active life. Third, contemplation should yield to action when the neighbor is in need. Some mystics advocated both ways, contemplation that expresses love for the Divine and activities that show love for everyone. Others realized that these two oscillate back and forth.[699]

As mystics, we alternate between spiritual experiences and love for all, between contemplation and action, between solitude and work, between retreat from the world and return to it, between illumination and public service that expresses our love for humanity, between union with the ONE and activities that produce social change. Our love for the Holy One transforms us so that we have a twofold destiny. Our inner spiritual life is to love and unite with the Sacred Spirit. Our outer career is to become Divine ambassadors by bringing spiritual teaching, loving actions, and social change to the world. To become Divine instruments means teaching spiritual wisdom and radiating love for all people and the cosmos by doing good works. It also means struggling against our own and others' selfish feelings, negative thoughts, critical words, materialist yearnings, dominating ways, and hostile actions. In addition, it involves creating a more loving world by changing social structures that discriminate, exploit, dominate, abuse, harm, and perpetuate violence.

When we as illuminated mystics become more contemplative, we are called to a more active and compassionate life. Our experience of the Holy One that is our spiritual way of life cannot be separated from our ethical way of life. Our moral way of life is a living manifestation of Infinite Love within us as our inner core of love. Illumination and union with the ONE produce as a minimum, moral actions, and as a maximum, a lifelong vocation of love for all. When we follow the moral law, we are practicing the law of life, the natural law, the universal law, and the Divine law. These laws are all the same. They are all the law of love. To live out the law of love is to express our inner core of love and thus fulfill our human nature. Our spirituality and human nature lead us to act only out of love because that is what we are.

After we experience illumination and union with the Holy One and get in touch with Infinite Love as our inner core of love, we want to follow the law of love which means practicing universal love. This love can also be called brotherly love, but to balance this male wording, it can also be referred to as sisterly love. Universal love means what it says; it means we love everyone and everything in the universe. Most of us love our family and friends. When we express universal love, we love our fellow students, work colleagues, religious members, and all the people in our community, state, nation, and the world. We are citizens of the world who care about everyone. We also love all of creation.

Jesus said, "love your enemies" which means love everyone. Besides religious founders, well known examples of people who practice universal love include Florence Nightingale, Gandhi, Dorothy Day, Albert Schweitzer, Martin Luther King, Mother Teresa, Nelson Mandela, and the Dalai Lama. The unknown names are innumerable.

Buddha described how to develop universal love. "When your mind is filled with love, send it in one direction, then a second, a third, and a fourth, then above, then below. Identify with everything without hatred, resentment, anger, or enmity. This mind of love is very wide. It grows immeasurably and eventually is able to embrace the whole world." Living in Confucius' time more than 2000 years ago, a philosopher Mo Tzu believed in universal love and said that the Chinese God, called Shang Ti and Heaven, "loves people dearly. . . . Heaven loves the whole world universally." In addition, "whoever loves others is loved by others; whoever benefits others is benefited by others; whoever injures others is injured by others." The solution to China's social problems is not force but love, universal love (*chien ai*). One should "feel toward all people under heaven exactly as one feels towards one's own people, and regard other states exactly as one regards one's own state."[700]

According to Mo Tzu, among the major calamities in the world are mutual harm among individuals and mutual attacks among states. These calamities "arise out of want for mutual love." The heads of houses only love their own house and the leaders their own state. "Individuals have learned only to love themselves and not others." How can we change this? "It is to be altered by the way of universal love and mutual aid." How is this done? The way is "to regard the state of others as one's own, the houses of others as one's own, and the person of others as one's self. When all the people in the world love one another, then the strong will not overpower the weak, the many will not oppress the few, the wealthy will not mock the poor, . . . the cunning will not deceive the simple. And it is all due to mutual love that calamities, strife, complaints, and hatred are prevented." Mo Tzu's thoughts became a Chinese social philosophy called Mohism.[701]

The nineteen-century philosopher August Comte said that cooperation between people is based on "their own inherent tendency to universal love." Chardin said, "universal love is not only psychologically possible; it is the only complete and final way in which we are able to love." William Johnson, a contemporary Jesuit priest, writes about the goal of mysticism as "union with God through charity." He stresses "charity as the most important" of the interior gifts. "Wisdom is mystical love." This love is all-consuming, unlimited love, and unrestricted" as well as without "qualifications or conditions or reservations." This love needs to express itself in deeds that show love for God and love for the world. It needs to be "a universal love which includes love for one's enemies."[702]

While I contend that our inner core of love is the source of our ability to practice universal love, Karen Armstrong says that maternal affection "in all likelihood gave birth to our capacity for unselfish, unconditional altruism. . . . We humans are more radically dependent on love than any other species. Our brains have evolved to be caring and to need to care—to such an extent that they are impaired if this nurturing is lacking." Universal love usually begins when we see the suffering of needy people, including our own children, and want to help by showing compassion. It deepens when we perceive all people as our own flesh and blood. The basis of universal love is the belief that all people are one. Of course, there are important differences between races, sexes, classes, disabilities, sexual preferences, religions, and nationalities that we need to acknowledge and respect. However, we who practice universal love feel and think that the unity because of our common humanity is greater than the divisions because of our individual and group differences. If we live on the surface, we see mainly the differences that separate us. When we have mystical experiences and penetrate to the depths, we encounter the common loving inner core that unites us. This helps us promote human solidarity.[703]

It is crucial to recognize our important differences. However, according to contemporary African American poet Audre Lorde, it is not these differences that separate us. "It is rather our refusal to recognize those differences, and to examine the distortions which result from our misnaming them and their effects upon human behavior and expectation." Unacknowledged differences distort our vision, make it difficult to see our different problems, and rob us of our creative insight and energy. "Community must not mean a shedding of our differences, nor the pathetic pretense that these differences do not exist." Community must accept, respect, value, and appreciate them. "Difference is that raw and powerful connection from which our personal power is forged." We need to see difference as a strength, "as a springboard for creative change within our lives."[704]

All kinds of love drive us to self-realization and communion with others. Universal love is the creative life force and dynamic power that tries to unite us with all human beings and nature. Not only does it strive toward the unity of all, but it also seeks the personal fulfillment of every person. When we practice universal love, we promote respect, liberty, equality, and justice for all people. Former Congresswoman Pat Schroeder asks, what do people not understand about the word, 'all.' Universal love not only cares for the oppressed, but also the oppressor; the abused, but also the abusers. Because love is creative, it struggles against whatever damages love. Love uses its power to oppose what is against it. It attempts to heal not only the victims, but also those oppressors who have caused the harm, because their dominating actions have damaged their own loving inner core.

Since the Holy One as Infinite, Unconditional, Universal Love is within us, we are bearers of infinite, unconditional, universal Love. But what is unconditional love? When I love myself unconditionally, it means that I love myself not because I am good or because of what I do, but rather because I have life and love. I accept and love myself the way I am. We unconditionally love birds whether or not they can fly. We love the ocean whether it is calm or wild. We love our dogs whether they are healthy or sick, good or bad. Most parents love their newborn infants unconditionally because they have life and love. Later because unconditional love is difficult to sustain, many parents change and love conditionally, because of what their children do, how they act, whether they are good. We love them if they clean their room, if they do this, if they do that. Elizabeth Kubler-Ross, a twentieth-century medical doctor who wrote about the stages of dying, taught that unconditional love for everyone, everywhere, is "the only thing that matters in life." Our mystical experiences enable us to make our vocation in life to express universal, unconditional love for all.

Albert Schweitzer, a scholar in the early twentieth-century who became a missionary doctor in Africa, claimed that reverence for life is "the beginning and foundation for morality." Reverence for life is "the supreme law" and "the underlying principle of ethics." In his view, "reverence for life is the ethic of love widened into universality." Love for God, love for humans, and "love for all creatures, reverence for all being, compassion with all life" are all interconnected. Revering life means removing alienation and suffering, affirming and promoting life, and restoring empathy and compassion. When we have reverence for life, we injure and destroy life only when it cannot be avoided and never from thoughtlessness. We take responsibility for all life and devote ourselves to helping it.[705]

Daniel Maguire, a contemporary moral theologian, sees action-oriented love as a part of the moral core of Judaism and Christianity. "Love is an energy that must be incarnated in action." Good intentions that are not lived out are no substitute for action. "Love begets love. . . .. Love is a unitive force, a fusion of vitalities." By melting the barriers, love unites without any loss of individuality. "True love accentuates our differences as it bonds us into a fruitful union and is a boon to both lover and beloved." For members of Alcoholics Anonymous (AA), it is not enough to have a spiritual experience. The twelfth step teaches that a spiritual awakening leads to the action of practicing the AA "principles in all our affairs," carrying the AA message to others, and helping other alcoholics become sober.[706]

Although Underhill said that there are five stages on the mystical way to the Divine, she actually described what I call the sixth stage, even though she did not call it a stage, but rather a movement. According to Underhill, every complete spiritual life has two movements. Union with the Divine is the first movement. Mystics going into the world to do spiritual work and to express love for all is the second movement. What is primary is "the achievement and maintenance of a right attitude toward God; the profound and awestruck sense of God's Transcendent Reality." A prayer of awe and wonder is better than all other kinds. It alone is able to overcome our persistent selfishness and to expand our awareness of the Sacred Spirit. This first movement includes the whole range of spiritual communion with the Holy One. Union with the Infinite ONE, not petitioning, is the very heart of the spiritual life. The first movement acknowledges the Divine law that the soul "comes from God, belongs to God, and is destined for God."[707]

For Underhill, the soul's inward movement of deepening communion with the Sacred Spirit precedes the second outward movement of active love for everyone and everything in the universe. After we experience union, we move into the world with increased energy to express love and to do social change and spiritual work. "Our ultimate effect as transmitters of heavenly light and love" depends directly on how much we have given ourselves to the Ultimate Reality. Only when our souls are filled with love for the Holy One and achieve self-forgetfulness can we communicate spiritual gifts to others.[708]

Henri Bergson's Two Stages of Mysticism

In trying to fathom the depths of life, the twentieth-century French philosopher Henri Bergson called the driving force of evolution *elan vital*. These French words mean "the vital impetus of life," "the impulse of life to movement," "the vital impulsion," the "original impetus," and the "inner vital movement." The elan vital as "an imperative demand for creation" dwells within the soul. "It is always there, a unique emotion, an impulse, an impetus received from the very depths of things." The elan vital is the inner directing, transforming, creative, vital principle of evolution. "This impetus, sustained right along the line of evolution, . . . is the fundamental cause of the variations . . . that accumulate and create a new species." In addition, his Universal *Elan Vital* is the Universal Vital Impetus.[709]

My interpretation of the meaning of Bergson's words, 'elan vital,' is the vital spirit, soul, the inner core of love, and the Divine within all people and things. In addition, his Universal *Elan Vital* or the Universal Vital Impetus refers to the Universal Vital Spirit or Soul.

Bergson's philosophy sees "the organized world as a harmonious whole" even though there is much discord. He traces the elan vital, the vital principle, further and further back to the individual's remotest ancestors and finds that it is in "solidarity with each of them, solidarity with . . . the root of the genealogical tree of life." Thus, "each individual may be said to remain united with the totality of living beings by invisible bonds." In addition, the Universal Vital Impetus is the Energy that each individual and species utilizes for its own self-interest. "Each species, each individual even, retains only a certain impetus from the Universal Vital Impulsion and tends to use this energy in its interest."[710]

According to Bergson, a mystic is "an individual being, capable of transcending the limitations imposed on the species by its material nature, thus continuing and extending Divine action." With their increased vitality, mystics radiate "an extraordinary energy, daring, power of conception and realization" as well as superabundant activity. Being mentally healthy and having the capacity to adapt and re-adapt themselves to circumstances, they have "the prophetic discernment of what is possible and what is not" and "the spirit of simplicity which triumphs over complications."[711]

Bergson presents two stages of mysticism. Mysticism first lifts souls to another plane that transcends human reason and second it leads to action. In Bergson's first stage, mystics achieve "contact with the very Principle of nature," union with the Universal Elan Vital, and "Oneness with the Creative Impetus." They experience visions, rapture, and "ecstasy, a state in which the soul feels . . . in the presence of God." After being shaken to its depths, sometimes going into its darkest night, mystics experience the indefinable Divine presence and "a boundless joy, an all-absorbing ecstasy, or an enthralling rapture: God is there, and the soul is in God." With these thoughts and feelings, the soul becomes absorbed in and united with the Holy One.[712]

Action is Bergson's second stage. When mystics experience illumination and union with the Divine, they produce "action, creation, love." This makes them feel "that they are the instrument of God who loves all men with an equal love, and who bids them to love each other." At a minimum, mystics want to teach humankind what they have experienced, seen, and known about the Sacred Spirit. They also "effect a radical transformation of humanity by setting an example." Mystics are ambassadors of the Holy One. In their actions, "it is God who is acting through the soul, in the soul; the union is total." When their "contemplation is engulfed in action, the human will become One with the Divine will." Then mystics feel a boundless impetus, a superabundance of life, an irresistible impulse which drives them into vast activities. "The superabundance of vitality... flows from a spring which is the very Source of life," the Universal Elan Vital. Their soul is replete with the Sacred essence. Their purpose is to attain "a Divine humanity."[713]

According to Bergson, in the second stage, mystics "embrace all humanity in one simple indivisible love." Their love, which lies at the root of all things, coincides with God's Love for creation, which is the Source of everything. Capable of yielding the secret of creation, their love wants "to complete the creation of the human species." Their love's "direction is exactly that of the Vital Impetus; it is this Impetus Itself." Their love is the Elan Vital, "communicated in its entirety to exceptional men who in their turn would fain impart it to all humanity."[714]

For Bergson, God is Creative Energy. In addition, Creative Energy is defined as Love. Love is the Universal Elan Vital and the very essence of the Divine. Creative Energy as Love "desires to produce from Itself beings worthy to be loved" as well as beings destined to love. Creation appears to be "God undertaking to create creators that He may have, besides Himself, beings worthy of His Love." The universe is "the mere visible and tangible aspect of Love and the need of loving, together with all the consequences entailed by this creative emotion." In addition, "the creation of a Divine humanity" has been prevented so far because people are subject to the laws of animal nature. However, humans can turn heavenward. By imparting the Vital Impetus to a handful of gifted souls who are mystics, a spiritual society of mystics will be formed. Such societies might multiply until profound changes take place. The impetus of love will drive mystics, with the help of the Sacred Spirit whose instruments they are, "to lift humanity up to God and complete the Divine creation."[715]

Bergson believed that mystics experience a "God common to all mankind." If all people could attain this vision of the Divine, war would be immediately abolished. The love which consumes mystics is not just the love of humans for God, but also it is the Love of God for all humankind. Through the Holy One, mystics love all humanity with a Divine Love. This love is more than a philosophical "principle that all men share by birth in one rational essence," that all people participate equally in a higher essence. Mystics' "love lies at the very root of feeling and reason." Coinciding with God's Love for His creation that is the Source of everything, what mystics' love wants to do, with Divine help, is "to complete the creation of the human species" and make it what it was meant to be, "a Divine humanity."[716]

Illuminated Mystics Move from Spiritual Experiences to Love for All

When illuminated mystics become more contemplative, many want to have a more active, compassionate life. Their experience of being within the Holy One that is their spiritual way of life produces love for everyone and everything that is their moral life. Moses' spiritual experiences produced the ten commandments and the commandments to love. "The Lord is our God, the Lord alone. 'You shall love the Lord your God with all your heart, and all your soul, and all your might.'" In addition, "you shall love your neighbor as yourself."[717]

In the Hindu *Bhagavad Gita*, the Divine Krishna said to his disciple Arjuna, the person "whose *love is the same for his enemies or his friends*, whose soul is the same in honor or disgrace, who is beyond heat or cold or pleasure or pain, who is free from the chains of attachment; . . . who is happy with whatever he has, whose home is not in this world, and who has love—this man is dear to Me." People "who have all the powers of their soul in harmony, and *the same loving mind for all*, who find *joy in the good of all beings*—they reach in truth My very Self." The individual who "dwells in his inner self," who "has *the same love for enemies or friends*, who surrenders all selfish undertakings, . . . and he who with never-failing love adores Me and works for Me, . . . can be One with Brahman, the ONE." The person "who works for Me, who loves Me, whose End Supreme I am, free from attachment to all things, and with *love for all creation*, he in truth comes unto Me."[718]

Buddha was a mystic who experienced Nirvana and then taught the four Noble Truths and the Eightfold Path to Nirvana. These truths and their path teach us how to end suffering and live a compassionate life. One of the central disciplines that Buddha also advocated was "a meditation on the four elements of the 'immeasurable' love that exists within everyone and everything." First is 'loving-kindness' (*maitri*), the desire to have "friendship for everything and everybody" and "to bring happiness to all sentient beings." The second element is 'compassion' (*karuna*), the aspiration to free all creatures from their sorrow and pain. Third is 'sympathetic joy' (*mudita*), the yearning for the happiness and joy of all creatures. The fourth element is 'even-mindedness' (*upeksha*), the longing to be free from personal attachments and to have "an equanimity that enables us to love all beings equally."[719]

Jesus was a mystic who experienced awakening and taught that "the kingdom of God is within you," the presence of God is within you. He also experienced union with God. Twice he said in John's gospel, "I am in the Father and the Father is in me." Jesus became a messenger for the Divine. What two messages did he communicate? First, Jesus taught the Divine presence within all people and second, love for all. Not only did he preached that "you shall love your neighbor as yourself," but also "love your enemies." His actions in the world were to live out these two teachings by helping the poor and the sick and trying to transform people and society through love. He preached that social structures need to change their highest value from being dominating to being a servant for all people. Jesus said to his disciples, "you know that among the Gentiles those whom they recognize as their rulers *lord it over them. But it is not so among you*; but whoever wishes to become great among you must be your servant. . . .. For the Son of Man came not to be served but to serve." Thus, Jesus was a mystic and a lover of all people.[720]

Paul was a mystic who experienced the Divine and then taught love. "Let love be genuine; hate what is evil, hold fast to what is good; love one another with mutual affection. . . . be ardent in spirit, serve the Lord. Rejoice in hope, be patient in suffering. . ... Contribute to the needs of the saints; extend hospitality to strangers. Bless those who persecute you, . . . weep with those who weep. . . . associate with the lowly." Paul also said, "do not repay anyone evil for evil. . . . live peaceably with all. Beloved, never avenge yourselves. . . . If your enemies are hungry, feed them; if they are thirsty, give them something to drink. . . . Do not be overcome by evil, but overcome evil with good. . . . Owe no one anything, except to love one another; for the one who loves another has fulfilled the law. The commandments, 'you shall not commit adultery,' . . . and any other commandment, are summed up in this word, 'love your neighbor as yourself.' Love does no wrong to a neighbor; therefore, love is the fulfilling of the law."[721]

In the thirteenth century, Francis of Assisi heard God's call to repair the Catholic Church and founded the Franciscan religious order based on living Jesus' message of love. In the thirteenth century, Rumi, an Islamic Sufi mystic, said that "while the thought of the Beloved fills our heart, all our work is to do Him service and spend our life for Him." In the fourteenth century, Ruysbroeck, a Flemish spiritual seeker, said that "the possession of God . . . demands and supposes active love. . . . All our life as it is in God is immersed in blessedness; all our life as it is in ourselves is immersed in active love. And though we live wholly in ourselves and wholly in God, it is but one life." Our life is only whole "when contemplation and work dwell in us side by side, and we are perfectly in both of them at once." As mystics, we dwell in God and yet we go out "in a spirit of love towards all things, in virtue and in works of righteousness. This is the supreme summit of the inner life."[722]

In the fourteenth century, Catherine of Siena wrote about her dialogues with God as well as led an active life that included political and religious reform. Besides taking care of her family's needs, she nursed the ill in two charitable hospitals, including working with plague victims; attempted to solve feuds between quarreling families; tried to stop the war and make peace between Florence and the papacy; encouraged the pope to return from Avignon, France to Rome; and urged the pope to initiate sweeping clerical reforms. In the fifteenth century, Joan of Arc, a French peasant, heard the voices of saints telling her that she had a Divine mission to lead the army to expel the occupying British and crown the King of France. After her experiences with the Sacred Spirit, Teresa of Avila reformed the Carmelite religious order and founded new convents and monasteries. Francis de Sales, a seventeenth-century French priest, said that for a person who is truly free, "it is all the same—serving God by meditating or serving Him by responding to the neighbor. Both are the will of God."[723]

Being unselfish and useful, mystics try to bring the Sacred Spirit into the secular world, not because they seek anything for themselves, but solely because they practice universal love. Elizabeth de la Trinity, a nineteenth-century French mystic, said that I want "to be all silence, all adoration, that I may penetrate more and more deeply into God; and become so full of Him that I can give Him in my prayers to those poor souls still ignorant of His gift." She wanted to be a channel so that her love for God could flow out to other souls. Elizabeth was not working for herself, but for the world. Writing to young people in 1932, Einstein said, "yours is not the first generation to yearn for a life full of beauty and freedom. . . . Your fervent wishes can only find fulfillment if you succeed in attaining love and understanding of men, and animals, and plants, and stars, so that every joy becomes your joy and every pain your pain. Open your eyes, your hearts, your hands, . . . Then will all the earth be your fatherland, and all your work and effort spread forth blessings."[724]

Contemporary American McKeever writes about union and love for all. "To love another person unconditionally is a wonderful feeling of oneness and acceptance. To offer service to that person is doubly powerful." Union with the Divine leads to love and the practice of self-giving by which he means serving others. When we feel connected and experience oneness, "we come to know that no one is any better or more important than another; we simply differ outwardly but within we are all manifestations of God." We are troubled when people suffer because of poverty and other destructive causes and we try to help others. "True self-giving is founded upon a realization of oneness" and not upon pride. Pride includes "the belief that we are better than others and they need our help." Assisting others out of pride is a mistake because we are shifting our awareness to our ego's importance and away from the spiritual Essence of existence. "We are forgetting the Reality of Oneness pulsing though all of creation." When "we have a pure heart and humility, our actions will stem from a feeling of Oneness. . . . Since we are compelled by life to act, let us have as the basis of our actions a feeling of love and humility based on Oneness." Moreover, "to act upon the feeling of Oneness serves to strengthen our awareness of Oneness."[725]

Exemplary Heroes and Contemporary Mystics Advocate and Express Love for All

Mother Teresa urged all of us to love the Divine "through that intimate union of love." Wanting a "love union" with the Holy One, she loved God with "an undivided love." However, love is connected to service. "If we love, we will learn to serve. . . . The first fruit of love is service." Love leads us to serve. We are to give our all as we strive to demonstrate the Divine in our communities. We are to "see the face of God in everything, everyone, and everywhere at all times." Mother Teresa told a story that shows how we are to love. A man came to Mother Teresa's Missionaries of Charity house in India to tell her about a Hindu family with eight children who had not eaten anything for days. Mother Teresa went to their house with enough rice for one meal. She could see the hunger in the faces of the whole family. The Hindu mother took the rice, divided it in half, and left. When she came back, Mother Teresa asked where she went? The mother said that she went next door to a Muslim family with eight children to give them half the rice, because they were hungry too. The next day Mother Teresa took enough rice for both families.[726]

Seeing herself as God's "willing instrument," Mother Teresa wanted the Missionaries of Charity to be "true carriers of God's Love." Because the Holy One loves the world, "it is we who have to be His Love, His Compassion in the world of today." She described working in the slums as "His work, and not my work." Repeating this in different words, she said, "God is so very wonderful to bless His own works in so many ways. Now more than ever I not only feel but know for certain—that really the work is His." She insisted to the Missionaries of Charity that "our Lord does not want us to use our energy in doing penance—in fasting, etc. for our sins—but rather in spending ourselves in giving Christ to the poor."[727]

Mother Teresa said, "I long, I desire to bring to Him many, many souls—to make each soul love the Good God with a burning love—to carry His love into every street and slum, every home and heart." As a channel of God's Love, she said, "I am happy to open all the houses the Good God wants and light the fire of love in as many cities." In addition, "God is in love with us and keeps giving Himself to the world through you—through me. . . . May you continue to be the sunshine of His Love to your people and thus make your life something truly beautiful for God." Following her patron saint, Therese of Lisieux, Mother Teresa believed in doing "all the smallest things and doing them with love." In addition, she said, "to the Good God nothing is little because He is so great and we so small. . . . Be faithful in little practices of love . . . which will build in you the life of holiness—make you Christ-like." Again, she insisted, "don't look for big things, just do small things with great love. . . . The smaller the thing, the greater must be our love."[728]

To her Missionaries of Charity, Mother Teresa wrote that "you have to be in the world and yet not of the world. The light you give must be so pure, the love you love must be so burning, the faith you believe must be so convincing—that in seeing you they really see only Jesus." Although she mainly worked with the poor, she also saw the problems of the affluent. "Tuberculosis and cancer are not the great diseases. I think a much greater disease is to be unwanted and unloved." In addition, "the greatest evil is the lack of love and charity, the terrible indifference toward one's neighbor who lives at the roadside assaulted by exploitation, corruption, poverty, and disease." Individuals not only have material needs but also "people today are hungry for love, for understanding, for love . . . which is the only answer to loneliness and great poverty."[729]

After Mother Teresa was invited to the United States in 1960 to speak, she said that she would "die of fear and shyness," because this would be the first time she ever spoke in public. Speaking to over 3,000 women in Las Vegas, she told them "of the love story of God's Mercy for the poorest of the poor, . . . With my whole heart I offer you to share in these Works of Love." The Missionaries of Charity grew under Mother Teresa's stewardship. Beginning in 1948, she was alone in the slums, in 1949 there were three nuns, and in 1950 seven sisters in five centers. By 1975 there were over 1,000 nuns in 85 foundations in 15 countries and today 4,500 sisters in 133 countries.[730]

There were similarities between Mother Teresa and Dorothy Day. Both were twentieth century Catholic mystics who loved and served both God and the poorest of the poor. Both created organizations to do this work, although Mother Teresa founded many more houses in many more countries than Day. One major difference was that Day not only served the poor but she was also a social change activist who worked to transform our world to stop poverty, injustice, violence, and war. She asked, "where are the saints to try to change the social order, not just to minister to the slaves, but to do away with slavery?" Day was committed to the Divine, worked to help the suffering, and tried to transform the world. Her work for women's right to vote caused her to be arrested. With Peter Maurin, she founded the Catholic Worker movement to share what she had with the poor. In their Catholic

Worker houses of hospitality and farms, the unpaid workers lived with the poor, ate the same food, and shared the same chores. Day created and published the monthly *Catholic Worker* newspaper that sold for a penny a copy. In it, she wrote about Jesus' gospel of love, condemned injustice, advocated for nonviolence and love, and explained how to apply them to world problems.[731]

Day was critical of the Catholic Church for not feeding its flocks, but remained faithful to it. The Catholic hierarchy tried unsuccessfully to close down the Catholic Worker houses because of their belief in nonviolence and in sharing all things. Day's antiwar protests expressed her belief that humans are meant to live in nonviolence and love. When the Catholic Worker houses refused to participate in World War II air raid drills, Day and her workers were jailed on and off for five years. Day participated in civil rights actions and was shot at during a southern march. She was jailed while protesting with the California farm workers.[732]

Day's writings combined her mysticism and her work for social change. Answering a question about what one person can do, she said, "we must lay one brick at a time; . . . we can beg for an increase of love in our heart that will vitalize and transform all our individual actions, and know that God will multiply them." Being an activist, Day said, "on one hand, we have to change the social order in order that people might lead decent Christian lives; on the other hand, we must remake people to remake the social order." Seeing life as a "journey to God," Day said, "we are all called to be saints. God expects something from each one of us that no one else can do. If we don't do it, it will not be done." Day admitted that she "failed in love" on her first night in a New York City prison when she "failed to see that we are all one people, seeking love, and seeking God." Besides living a life of compassion for all, Day preached love. "We are walking in love and love is all we want . . . The final word is love. . . . We cannot love God unless we love each other. . . . We have all known the long loneliness and we have learned the only solution is love. Love comes in community."[733]

Since the 1960s, feminist theologians have joined with liberation theologians to advocate that we not only love the Divine and work for our own personal transformation, but also love our neighbors. In addition, we need to love our enemies and to work for social change that liberates all from oppression. We need to realize that changing our inner selves and the outer social structures must proceed together to create a more just, free, equal, and loving world. A contemporary Korean feminist liberation theologian, Cho Wha Soon, says that "Jesus' liberation is a movement for the simultaneous achievement of social revolution and the inner revolution of the person." We need to break the present evil social structures to create a new society and a new future. "True human liberation can be accomplished only when the women's liberation movement is realized at the same time."[734]

Mercy Amba Oduyoye, a contemporary African feminist liberation theologian, says that "with African culture, Islamic norms, Western civilization, and the church's traditional antifeminism piled on African women, the world has been led to see African women as . . . the quintessence of . . . the oppressed." In Africa, "patriarchy has distorted partnership" in the family, society, and religion. "Where there is religious fundamentalism, women's traditional place and roles are curtailed in ways that seriously limit possibilities of personal development." Oduyoye gets depressed because the church in Africa is so little concerned with social liberation.[735]

In an anthology of spiritual writings by women mystics, visionaries, and prophets of the last 2,000 years, the editor said that "for all the women, regardless of their time or place, love is the guiding and integrating force of all things." Underhill said that union with the Holy One is, "in essence, a fulfillment of love" and "the only proper end of love." The bond of love between the soul and the Divine always existed in the past, always exists in the present, and will always exist in the future. It can never be broken or lost. The authentic mystical way is always based on love; it is a way of love and a journey of love. Thus, we mystics have a twofold task. First, our love unites us with the Sacred making us ONE. Second, after experiencing the Holy One, we carry the message of Divine Infinite Love to humanity and we act out that love by trying to transform people and social structures. Underhill said that love is the driving power as well as "the business and method" of mystics. Love is one of the distinctive marks of mystics that sets their work off from other kinds of spiritual activities.[736]

Martin Luther King said, "I still believe that love is the most durable power in the world." For over two thousand years, humans tried to discover the highest good. "I think I have discovered the highest good. It is love. As John says, 'God is Love.' He who loves is a participant in the Being of God. He who hates does not know God." In addition, he offered practical advice. "In your struggle for justice, let your oppressor know that you are not attempting to defeat or humiliate him, . . . Let him know that you are merely seeking justice for him as well as yourself." To bring change through a nonviolent campaign, use the "four basic steps: (1) collection of the facts to determine whether injustices are alive, (2) negotiation, (3) self-purification, and (4) direct action."[737]

Armstrong says that all faiths have a version of the Golden Rule in its negative or positive form. In its positive form, it is "always treat others as you would wish to be treated yourself." These faiths insist that "you cannot confine your benevolence to your own group, you must have concern for everybody—even your enemies." In addition, spirituality results in compassion. "All the great world religions insist that the single test of any theology or spiritual practice is that it issues in practical compassion." The Jewish prophets taught that the Israelites needed to "care for the poor, the widows, and the orphans." Christianity stressed charity. Buddha urged monks, nuns, and lay people to "radiate feelings of benevolence, sympathy, and compassion" to all the world. "A habit of universal compassion breaks down the selfishness that holds us back from our best selves and the experience of the Sacred" and "the boundless dimension of Nirvana."[738]

According to Armstrong, "we begin with ourselves. We often have a myopic view of the history of our own country or religious tradition and criticize others for behavior of which 'we' have been guilty in the past" or present. For example, some Christians condemn Muslims for their violence, when their own religion has been guilty of crusades, persecutions, inquisitions, and wars of religion. We need to realize that "we are not alone in our suffering but that everybody is in pain." We need to look at a fellow sufferer and see ourselves. "There is no 'us' and 'them.'" We need to "regard our exposure to global suffering as a spiritual opportunity" to show concern for everybody and "to work practically to alleviate the pain of others." We need to realize that "in our global village, everybody is our neighbor, and it is essential to make allies of our enemies. We need to create a world democracy in which everybody's voice is heard and everybody's aspirations are taken seriously. In the last resort, this kind of 'love' and 'concern for everybody' will serve our best interests better than short-sighted and self-serving policies."[739]

For Armstrong, becoming compassionate is a lifelong project. "Nearly every day we will fail, but we cannot give up." We need to begin again. However, being loving is possible for us all. "Some people have achieved heroic levels of empathy, forgiveness, and 'concern for everybody.'" They touch our hearts and awaken our deepest yearnings. "We are not doomed to live in misery, hatred, greed, and envy. . . . Any one of us can become a sage, an avatar of compassion" and thus "a person who is impartial, fair, calm, gentle, serene, accepting, and openhearted."[740]

According to contemporary scholar Jean Houston, seekers say that their spiritual experiences result in "a joy that passes understanding, an immense surge of creativity, an instant up-rush of kindness and tolerance that makes them impassioned champions for the betterment of all, bridge builders, magnets for solutions, peacemakers, pathfinders. Best of all, other people feel enriched and nourished around them." Those who achieve the deepest spiritual experience, union with the One Reality, "become world changers and world servers. They become powers for life, centers for energy, partners and guides for spiritual vitality in other human beings. They glow and set others glowing. . . . They are force fields. . . . They are fields of being, for they have moved from Godseed to Godself."[741]

When Nelson Mandela, the freedom fighter against apartheid who was elected President of South Africa, was freed after spending 27 years, almost 10,000 days, in prison, he said, "friends, comrades, and fellow South Africans, I greet you *all* in the name of peace, democracy, and freedom for all! I stand here before you not as a prophet but as a humble servant of you, the people. Your tireless and heroic sacrifices have made it possible for me to be here today. I therefore place the remaining years of my life in your hands." In his inaugural address after being elected President, he spoke of our victory for justice, peace, and human dignity that "belonged to everyone. . . . Never, never, and never again shall it be that this beautiful land will again experience the oppression of one by another."[742]

Thich Nhat Hanh, a Vietnamese Buddhist monk, advocates mindfulness, insight, peace, nonviolence, and love as he protests against violence and war. "The harmony and equilibrium in the individual, society, and nature are being destroyed. Individuals are sick, society is sick, and nature is sick. . . . How do we begin the work of healing?" How do we stop the violence and war? "The roots of war are in the unmindful ways we have been living," including blaming and arguing that are forms of violence. We who want peace must have a peaceful heart. "To practice *ahimsa* (nonviolence), we must first of all learn to deal peacefully with ourselves. To practice ahimsa, we need gentleness, loving-kindness, compassion, joy, and equanimity directed at our bodies, our feelings, and other people." Love is "the essence of nonviolence. . . . Out of love and willingness to act selflessly, strategies, tactics, and techniques for nonviolence struggle arise naturally. . . . Nonviolent action, born of the awareness of suffering and nurtured by love, is the most effective way to confront adversity."[743]

The current Dalai Lama, the exiled Buddhist leader of the Tibetan people whose name is Tenzin Gyatso, says that "the purpose of religion is not to build beautiful churches or temples, but to cultivate positive human qualities such as tolerance, generosity, and love." He advocates "universal responsibility" which is "rooted in a very simple fact—in general terms, all others' desires are the same as mine. Every human being wants happiness and does not want suffering." First our purpose is "generating the mind of enlightenment," of awakening, of wishing the freedom of all sentient beings from suffering. Then we need to cultivate compassion and a good heart. "Love and compassion predominate in the world. . . . Interdependence is a natural law," our human nature, "a fundamental law of nature," and "the key to happiness." Interdependence means "giving and receiving affection" and depending on others to live. "Ultimately, the reason why love and compassion bring the greatest happiness is simply that our nature cherishes them above all else."[744]

The Dalai Lama's "main concern is always how to promote an understanding of deeper human values. These deeper human values are compassion, a sense of caring, and commitment." In Buddhism, "compassion and love are two aspects of the same thing: compassion is the wish for another being to be free from suffering; love is wanting them to have happiness." Given enough time and patience, "it is within our power to develop this kind of *universal compassion*." Moreover, "we are now so interdependent that the concept of war has become outdated. . . . We must strive for reconciliation and always remember the interests of others."[745]

Templeton's Spiritual Experiences Produces Unlimited Love for All

Although he did not use the framework of stages, Sir John Templeton, a financier and philanthropist who died in 2008, gave concrete examples of them, including awe and wonder, awakening, illumination, and love for all. After amassing millions on Wall Street, he created the Templeton Foundation to promote scientific research to help "spiritual information to multiply hundredfold about every two centuries." This "new additional spiritual information" was "to supplement ancient scriptures." This research was not limited "to things visible or tangible but also . . . vastly greater spiritual realities." These basic spiritual realities included "love, purpose, creativity, intellect, thanksgiving, prayer, humility, praise, thrift, compassion, invention, truthfulness, giving, and worship" as well as altruism, mercy, loyalty, consciousness, honesty, forgiveness, ethics, and "unselfish love unlimited." This research was also to learn about spiritual principles and laws, such as "the more love we give away, the more we have left" and Buddha's law, "hatred does not cease by hatred at any time; hatred ceases by love."[746]

Templeton was concerned with "how little we know." Practicing humility, his writing was filled with questions as well as statements. As an adult, he seemed to have experienced both awe and awakening as shown in his questions and statements about the stars and people's concept of God being too small. "Is God billions of stars in the Milky Way, and yet is God much more? Is God billions and billions of stars in other galaxies, and yet is God much more?" About religions, he said, "it is unlikely any religion could know more than a tiny bit about an Infinite God." Is "God even more awesome than comprehended by the ancients?" In Templeton's opinion, "every person's concept of God is too small." He asked, "is it egotistical to think that humans can ever comprehend all of Reality or of God or of His nature or of His methods and purposes?" In addition, "is the ability of humans to understand God just as tiny as the ability of a clam to understand the ocean" in which it lives. It seems difficult for us to realize that "our perspective might itself be limited relative to something vastly greater and more wise and powerful and creative than we." However, "when we no longer limit God," we may find Him if we "humbly search for Unlimited Love and Purpose and Creativity vastly beyond limited ancient human concepts."[747]

Beyond belief in the Holy One, Templeton had the advanced awakening that the Sacred Spirit is within all of us. Besides saying that God is Omnipresent, which means all present, he said that "the Divine dwells in various ways in every human being." Christian theologians conceive of God as "both Immanent and Transcendent—within the universe at all places and times, but also beyond and above it." Does discovering God within our consciousness, increase our capacity for humility, thanksgiving, forgiveness, compassion, and unlimited love?[748]

Templeton had an illumination that we and all of creation are within the Unlimited Spirit, which he also called "the Total Reality" and "the Totality." Stating this humbly, he said that we may reach our spiritual potential "simply by being open to "the possibility of our existence within a Divine Reality." Are "our individual realities only tiny temporary outward manifestations of a vast universe of being which subsists in the Eternal and Infinite Reality, which some call God? . . . Humanity on this little earth may be an aspect of Unlimited Spirit. . . . A wave is part of the ocean, having no existence apart" from it. "When it dies, it returns to and continues to be a part of the surging ocean." Phrased as a question, "if a wave is a tiny temporary manifestation of the ocean of which it is a part," are we tiny temporary manifestations of God of whom we are a part? Are humans "only tiny temporary parts of Reality, parts of a limitless, timeless Creator?" In addition, he states that "nature in all its complexity and beauty is only a contingent and partial manifestation of His Creativity and Power."[749]

Humbly Templeton asked, "is God all of you and are you a little part of Him?" His Foundation supported publications that say, "God may be all of Reality and man only a tiny part of God." Furthermore, he inquired, "what evidence is there that God lives in you and you in Him?" However, he also said that "profound mutual indwelling between man and Divinity may be better stated by the Unity School of Christianity, 'God is all of me and I am a little part of Him.' Such a notion implies an inseparable relationship between God and us." In addition, "we may realize the mutual unity of God and His creation." Another image he used was a caterpillar developing the

Love for All People and All of Creation Is the Sixth Stage on the Mystical Way

chrysalis, then shedding it and becoming a butterfly flying away. Does a caterpillar deny it can become a butterfly?[750]

While Templeton recognized the inadequacy of our understanding, he described God as "a limitless, timeless, Total Reality," Spirit, and Creator who is Infinite, Omnipresent, Omniscient, and increasingly Creative. Other theologians say that He is "perfect, unchanging." God is "a vast Creative Consciousness" and "Infinite Intellect." Furthermore, "is God the only Reality? Can anything ever be separate from God" who is the Totality?[751]

Templeton asked, can atheists recognize God as the "Fundamental Reality or Unlimited Mind or Unlimited Love?" Besides being "the Source of Love," God gives His "Unlimited and Undeserved Love." He is "Pure, Limitless, Timeless Love" and "Eternal Divine Love." As John said in the New Testament, "God is Love." Theologian Emil Brunner said that He is "the One who has created us in love, by love, for love." His "Love is Infinite." It is directed equally and unceasingly to all of us.[752]

Since Templeton saw God as the Source of Love and Unlimited Love, he advocated for us to love all people and all creation. Each child "should seek to find and serve the Creator's purpose." He called for and encouraged "the expression of the highest and noblest qualities of the human spirit." He claimed that "almost everyone agrees that one of the greatest forces on earth is *love*" and that "maybe we will discover that love is indeed the basic force in the spiritual world." After citing Jesus' two greatest commandments to love God and to love our neighbor as ourselves that he called "basic laws of the spirit," he said that "opening our hearts allows God's Love to flow through us like a mighty river.... The happiest people on earth seem to be those who give love wholeheartedly always." It is "the Divine life of the soul, love to God and love to man." Furthermore, "the real wealth of a nation does not come from mineral resources but from the way it develops and harnesses the lovepower in the minds and hearts of its people."[753]

According to Templeton, sometimes churches make dogmatic pronouncements even when they are poorly informed. "Can this create even more division, hatred, and strife?" Won't they get better results "if they expressed love for all, welcomed diversity, and avoided the sin of self-righteousness?" Moreover, can we be "an expression or agent of God in love and creativity?" When "the Divine Spirit moves into our life, ... love for all becomes the spontaneous expression of a spirit-filled soul." In addition, "we are spirits. ... Love, understanding, loyalty, friendship, patience, mercy—these are spiritual realities the Lord seeks to instill in our lives here and now." In addition, "one of the spiritual principles seems to be that self-improvement comes mainly from trying to help others." Templeton claimed that "*a vision of spiritual progress ... calls us to do our best work, to serve others, to love, to aspire beyond the merely human."* We need to realize that "giving love, not receiving, is important."[754]

Templeton claimed that our purpose is to get rid of ego-centeredness and "become clear channels for God's Love and Wisdom to flow through us, just as sunlight pours through an open window." Stated humbly, "should we radiate love and happiness as faithfully as the sun radiated light and warmth?" We can become servants and "helpers in Divine Creativity" and "co-creators with God." We need to try "learning unselfish unlimited love." Then "gradually each of us may learn to feel unlimited love for every person, with never any exception." Slowly each of us begins to participate in small ways in "expressing love for all" and in "accelerating God's Creativity." At the close of each day, "can we say we have learned to radiate all pure unlimited love and to help our neighbor?" Moreover, "above all, should we not only radiate love but also help others to become alive with love? Can school children be taught some of the laws of the spirit" and how to give love?[755]

For Templeton, "even the saints need to work daily to maintain continuous overflowing love for friends and foes alike. . . . Love given multiplies. Love hoarded disappears." Furthermore, "love professed in expectation of any reward is not authentic love." How can we learn to radiate love? One way to learn is "first we must practice using loving words and loving thoughts. If we keep our minds filled with good thoughts of love, giving, and thanksgiving, they may spill over into our words and deeds. If we are not very careful to weed out all evil thoughts, such as envy or hate or selfishness, they too may overflow into our words and deeds." To learn to radiate love, "one of the simplest ways is by beginning to practice a habit of thanksgiving. A heart of gratitude is ready and prepared to radiate love" to all.[756]

Gandhi's Mystical Experiences Produced His Nonviolence and Love for All People

Mohandas Gandhi was given the title *Mahatma* which means 'great soul.' In his writings, Gandhi did not attempt to develop a comprehensive philosophy, because he simply wanted "to tell the story of my numerous experiments with Truth." His life exemplifies how mystical experiences of the Divine produce nonviolence and love that caused him to become a political activist who helped liberate India from British colonialism. "Once an agnostic," he later said, "I believe in an indefinable mysterious Power that pervades everything. I feel It although I do not see It." This unseen Power is "unlike and infinitely superior to anything we perceive through our senses" because "It transcends the senses." Underlying the universe that is ever-changing is

God, a benevolent Spirit, "a living Power that is changeless, that holds all together, that creates, dissolves, and re-creates.... He alone is."[757]

The definitions of God for Gandhi are innumerable, "because His manifestations are innumerable." God is One, "a self-existent, all-knowing, living Force which inheres in every other force." He is "all-pervading and where He is, all is well." He is "pure and undefiled Consciousness. He is eternal" and perfect, but "His perfection is indescribable, untranslatable." Since "this universe of sentient beings is governed by a law, ... the law is the Law-giver, that is God." Furthermore, "God is at the bottom of both good and evil. He directs the assassin's dagger no less than the surgeon's knife." God is "the only Reality" and "He alone is real and all else is unreal." Hindu philosophy teaches that "God alone is and nothing else exists." *Sat*, the Sanskrit word for truth, "literally means that which exists," that is being. God is *Sat-Chit-Ananda*, the One who combines in Himself Being, Truth, and Bliss. "In the midst of death, life persists; in the midst of untruth, truth persists; in the midst of darkness, light persists.... God is Life, Truth, Light. He is Love. He is the Supreme God." In addition, "God is the Source of Light and Life and yet He is above and beyond all these.... He is a personal God."[758]

Gandhi stresses that "God is Truth above all" and "the universal all-pervading Spirit of Truth." Furthermore, "there is no other God than Truth," Absolute Truth. "God and Truth are convertible terms." Finite human beings shall never know "in Its fullness Truth and Love which is in Itself Infinite." In addition, "Truth is God. God is, because Truth is. His names are legion. Truth is the crown of them all." In reply to the question, what is Truth, Gandhi answered, "it is what the voice within tells you." God who is "Truth resides in every human heart, and one has to search for It there, and to be guided by Truth." Furthermore, "Truth is the law of our being."[759]

According to Gandhi, it is "difficult to define God, but the definition of Truth is deposited in every heart." The maxim, Truth is God, enabled Gandhi to have a mystical experience and thus "to see God face to face.... I feel Him pervade every fiber of my being." In addition, "He is in us and yet above and beyond us." Thus, "God dwells in the heart of every human being" and is "the Light within me." Furthermore, "we can feel Him, ... The Divine music is incessantly going on within ourselves, but the loud senses drown the delicate music." Searching for Truth is searching for God. "I am but a seeker after Truth" and God. "I know the path. It is straight and narrow. It is like the edge of a sword. I rejoice to walk on it." As we search for relative truth, we are "sure to attain Absolute Truth, i.e., God, in the course of time."[760]

Because God is "the all-pervading living Presence," Gandhi claimed that "when Soul-force is awakened in us, it becomes irresistible. But the test and condition of full awakening is that it must permeate every pore of our being and emanate with every breath that we breathe." As "I am journeying Godward, . . . I feel the warmth of the sunshine of His presence." Although "I have no revelation of God's will, . . . He reveals Himself daily to every human being, but we shut our ears to the 'still small voice.'" In addition, "if we could completely obliterate in us the consciousness of our physical body, we would see Him face to face."[761]

Gandhi said, my "trust is solely in God" and "I may live without air and water but not without Him." He had "God as my only guide." We "who believe in God's guidance just do the best we can and never worry. The sun has never been known to suffer overstrain. . . . If we completely surrender to His will" and not worry, we will experience "no wear and tear." Besides being "an irrepressible optimist," Gandhi was "a practical idealist" who described a number of paths to God, to Truth. "Means and ends are convertible terms" and "means are after all everything. As the means so the end. . . . the Creator has given us control . . . over the means, none over the end."[762]

Faith and prayer are two of Gandhi's paths to God. When my faith "has become as immovable as the Himalayas," I will be even nearer to Him. "A living immovable faith is all that is required for reaching the full spiritual height attainable to human beings." In addition, "we become what we yearn after, hence the necessity of prayer." Furthermore, "my austerities, fasts, and prayers . . . have spiritual value." They are "the yearnings of a soul, striving to . . . his Maker." Prayer is as indispensable for the soul as food was for the body. "Prayer has saved my life . . . If I was able to get rid of despair, it was because of prayer." Moreover, "prayer from the heart can achieve what nothing else can." My "peace comes from prayer. I am indifferent as to the form." In addition, "silence is a part of spiritual discipline" and it is necessary to surmount weakness. Silence has spiritual value and is "the time when I could best hold communion with God."[763]

For Gandhi, spiritual training means "education of the heart." Education means "an all-round drawing out the best in the child," including body, mind, and spirit. "Constant development is the law of life." To learn about God, gaze at His creation, the goodness of people, the shining stars, and the unending expanse of the infinite beauty of Nature. A person "should do his duty" and "leave the results in God's hands. . . . He can make his own destiny only in so far as he is allowed by the Great Power which overrides all our intentions, all our plans, and carries out His own plan." An individual or nation will be truly spiritual only when they "show more truth than gold, greater fearlessness than pomp and wealth, greater charity than love of self."[764]

Gandhi said, "mine must be a state of complete resignation to the Divine will." A person's "ultimate aim is the realization of God, and all his activities . . . have to be guided by the ultimate aim of the vision of God." What Gandhi wanted and strived for was "self-realization, to see God face to face, to attain *moksha*." The Sanskrit word *moksha* or *mukti* means liberation, "emancipation from earthly attachments," from reincarnation, and from the cycle of birth, death, and rebirth. "I live and move and have my being in pursuit of this goal. All I do . . . and all my ventures in the political field are directed to this same end." Gandhi was "in search of God and striving for self-realization." This striving "helps the soul to realize its inner self," including "the hidden forces within" and "the Godliness of human nature." Aware that he might be assassinated, Gandhi's constant prayer was that he would die with "remembrance of God upon my lips." After he was shot, his last words were "Oh God, Oh God."[765]

Religions are different paths to God. According to Gandhi, "there are as many religions as there are individuals." Gandhi thought, "it is our duty to blend into our faith every acceptable feature of other faiths." To seek God, we "need not go on a pilgrimage or light lamps and burn incense to . . . the image of the Deity. . . . For He resides in our hearts."[766]

For Gandhi, *Satyagraha* is a way to God who is Truth. It is "purely an inward and purifying movement" that practices "self-discipline, self-control, and self-purification." It advocates "self-introspection and self-analysis" to ensure freedom from anger, ill will, and other vices. It teaches "the distinction between evil and the evil-doer." We are to "hate the sin and not the sinner," because we are all children of God and we have Divine powers within us. "To slight a human being is to slight those Divine powers, and thus to harm not only that being but within him the whole world." Satyagraha includes "fasts, prayer, and suspension of all work on one day" and requires Truth in thought, speech, and action. It realizes Truth "by single-minded devotion and indifference to all other interests in life." The soul-force of Satyagraha is "to violence, and therefore to all tyranny, all injustice, what light is to darkness." Furthermore, "Satyagraha is the noblest and best education. . . . a child should learn that in the struggle of life, it can easily conquer hate by love, untruth by truth, violence by self-suffering."[767]

As "an attribute of the Spirit within" and a "search for Truth," Gandhi's meaning of "Satyagraha is literally holding on to Truth" and it is "therefore, Truth-force," Soul-force, and Love-force. As a method of social change, Satyagraha "includes all non-violent resistance for the vindication of Truth." It involves "not inflicting suffering on the opponent but on one's self." Satyagraha tries to convert the evil-doer by love and to "overcome evil by good, anger by love, untruth by truth, *himsa* (violence) by *ahimsa* (nonviolence)."

One branch of Satyagraha is Civil Disobedience, also called Civil Resistance, which means openly breaking unjust, immoral laws in "a civil, i.e., nonviolent manner" and quietly suffering the penalty, including being arrested. Another branch of Satyagraha is non-cooperation which means "withdrawing cooperation from the State" that has become corrupt. "Non-cooperation is a protest against unwitting and unwilling participation in evil." Gandhi does not call passive resistance a branch of Satyagraha because he said, "nonviolence is not passivity in any shape or form. Nonviolence . . . is the most active force in the world." In addition, "Satyagraha differs from passive resistance as the North Pole from the South."[768]

Gandhi experienced awakening as having "faith, . . . a living, wide-awake consciousness of the God within." His mystical awakening led him to advocate nonviolence and universal love. *Ahimsa* which means nonviolence and love is a way to God and Truth. Both ahimsa and truth "mean one and the same thing." Thus, ahimsa is Love-force, Soul-force, and Truth-force. "Ahimsa is the means; Truth is the end. Ahimsa is our supreme duty. If we take care of the means, we are bound to reach the end." In other words, "the only means for the realization of Truth is ahimsa." Nonviolence's "spread is my life mission."[769]

For Gandhi, in its negative form, *ahimsa* means harmlessness and nonviolence. "In its positive form, ahimsa means the largest love, the greatest charity," and "Universal Love." It means "doing good even to the evil-doer" but resisting his wrong actions. "Nonviolence begins and ends by turning the searchlight inward." It is "a quality of the heart." Nonviolence is "the law of life" and "the rule and the breath of my life. . . . It is a matter not of the intellect but of the heart." It is "the most active force in the world. . . . Nonviolence is the supreme law." Love is "the law of our being." Thus, "we are drops in the limitless ocean of mercy." Nonviolence, that is love, is "the law of our species as violence is the law of the brute." In fact, "it is the law of love that rules mankind. Had violence, i.e., hatred ruled us, we should have become extinct long ago." A human "as animal is violent, but as spirit is nonviolent. The moment he awakes to the Spirit within, he cannot remain violent. Either he progresses toward ahimsa or rushes to his doom."[770]

According to Gandhi, service is a road to God. Love leads to selfless service. Gandhi practiced "the religion of service" because he believed that "God could be realized only through service." He endeavored "to see God through service to humanity." Gandhi said, "I love mankind . . . because God dwells in the heart of every human being, and I strive to realize the highest in life through the service to humanity." In addition, "service, not bread, becomes with us the staff of life. We eat and drink, sleep and wake, for service alone. Such an attitude of mind brings us real happiness and the beatific vision." Furthermore, "the immediate service of all human beings becomes a necessary part of the endeavor simply because the only way to find God is to see Him in His creation and be one with it. This can only be done by service of all."[771]

Love is the path to God. Gandhi said, "when you want to find Truth as God, the only inevitable means is love, that is, nonviolence" and "the nearest approach to Truth was through love." In addition, "there only is life where there is love. Life without love is death." A person who wants to be friends with God must "make the whole world his friend." To realize God, an individual should identify with everything that lives, "earnestly desire the well-being of all God's creation," and treat all beings as his own closest relatives. "All my activities . . . have their rise in my insatiable love of mankind." We need to "look upon all mankind as kith and kin" and even regard thieves as our kin, "our brethren, our friends." When the Japanese invaded during World War II, Gandhi advised the Chinese to "develop love for the Japanese in your hearts." To see God face to face, one must be able "to love the meanest of creation as oneself." This is because love is "the law of our being" and "real love is to love them that hate you, to love your neighbor even though you distrust him." We must not "hurt any living thing" and be "free from hatred toward any individual" because "it is love that sustains the earth. There only is life where there is love. . . . Love is the reverse of the coin of which the obverse is Truth. . . . we can conquer the whole world by Truth and Love." Violence can be overcome only by nonviolence. "Hatred can be overcome only by Love."[772]

We Need to Follow Our Own Spiritual Path to the Holy One

Contemporary author Robert Ellsberg says that learning to love is "the final goal of all spiritual practice." According to Underhill, mystical education, development, and life are "a progressive surrender of selfhood under the steady advance of conquering love." Thus, "the measure of the mystic's real progress is and must always be his progress in love." The simplest expression of union with the Sacred Spirit is "the complete and conscious fulfillment here and now of this Perfect Love." Mystics are lovers and friends of the Holy One and the human race. They are the messengers and ambassadors of Divine Love. The mystic way is "the crown of human evolution." The evolution of mystical consciousness is "a progress, a growth in love." Mystics love not only the Sacred Spirit but also everyone and everything.[773]

Thomas Merton, the twentieth-century Trappist monk, answered the question, "what is the one thing necessary?" Although it is different for each of us, it is "to fulfill our own destiny, according to God's will, to be what God wants us to be." But what is our destiny? What does the Holy One want us to be? The Hebrew scripture said that "God created humankind in His image, in the image of God He created them." Thus, we are created in the image of Infinite Love. We have an inner core of love. To fulfill our own destiny and purpose, to be what the Sacred Spirit intended, and to be true to our loving inner core and human nature, we need to be as loving as we can locally, nationally, and globally, we need to love everyone and everything.[774]

What is our own spiritual path? There is no single right way to the Sacred Spirit. Because there are many paths and stages, we need to choose our own way. Although the spiritual routes of great women and men in the past serve as examples, they are not models to be copied. Since we are all unique, there has never been anyone exactly like us in the world before. Each of us has a different road to the Divine. As I travel my path, I am not trying to repeat something that another person accomplished, not even the greatest human achievement. If I do not climb up to my own rung on the ladder, but instead seize someone else's rung and abandon my own, I will achieve neither. Only within myself will I find my own distinctive way. My strongest feelings, thoughts, words, values, actions, talents, experiences, and my loving nature reveal what is most precious to me. These stir my innermost spirit and point to my path. I must recognize the way to the Holy One that touches my heart and then choose it and follow it wholeheartedly with all my dedication, passion, strength, and determination.

The path that I discovered is the six stages on the mystical way to Infinite Love. There is always more to learn and experience on the six stages as we progress through our lives. The six stages help us fulfill our two purposes, missions, and goals in life. Our first purpose is to try to learn about, experience, and love the Holy One in our own way. To learn about the Creator, study the creation. To experience and love the Sacred Spirit, we need to delve deeper and deeper into Infinite Love within ourselves and others as well as realize and explore what it means to be within the ONE. Our second purpose is to love passionately ourselves, all people, and all creation. We are not to turn away from people who attract our heart, but to form nurturing relationships and build communities of love, so that together we can express our spirit and love. Flowing out of our love for all people is our work that is to devote our whole being to taking suffering out of life, nurturing loving individuals, creating communities of love, producing social change, and transforming the world so that it promotes respect, equality, freedom, justice, and love for all people and all creation.

The six stages on the spiritual path work for me, but you can choose any mystic way you want: prayer, faith, learning, reading spiritual books, participating in religious rituals, singing hymns, listening to sermons, fasting, asceticism, silence, detachment from life, involvement in life, work, play, leading a moral life, doing good deeds, helping others, fighting all forms of oppression, opposing violence and war. All these can be roads to the Sacred Spirit or barriers on the path depending on whether they are done in a loving or unloving way.

To conclude, our two purposes in life are mystical experiences and love. Our first purpose is to have mystical experiences of the Divine so that we develop spiritual awareness. In the first stage, we experience awe and wonder. In the third stage, we become awakened that Infinite Love is within us as our inner core of love. We become conscious that the Holy One is within all people and all of creation. In the fifth stage, we experience illumination, we become aware that we are within the ONE, and we realize that we have always been in union with the Divine.

Our second purpose is love. Our mystical experiences produce love for our neighbors and ourselves in the fourth stage and love for everyone and everything in the sixth stage. Our spiritual experiences of the Sacred Spirit help us love ourselves, all people, and all of creation. There is a dialogue between these two purposes. The more conscious we are that the Holy One is within us and that we are within the ONE, the greater our love for all people and all of the universe. The more abundant our love, the more extensive and deeper our mystical consciousness.

Endnotes

Chapter 1: Awe and Wonder Are the First Stage on the Mystic Way

1. Cox, *Future of Faith*, 23.
2. Dukas and Hoffman, *Albert Einstein*, 3–5.
3. Fox, *Coming of the Cosmic Christ*, 51; Fox, *Christian Mystics*, 5; and Underhill, *Mysticism*, 258.
4. Tolle, *New Earth*, 2–3, 25–26.
5. Tolle, *New Earth*, 3–4, 26.
6. Otto, *Idea of the Holy*, 14–18.
7. Otto, *Idea of the Holy*, 31–32, 36–39, 50–51, 143.
8. Otto, *Idea of the Holy*, 31–32, 36–39, 50–51, 143.
9. Mother Teresa, *Come Be My Light*, 14–15.
10. Coles, *Spiritual Life of Children*, 326–329.
11. Coles, *Spiritual Life of Children*, 326–329.
12. Otto, *Idea of the Holy*, 115–116.
13. Coles, *Spiritual Life of Children*, 148–149.
14. Coles, *Spiritual Life of Children*, 136–137.
15. Coles, *Spiritual Life of Children*, 136–137.
16. Coles, *Spiritual Life of Children*, 148–150.
17. Coles, *Spiritual Life of Children*, 156–157.
18. Feibleman, *Understanding Oriental Philosophy*, 100–101
19. Emerson, *Selections from Ralph Waldo Emerson*, 23–24, 27.
20. Emerson, *Selections from Ralph Waldo Emerson*, 24–27 30–31.
21. *Bhagavad Gita*, 116–117, 18:20–22.
22. Luke 9:46–48, 12:22–33, 18:15–17; Matthew 6:19–34, 18:1–5, 19:13–15; and Mark 9:33–37, 10:13–16.
23. Juan Mascaro, "Introduction," *Upanishads*, 8 and *Teaching of Rumi*, 102–103, 114.
24. Dukas and Hoffman, *Albert Einstein*, 18, 33, 66, 165 and Cox, *Future of Faith*, 21–23.
25. Dukas and Hoffman, *Albert Einstein*, 18, 33, 66, 165 and Cox, *Future of Faith*, 21–23.
26. Tolle, *New Earth*, 3–4, 26–27.
27. Tolle, *New Earth*, 3–4, 26–27.

28. Chardin, *Divine Milieu*, 23, 27, 31, 55, 59.
29. Chardin, *Divine Milieu*, 59, 77-78, 85.
30. Chardin, *Divine Milieu*, 58-59.
31. Buber, *I and Thou*, 3, 9, 11, 14-15. Throughout his book, he italicized the words *I-Thou* and *I-It*.
32. Buber, *I and Thou*, 7-9.
33. Buber, *I and Thou*, 11-13, 15-17.
34. Fromm, *To Have and To Be*, xxxiii, 3-4, 10, 12, 87-88.
35. Fromm, *To Have and To Be*, 3-4, 7, 10, 12, 15, 75-76.
36. Fromm, *To Have and To Be*, 3-4, 7, 10, 12, 15, 75-76.
37. Fromm, *To Have and To Be*, 10-11, 76-77, 93.
38. Juan Mascaro, "Introduction," *Upanishads*, 17.
39. Otto, *Idea of the Holy*, 15-16, 27-28.
40. Otto, *Idea of the Holy*, 15-16, 27-28.
41. Otto, *Idea of the Holy*, 1-8, 12-21, 112.
42. Fisher, *West African Traditional Religions*, 5, 15-16; Parrinder, *World Religions from Ancient History to the Present*, 24-25, 28; Goode, *Religion among the Primitives*, 24-25; and Palmer, *World Religions*, 8-17.
43. Hartmann, *Last Hours of Ancient Sunlight*, 180-185. Scholars call the earliest religions by a number of different names, including primal, primitive, prehistoric, pre-literate, non-literate, archaic, indigenous, native, aboriginal, tribal, folk, and traditional. Some even referred to them as savage, undeveloped, uncivilized, superstitious, and pagan. Robert Fisher claims that "African Traditional Religion should be ranked and treated together with world religions." Fisher, *West African Traditional Religions*, 5-8.
44. Hartmann, *Last Hours of Ancient Sunlight*, 176, 190.
45. Hartmann, *Last Hours of Ancient Sunlight*, 174-175, 177, 194-196, 209-210.
46. Hartmann, *Last Hours of Ancient Sunlight*, 174-175, 177, 194-196, 209-210.
47. Evelyn Underhill, *Practical Mysticism*, 11-14.
48. Underhill, *Practical Mysticism*, 11-12.
49. Buber, *I and Thou*, 9-10, 14.
50. *Bhagavad Gita*, 17-18, 116-117 and Underhill, *Practical Mysticism*, 11-14.
51. Walker, "God Is Inside You and Inside Everybody Else," *Weaving the Visions*, 101-104.
52. Walker, "God Is Inside You and Inside Everybody Else," *Weaving the Visions*, 101-104.
53. Walker, "God Is Inside You and Inside Everybody Else," *Weaving the Visions*, 101-104.
54. Huxley, "Perennial Philosophy," *The Highest State of Consciousness*, 76.
55. Robert Fulghum, *All I Really Need to Know I Learned in Kindergarten*, pp. 4-5.

Chapter 2: Do We All Have a Spiritual Path?

56. Fox, *Coming of the Cosmic Christ*, 63-64.
57. Whitney, *Feminism and Love*, 13-22.
58. Tolle, *Practicing the Power of NOW*, 15-17, 43.
59. Underhill, *Mysticism*, 55, 135, 142-143, 145. Some scholars including Underhill capitalize the words for the Divine, while others do not. In this book all words for the Sacred Spirit are capitalized even in quotations where they are not.
60. Underhill, *Mysticism*, 100, 103, 113, 120, 132-133, 144, 446.

61. Otto, *Idea of the Holy*, 36, 62, 194–196.
62. Julian of Norwich, *Revelations of Divine Love*, 158, 160–162.
63. Catherine of Genoa, *Purgation and Purgatory*, 73, 102–103, 106, 138–139.
64. Gandhi, *All Men Are Brothers*, 3, 48–49, 61–62, 64–65, 80, 90; Gandhi, *Nonviolent Resistance (Sayagraha)*, 3, 15, 88; and Gandhi, *Gandhi on Nonviolence*, 38–39.
65. Matthew Fox, *Coming of the Cosmic Christ*, 58–59, 61.
66. Underhill, *Mysticism*, 34–37, 65, 67–68.
67. Underhill, *Mysticism*, 23, 34–37, 41, 44–45, 53–55, 67, 75–76, 82–83, 133, 175, 427, 447–448, 450.
68. Underhill, *Mysticism*, 23, 34–37, 39, 41, 53–55, 72, 75–76, 82–83, 133, 447–448, 450.
69. Underhill, *Practical Mysticism*, 2–3 and Underhill, *Mysticism*, 23, 34–37, 39, 41, 53–55, 72, 75–76, 82–83, 133, 447–448, 450.
70. Fox, *Coming of the Cosmic Christ*, 48–49, 59, 63–64. Italics added.
71. Fox, *Coming of the Cosmic Christ*, 48–49, 61, 63–64.
72. Bucke, *Cosmic Consciousness*, 1–2, 13–14.
73. Radhakrishnan, *The Hindu View of Life*, 20–25.
74. Whitney, *Heart of Jesus' Teaching*, 123–124.
75. Whitney, *Heart of Jesus' Teaching*, Chapter 6.
76. Otto, *Idea of the Holy*, 14–18, 31–32, 36–37, 39.
77. Walsh, *Essential Spirituality*, pp. 196–197.
78. Matthew 18:3 and Underhill, *Mysticism*, 446–447.
79. Underhill, *Mysticism*, 298, 306, 308–310, 312, 317.
80. Schneiders, "Feminist Spirituality," *Women's Spirituality*, 30–31 and Conn, "Dancing in the Dark," *Women's Spirituality*, pp. 9–10.
81. King, *Christian Mystics*, 6, 8, 15, 20 and King, *Women's Spirituality*, 5–6, 81, 99, 114, 118.
82. King, *Women's Spirituality*, 5–6, 81, 99, 114, 118 and King, *Christian Mystics*, 6, 8, 15, 20.
83. Brussat, *Spiritual Literacy*, 18, 28–29.
84. James, *Varieties of Religious Experience*, 24, 40–42, 44–45, 218.
85. Fredrickson, "What Is This Thing, Love?" *Psychotherapy Networker*, 42–47. Fredrickson writes about love, but her insights apply to spiritual experiences.
86. Fredrickson, "What Is This Thing, Love?" *Psychotherapy Networker*, 42–44.
87. Taylor, *My Stroke of Insight*, 15–16, 44–45, 71–72, 157.
88. Taylor, *My Stroke of Insight*, 46–47, 49–50, 55, 67, 69–71, 78.
89. Taylor, *My Stroke of Insight*, 10, 29–30, 42, 47–48, 65, 67–72, 159.
90. Taylor, *My Stroke of Insight*, 30–31, 74, 139–141, 152, 172.
91. Taylor, *My Stroke of Insight*, 30, 41, 49, 54, 61, 65–66, 73, 82, 111, 135–136, 140, 171, 173.
92. Taylor, *My Stroke of Insight*, 41, 54, 61, 65–67, 70–71, 82, 110–111, 140.
93. Taylor, *My Stroke of Insight*, 41, 49, 54, 61, 65–67, 70–71, 82, 110–111, 140.
94. Taylor, *My Stroke of Insight*, 130, 133–135, 141, 170–171, 177.
95. Taylor, *My Stroke of Insight*, 30–31, 74, 130, 133–135, 139–141, 170–171, 177.
96. Taylor, *My Stroke of Insight*, 49, 111, 132, 135, 166.
97. Dyer, *There's a Spiritual Solution to Every Problem*, pp. xi, 9–16, 139–141.
98. Dyer, *Manifest Your Destiny*, 169–171.
99. Thurman, *Infinite Life*, 252–253.
100. Chopra, *Seven Spiritual Laws of Success*, 1–2, 9–10, 27–30, 39 and Chopra, *Seven Spiritual Laws of Yoga*, 192–193.
101. Chopra, *Seven Spiritual Laws of Success*, 53, 55, 67–68, 83–84.

102. Chopra, *Seven Spiritual Laws of Success*, 95, 97–98, 101.
103. James, *Varieties of Religious Experience*, 51, 53–53.
104. Emerson, *Selections from Ralph Waldo Emerson*, 103–104 and James, *Varieties of Religious Experience*, 46, 49, 54, 56.
105. Walsh, *Essential Spirituality*, 23–24 and John White, "Introduction," *The Highest State of Consciousness*, vii-viii.
106. White, "Introduction," *The Highest State of Consciousness*, vii-viii, x.
107. Tolle, *The Power of NOW*, 98–99.
108. Tolle, *Practicing the Power of NOW*, 14, 16, 23, 140.
109. Tolle, *Practicing the Power of NOW*, 195–196.
110. Walsh, *Essential Spirituality*, 9–10.
111. Ferguson, *Aquarian Conspiracy*, 217–218, 364–366; Underhill, *Mysticism*, 37, 40–41, 73, 81, 170, 172–173, 435.
112. Fox, *Coming of the Cosmic Christ*, 47–50.
113. Eckhart, *Everything as Divine*, 8, 27–28, 54–55, 64, 78, 81 and Johnson, *Mystical Theology*, 217–218, 244, 264.
114. King, *Christian Mystics*, 8–9 and Underhill, *Mysticism*, 70.
115. Brussat, *Spiritual Literacy*, 18.
116. Elwood and McGraw, *Many Peoples, Many Faiths*, 7–12.
117. Aurobindo, *Essential Aurobindo*, 23–24.
118. Whitney, *Heart of Jesus' Teaching*, Chapters 1 and 2.
119. *Bhagavad Gita*, 99–101 and Gandhi, *Gandhi on Nonviolence*, 38–39.

Chapter 3: Mystics Explained Different Versions of Stages on the Spiritual Path

120. Catherine of Genoa, *Purgation and Purgatory*, 40–41 and Underhill, *Mysticism*, 441–442.
121. Chardin, *Phenomenon of Man*; Aurobindo, *Mind of Light*; and Aurobindo, *Essential Aurobindo*.
122. Chardin, *Human Energy*, 32–44, 57–64, 78–81.
123. Chardin, *Phenomenon of Man*, 264–268 and Chardin, *Human Energy*, 32–44, 57–64, 78–81.
124. Chardin, *Human Energy*, 32–44, 57–64, 78–81 and Chardin, *Phenomenon of Man*, 264–268, 300–302.
125. Aurobindo, *Mind of Light*, 8–9, 13–14, 46–48, 53, 79, 81, 100 and *Essential Aurobindo*, 22, 29, 47–48, 74, 76.
126. Aurobindo, *Mind of Light*, 8–9, 13–14, 52–63; *Essential Aurobindo*, 29–30; Aurobindo, *Life Divine*, 53–54; and Chardin, *Phenomenon of Man*, 300–302.
127. Aurobindo, *Mind of Light*, 13–14, 52–63; *Essential Aurobindo*, 29–30; and Aurobindo, *Teachings of the Mystics*, 53–54.
128. Chardin, *Phenomenon of Man*, 165–166, 302.
129. Chardin, *Phenomenon of Man*, 180, 258, 306–307.
130. Chardin, *Phenomenon of Man*, 262–263, 305–307.
131. Aurobindo, *Mind of Light*, 13–14, 52–63, 70, 94, 116–118 and *Essential Aurobindo*, 55–56.
132. Aurobindo, *Mind of Light*, 13–17, 52–63, 70 and Aurobindo, *The Teaching of Hindu Mystics*, 121–133.
133. Aurobindo, *Teaching of Hindu Mystics*, 121–133.

134. Aurobindo, *Mind of Light*, 87–90, 102, 110–111.
135. Aurobindo, *Teaching of Hindu Mystics*, 121–133 and Aurobindo, *Mind of Light*, 89–90, 102–103.
136. Wilber, *Integral Psychology*, 194 and Wilber, *The Religion of Tomorrow*, 239, 241–246, 523.
137. Wilber, *Religion of Tomorrow*, 129–130 and Wilber, *Integral Psychology*, 60–62.
138. Wilber, *Integral Psychology*, 197–217.
139. Wilber, *Integral Psychology*, 113–114 and Wilber, *The Religion of Tomorrow*, pp. 56, 120–122.
140. Wilber, *The Religion of Tomorrow*, 56–57, 117–119.
141. Wilber, *The Religion of Tomorrow*, 117–119.
142. Wilber, *The Religion of Tomorrow*, 54, 56–57, 74, 76.
143. Wilber, *The Religion of Tomorrow*, 12–13.
144. Wilber, *The Religion of Tomorrow*, 12–13.
145. Wilber, *The Religion of Tomorrow*, 8–11, 14, 56, 121.
146. Wilber, *The Religion of Tomorrow*, 526–527, 531.
147. Wilber, *The Religion of Tomorrow*, 39–40, 66–67.
148. Wilber, *The Religion of Tomorrow*, 43–53, 59, 121, 143, 215, 220, 495–504, 517–524 and Wilber, *Integral Psychology*, 41, 209.
149. Wilber, *The Religion of Tomorrow*, 36–37, 39–40.
150. Wilber, *The Religion of Tomorrow*, 220, 243–244, 517, 523.
151. Wilber, *The Religion of Tomorrow*, 33, 38–40.
152. Wilber, *The Religion of Tomorrow*, 245–246.
153. Wilber, *The Religion of Tomorrow*, 243–244, 523.
154. Wilber, *The Religion of Tomorrow*, 239, 241–242, 523.
155. Wilber, *The Religion of Tomorrow*, 57, 62–63, 73, 83, 526.
156. Prabhavananda, *Vedic Religion and Philosophy*, 109–110 and *Bhagavad Gita*, 52–53, 56, 96.
157. *Bhagavad Gita*, 52–53, 58.
158. *Bhagavad Gita*, 81–82, 96.
159. Patanjali, *How to Know God*, 7–8, 147–148, 151, 163–164, 171–174.
160. Patanjali, *How to Know God*, 171–174, 181, 183–184, 222 and Chopra, *Seven Spiritual Laws of Yoga*, 41–42.
161. *Buddhist Scriptures*, 56, 112–113, 186–187, 242 and Burtt, *Teaching of the Compassionate Buddha*, 20, 28–31.
162. *Dhammapada*, 35, 75.
163. *Dhammapada*, 36–37, 42, 45, 51.
164. McGinn, *Essential Writings of Christian Mysticism*, 7, 55–57, 150.
165. Denys the Areopagite, *Pseudo-Dionysius*, "Mystical Theology," 136–137, and "Celestial Hierarchy," 143–148; King, *Christian Mystics*, 57–63; Armstrong, *History of God*, 125–130; and Armstrong, *The Case for God*, 123–129.
166. King, *Christian Mystics*, 57–63 and Johnson, *Mystical Theology*, 129–220.
167. Genesis 18:12 and Climacus, *Ladder of Divine Ascent*, 11–13.
168. *Koran*, trans. Dawood, 24, 63–69, 104–105, 115, 117, 120, 122, 132–133, 326, 373 and *Meaning of the Glorious Koran*, trans. Pickthall, 34.
169. Baldock, *Essence of Sufism*, 135–155, 227.
170. Baldock, *Essence of Sufism*, 148–151.
171. Baldock, *Essence of Sufism*, 151–155.
172. McGinn, *Essential Writings of Christian Mysticism*, 151–154.
173. McGinn, *Essential Writings of Christian Mysticism*, 151–154.
174. Bonventure, *Soul's Journey into God, the Tree of Life, the Life of St. Francis*, 20,

54-55, 61, 63, 65.
175. Bonventure, *Soul's Journey into God*, pp. 69-73, 79-84, 87, 89.
176. Bonventure, *Soul's Journey into God*, pp. 94, 97, 102-104, 110, 113-116.
177. Porete, *Mirror of Simple Souls*, 5, 27-28, 136-139, 189.
178. Porete, *Mirror of Simple Souls*, 28, 136, 139-141, 189-190.
179. Porete, *Mirror of Simple Souls*, 28, 190-193.
180. Porete, *Mirror of Simple Souls*, 28, 193-194.
181. McGinn, *Essential Writings of Christian Mysticism*, 180-182.
182. McGinn, *Essential Writings of Christian Mysticism*, 182-183.
183. Catherine of Siena, *Dialogue*, 64-65, 67-68, 83, 89, 158-159.
184. Catherine of Siena, *Dialogue*, 64-65, 67-68, 83-85, 89, 110, 158-159.
185. Teresa of Avila, *Interior Castle*, 35-36, 38-40, 42-43, 45.
186. Teresa of Avila, *Interior Castle*, 48-49, 52.
187. Teresa of Avila, *Interior Castle*, 55, 57-59, 62-65.
188. Teresa of Avila, *Interior Castle*, 67-69, 73-76.
189. Teresa of Avila, *Interior Castle*, 70, 77-82.
190. Teresa of Avila, *Interior Castle*, 86-89, 91, 93, 96, 100, 103-103.
191. Teresa of Avila, *Interior Castle*, 108-109, 114-117, 166-167.
192. Teresa of Avila, *Interior Castle*, 118, 127-118, 137, 166.
193. Teresa of Avila, *Interior Castle*, 175, 178-180.
194. Teresa of Avila, *Interior Castle*, 183-184, 190, 193-194.
195. Campbell, *Myths to Live By*, 209-210, 234, 236-237 and Joseph Campbell, *Hero with a Thousand Faces*, 30-31.
196. Borysenko, *Saying Yes to Change*, 14-18 and Borysenko, *Seven Paths to God*, 1, 7-15.
197. Myss, *Anatomy of the Spirit*, 29-30, 103, 129, 167, 197, 219, 137, 165 and Harris, *Dance of the Spirit*, 1, 28, 58, 86, 114, 145, 179.
198. *Essential Aurobindo*, 138-139, 150-151.
199. *Essential Aurobindo*, 138-139, 147, 150-151, 155-156.
200. *Essential Aurobindo*, 135, 138-139.
201. Chopra, *Book of Secrets*, 37-44.
202. Underhill, *Mysticism*, 55, 81, 169-179, 446-447.
203. Underhill, *Mysticism*, 91-92, 169-179, 446-447.
204. Underhill, *Mysticism*, 91-92, 169-179, 446-447; Teresa of Avila, *Interior Castle*, 35-36; and Teresa of Avila, *Collected Works of St. Teresa of Avila*, 48-49.

Chapter 4: The Second Stage Is Parents and Religious Leaders Teaching Children about God

205. Maslow, *Religions, Values, and Peak Experiences*, 19-21, 28-29.
206. Maslow, *Religions, Values, and Peak Experiences*, 20-21, 28-29.
207. Maslow, *Religions, Values, and Peak Experiences*, 20-21, 28.
208. Whitney, *Feminism and Love*, 127-163.
209. 5 Liebert, "Changing Life Patterns," *Women's Spirituality*, 349-351.
210. Maslow, *Religions, Values, and Peak Experiences*, 21-22.
211. Maslow, *Religions, Values, and Peak Experiences*, 25-26.
212. Otto, *Idea of the Holy*, 215-216.
213. Ruether, *Catholic Does Not Equal the Vatican*, 4, 11-12.
214. Armstrong, *History of God*, 239-240.

215. Mother Teresa, *Come Be My Light*, 14–15.
216. King, "What Is Spirituality?" *Spiral Path*, 7–8 and Underhill, *Mysticism*, 445–446.
217. Kimball, *When Religion Becomes Evil*, 44, 72; King, *Spiral Path*, 7–8; and Gallagher, *Working on God*, p. xv.
218. Das, *Essential Unity of All Religions*, 517–522; Maslow, *Religions, Values, and Peak Experiences*, 13–14; Kimball, *When Religion Becomes Evil*, 44, 72; Smith, *World's Religions*, 74–75; Radhakrishnan, *Hindu View of Life*, 37–38; and "Lord Jesus," Vatican Congregation for the Doctrine of the Faith, #4–9, 16–17.
219. Kung, *Church*, 403–411; Brennan, *Radical Reform of Christianity*, 79–80; Armstrong, *History of God*, xix-xx; and Harkness, *Understanding the Christian Faith*, 11–12.
220. Walker, "God Is Inside You and Inside Everybody Else," *Weaving the Visions*, 103–104.
221. Borg, *Heart of Christianity*, 73–74; Smith, *World's Religions*, 60–63, 74–75; Underhill, *Mysticism*, 337–357; Armstrong, *History of God*, 339, 389–390; and Spencer, *Mysticism in World Religions*, 54–55.
222. *Cloud of Unknowing*, 62, 67, 74.
223. Happold, *Mysticism*, 339–340.
224. Smith, *World's Religions*, 60–61 and Burtt, *Teachings of the Compassionate Buddha*, 194–195.
225. Ruether, *Sexism and God-talk*, 68–69; Daly, *Beyond God the Father*, 19–20; and Liebert, "Changing Life Patterns," *Women's Spirituality*, 350–351.
226. Maslow, *Religions, Values, and Peak Experiences*, 28–29.

Chapter 5: Awakening Is the Third Stage on the Spiritual Path

227. Rolle, *Fire of Love*, 76 and Underhill, *Mysticism*, 265.
228. Julian of Norwich, *Revelations of Divine Love*, 68–69; Underhill, *Mysticism*, 89, 241, 248–249; and Denys the Areopagite, "Divine Name," *Pseudo-Dionysius*, 54, 72, 75, 79.
229. Rumi, *Teachings of Rumi*, 6, 9, 34.
230. Smith, *Forgotten Truth*, 76–79 and Armstrong, *Case for God*, 9.
231. *Buddhist Scriptures*, 34–35; Stace, *Teachings of the Mystics*, 67–68; Dala Lama, *Essential Teachings*, 7, 122; and Hodge, *Tibetan Buddhism*, 10.
232. *Buddhist Scriptures*, 34–38; Conze, *Buddhism*, 34–35; and Bary, *Buddhism Tradition in India, China, and Japan*, 57–60.
233. *Buddhist Scriptures*, 34–38 and Bary, *Buddhism Tradition in India, China, and Japan*, 67–68.
234. *Buddhist Scriptures*, 55–56.
235. *Buddhist Scriptures*, 47–53; Stace, *Teachings of the Mystics*, 20–24; and Bary, *Buddhism Tradition in India, China, and Japan*, 71–72.
236. *Buddhist Scriptures*, 56, 112–116, 186–187.
237. *Buddhist Scriptures*, 56, 112–116, 186–187.
238. *Buddhist Scriptures*, 47–53; Stace, *Teachings of the Mystics*, 20–24, 67–71; Smith, *World Religions*, 113–114; and Bary, *Buddhism Tradition in India, China, and Japan*, 71–72.
239. Julian of Norwich, *Revelations of Divine Love*, 21–22, 76–77, 191–192, 211–212.

240. Julian of Norwich, *Revelations of Divine Love*, 63, 136, 152, 164, 184, 189–190, 206, 211.
241. Julian of Norwich, *Revelations of Divine Love*, 75, 80, 175, 179–180, 206.
242. Julian of Norwich, *Revelations of Divine Love*, 49–50, 67–68, 73, 153–157, 211–212.
243. McGinn, *Essential Writings of Christian Mysticism*, 361–362.
244. Matthew Lee, Margaret Poloma, and Stephen Post, *Heart of Religion*, 8–9, 96.
245. Lee, et al., *Heart of Religion*, 18–19, 49, 96, 130.
246. Lee, et al., *Heart of Religion*, 100, 102–103, 105, 183.
247. Lee, et al., *Heart of Religion*, 96–97, 102–104, 133.
248. Lee, et al., *Heart of Religion*, 76–78, 96, 118.
249. Lee, et al., *Heart of Religion*, 44, 46–47, 49–51, 74.
250. Lee, et al., *Heart of Religion*, 44, 46–47, 49–51, 74.
251. Lee, et al., *Heart of Religion*, 53, 74, 92, 126, 134–135, 202, 241.
252. Underhill, *Mysticism*, 299, 308, 380.
253. Armstrong, *Case for God*, 270, 327.
254. Heschel, *Man's Quest for God*, 59, 61–62, 93–94.
255. Exodus 3:17–21, 6:4–7, 20:5–6; Deuteronomy 5:9, 6:4–5; Genesis 22:1–19; Numbers 31:1–54; Hosea 1:1–3:5; and Borg, *God We Never Knew*, 58–61.
256. Exodus 3:1–5 and Borg, *God We Never Knew*, 58–61.
257. Luke 13:20–21, 34, 15:31–32; Matthew 13:33, 18:10–14, 23:37 and John 4:24.
258. Romans 1:25, 8:9–14, 23–27, 9:1; 1 Corinthians 9:21; Ephesians 3:9; and 1 John 4:8–16.
259. John 3:16, 14:16–17, 26–27.
260. Borg, *God at 2000*, 10–12, 16–17; Borg, *God We Never Knew*, 58–61; and Borg, *Heart of Christianity*, 75–76.
261. Exodus 3:7–8; Psalms 82:3–4; and Nelson-Pallmeyer, *Jesus against Christianity*, 104–105.
262. Julian of Norwich, *Revelations of Divine Love*, 61, 68, 110, 114, 117, 138, 165–170, 172, 192.
263. Julian of Norwich, *Revelations of Divine Love*, 102, 165–167, 174.
264. Julian of Norwich, *Revelations of Divine Love*, 63, 66–69, 71, 76, 82, 85, 137, 145, 193 203.
265. Julian of Norwich, *Revelations of Divine Love*, 67, 72, 133, 144–145, 154–155, 114, 171, 183, 188, 193.
266. Julian of Norwich, *Revelations of Divine Love*, 199–200.
267. Mother Teresa, *Come Be My Light*, 18–19, 42, 58, 185.
268. Mother Teresa, *Come Be My Light*, 22–29.
269. Mother Teresa, *Come Be My Light*, 18–19, 42, 58, 185.
270. Lee, et al., *Heart of Religion*, 25, 30.
271. Whitney, *Feminism and Love*, 208–209.
272. Thomas, *Sacred Pathways*, 23–25, 39–58.
273. Proverbs 1:5–7; Psalms 49:1–4; *Bhagavad Gita*, 64–65, 108, 116; Mother Teresa, *My Life among the Poor*, 19, 107–108; and Thomas, *Sacred Pathways*, 26–32, 82–113, 182–256.
274. Mother Teresa, *My Life among the Poor*, 108–109; Thomas, *Sacred Pathways*, 29–30, 160–181; Whitney, *Feminism and Love*, 164–224; and *Dhammapada*, 35.
275. *Bhagavad Gita*, 95.
276. *Bhagavad Gita*, 56–59, 63–64, 67, 108, 116–117.
277. *Bhagavad Gita*, 96–97.
278. *Bhagavad Gita*, 73, 97–98.

279. Tolle, *Power of NOW*, 133–134, 138, 194–195.
280. Tolle, *Power of NOW*, 107–111, 120, 131–132.
281. Tolle, *Power of NOW*, 131–134.
282. Tolle, *Power of NOW*, 131–134.
283. Otto, *Idea of the Holy*, 15–16, 27–28.
284. Otto, *Idea of the Holy*, 15–16, 27–28.
285. Otto, *Idea of the Holy*, 31–32, 36–39, 50–51, 143.
286. Otto, *Idea of the Holy*, 1–8, 12–21, 25–26, 31–32, 36–39, 50–51, 60–61, 65–68, 143, 146–147.
287. Whitney, *Feminism and Love*, 214–224; Parrinder, *World Religions*, 26–32; and Palmer, *World Religions*, 12–13.
288. Whitney, *Feminism and Love*, 76–77, 80–81 and Parrinder, *World Religions*, 30–36.
289. Goode, *Religion among the Primitives*, 45–49, 233, 244–245; Parrinder, *World Religions from Ancient History to the Present*, 32–33, 114–115; Parrinder, *Religion in Africa*, 26–27; Mitchell, *African Primal Religion*, 30–31; Frazer, *New Golden Bough*, 36–39; Palmer, *World Religions*, 44–51, 58–59; and Spencer, *Mysticism in World Religions*, 10–13.
290. Parrinder, *World Religions from Ancient History to the Present*, 24–25; Parrinder, *Religion in Africa*, 26–27; Mitchell, *African Primal Religion*, 30–31; Goode, *Religion among the Primitives*, 45–49, 233, 244–245; Frazer, *New Golden Bough*, 44–45; and Palmer, *World Religions*, 44–51.
291. Goode, *Religion among the Primitives*, 45–49, 233, 244–245; Parrinder, *World Religions from Ancient History to the Present*, 32–33, 114–115; Parrinder, *Religion in Africa*, 26–27; Mitchell, *African Primal Religion*, 30–31; Frazer, *New Golden Bough*, 61–66; Palmer, *World Religions*, 44–51, 58–59; and Sidney Spencer, *Mysticism in World Religions*, 10–13.
292. Fisher, *West African Traditional Religions*, 8, 64–68, 86–87, 92, 106–107, 112, 139–141, 185–189.
293. Fisher, *West African Traditional Religions*, 139–140; Parrinder, *Religion in Africa*, 26–27; Mitchell, *African Primal Religion*, 30–31; and Palmer, *World Religions*, 88–89.
294. Spencer, *Mysticism in World Religions*, 10–17.
295. Fisher, *West African Traditional Religions*, 45–49, 64–65, 138–140.
296. Hultkrantz, *Native Religions of North America*, 22–27 and Palmer, *World Religions*, 76–77.
297. Hartmann, *Last Hours of Ancient Sunlight*, 183–184.
298. Hultkrantz, *Native Religions of North America*, 24–28; Gabriel Horn, *Contemplation of a Primal Mind*, 2, 6, 9–11, 23–28, 35; and Sun Bear and others, *Walk in Balance* (NY: Fireside, 1992), pp. ix-x, 1–7.
299. Hultkrantz, *Native Religions of North America*, 17, 20–23; Parrinder, *World Religions from Ancient History to the Present*, 76–77; Palmer, *World Religions*, 76–77; Horn, *Contemplation of a Primal Mind*, 28–29; Jensen, *Myth and Cult among Primitive Peoples*, 163–164; and Hartmann, *Last Hours of Ancient Sunlight*, 171, 189.
300. Spencer, *Mysticism in World Religions*, 9–10.
301. Hartmann, *Last Hours of Ancient Sunlight*, pp. 171, 189 and Frazer, *New Golden Bough*, 108–112.
302. Frazer, *New Golden Bough*, 108–112.
303. Goode, *Religion among the Primitives*, 45–49; Parrinder, *Religion in Africa*, 8–9, 40–41, 47; Mitchell, *African Primal Religion*, x-xi; and Hultkrantz, *Native Religions of North America*, 22–24.

304. Parrinder, *Religion in Africa*, 8-9, 40-41, 47; Mitchell, *African Primal Religion*, 1-2; Fisher, *West African Traditional Religions*, 5, 15-16, 28; and Hultkrantz, *Native Religions of North America*, 24-26.

Chapter 6: The Awakenings of Mystics of Eastern Religions

305. Prabhavananda, *The Spiritual Heritage of India*, 3-5; Sen, *Hinduism*, 46-47; and Prabhavananda, *Vedic Religion and Philosophy*, 30-31.
306. *Rig Veda* X:129; Mascaro, "Introduction," *Upanishads*, 9-10; Prabhavananda, *Vedic Religion and Philosophy*, 30-31; Sen, *Hinduism*, 116-117; Louis Renou, *Hinduism*, 47-48; Ainslie Embree, *The Hindu Tradition*, 26-27; and Prabhavananda, *The Spiritual Heritage of India*, 3-5.
307. *Upanishads*, trans., Mascaro, 79, 83 and *Upanishads*, trans., Prabhavananda and Manchester, 50-51, 87.
308. *Upanishads*, trans., Prabhavananda and Manchester, 50-51, 62 and *Upanishads*, trans., Mascaro, 57-58, 64, 75, 79, 85, 87, 109-110, 118.
309. *Upanishads*, trans., Mascaro, 57-58, 64, 75, 77, 79, 83, 87, 89-90, 92, 94-96, 101, 109-110, 114, 118 and *Upanishads*, trans., Prabhavananda and Manchester, 50-51.
310. *Upanishads*, trans., Mascaro, 83, 89-90, 92, 94-96, 101, 109-110, 114.
311. Embree, *The Hindu Tradition*, 48-49 and Prabhavananda, *Vedic Religion and Philosophy*, 42-43.
312. Shankara, *Crest-Jewel of Discrimination*, 45, 52, 54-56, 58, 61, 63, 67.
313. Shankara, *Crest-Jewel of Discrimination*, 52-53, 56, 63.
314. Shankara, *Crest-Jewel of Discrimination*, 34, 53-54, 56, 63, 65.
315. *Upanishads*, trans., Mascaro, 49-50, 67, 78-81, 84-88, 90-92, 99 and *Upanishads*, trans., Prabhavananda and Manchester, 18, 62.
316. *Upanishads*, trans., Prabhavananda and Manchester, 50-51 and *Upanishads*, trans., Mascaro, 83-84.
317. *Upanishads*, trans., Mascaro, 57-58 and *Upanishads*, trans., Prabhavananda and Manchester, 16-17.
318. *Upanishads*, trans., Prabhavananda and Manchester, 17, 62 and *Upanishads*, trans., Mascaro, 52, 58-59, 62.
319. *Upanishads*, trans., Mascaro, 64, 81, 86.
320. *Bhagavad Gita*, 50, 95-96, 102.
321. *Bhagavad Gita*, 85-87, 94, 100, 105, 107.
322. *Bhagavad Gita*, 49-50, 53-54, 100-101, 107, 116.
323. *Bhagavad Gita*, 49-50, 53-54, 100-101, 107, 116.
324. *Bhagavad Gita*, 95-96.
325. *Bhagavad Gita*, 56-59, 63-64, 67, 107, 116-117.
326. *Bhagavad Gita*, 73, 96-98.
327. Ghanananda and Stewart-Wallace, *Women Saints: East and West*, 40-41 and Star, *Inner Treasure*, 182-184.
328. Cahill, *Wise Women*, 102-103; Ghanananda and Stewart-Wallace, *Women Saints: East and West*, 55-57; and Star, *Inner Treasure*, 190-191.
329. Cahill, *Wise Women*, 102-103; Ghanananda and Stewart-Wallace, *Women Saints: East and West*, 55-57; and Star, *Inner Treasure*, 190-192.
330. Ramakrishna, *Teachings of Sri Ramakrishna*, 3, 148-149, 161-162, 175-176, 179, 301, 314, 319-320.
331. Ramakrishna, *Teachings of Sri Ramakrishna*, 11, 251, 275, 321.

332. Ramakrishna, *Teachings of Sri Ramakrishna*, 259–260, 269, 272, 302.

333. Ramakrishna, *Teachings of Sri Ramakrishna*, 161–162, 171–172.

334. Ramakrishna, *Teachings of Sri Ramakrishna*, 161–162, 171–173.

335. Ramakrishna, *Teachings of Sri Ramakrishna*, 173–175, 207–208, 218, 274, 287, 289.

336. Star, *Inner Treasure*, 219, 221–222.

337. Eck, *India: Sacred Geography*, 1, 10, 18, 26–29, 31, 36, 53.

338. Parrinder, *World Religions*, pp. 351–352; Miller, *Daoism*, xii-xiii, 188–193; and Renard, *Confucianism, Daoism, and Shinto*, 217–218. When both systems are used, the Pinyin is in parentheses.

339. Ellwood and McGraw, *Many Peoples, Many Faiths*, 182–183 and Parrinder, *World Religions*, 351–352.

340. Novak, *World's Wisdom*, 146–149; *I Ching: The Chinese Book of Changes*, 21–22; Parrinder, *World Religions*, 316, 337, 352–353; Campbell, *Masks of Gods*, 334–339, 395–396, 461–464; Ellwood and McGraw, *Many Peoples, Many Faiths*, 182–183; and Smith, *World's Religions*, 198–199.

341. Parrinder, *World Religions*, 352–353.

342. Hu, "Rectification of the Four Teachings in Chinese Culture," *Violence against Women in Contemporary World Religions*, 109–110; Renard, *Confucianism, Daoism, and Shinto*, 75–78, 80, 95; Novak, *World's Wisdom*, 111–113, 119; Ellwood and McGraw, *Many Peoples, Many Faiths*, 182–194, 210–212; Smith, *World's Religions*, 183, 185–186; Lao Tzu, *Tao Te Ching*, 22–23; Confucius, *Analects of Confucius*, 110, 162, 198; and Confucius, *Sayings of Confucius*, 16–17.

343. Confucius, *Analects of Confucius*, 127–128; Confucius, *Sayings of Confucius*, 53, 72; Smith, *World's Religions*, 172–173; Ellwood and McGraw, *Many Peoples, Many Faiths*, 186–187; Hu, "Rectification," *Violence against Women*, 111–113.

344. Confucius, *Analects of Confucius*, 102–103, 105, 110, 162, 198; Confucius, *Sayings of Confucius*, 40, 76, 101; and Novak, *World's Wisdom*, 125–126.

345. Confucius, *Analects of Confucius*, 34–38; Confucius, *Sayings of Confucius*, 17–19; and Novak, *World's Wisdom*, 129–130; Smith, *World's Religions*, 173, 182; and Ellwood and McGraw, *Many Peoples, Many Faiths*, 188–189. Although *chun tzu* in the *Analects* is male, some gender-neutral translations avoid the sexist language.

346. Confucius, *Analects of Confucius*, 41, 88, 91, 105, 119; Confucius, *Sayings of Confucius*, 51–52; and Novak, *World's Wisdom*, 125–126.

347. *Analects of Confucius*, pp. 189, 197; Confucius, *Sayings of Confucius*, pp. 22, 36, 47, 77, 79; and Novak, *World's Wisdom*, 125–126.

348. Hu, "Rectification," *Violence against Women*, 13–114 and Novak, *World's Wisdom*, 134–136.

349. Miller, *Daoism*, 4–5, 189; Renard, *Confucianism, Daoism, and Shinto*, 13, 217; Ellwood and McGraw, *Many Peoples, Many Faiths*, 197–200; Smith, *World's Religions*, 197–198; and Hu, "Rectification," *Violence against Women*, 110–124.

350. Chia and Wei, *Living in the Tao*, 1–3, 6, 8; Renard, *Confucianism, Daoism, and Shinto*, pp. 95–96; Ellwood and McGraw, *Many Peoples, Many Faiths*, 184–184, 196–197; Smith, *World's Religions*, 172–184, 196; and Novak, *World's Wisdom*, 125–126.

351. Lao Tzu, *Tao Te Ching*, 22–23; Lao Tzu, *Way of Life according to Lao Tzu*; Novak, *World's Wisdom*, 146–148; and Dyer, *Changing Your Thoughts—Changing Your Life*, 2–3. Dyer presents ten different translations of *Tao Te Ching*.

352. Novak, *World's Wisdom*, 148–149 and Star, *Inner Treasure*, 31–32.

353. Lao Tzu, *Way of Life according to Lao Tzu*, 26–27 and Novak, *World's Wisdom*, 151–153. Again there is sexist language.

354. Lao Tzu, *Way of Life according to Lao Tzu*, 29–30 and Novak, *World's Wisdom*,

151, 155.

355. Star, *Inner Treasure*, 33-34; Lao Tzu, *Way of Life according to Lao Tzu*, 48, 55; Novak, *World's Wisdom*, 153, 157-158; and Dyer, *Changing Your Thoughts*, 14-15.

356. Lao Tzu, *Way of Life according to Lao Tzu*, 33-34, 37, 60 and Novak, *World's Wisdom*, 153-154.

357. Star, *Inner Treasure*, pp. 38-39 and Novak, *World's Wisdom*, pp. 149-150.

358. Harvey, *Essential Mystics*, 18-19; Miller, *Daoism*, 7-8, 189; Star, *Inner Treasure*, 28-29; Ellwood and McGraw, *Many Peoples, Many Faiths*, 201-202; and Novak, *World's Wisdom*, 164-165.

359. Star, *Inner Treasure*, 40-41 and Novak, *World's Wisdom*, 164, 168.

360. Harvey, *Essential Mystics*, 28-29 and Star, *Inner Treasure*, 43-44.

361. Renard, *Confucianism, Daoism, and Shinto*, 11, 114-115; Miller, *Daoism*, 133-135; Harvey, *Essential Mystics*, 30-31; Novak, *World's Wisdom*, 146-147; Ellwood and McGraw, *Many Peoples, Many Faiths*, 201-202; and *I Ching*, 9-15.

362. Campbell, *Masks of Gods*, 334-339, 395-396, 461-464 and Parrinder, *World Religions*, 353-354.

363. G. Bownas, "Shinto," *The Concise Encyclopedia of Living Religions*, 348-349; Parrinder, *World Religions*, 355-356, 363; Ellwood and McGraw, *Many Peoples, Many Faiths*, 180, 233; Lew Hopfe, *Religions of the World*, 148-149; and Joseph Kitagawa, *Religions of the East*, 280-281.

364. Bownas, "Shinto," *The Concise Encyclopedia*, pp. 358-359; Parrinder, *World Religions*, pp. 355-356, 363; and Campbell, *Masks of God*, pp. 334-339, 395-396, 461-464.

365. Kitagawa, *Religions of the East*, 278, 283; Bownas, "Shinto," *The Concise Encyclopedia*, 363-364; and Hopfe, *Religions of the World*, 150-151.

Chapter 7: Jewish and Christian Mystics' Awakenings

366. Genesis 12:1-4, 15:1-6, 17-18. The *Bible* (NRSV). NRSV translation is used throughout unless other translations are mentioned.
367. Genesis 17:1-12.
368. Exodus 3:1-8, 13-15.
369. Exodus 20:1-17 and Deuteronomy 5:1-21.
370. Isaiah 6:1-8.
371. Isaiah 1:1-4, 15, 19, 5:16-19, 6:8-13.
372. Isaiah 1:1-4, 7:14-15, 9:6-7, 10:20, 11:2-4, 12:2, 14:1.
373. Isaiah 39:7, 41:10, 42:6, 16, 48:5,17, 49:13, 52:1, 54:8, 55:3.
374. Isaiah 56:1, 58:9-11, 61:1-2, 6,8, 63:7-11, 16, 65:17, 66:13.
375. Jeremiah 1:1-8, 2:13.
376. Jeremiah 4:1-2, 7:5-8, 9:24, 10:10, 24:7.
377. Jeremiah 26:8, 31:1-3, 31-33.
378. Amos 5:14-15, 24, 7:14-1-6, 8:4,7.
379. Hosea 2:16-23, 4:1-2, 12, 6:6, 11:1, 4.
380. Micah 3:1-2, 8, 6:8, 7:7, 19.
381. Psalms 5:7-8, 23:1-4, 25, 4, 10.
382. Psalms 40:5-11, 46:1-2, 7-8, 51:1-2, 10-11, 16.
383. Psalms 68:5-10, 86:5, 15, 89:2, 14, 33-35, 136:1-16.
384. "From the Book of Judith," *Wise Women*, 23-24 and Peter Ellis, *The Men and the Message of the Old Testament*, 526-527.

385. Cohen, *Everyman's Talmud*, x-xii, xix, xxx, xiv-xlviii, 1-2 and Judah Goldin, *Living Talmud*, 10, 16, 20, 179-189.
386. *Pirte Avot* 4:22 in Harvey, *Essential Mystics*, pp. 99-100.
387. Scholem, *Kabbalah*, 88-89, 99, 106; Matt, *The Essential Kabbalah*, xvii, 1, 6-10, 39-40; Goldwag, *Beliefnet Guide to Kabbalah*, xvi, xix, 54-59, 108-109; and Harvey, *Essential Mystics*, 103-104.
388. Hoffman, *Kabbalah Reader*, 3-5; Scholem, *Kabbalah*, 88-89, 99 106; Matt, *Essential Kabbalah*, xvii, 1, 6-10, 39-40; Goldwag, *Beliefnet Guide to Kabbalah*, xvi, xix, 54-59, 108-109; and Harvey, *Essential Mystics*, 103-104.
389. Hoffman, *Kabbalah Reader*, 22-23, 25-26 and Matt, *Essential Kabbalah*, 29-30.
390. Matt, *Essential Kabbalah*, 25, 158 and Hoffman, *Kabbalah Reader*, 80-81.
391. Gluckel of Hameln, *Wise Women*, 109-110.
392. Hoffman, *Kabbalah Reader*, 116, 119.
393. Matt, *Essential Kabbalah*, 31, 128 and Goldwag, *Beliefnet Guide to Kabbalah*, 90-91.
394. Buber, *I and Thou*, 76-81, 106.
395. Buber, *I and Thou*, 99, 101-102; Heschel, *Man's Quest for God*, 59, 61-62, 93-94; Heschel, *Who Is Man?* 75-76.
396. Natalia Ginzburg and Judith Plaskow, *Wise Women*, pp. 200-201, 321-322.
397. Maguire, *Moral Creed for All Christians*, 32; Maguire, *Moral Core of Judaism and Christianity*, 116-117; McGrath, *Christian Theology*, 542; Funk, et al., *Five Gospels: What Did Jesus Really Say?* 11; Borg, *Heart of Christianity*, 131; and Fiorenza, *In Memory of Her*, 111-112, 148.
398. Luke 17:21 and Funk, *Five Gospels*, 40, 134-137, 166, 192, 318, 364-365.
399. Luke 6:20, 11:2 and Matthew 5:3, 6:9-10.
400. Matthew 6:25-33, 7:21, 19:13-15; Luke 12:22-32, 18:15-17; and Mark 10:13-16.
401. Matthew 13:31-33, 13:44; Mark 4:30-32; and Luke 13:18-21.
402. John 10:30, 38, 14:10-20, 31, 15:10-15, 16:27-28, 17:4-26, and Luke 17:20-21.
403. Deuteronomy 6:4-5; Leviticus 19:18; Mark 12:28-31; Matthew 5:43-44, 22:34-40; and Luke 6:27-28, 32-36, 10:25-27.
404. John 7:16, 12, 12:44-49, 14:24, 16:5, 27-28, 17:4-26.
405. Matthew 4:10, 6:9, 26-30, 12:20-29, 32, 19:17, 25-26, 22:31-32; Mark 3:29, 10:18, 12:26-27, 13:11; Luke 1:47, 48, 11:2, 12:24-28, 18:19, 26-27, 20:37-38; and John 4:24.
406. Acts 17:24-29; Romans 1:23-25, 2:1-4, 7, 3:7, 21, 30, 5:5, 9, 8:15, 9:15-16, 11:22, 15:5; and 1 Corinthians 1:3, 9, 29, 8:4-6, 10:13.
407. 1 John 4:7-16.
408. Augustine, *Confessions of St. Augustine*, 17, 19, 58, 139-140, 149, 235-236, 316.
409. Augustine, *Confessions of St. Augustine*, 58, 139-140, 149, 235-236, 316.
410. Denys the Areopagite, "Divine Names," *Pseudo-Dionysius*, 54-56, 60, 65, 67-68, 103, 105, 110, 128.
411. *The Little Flowers of St. Francis*, 201-202 and Clare of Assisi, *Wise Women*, 65-66.
412. Rolle, *The Fire of Love*, pp. 41, 49, 56, 59, 63, 65, 105, 165, 187-188.
413. Catherine of Siena, *Dialogue*, pp. 25, 33-38, 49-50, 101-102, 114, 121, 126, 147, 151-157, 274-278, 325-327, 366.
414. Underhill, *Mysticism*, 100-101, 133.
415. Catherine of Genoa, *Purgation and Purgatory*, 27, 34, 76-81, 107-110.

416. Ignatius of Loyola, *Spiritual Exercises*, 177, 251.
417. Teresa of Avila, *The Interior Castle*, 116, 119–121.
418. Lawrence, *Practice of the Presence of God*, 88, 93–94, 125.
419. Lawrence, *Practice of the Presence of God*, 86–88, 94–96, 103, 105, 108, 111.
420. Stahl, *Most Surprising Song*, 157, 168 and McKeever, *Paths Are Many, Truth Is One*, 26, 34–35, 37, 46, 55, 72, 96.
421. Desmond Tutu, "The Prodigal God," *God at 2000*, 122–128, 130–131.

Chapter 8: Muhammad and Islamic Mystics' Awakenings

422. Armstrong, *Islam*, 3–6; Armstrong, *History of God*, 132–142; Smith, *World's Religions*, 218–222; Ernst, *Shambhala Guide to Sufism*, 32–42; and Jeffery, *Islam: Muhammad and His Religion*, 3–5, 15–17, 47–51.
423. Armstrong, *History of God*, 132–142; Armstrong, *Islam*, 3–6; Smith, *World's Religions*, 218–222; Ernst, *Shambhala Guide*, 32–42; Jeffrey, *Islam*, 3–5, 15–17, 47–51; *Koran*, trans., Dawood, 9–10; *Meaning of the Glorious Koran*, trans., Pickthall, 287; *Koran*, trans., J.M. Rodwell (NY: Ballantine, 1993); and *Koran*, trans., Jeffery.
424. Jeffery, *Islam*, 3–5, 15–17, 47–51; Armstrong, *Islam*, 3–6; Armstrong, *History of God*, 132–142; Smith, *World's Religions*, 218–222; *Koran*, trans., Dawood, 9–10, 16; and *Glorious Koran*, 287–288.
425. Nasr, *Heart of Islam*, 4–5; Smith, *World's Religions*, 218–222, 227–230; Armstrong, *Islam*, 3–6; Armstrong, *History of God*, 132–142; Jeffery, *Islam*, 3–5, 15–17, 47–51; *Koran*, trans., Dawood, 14–15, 336, 345; *Glorious Koran*, 31–32; and *Koran*, trans., Jeffery, 9, 17.
426. *Koran*, trans., Dawood, 24, 63–69, 104–105, 115, 117, 120, 373.
427. Williams, *Islam*, 152–153; Armstrong, *History of God*, 146–150; Jeffery, *Islam*, 93–98, 166; *Koran*, trans., Dawood, 14–17, 47, 194, 256, 259, 313; and *Glorious Koran*, 133, 135, 145, 286, 432.
428. Nasr, *Heart of Islam*, 3–4, 210; Armstrong, *History of God*, 146–150; Jeffery, *Islam*, 93–98, 166; *Glorious Koran*, 133, 135, 145, 286, 432; and *Koran*, trans., Dawood, 14–17, 47, 194, 256, 259, 313.
429. Smart and Hecht, *Sacred Texts*, 142–144; Baldock, *Essence of Sufism*, 213–221; Armstrong, *History of God*, 149–150; Jeffery, *Islam*, 93–98, 166; Ernst, *Shambhala Guide*, 82–84; *Glorious Koran*, 135, 145; and *Koran*, trans., Dawood, 14–17, 256, 313; and Williams, *Islam*, 152, 153.
430. Baldock, *Essence of Sufism*, 213–221; Smart and Hecht, *Sacred Texts*, 142–144; Jeffery, *Islam*, 93–98, 166; and Ernst, *Shambhala Guide*, 82–84. Different authors present various 99 names.
431. Smart and Hecht, *Sacred Texts*, 142–144; Baldock, *Essence of Sufism*, 213–221; Jeffery, *Islam*, 93–98, 166; Ernst, *Shambhala Guide*, 82–84; and Otto, *Idea of the Holy*, 154.
432. *Koran*, trans., Dawood, 120, 151, 342–343, 368.
433. Novak, *The World's Wisdom*, 321–322; Armstrong, *History of God*, 142–144, 149–150; *Glorious Koran*, 47–48; and *Koran*, trans., Dawood, 336–337.
434. Smart and Hecht, *Sacred Texts*, 142–144; Jeffery, *Islam*, 93–98; Armstrong, *History of God*, 142–144, 149–150; and *Koran*, trans., Dawood, 107, 120, 336.
435. Ibrahim, *Brief Illustrated Guide to Understanding Islam*, 45–49; Novak, *The World's Wisdom*, 321–322; Smith, *World's Religions*, 230–234; *Glorious Koran*, 91–92; and *Koran*, trans., Jeffery, 72–73.

436. Smart and Hecht, *Sacred Texts*, 129, 152; Ibrahim, *Brief Illustrated Guide*, 65-68; Novak, *World's Wisdom*, 286, 296-299; Jeffery, *Islam*, 155-156, 165; and *Glorious Koran*, 89, 287.

437. Williams, *Islam*, 44-45; Smart and Hecht, *Sacred Texts*, 154-157; Ibrahim, *Brief Illustrated Guide*, 65-68; Novak, *World's Wisdom*, pp. 288, 296-299; Jeffery, *Islam*, pp. 184-186, 193; *Koran*, trans., Dawood, pp. 344-345; and *Glorious Koran*, 48-49, 243.

438. Armstrong, *History of God*, 226-227 and Baldock, *Essence of Sufism*, 9, 64, 67, 88.

439. Star, *Inner Treasure*, pp. 138-139 and Baldock, *Essence of Sufism*, pp. 39-40.

440. Baldock, *Essence of Sufism*, 75-80, 213-214.

441. Sharma, *Our Religons*, 468-469 and Baldock, *Essence of Sufism*, 9, 63, 227.

442. Ellwood and McGraw, *Many Peoples, Many Faiths*, 409-410; Armstrong, *History of God*, 226-227; and Baldock, *Essence of Sufism*, 91-92.

443. Harvey, *Essential Mystics*, 144-145; Baldock, *Essence of Sufism*, 91-92; and Spencer, *Mysticism in World Religion*, 308-309.

444. Baldock, *Essence of Sufism*, 92-94.

445. Baldock, *Essence of Sufism*, 99-100.

446. Happold, *Mysticism*, 251-252 and Baldock, *Essence of Sufism*, 105-106, 108-109.

447. Spencer, *Mysticism in World Religion*, 308-309 and Baldock, *Essence of Sufism*, 129-130.

448. Baldock, *Essence of Sufism*, 130-131.

449. Armstrong, *History of God*, 232-233.

450. Armstrong, *History of God*, 234-235 and Baldock, *Essence of Sufism*, 160-161.

451. Star, *Inner Treasure*, 130-131 and Baldock, *Essence of Sufism*, 161-162.

452. Baldock, *Essence of Sufism*, 161-163.

453. Harvey, *Essential Mystics*, 145-146; Armstrong, *History of God*, 42-43 and Baldock, *Essence of Sufism*, 156-157; and *Glorious Koran*, 42-43.

454. Ernst, *Shambhala Guide*, 166-167; Rumi, *Teachings of Rumi*, 17, 36; and Armstrong, *History of God*, 240-241, 403.

455. Rumi, *Teachings of Rumi*, 7, 26-27.

456. Rumi, *Teachings of Rumi*, 11-12, 22, 38.

457. Star, *Inner Treasure*, 111-112; Rumi, *Teachings of Rumi*, 56-57; and Baldock, *Essence of Sufism*, 179-180.

458. Star, *Inner Treasure*, 107, 118 and Rumi, *Teachings of Rumi*, 15, 35, 52.

459. Rumi, *Teachings of Rumi*, 15, 35, 52, 75, 141, 153.

460. Happold, *Mysticism*, 259-260 and Star, *Inner Treasure*, 135-136.

461. Novak, *World's Wisdom*, 331-331.

462. Novak, *World's Wisdom*, 331-332.

Chapter 9: Love for Our Neighbors and Ourselves Is the Fourth Stage

463. Karen Armstrong, *Twelve Steps to a Compassionate Life*, 3-4, 9.

464. Whitney, *Feminism and Love*, 214-220; Armstrong, *Twelve Steps to a Compassionate Life*, 23-24; Einstein, *Albert Einstein, the Human Side*, 66-67; and *Bhagavad Gita*, 79-80.

465. Armstrong, *Twelve Steps to a Compassionate Life*, pp. 4-6. The Charter for Compassion can be found at www.charterforcompassion.org.

466. *Dhammapada*, 335 and John Maxwell, *Ethics 101*, 16-17.

467. Confucius, *Sayings of Confucius*, 40, 76–77, 101 and Confucius, *Analects of Confucius*, 110, 162–164, 198.
468. *Bhagavad Gita*, 62, 73, 79, 96–98, 105 and Maxwell, *Ethics 101*, 16–17.
469. Deuteronomy 6:4–5; Leviticus 19:17–18; and Neusner, *The Way of the Torah*, 87–88.
470. Matthew 5:17, 43–48; 7:12, 22:34–40; Mark 12:28–34; Luke 6:27–36, 10:25–28; John 13:34–35, 15:12–13.
471. *Koran*, 23–24; Armstrong, *Twelve Steps to a Compassionate Life*, 100; and Maxwell, *Ethics 101*, 16–17.
472. Maxwell, *Ethics 101*, 16–17 and Schweitzer, *Treasury of Albert Schweitzer*, 48.
473. Underhill, *Mysticism*, 198–199.
474. Underhill, *Mysticism*, 198–199.
475. Mother Teresa, *Come Be My Light*, 6, 15, 49, 51, 58, 66.
476. Mother Teresa, *Come Be My Light*, 66–67, 71, 85–86.
477. Mother Teresa, *Come Be My Light*, 96–98, 260, 271–274, 278, 305, 354, 362.
478. Underhill, *Mysticism*, 168–169, 198–200, 204–205.
479. Underhill, *Mysticism*, 201–202.
480. Catherine of Genoa, *Purgation and Purgatory*, 71–72.
481. Gandhi, *All Men Are Brothers*, 22, 46, 52–53, 58, 60, 99–100, 102; Gandhi, *Gandhi on Non-violence*, 45–46; and Gandhi, *Non-violent Resistance*, 42, 45–49.
482. Reinhold, *Soul Afire*, 97–98; Underhill, *Mysticism*, 205–212; and *Bhagavad Gita*, 97–98, 119–120.
483. Underhill, *Mysticism*, 205–212, 223 and Catherine of Siena, *Dialogue*, 97.
484. Underhill, *Mysticism*, 210–213, 215–216, 220.
485. Mother Teresa, *No Greater Love*, 81; McGinn, *Essential Writings of Christian Mysticism*, 77; Underhill, *Mysticism*, 201–202; and Johnson, *Imprisoned Splendor*, 89–90.
486. Reinhold, *Soul Afire*, 86–87, 97–98 and Underhill, *Mysticism*, 205–213.
487. Gandhi, *All Men Are Brothers*, 22, 46, 52–53, 58, 60, 99–100, 102; Gandhi, *Gandhi on Non-violence*, 45–46; and Gandhi, *Non-violent Resistance*, 42, 45–49.
488. Plato, *Dialogues of Plato*, 190–192.
489. Whitney, *Feminism and Love*, 23–43.
490. Teresa of Avila, *Interior Castle*, 70.
491. Bernard of Clairvaux, *Twelve Steps of Humility and Pride, On Loving God*, 78–126; Armstrong, *Twelve Steps to a Compassionate Life*, 3–4, 6, 10–11, 17, 23–25, 84–85; Johnson, *Mystical Theology*, 45–46, 166–167; and Erich Fromm, *The Art of Loving*, 22–28.
492. Whitney, *Feminism and Love*, 46–68.
493. Whitney, *Feminism and Love*, 46–68.
494. Williamson, *The Law of Divine Compensation*, 49–50 and Whitney, *Feminism and Love*, 46–68.
495. 1 Corinthians 13:7–13 and Whitney, *Feminism and Love*, 46–68.
496. Augustine, *Confessions of St. Augustine*, 214–217; Augustine, *Enchiridion of Faith, Hope, and Love*, 3, 10, 132; and Bernard of Clairvaux, *Twelve Steps of Humility and Pride, On Loving God*, 81–120.
497. Augustine, *Enchiridion of Faith, Hope, and Love*, 3, 10, 132; 1 Timothy 1:5; and 1 John 4:8–16.
498. *Bhagavad Gita*, 97–98, 119–120.
499. Deuteronomy 5:6–21, 6:4–5; Leviticus 19:17–18; and Exodus 20:7–21.
500. Matthew 19:20–21, 25:31–46; Mark 10:20–21; and Luke 18:21–22.
501. Augustine, *Enchiridion of Faith, Hope, and Love*, 85–86, 89–90; Luke 6:27–28,

35; Matthew 5:43; and Ecclesiasticus 30:24.

502. *Koran*, 23, 27, 35, 50, 63–64, 132, 153, 181, 184, 335, 344.

503. *Koran*, 24, 158, 187, 190–191, 216, 220, 231, 342–343. The Quran also says, "believers, retaliation is decreed for you in bloodshed: a free man for a free man, a slave for a slave, and a female for a female." Furthermore, "fight for the sake of Allah those that fight against you, but do not attack them first. Allah does not love aggressors. Kill them wherever you find them. . . . If they attack you put them to the sword. . . . Fight against them until idolatry is no more and Allah's religion reigns supreme. But if they mend their ways, fight none except the evil-doers."

504. Augustine, *Enchiridion of Faith, Hope, and Love*, 8, 195, 202.

505. *Little Flowers of St. Francis*, 199–200.

506. Hadewijch, *Hadewijch*, 128, 148, 271.

507. Hadewijch, *Hadewijch*, 141–142, 153, 158.

508. Rumi, *Teachings of Rumi*, 31, 59, 72, 105.

509. Rumi, *Teachings of Rumi*, 69, 73, 76-7, 89–90.

510. Paul and Marillac, *Rules, Conferences, and Writings*, 13–14, 225, 240, 244.

511. Bernard Christensen, *The Inward Pilgrim: Spiritual Classics from Augustine to Bonhoeffer*, 94–45.

512. Jesuit General Congregation, 1995, "Jesuits and the Situation of Women in Church and Society," *Women's Spirituality*, pp. 96–102.

513. Jesuit General Congregation, "Jesuits and the Situation of Women in Church and Society," *Women's Spirituality*, 96–102.

514. Margaret Wheatley, *Leadership and the New Science*, 9–10, 12, 19, 32–34, 38–39, 81, 120, 139–140, 143.

515. Wheatley, *Leadership and the New Science*, 10, 32–34, 36, 38–39, 139–140, 143.

516. McKeever, *Paths Are Many, Truth Is One*, 98–192.

517. Williamson, *The Law of Divine Compensation*, xi, xiii, 2, 5, 8, 37–38, 79, 88–89.

518. Williamson, *The Law of Divine Compensation*, 5, 35, 78, 80, 89, 99–100, 117–119.

519. Williamson, *The Law of Divine Compensation*, 2, 7–10, 19–20, 24–25, 27, 34, 37.

520. Williamson, *The Law of Divine Compensation*, x-xiv, 78–79.

521. Williamson, *The Law of Divine Compensation*, xiv-xv.

522. Whitney, *Feminism and Love*, 170–176.

523. Whitney, *Feminism and Love*, 170–176.

524. Underhill, *Mysticism*, 221, 226–230.

Chapter 10: Illumination and Union with the Holy One Are the Fifth Stage

525. Underhill, *Mysticism*, 234, 238, 254.

526. Underhill, *Mysticism*, 169, 227–229, 232–234, 242, 258–259, 262.

527. Underhill, *Mysticism*, 258–259.

528. King, *Christian Mystics*, 65–166 and Underhill, *Mysticism*, 258–259, 263.

529. Gandhi, *All Men Are Brothers*, 76 and Mother Teresa, *Come Be My Light*, 73–74, 93, 146, 242–243, 266, 283.

530. Underhill, *Mysticism*, 169, 227–229, 232–234, 240–242, 420.

531. Underhill, *Mysticism*, 252–253, 445.

532. *Upanishads*, 83, 91–93, 116–118, 120.
533. *Upanishads*, 49, 67, 78–79, 84–87, 90–92, 99.
534. *Upanishads*, 12, 62–65, 91–96, 117–118.
535. *Upanishads*, 65, 80–81, 117–118.
536. *Bhagavad Gita*, 40–45, 90.
537. *Bhagavad Gita*, 52, 77, 80–81.
538. *Bhagavad Gita*, 71, 82, 89, 102, 120.
539. Novak, *World's Wisdom*, 148–149; Star, *Inner Treasure*, 31; Miller, *Daoism*, 7; and Stahl, *Most Surprising Song*, 167–168.
540. 1 John 4:7–16a.
541. Augustine, *Confessions of St. Augustine*, 140–141, 152, 236.
542. Augustine, *Confessions of St. Augustine*, 140–141, 152, 236.
543. Denys the Areopagite, "Divine Names," *Pseudo-Dionysius*, 56, 68, 79, 99, 101, 128–129; Underhill, *Mysticism*, 420, 423–424; Fox, *Coming of the Cosmic Christ*, 57–58; and Armstrong, *History of God*, 228, 243.
544. Julian of Norwich, *Revelations of Divine Love*, 138, 159–161, 164, 202–203.
545. Julian of Norwich, *Revelations of Divine Love*, 138, 159–162, 164,190, 201.
546. Star, *Inner Treasure*, 191.
547. Matt, *Essential Kabbalah*, 24, 59.
548. Buber, *I and Thou*, 75, 79–80, 99, 101 and Fox, *Coming of the Cosmic Christ*, 57–58.
549. Reinhold, *Soul Afire*, 289–290.
550. Johnson, *Imprisoned Splendor*, 305, 326.
551. Johnson, *Imprisoned Splendor*, 302, 327.
552. Underhill, *Mysticism*, 298, 306, 308–310, 312, 317.
553. Underhill, *Mysticism*, 298, 306, 308–310, 314–315, 317.
554. Underhill, *Mysticism*, 317–321, 323, 327.
555. Underhill, *Mysticism*, 299–301, 304, 312, 328–330, 333.
556. Underhill, *Mysticism*, 64–65, 299–301, 304, 312, 328–330, 333.
557. Fleming, *Fire and Cloud*, 134–135; Berdyaev, *The Nature of Man*, 278–279; Underhill, *Mysticism*, 299–302, 304–306; and Fritjof Capra, *Tao of Physics*, 25–26.
558. Johnson, *Mystical Theology*, 168–169 and Underhill, *Mysticism*, 381–384.
559. Underhill, *Mysticism*, 9–10, 16–17, 19–20, 86, 238, 247, 413–414, 416–417.
560. Underhill, *Mysticism*, 9–10, 16–17, 19–20, 86, 238, 247, 413–414, 416–417.
561. Ramakrishna, *Teaching of Ramakrishna*, 31–32 and Underhill, *Mysticism*, 245–246, 425.
562. Underhill, *Mysticism*, 424–425.
563. Underhill, *Mysticism*, 423–424.
564. Therese of Lisieux, *Autobiography of St. Therese of Lisieux*, 52–53 and Underhill, *Mysticism*, 423–424.
565. Underhill, *Mysticism*, 420–423.
566. Buber, *I and Thou*, 78–87.
567. *Upanishads*, 49–51, 78–81, 93.
568. *Upanishads*, 49–51, 78–81, 93.
569. *Bhagavad Gita*, 81–82, 101–102, 107, 120 and Ramakrishna, *Teaching of Ramakrishna*, 22–24, 31.
570. Smith, *World Religions*, 113–119 and Ellwood and McGraw, *Many Peoples, Many Faiths*, 131–132.
571. Carmody, *How to Live Well*, 118–119, 145–146; Smith, *World Religions*, 113–119; Ellwood and McGraw, *Many Peoples, Many Faiths*, 130–132; and Baldock, *Essence of Islam*, 75–80, 213–214.

572. Carmody, *How to Live Well*, 145–148; Smith, *World Religions*, 117–119; and Ellwood and McGraw, *Many Peoples, Many Faiths*, 147–148.
573. Ellwood and McGraw, *Many Peoples, Many Faiths*, 132–135 and Smith, *World Religions*, 117–119.
574. Smith, *World Religions*, 117–119.
575. Smith, *World Religions*, 117–119.
576. Novak, *World's Wisdom*, 165–166 and Star, *Inner Treasure*, 41.
577. John 14:7–11, 20, 24, 31; 15:1–10; 16:32; 17:3, 6, 20–23.
578. John 5:19–20, 30, 36; 6:38–39; 8:16, 26, 28; 12:49–50; 14:7–11, 24, 31; 16:13; and Matthew 10:1–20.
579. Denys the Areopagite, *Pseudo-Dionysius*, 49–51, 72, 135–141, 154–155, 162–168, 173–174, 235–239.
580. Harvey, *Essential Mystics*, 101–103 and Armstrong, *History of God*, 228, 243.
581. Harvey, *Essential Mystics*, 101–103 and Armstrong, *History of God*, 228, 243.
582. Rumi, *Teachings of Rumi*, 50, 61, 132–133, 147, 169.
583. Hadewijch, *Hadewijch*, 148, 181, 187, 199.
584. Hadewijch, *Hadewijch*, 167, 272.
585. 2 Peter 1:4 and Hadewijch, *Hadewijch*, 66, 147, 159, 161, 198.
586. McGinn, *Essential Writings of Christian Mystics*, 423–424; Underhill, *Mysticism*, 419–420, 422, 427–428; and Armstrong, *History of God*, 228, 243.
587. Underhill, *Mysticism*, 422–423.
588. Underhill, *Mysticism*, 422–424.
589. Capps and Wright, *Silent Fire*, l39–140.
590. McGinn, *Essential Writings of Christian Mystics*, 367–368 and Underhill, *Mysticism*, 320–321.
591. Julian of Norwich, *Revelations of Divine Love*, 61, 133, 137, 139, 155, 159–160, 163, 165, 188 and Underhill, *Mysticism*, 247–248.
592. Marie of the Incarnation, "Autobiograhy," Capps and Wright, *Silent Fire*, 206–208.
593. Ramakrishna, *The Teaching of Ramakrishna*, 31–33, 37–39.
594. Ramakrishna, *The Teaching of Ramakrishna*, 22–24.
595. Ramakrishna, *The Teaching of Ramakrishna*, 22–24, 28–31.
596. Mother Teresa, *Come Be My Light*, 83, 98–99. 168, 257, 260.
597. Mother Teresa, *Come Be My Light*, 231, 341.
598. Mother Teresa, *Come Be My Light*, 202–203, 223 ,245.
599. Radhakrishnan quoted in Johnson, *Imprisoned Splendor*, 331 and Whitney, *Feminism and Love*, 203–204.
600. Isherwood, *Where Joy Resides*, 290–291; Fox, *Coming of the Cosmic Christ*, 50–51; and McKeever, *Paths Are Many, Truth Is One*, 71, 96.
601. Underhill, *Mysticism*, 413, 415, 418–420, 425–427.
602. *Philokalia: Eastern Christian Spiritual Texts*, vii–viii, 190–191 and McGinn, *Essential Writings of Christian Mystics*, 400–401.
603. Genesis 1:27–28; *Philokalia*, pp. 197, 199; and McGinn, *Essential Writings of Christian Mystics*, pp. 401, 408–409.
604. *Philokalia*, pp. 214, 219.
605. Acts 17:28 and Underhill, *Mysticism*, 413, 415, 418–420, 425–427.
606. Teresa of Avila, *Interior Castle*, 179–180.
607. Teresa of Avila, *Interior Castle*, 178–181.
608. John of the Cross, *Collected Works of St. John of the Cross*, 496–499 and McGinn, *Essential Writings of Christian Mystics*, pp. 461–463.
609. McGinn, *Essential Writings of Christian Mystics*, 400–401, 466–467.

610. Mechthild of Magdeburg, *Flowing Light of the Godhead*, 4–5, 39–42, 195.
611. Mechthild of Magdeburg, *Flowing Light of the Godhead*, 5, 193–194.
612. Mechthild of Magdeburg, *Flowing Light of the Godhead*, 44–45, 47–48, 61, 194.
613. Mechthild of Magdeburg, *Flowing Light of the Godhead*, 43–44.
614. Mechthild of Magdeburg, *Flowing Light of the Godhead*, 53, 69, 76, 78, 98.
615. Mechthild of Magdeburg, *Flowing Light of the Godhead*, 53, 69, 76, 78, 98.

Chapter 11: Transpersonal Images of the Divine during Illumination and Union

616. King, *Christian Mystics*, 93–95.
617. Smith, *World's Religions*, 114–115; Ramakrishna, *Teachings of Sri Ramakrishna*, and Otto, *Idea of the Holy*, 200–213.
618. Huston Smith, *Forgotten Truth*, 79–80; Smith, *World's Religions*, 114–115; Ramakrishna, *Teachings of Sri Ramakrishna*, and Otto, *Idea of the Holy*, 200–203.
619. Bede Griffins, *Universal Wisdom*, 40–4; Smith, *Forgotten Truth*, 79–80; Smith, *World's Religions*, 114–115; and Ramakrishna, *Teachings of Sri Ramakrishna*.
620. Armstrong, *History of God*, 210–211.
621. Kishore, *Hinduism*, 15, 191 and Ramakrishna, *Teachings of Sri Ramakrishna*, 49–50, 292, 310, 317.
622. Ramakrishna, *Teachings of Sri Ramakrishna*, pp. 49–50, 292, 310, 317; Smith, *World's Religions*, 60–63, 74–75; and Underhill, *Mysticism*, 337–357.
623. Ramakrishna, *Teachings of Sri Ramakrishna*, 49- 50, 292, 310, 317; Smith, *World's Religions*, 60–63, 74–75; and Spencer, *Mysticism in World Religions*, 54–55.
624. Mother Teresa. *Come Be My Light*, 41–42.
625. Underhill, *Mysticism*, 3–4, 24, 444–446 and Armstrong, *History of God*, 210–211.
626. Griffins, *Universal Wisdom*, 40–41.
627. Armstrong, *History of God*, xxii, 396.
628. 1 John 4:7, 16; Simmons, *In the Footsteps of the Mystics*, 21, 26; and Underhill, *Mysticism*, 87–88.
629. Denys the Areopagite, *Pseudo-Dionysius*, "Mystical Theology," 136–137, and "Divine Names," 54, 57, 61, 66, 68, 71, 79, 96–97, 99, 107.
630. Denys the Areopagite, *Pseudo-Dionysius*, "Divine Names," 53–54, 56, 59, 62, 65–66, 73, 91, 99, 103, 110–111, 127–128.
631. Denys the Areopagite, *Pseudo-Dionysius*, "Mystical Theology," 136–137, 139–141 and "Divine Names," 96–97, 106.
632. Denys the Areopagite, *Pseudo-Dionysius*, "Divine Names," 106, 141 and "Mystical Theology," 136–137, 139–140.
633. Evelyn Underhill, *Essentials of Mysticism*, 179–180; Underhill, *Mysticism*, 252, 342–343; and Johnson, *Imprisoned Splendor*, 317–318.
634. Underhill, *Essential Mysticism*, 179–180; Underhill, *Mysticism*, 252, 342–343; *True Joy: Wisdom of Francis and Clare*, 35–36; and Johnson, *Imprisoned Splendor*, 317–318.
635. Mechthild of Magdeburg, *Flowing Light of the Godhead*, pp. 18, 22–24, 35–48, 50–56, 70–73, 86–87, 111, 115, 124.
636. Rolle, *Fire of Love*, 47–49, 55–65, 76–77, 144–146, 181–188.
637. Catherine of Siena, *Dialogue*, 33–38, 49–56, 101–102, 274–278, 325–327.

638. Catherine of Siena, *Dialogue*, 40–46, 92–93, 102–103, 114–115, 147–157.

639. Thomas a Kempis, *Imitation of Christ*, 98–99; Simmons, *In the Footsteps of the Mystics*, 21, 26; and Underhill, *Mysticism*, pp. 65, 87–88, 93.

640. Simmons, *In the Footsteps of the Mystics*, 21, 26; and Underhill, *Mysticism*, 65, 87–88, 93.

641. Julian of Norwich, *Revelations of Divine Love*, 40–50, 66–68, 115–118, 130–137, 151–157, 210–213.

642. Julian of Norwich, *Revelations of Divine Love*, 62, 69, 74, 102, 130, 133, 163–164, 167, 171, 174, 206.

643. Julian of Norwich, *Revelations of Divine Love*, 184, 208–210.

644. Underhill, *Mysticism*, 232–239, 249–252.

645. Underhill, *Mysticism*, 232–239, 249–252.

646. Catherine of Genoa, *Purgation and Purgatory*, 27, 34, 76–81, 107–110.

647. Reinhold, *Soul Afire*, 104–105; Underhill, *Mysticism*, 87–88, 248–249; and Simmons, *In the Footsteps of the Mystics*, 23–24.

648. Cady, *Complete Works of H. Emilie Cady*, 138–144, 149, 154–157, 163–169, 170–177, 180–187, 191–193 and Cady, *Lessons in Truth*, 12, 18, 37–39, 50, 62–65, 98, 126, 165–168.

649. Tillich, *Systematic Theology*, and Armstrong, *History of God*, 281–282.

650. Chardin, *Hymn of the Universe*, 4–31; Chardin, *How I Believe*, 19, 27–36; and McGinn, *Essential Writings of Christian Mysticism*, 303–308.

651. Chardin, *Hymn of the Universe*, 4–31 and McGinn, *Essential Writings of Christian Mysticism*, 306–308.

652. Joan Chittister, *God at 2000*, 62–69 and Desmond Tutu, *God at 2000*, 122–123.

653. *Upanishads*, 83–84 and *Bhagavad Gita*, 89–90, 96–97.

654. *Bhagavad Gita*, 90–91, 93–94.

655. Lao Tzu, *Tao Te Ching*, 1–2.

656. Conze, *Buddhism*, 39–40; Smith, *World's Religions*, 113–114; and Ellwood and McGraw, *Many Peoples, Many Faiths*, 132–133.

657. Scholem, *Kabbalah*, 88–89, 99, 106 and Matt, *The Essential Kabbalah*, xvii, 1, 6–10, 39–40.

658. Armstrong, *Case for God*, 71–72.

659. Williams, *Islam*, 152–153; Jeffery, *Islam*, 93–98, 166; Armstrong, *History of God*, 149–150; *Koran*, trans., Dawood, 14–17, 47, 194, 265, 259, 313; and *Glorious Koran*, 133, 135, 145, 286, 432; and Nasr, *Heart of Islam*, 3, 210.

660. Williams, *Islam*, 152–153; Jeffery, *Islam*, 93–98, 166; Armstrong, *History of God*, 149–150; Smart and Hecht, *Sacred Texts of the World*, 132–144; Ernst, *Shambhala Guide*, 82–84; and Baldock, *Essence of Sufism*, 213–221.

661. Armstrong, *Case for God*, 229–230.

662. Gandhi, *All Men Are Brothers*, 51–53, 59–60.

663. Tolle, *Power of NOW*, 132, 139–142.

664. Underhill, *Mysticism*, 97–99, 102–104, 337.

665. Underhill, *Mysticism*, 97–99, 102–104, 337.

666. Armstrong, *Case for God*, 110, 326.

667. Underhill, *Mysticism*, 318–320, 323, 327.

668. Underhill, *Mysticism*, 319–320, 323, 327.

669. Denys the Areopagite, *Pseudo-Dionysius*, "Mystical Theology," 135–141, and "Divine Names," 49–50, 57, 66–68, 73, 106, 127–128.

670. Denys the Areopagite, *Pseudo-Dionysius*, "Mystical Theology," 135–141.

671. Denys the Areopagite, *Pseudo-Dionysius*, "Mystical Theology," 135–141.

672. Denys the Areopagite, *Pseudo-Dionysius*, "Divine Names," 49–50, 56, 105 and

"Mystical Theology," 135–141.

673. Armstrong, *Case for God*, 155–156 and Underhill, *Mysticism*, 319–320.
674. Armstrong, *Case for God*, 156–157.
675. McGinn, *Essential Writings of Christian Mysticism*, 385–387 and Underhill, *Mysticism*, 324–325.
676. Stephen, "Quaker Strongholds," *Quaker Spirituality*, 241, 243–244.
677. Stephen, "Quaker Strongholds," *Quaker Spirituality*, 246, 250.
678. Stephen, "Quaker Strongholds," *Quaker Spirituality*, 247–249.
679. Otto, *Idea of the Holy*, 220–221.
680. Otto, *Idea of the Holy*, 221.
681. Ramakrishna, *Teachings of Sri Ramakrishna*, 293–294.
682. Tolle, *Power of NOW*, 126, 138, 141.
683. Saint John of the Cross, *Dark Night of the Soul*.
684. McGinn, *Essential Writings of Christian Mysticism*, 385–387 and John of the Cross, *Dark Night of the Soul*, 33–44, 69–108.
685. Underhill, *Mysticism*, 383–389, 393, 395–398, 402 and Catherine of Siena, *Dialogue*, 274–278, 325–327.
686. Underhill, *Mysticism*, 384–385.
687. Underhill, *Mysticism*, 325, 396–398.
688. Mother Teresa. *Come Be My Light*, 50, 57, 61–62, 67, 74, 126, 136.
689. Mother Teresa. *Come Be My Light*, 50, 57, 61–62, 67, 74, 126, 136.
690. Mother Teresa. *Come Be My Light*, 1–2, 20, 22, 210.
691. Mother Teresa. *Come Be My Light*, 207, 214, 219, 221–222.
692. Underhill, *Mysticism*, 381–389, 400.
693. Underhill, *Mysticism*, 381–389, 393, 395–398, 402.
694. Underhill, *Mysticism*, 169–170, 381–389
695. Johnson, *Mystical Theology*, 62–163, 166–167.

Chapter 12: Love for All People and All Creation Is the Sixth Stage on the Mystic Way

696. Underhill, *Mysticism*, 246–247.
697. 2 Peter 1:4–5; Whitney, *Feminism and Love*, 214–218; and Underhill, *Mysticism*, 246–247.
698. Underhill, *Essentials of Mysticism*, 23, 38, 58–64 and Underhill, *Mysticism*, 173–174, 414–415, 433.
699. Luke 10:38–42 and McGinn, *Essential Writings of Christian Mysticism*, 521–522.
700. Armstrong, *Twelve Steps to a Compassionate Life*, 19–20 and Smith, *World's Religions*, 166–167.
701. Smith, *World's Religions*, 166–167; Whitney, *Feminism and Love*, 186–190; and Armstrong, *Twelve Steps to a Compassionate Life*, 11–12, 15.
702. Armstrong, *Twelve Steps to a Compassionate Life*, 11–12, 15 and Johnson, *Mystical Theology*, 217–218, 244, 264.
703. Armstrong, *Twelve Steps to a Compassionate Life*, 19–20 and Whitney, *Feminism and Love*, 186–190.
704. Whitney, *Feminism and Love*, 186–190.
705. Whitney, *Feminism and Love*, 217–218.
706. Alcoholics Anonymous, *Alcoholics Anonymous: The Big Book*, 101–116;

Alcoholics Anonymous, *Twelve Steps and Twelve Traditions*, 79–80; Maguire, *Moral Core of Judaism and Christianity*, 212, 220, 230.

707. Underhill, *Contemporaries Meet the Classics on Prayer*, 19–20.

708. Underhill, *Contemporaries Meet the Classics on Prayer*, 20–21.

709. Henri Bergson, *Creative Evolution*, xx–xxiii, 31–38, 56–58, 97–98, 145, 277 and Bergson, *Two Sources of Morality and Religion*, 39–59, 233–235.

710. Bergson, *Creative Evolution*, 49–50, 57–58 and Bergson, *Two Sources of Morality and Religion*, 39–59.

711. Bergson, *Two Sources of Morality and Religion*, 213, 219–220, 227–228.

712. Bergson, *Two Sources of Morality and Religion*, 213, 219–221, 227–232, 252–253.

713. Bergson, *Two Sources of Morality and Religion*, 221, 230–232, 252–253.

714. Bergson, *Two Sources of Morality and Religion*, 252–253.

715. Bergson, *Two Sources of Morality and Religion*, 236–237, 252–257.

716. Bergson, *Two Sources of Morality and Religion*, 215, 233–235.

717. Deuteronomy 5:1–21, 6:4–5; Exodus 20:7–17; and Leviticus 19:17–18.

718. *Bhagavad Gita*, 95–98, 105, 119–120. Italics added.

719. Armstrong, *Twelve Steps to a Compassionate Life*, 3–4, 6, 10–11, 17, 23–25, 39, 84–85.

720. Matthew 5:43–48, 22:34–40; Luke 6:29–31, 10:25–28; and Mark 10:42–45, 12:28–34. Italics added.

721. Romans 12:9–21, 13:8–10.

722. Underhill, *Essentials of Mysticism*, 23, 38, 58–64; Underhill, *Mysticism*, 187, 173–174, 325, 396–398, 414–415, 429–441; Simmons, *In the Footsteps of the Mystics*, 39–40; and Leigh Schmidt, "Making of Modern Mysticism," *JAAR*, vol. 71-2 (June 2003), 292–293.

723. Catherine of Siena, *Dialogue*, 3–7; Flinder, *Enduring Grace*, 115–124; Underhill, *Mysticism*, 87, 173–174, 414–415, 429–431; Underhill, *Essentials of Mysticism*, 23, 38, 64–65; Simmons, *In the Footsteps of the Mystics*, 39–40; and Leigh Schmidt, "Making of Modern Mysticism," *JAAR*, 292–293.

724. Underhill, *Essentials of Mysticism*,. 35–39 and Einstein, *Albert Einstein, the Human Side*, 30–31.

725. McKeever, *Paths Are Many, Truth Is One*, 98–103.

726. Mother Teresa, *No Greater Love*, 71–72, 86 and Mother Teresa, *In My Own Words*, 16.

727. Mother Teresa, *Come Be My Light*, 55, 147, 184, 206, 231, 234, 236, 260, 279, 338, 341.

728. Mother Teresa, *Come Be My Light*, 34–35, 94, 248, 325.

729. Mother Teresa, *Come Be My Light*, 231, 233.

730. Mother Teresa, *Come Be My Light*, 40, 184, 203–204, 267, 331.

731. Dorothy Day, *Long Loneliness*, 50–51 and Dorothy Day, *Mystics, Visionaries, and Prophets*, 345–361.

732. Day, *Mystics, Visionaries, and Prophets*, 345–361.

733. Day, *Mystics, Visionaries, and Prophets*, 345–361.

734. Cho Wha Soon, *Mystics, Visionaries, and Prophets*, 434–453.

735. Oduyoye, *Mystics, Visionaries, and Prophets*, 454–472.

736. Johnson, *Mystical Theology*, 44, 51, 53, 67; Underhill, *Mysticism*, 85, 427–428, 437; and Madigan, *Mystics, Visionaries, and Prophets*, 85, 427–428, 437.

737. Martin Luther King, Jr., *A Testament of Hope*, 110–11, 290.

738. Armstrong, *God at 2000*, 108–109 and Armstrong, *Twelve Steps to a Compassionate Life*, 4–6.

739. Armstrong, *Twelve Steps to a Compassionate Life*, 157, 166–168, 184.
740. Armstrong, *Twelve Steps to a Compassionate Life*, 192–193.
741. Houston, "Spirituality and the Meaning of Mysticism for Our Time, *New Science and Spirituality Reader*, 19–21.
742. Nelson Mandela, *Long Walk to Freedom*, 134–151.
743. Hanh, *Love in Action*, 39, 66–70, 73, 101, 105, 122.
744. Dalai Lama, *Heart of Compassion*, 1, 109–110, 144, 147 and Dalai Lama, *Compassionate Life*, 3–4, 8.
745. Dalai Lama, *Compassionate Life*, 12, 17, 23 and Armstrong, *Twelve Steps to a Compassionate Life*, 145–146.
746. John Templeton, *Possibilities for Over One Hundredfold More Spiritual Information*, vii, 11, 13, 127, 145, 158–163, 175, 179–181, 184.
747. Templeton, *Possibilities*, 7–8, 17, 19–20, 175–176.
748. Templeton, *Possibilities*, 85, 142, 151, 175.
749. Templeton, *Possibilities*, 6, 15–16, 167, 174.
750. Templeton, *Possibilities*, 20, 89, 85–86, 132, 176–177, 184.
751. Templeton, *Possibilities*, 92, 126–127, 143, 148, 159, 162, 164, 166, 172–176, 178.
752. Templeton, *Possibilities*, 92, 126–127, 143, 148, 159, 162, 164, 166, 172–176, 178.
753. Templeton, *Possibilities*, 33, 160–161, 163–164, 166.
754. Templeton, *Possibilities*, 28, 34, 45–46, 127–128, 131, 135, 159, 177.
755. Templeton, *Possibilities*, 10, 20, 28, 34, 44–45, 88, 132, 136, 140, 151, 164, 177.
756. Templeton, *Possibilities*, 138, 141, 146.
757. Gandhi, *All Men Are Brothers*, 9, 29, 45, 51–53, 55–56, 60, 63, 66, 71 and Gandhi, *Gandhi on Nonviolence*, 32–33.
758. Gandhi, *Gandhi on Nonviolence*, pp. 32–33, 49; Gandhi, *Nonviolent Resistance (Satyagraha)*, pp. 38–39; and Gandhi, *All Men Are Brothers*, pp. 9, 29, 45, 51–53, 55–56, 58, 60, 62–64, 66, 71.
759. Gandhi, *Nonviolent Resistance (Satyagraha)*, 3, 6, 43, 161; Gandhi, *All Men Are Brothers*, 17, 34–35, 48, 51–52, 60, 62, 67, 72, 88, 119; and Gandhi, *Gandhi on Nonviolence*, 25, 27–28, 45, 383.
760. Gandhi, *All Men Are Brothers*, 17, 34–35, 48, 51–52, 54, 60, 62, 66–67, 72, 74, 88, 119, 133.
761. Gandhi, *Gandhi on Nonviolence*, 28–29; Gandhi, *All Men Are Brothers*, 17, 34, 41, 48, 51–53, 61, 63, 79, 90; and Gandhi, *Nonviolent Resistance (Satyagraha)*, 3, 6.
762. Gandhi, *All Men Are Brothers*, 54, 60, 62–67, 72, 74, 88, 119, 133.
763. Gandhi, *Gandhi on Nonviolence*, 28–29 and Gandhi, *All Men Are Brothers*, 41, 52–53, 56–58, 101.
764. Gandhi, *All Men Are Brothers*, 138, 154–155, 160, 163.
765. Gandhi, *Gandhi on Nonviolence*, 24, 76 and Gandhi, *All Men Are Brothers*, 3–4, 17, 57, 111, 163.
766. Gandhi, *All Men Are Brothers*, 35, 58–59, 64, 67, 73–74.
767. Gandhi, *All Men Are Brothers*, 23–24 and Gandhi, *Nonviolent Resistance (Satyagraha)*, 7–8, 35–36, 39, 77.
768. Gandhi, *Nonviolent Resistance (Satyagraha)*, 3–4, 6–7, 163, 167 and Gandhi, *All Men Are Brothers*, 88–89.
769. Gandhi, *Gandhi on Nonviolence*, 28–29; Gandhi, *All Men Are Brothers*, 17, 34–35, 41, 48, 51–53, 58–59, 61, 63–64, 67, 73–74, 79, 90; and Gandhi, *Nonviolent Resistance (Satyagraha)*, 3, 6.
770. Gandhi, *Nonviolent Resistance (Satyagraha)*, 3, 6, 43, 161; Gandhi, *All Men Are*

Brothers, 17, 34–35, 48, 51–53, 60–1, 63–67, 72, 79, 88, 90, 119; and Gandhi, *Gandhi on Nonviolence*, 25, 27–28, 45, 383.

771. Gandhi, *All Men Are Brothers*, 17, 48, 54, 64 and Gandhi, *Gandhi on Nonviolence*, 38–39.

772. Gandhi, *Gandhi on Nonviolence*, 32, 37, 58; Gandhi, *All Men Are Brothers*, 7, 53–54, 64–65, 72; and Gandhi, *Nonviolent Resistance (Satyagraha)*, 41, 43.

773. Robert Ellsberg, *Saints Guide to Happiness*, xiv; Underhill, *Mysticism*, 37, 40–41, 71, 73, 85, 94, 167–171, 311–312, 424–428, 437, 446–448; and Simmons, *In the Footsteps of the Mystics*, 3, 5.

774. Genesis 1:26–27 and Ellsberg, *Saints Guide to Happiness*, xvi-xvii.

Bibliography

Alcoholics Anonymous. *Alcoholics Anonymous: The Big Book*. Mineola, NY: Dover, 2011, 1939.
———. *Twelve Steps and Twelve Traditions*. New York: Alcoholics Anonymous World Services, 1953.
Armstrong, Karen. *The Case for God*. New York: Random House, 2009.
———. *The History of God*. New York: Ballantine, 1994.
———. *Islam: A Short History*. New York: Modern Library, 2000.
———. *Twelve Steps to a Compassionate Life*. New York: Random House, 2011.
Augustine. *Confessions of St. Augustine*. New York: Penguin, 1963.
———. *Enchiridion of Faith, Hope, and Love*. Edited by Henry Paulucci. Chicago: Henry Regnery, 1966.
Aurobindo, Sri. *Essential Aurobindo*. Edited by Robert McDermott. New York: Schocken, 1973.
———. *The Mind of Light*. New York: E.P. Dutton, 1971.
Baldock, John. *The Essence of Sufism*. Edison, NY: Chartwell, 2004.
Bary, William Theodore de, ed. *Buddhism Tradition in India, China, and Japan*. New York: Random House, 1972.
Berdyaev, Nicolas. *The Nature of Man*. Edited by Erich Fromm. New York: Macmillan, 1971.
Bergson, Henri. *Creative Evolution*. New York: Modern Library, 1944.
———. *Two Sources of Morality and Religion*. Garden City, NY: Doubleday, 1935.
Bernard of Clairvaux. *Twelve Steps of Humility and Pride, On Loving God*. London: Hodder and Stoughton, 1985.
Bhagavad Gita. Translated by Juan Mascaro. New York: Penguin, 1962.
Bible, the New Revised Standard Version (NRSV) Translation. Nashville, TN: Thomas Nelson, 1989.
Bonventure. *The Soul's Journey into God, the Tree of Life, the Life of St. Francis*. Translated by Ewert Cousins. NY: Paulist, 1978.
Borg, Marcus. *God at 2000*. New York: Church, 2002
———. *The God We Never Knew*. New York: HarperCollins, 1998
———. *The Heart of Christianity*. San Francisco: HarperSanFrancisco, 2003.
Borysenko, Joan. *Saying Yes to Change*. Carlsbad, CA: Hay House, 2006.
———. *Seven Paths to God*. Carlsbad, CA: Hay House, 1997.
Bownas, G. *The Concise Encyclopedia of Living Religions*. Edited by R.C. Zaehner. Boston: Beacon, 1959.

Brennan, Edward. *The Radical Reform of Christianity*. Notre Dame, IN: Cross Cultural, 1995.
Brussat, Frederic and Mary. *Spiritual Literacy*. New York: Scribner, 1996.
Buber, Martin. *I and Thou*. New York: Charles Scribner's Sons, 1958.
Bucke, Richard. *Cosmic Consciousness*. Secaucas, NJ: Citadel, 1973.
Burtt, E.A, ed. *The Teachings of the Compassionate Buddha*. NY: New American Library, 1995.
Cady, H. Emilie. *Complete Works of H. Emilie Cady*. Unity Village, MO: Unity, 1995.
———. *Lessons in Truth*. Unity Village, MO: Unity, 1999, 1903.
Cahill, Susan. *Wise Women: Over Two Thousand Years of Spiritual Writing by Women*. New York: W.W. Norton, 1996.
Campbell, Joseph. *The Hero with a Thousand Faces*. New York: Pantheon, 1949.
———. *Masks of Gods: Oriental Mythology*. New York: Viking, 1973.
———. *Myths to Live By*. New York: Bantam, 1973.
Capps, Walter, and Wendy Wright, eds. *Silent Fire*. New York: Harper and Row, 1978.
Capra, Fritjof. *Tao of Physics*. New York: Bantam, 1976.
Carmody, Denise and John. *How to Live Well: Ethics in World Religions*. Belmont, CA: Wadsworth, 1988.
Catherine of Genoa. *Purgation and Purgatory, the Spiritual Dialogue*. Mahwah, NJ: Paulist, 1979.
Catherine of Siena. *The Dialogue*. New York: Paulist, 1980.
Chardin, Pierre Teilhard de, *The Divine Milieu*. New York: Harper and Row, 1960.
———. *How I Believe*. New York: Harper & Row, 1969.
———. *Human Energy*. New York: Harcourt Brace Jovanovich, 1969.
———. *Hymn of the Universe*. New York: Harper & Row, 1972.
———. *The Phenomenon of Man*. New York: Harper Torchbook, 1959.
Chia, Mantak, and William Wei. *Living in the Tao: The Effortless Path of Self-Discovery*. Rochester, VT: Destiny, 2009.
Chopra, Deepak. *The Book of Secrets*. New York: Harmony, 2004.
———. *The Seven Spiritual Laws of Success*. San Rafael, CA: Amber-Allen, 1994.
———. *The Seven Spiritual Laws of Yoga*. New York: John Wiley, 2004.
Christensen, Bernard. *The Inward Pilgrim: Spiritual Classics from Augustine to Bonhoeffer*. Minneapolis, MN: Augsburg, 1967.
Climacus, John. *The Ladder of Divine Ascent*. New York: Paulist, 1982.
Cloud of Unknowing. Karen Armstrong, ed. New York: Bantam, 1994.
Cohen, Abraham. *Everyman's Talmud: The Major Teachings of Rabbinic Sages*. New York: Schocken, 1995.
Coles, Robert. *The Spiritual Life of Children*. Boston: Houghton Mifflin, 1990.
Confucius. *Analects of Confucius*. Translated by Arthur Waley. New York: Vintage, 1938.
———. *The Saying of Confucius*. Translated by James Ware. New York: New American Library, 1955.
Conn, Joann, ed. *Women's Spirituality*. New York: Paulist, 1996.
Conze, Edward. *Buddhism: Its Essence and Development*. New York: Harper and Row, 1959.
———, ed. *Buddhist Scriptures*. New York: Penguin, 1959.
Cox, Harvey. *Future of Faith*. New York: HarperOne, 2009.
Dalai Lama. *The Compassionate Life*. Boston: Wisdom, 2001.

———. *Essential Teachings*. Berkeley: N. Atlantic, 1995.
———. *The Heart of Compassion: A Practical Approach to a Meaningful Life*. Twin Lakes, WI: Lotus, 1997.
Daly, Mary. *Beyond God the Father*. Boston: Beacon, 1973.
Das, Bhagavan. *The Essential Unity of All Religions*. Wheaton, IL: Theosophical, 1973.
Denys the Areopagite. *Pseudo-Dionysius: The Complete Works*. Mahwah, NJ: Paulist, 1987.
Dhammapada. Translated by Juan Mascaro. New York: Penguin, 1973.
Dorothy Day. *The Long Loneliness: The Autobiography of Dorothy Day*. New York: Harper and Row, 1952.
Dukas, Helen and Banesh Hoffman, eds. *Albert Einstein: The Human Side*. Princeton, NJ: Princeton University Press, 1981.
Dyer, Wayne. *Changing Your Thoughts—Changing Your Life*. Calsbad, CA: Hay House, 2007.
———. *There's a Spiritual Solution to Every Problem*. New York: Quill, 2003.
———. *Manifest Your Destiny*. New York: HarperCollins, 1997.
Eck, Diana. *India: Sacred Geography*. New York: Harmony, 2012.
Eckhart, Meister. *Everything as Divine*. Mahwah, NJ: Paulist, 1966.
Ellis, Peter. *The Men and the Message of the Old Testament*. Collegeville, MN: Liturgical, 1963.
Ellsberg, Robert. *The Saints Guide to Happiness*. New York: North Point, 2003.
Elwood, Robert, and Barbara McGraw, *Many Peoples, Many Faiths: Women and Men in the World Religions*. 6th edition. Upper Saddle River, NJ: Prentice Hall, 1999.
Embree, Ainslie, ed., *The Hindu Tradition*. New York: Vintage, 1972.
Emerson, Ralph Waldo. *Selections from Ralph Waldo Emerson: An Organic Anthology*. Boston: Houghton Mifflin, 1957.
Ernst, Carl. *The Shambhala Guide to Sufism*. Boston: Shambhala, 1997.
Feibleman, James. *Understanding Oriental Philosophy*. New York: New American Library, 1976.
Ferguson, Marilyn. *Aquarian Conspiracy*. Los Angeles: J.P. Tarcher, 1980.
Fiorenza, Elisabeth Schussler. *In Memory of Her*. New York: Crossroad, 1990.
Fisher, Robert. *West African Traditional Religions*. Maryknoll, NY: Orbis, 1998.
Fleming, David, ed. *Fire and Cloud*. New York: Paulist, 1978.
Flinder, Carol. *Enduring Grace*. San Francisco: HarperSanFrancisco, 1993.
Fox, Matthew. *The Coming of the Cosmic Christ*. San Francisco: Harper and Row, 1988.
———. *Christian Mystics*. Novato, California: New World Library, 2011.
Fredrickson, Barbara. "What Is This Thing, Love?" In *Psychotherapy Networker* (Jan/Feb, 2014), 42–47.
Fromm, Erich. *The Art of Loving*. New York: Bantam, 1956.
———. *To Have and To Be*. New York: Bantam, 1981.
Fulghum, Robert. *All I Really Need to Know I Learned in Kindergarten*. New York: Ivy, 1988.
Funk, Robert, et al. *Five Gospels: What Did Jesus Really Say?* New York: HarperCollins, 1997.
Gallagher, Winifred. *Working on God*. New York: Random House, 1999.
Gandhi, M.K. *All Men Are Brothers*, edited by Krishna Kripalani. New York: World without War, 1969.

———. *Gandhi on Nonviolence*, edited by Thomas Merton. New York: New Directions, 1965.
———. *Mahatma Gandhi*.
———. *Non-violent Resistance (Sayagraha)*. New York: Schocken, 1961.
Ghanananda, Swami, and John Stewart-Wallace, eds. *Women Saints: East and West*. Hollywood, CA: Vedanta, 1979.
Goldin, Judah, ed. *The Living Talmud: The Wisdom of the Fathers*. New York: New American Library, 1957.
Goldwag, Arthur. *The Beliefnet Guide to Kabbalah*. New York: Doubleday, 2005.
Goode, William. *Religion among the Primitives*. New York: Free, 1964.
Griffins, Bede, ed. *Universal Wisdom*. New York: Harper Collins, 1994.
Hadewijch. *Hadewijch: The Collected Works*. Mahwah, NJ: Paulist, 1980.
Hanh, Thich Nhat. *Love in Action: Writings on Nonviolent Social Change*. Berkeley, CA: Parallax, 1993.
Happold, F.C. *Mysticism*. New York: Penguin, 1990.
Harkness, Georgia. *Understanding the Christian Faith*. New York: Abingdon, 1948.
Harris, Maria. *The Dance of the Spirit*. New York: Bantam, 1991.
Hartmann, Thom. *The Last Hours of Ancient Sunlight*. New York: Three Rivers, 2004.
Harvey, Andrew, ed., *Essential Mystics: The Soul's Journey to Truth*. Edison, NJ: Castle, 1996.
———. *The Teaching of the Hindu Mystics*. Boston: Shambhala, 2002.
———. *The Teachings of the Mystics*. Boston: Shambhala, 2001.
Heschel, Abraham. *Man's Quest for God*. New York: Charles Scribner's Sons, 1954.
———. *Who Is Man?* Stanford, CA: Stanford University Press, 1965.
Hodge, Stephen. *Tibetan Buddhism*. London: Piatkus, 1999.
Hoffman, Edward. *The Kabbalah Reader: A Sourcebook of Visionary Judaism*. Boston: Trumpter, 2010.
Hopfe, Lew. *Religions of the World*. London: Collier Macmillan, 1976.
Horn, Gabriel. *Contemplation of a Primal Mind*. Gainesville, FL: University of Florida Press, 2000.
Houston, Jean. "Spirituality and the Meaning of Mysticism for Our Time." In *New Science and Spirituality Reader*, edited by Ervin Laszlo and Kingsley Dennis. Rochester, VT: Inner Traditions, 2013.
Hu, Hsiao-Lan. "Rectification of the Four Teachings in Chinese Culture." In *Violence against Women in Contemporary World Religions: Roots and Cures*, edited by Daniel Maguire and Sa' Diyya Shaikh. Cleveland: Pilgrim, 2007.
Hultkrantz, Ake. *Native Religions of North America*. New York: Harper & Row, 1987.
Huxley, Aldous. "Perennial Philosophy." In *The Highest State of Consciousness*, edited by John White. Garden City, NY: Doubleday, 1972.
Ibrahim, I.A. *A Brief Illustrated Guide to Understanding Islam*. Houston: Darussalam, 1997.
I Ching: The Chinese Book of Changes, edited by Clae Waltham. New York: Ace, 1969.
Ignatius of Loyola. *Spiritual Exercises and Selected Works*, edited by George Ganso. New York: Paulist, 1991.
Isherwood, Christopher. *Where Joy Resides*. New York: Farrar, Straus, and Giroux, 1989.
James, William. *The Varieties of Religious Experience*. New York: Mentor, 1958, 1902.
Jeffery, Arthur, ed. *Islam: Muhammad and His Religion*. New York: Bobbs Merrill, 1958.

Jensen, Adolf. *Myth and Cult among Primitive Peoples*. Chicago: University of Chicago Press, 1973.
Jesuit General Congregation, 1995, "Jesuits and the Situation of Women in Church and Society," In *Women's Spirituality*, edited by Joann Conn. pp. 96–102.
John of the Cross. *The Collected Works of St. John of the Cross*. Washington, D.C.: Institute of Carmelite Studies, 1973.
———. *Dark Night of the Soul*. Garden City, NY: Doubleday, 1959.
Johnson, Raynor. *Imprisoned Splendor*. Wheaton, IL: Theosophical/Quest, 1971.
Johnson, William. *Mystical Theology: Science of Love*. Maryknoll, NY: Orbis, 1995.
Julian of Norwich. *Revelations of Divine Love*. New York: Penguin, 1966.
Kimball, Charles. *When Religion Becomes Evil*. San Francisco: HarperSanFrancisco, 2002.
King, Martin Luther King Jr. *A Testament of Hope: The Essential Writings of Martin Luther King Jr.*, edited by James Washington. New York: Harper and Row, 1986.
King, Ursula. *Christian Mystics*. New York: Simon and Schuster, 1998.
———. *Women's Spirituality*. New York: New Amsterdam, 1989.
King, Theresa. "What Is Spirituality?" *The Spiral Path*, edited by Theresa King. Saint Paul, MN: Yes International, 1992.
Kishore, B.R. *Hinduism*. New Delhi, India: Diamond, 1994.
Kitagawa, Joseph. *Religions of the East*. Philadelphia: Westminster, 1968.
Koran. Translated by N.J. Dawood. New York: Penguin, 1968.
Koran. Translated by Arthur Jeffery. Mineola, NY: Dover, 2001.
Koran. Translated by J.M. Rodwell. New York: Ballantine, 1993.
Kung, Hans. *The Church*. Garden City, NY: Doubleday, 1976.
Lao Tzu. *Tao Te Ching*. Translated by James Legge. Mineola, NY: Dover, 1997.
———. *The Way of Life according to Lao Tzu*. Translated by Witter Bynner. New York: Capricorn, 1994.
Lawrence, Brother. *The Practice of the Presence of God*, edited by Hal Helms. Orleans, MA: Paraclete, 1985.
Lee, Matthew, et al. *The Heart of Religion: Spiritual Empowerment, Benevolence, and the Experience of God*. New York: Oxford University Press, 2013.
Liebert, Elizabeth. "Changing Life Patterns," In *Women's Spirituality*, 349–351.
The Little Flowers of St. Francis. Translated by Leo Price. Baltimore, MD: Penguin, 1959.
"Lord Jesus," Vatican Congregation for the Doctrine of the Faith, #4–9, 16–17.
Madigan, Shawn, ed. *Mystics, Visionaries, and Prophets*. Minneapolis, MN: Fortress, 1998.
Maguire, Daniel. *A Moral Creed for All Christians*. Minneapolis, MN: Fortress, 2005.
———. *The Moral Core of Judaism and Christianity*. Minneapolis, MN: Fortress, 1993.
Mandela, Nelson. *The Long Walk to Freedom: The Autobiography of Nelson Mandela*, edited by Coco Cachalia. New York: Little and Brown, 1996.
McGinn, Bernard. *Essential Writings of Christian Mysticism*. New York: Modern Library, 2006.
McGrath, Alister. *Christian Theology*. 2nd ed. Cambridge, MA: Blackwell, 1994.
McKeever, S.G. *Paths Are Many, Truth Is One*. San Diego, CA: McKeever, 1998.
Mascaro, Juan. "Introduction," *Upanishads*. Translated by Juan Marcaro. New York: Penguin, 1965.
Maslow, Abraham. *Religions, Values, and Peak Experiences*. Columbus, OH: Ohio State University Press, 1964.

Matt, Daniel. *The Essential Kabbalah: The Heart of Jewish Mysticism*. New York: Quality, 1995.
Maxwell, John. *Ethics 101: What Every Leader Needs to Know*. New York: Center Street, 2003.
Meaning of the Glorious Koran. Translated by Mohammad Pickthall. New York: New American Library, 1968.
Mechthild of Magdeburg. *The Flowing Light of the Godhead*. New York: Paulist, 1998.
Miller, James. *Daoism*. Oxford, England: One World, 2003.
Myss, Caroline. *The Anatomy of the Spirit*. New York: Three Rivers, 1996.
Nasr, Seyyed Hossein. *The Heart of Islam: Enduring Values for Humanity*. San Francisco: HarperSanFrancisco, 2002.
Neusner, Jacob. *The Way of the Torah*. Belmont, CA: Dickerson, 1970.
Novak, Philip. *World's Wisdom: Sacred Texts of the World's Religions*. New York: HarperSanFrancisco, 1994.
Otto, Rudolf. *The Idea of the Holy*. New York: Oxford University Press, 1917.
Palmer, Martin. *World Religions*. London: HarperCollins, 2004.
Parrinder, Geoffrey. *Religion in Africa*. New York: Penguin, 1969.
Parrinder, Geoffrey, ed. *World Religions from Ancient History to the Present*. New York: Facts on File, 1984.
Patanjali. *How to Know God*. Hollywood, CA: Vedanta, 2007.
Paul, Vincent de, and Louise de Marillac. *Rules, Conferences, and Writings*, edited by Frances Ryan and John Rybolt. New York: Paulist, 1995.
Philokalia: Eastern Christian Spiritual Texts, edited by Allyne Smith. Woodstock, VT: Skylight Paths, 2006.
Plato. *Dialogues of Plato*, edited by Justin Kaplan. New York: Washington Square, 1950.
Porete, Marguerite. *The Mirror of Simple Souls*. New York: Paulist, 1993.
Prabhavananda, Swami. *The Spiritual Heritage of India*. Garden City, NY: Doubleday, 1964.
———. *Vedic Religion and Philosophy*. Mylorpaore, India: Sri Ramakrishna Math, 1995.
Radhakrishnan, Sarvepalli. *The Hindu View of Life*. NewYork: Macmillan, 1926, 1973.
Ramakrishna, Sri. *Teachings of Sri Ramakrishna*. Calcutta, India: Advaita Ashrama, 1981, 1934.
Reinhold, H.A., ed. *Soul Afire: Revelations of the Mystics*. Garden City, NY: Doubleday, 1973.
Renard, John. *Confucianism, Daoism, and Shinto*. Mahwah, NJ: Paulist, 2002.
Renou, Louis, ed., *Hinduism*. New York: Washington Square, 1972.
Rolle, Richard. *The Fire of Love*. New York: Penguin, 1971.
Ruether, Rosemary. *Catholic Does Not Equal the Vatican: A Vision of Progressive Catholicism*. New York: New, 2008.
———. *Sexism and God-talk*. Boston: Beacon, 1983.
Rumi, Jalal-id-Din. *Teaching of Rumi*. Translated and edited by Andrew Harvey. Boston: Shambhala, 1999.
Schmidt, Leigh. "Making of Modern Mysticism." In *JAAR*, vol. 71-2 (June 2003), 292–293.
Schneiders, Susan. "Feminist Spirituality." In *Women's Spirituality*, edited by Joann Conn. New York: Paulist, 1996.
Scholem, Gershom. *Kabbalah*. New York: Penguin, 1974.

Schweitzer, Albert. *Treasury of Albert Schweitzer*, edited by Thomas Kiernan. New York: Gramercy, 1994, 1965.
Sen, K.M. *Hinduism*. New York: Penguin, 1973.
Shankara, *Crest-Jewel of Discrimination*. Translated by Swami Prabhavananda and Christopher Isherwood. Hollywood, CA: Vedanta, 1978.
Sharma, Arvind, ed., *Our Religions*. San Francisco: HarperSanFrancisco, 1995.
Simmons, Henry. *In the Footsteps of the Mystics*. Mahwah, NJ: Paulist, 1992.
Smart, Ninian and Rechard Hecht, eds. *Sacred Texts of the World: A Universal Anthology*. New York: Crossroad, 2004.
Smith, Huston. *Forgotten Truth: The Common Vision of the World Religions*. New York: HarperSanFrancisco, 1976.
———. *World's Religions*. New York: HarperSanFrancisco, 1991.
Spencer, Sidney. *Mysticism in World Religions*. Gloucester, MA: Peter Smith, 1971.
Stace, Walter. *The Teachings of the Mystics*. New York: New American Library, 1961.
Stahl, Louann. *A Most Surprising Song: Exploring Mystical Experience*. Unity Village, MO: Unity, 1992.
Star, Jonathan. *Inner Treasure*. New York: Penguin Putnam, 1999.
Stephen, Carolyn. "Quaker Strongholds." In *Quaker Spirituality: Selected Writings*, edited by Douglas Steere, 241–250. Mahwah, NJ: Paulist, 1989.
Sun Bear and others. *Walk in Balance*. New York: Fireside, 1992.
Taylor, Jill Bolte. *My Stroke of Insight*. New York: Viking, 1996.
Templeton, John. *Possibilities for Over One Hundredfold More Spiritual Information: The Humble Approach in Theology and Science*. Philadelphia: Templeton Foundation, 2000.
Teresa, Mother. *Come Be My Light: The Private Writings of the 'Saint of Calcutta,'* edited by Brian Kolodiejchuk. New York: Doubleday, 2007.
———. *In My Own Words*. New York: Gramercy, 1996.
———. *My Life among the Poor*. New York: Ballantine, 1985.
———. *No Greater Love*. Novato, CA: New World Library, 1977.
Teresa of Avila. *The Collected Works of St. Teresa of Avila*, vol. 2. Washington, DC: Institute of Carmelite Studies, 1980.
———. *The Interior Castle*. New York: Paulist, 1979.
Therese of Lisieux. *The Autobiography of St. Therese of Lisieux*. Garden City, NY: Doubleday, 1957.
Thomas a Kempis. *Imitation of Christ*. Baltimore, MD: Penguin, 1973.
Thomas, Gary. *Sacred Pathways*. Nashville, TN: Thomas Nelson, 1996.
Thurman, Robert. *Infinite Life: Seven Virtues for Living Well*. New York: Riverhead, 2004.
Tillich, Paul. *Systematic Theology*. Chicago: University of Chicago Press, 1967.
Tolle, Eckhart. *A New Earth: Awakening to Your Life's Purpose*. New York: Penguin, 2005.
———. *The Power of NOW*. Novato, CA: New World Library, 2004.
———. *Practicing the Power of NOW*. Novato, CA: New World Library, 2001.
Underhill, Evelyn. *Contemporaries Meet the Classics on Prayer*, edited by Leonard Monroe. Los Angeles: Howard, 2003.
———. *Essentials of Mysticism*. New York: E.P. Dutton, 1960, 1920.
———. *Mysticism: A Study in the Nature of Development of Man's Spiritual Consciousness*. New York: E.P. Dutton, 1911, 1961.
———. *Practical Mysticism*. Mineola, New York: Dover, 2000.

Upanishads. Translated by Juan Mascaro. NY: Penguin, 1965.
Upanishads. Translated by Swami Prabhavananda and Frederick Manchester. New York: New American Library, 2002.
Walker, Alice. "God Is Inside You and Inside Everybody Else." In *Weaving the Visions*, edited by Judith Plaskow and Carol Christ. New York: Harper and Row, 1989.
Walsh, Roger. *Essential Spirituality*. New York: John Wiley, 1999.
Wheatley, Margaret. *Leadership and the New Science: Learning about Organizations from an Orderly Universe*. San Francisco: Berrett-Koehler, 1994.
White, John, ed. *The Highest State of Consciousness*. Garden City, NY: Doubleday, 1972.
Whitney, Ruth. *Feminism and Love: Transforming Ourselves and Our World*. Notre Dame, IN: Cross Cultural, 1998.
———. *The Heart of Jesus' Teaching: The Key to Transforming Christianity and Our World*. Nevada City, CA: Blue Dolphin, 2016.
Ken Wilber. *Integral Psychology: Consciousness, Spirit, Psychology, Therapy*. Boston: Shambhala, 2000.
———. *The Religion of Tomorrow: A Vision for the Future of the Great Traditions—More Inclusive, More Comprehensive, More Complete*. Boulder, CO: Shambhala, 2017.
Williams, John, ed. *Islam*. New York: Braziller, 1962.
Williamson, Marianne. *The Law of Divine Compensation: On Work, Money, and Miracles*. New York: HarperOne, 2012.

Index

Abraham, 143
Allah's ninety-nine names, 165–67
Amos, 148
Angelo de Filigno, 244–45
Arabi, Muid ad-Din ibn al-, 172–73, 253
Aristotle, 252
Armstrong, Karen, 87, 103, 177–79, 239–240, 242, 255, 271, 282–83
Attar, Fariduddin, 68–69
Augustine, 158–59, 191
Aurbindo, Sri, 47, 52–55, 57, 78–79
Azriel, 151

Bahai, 180
Baldock, John, 68, 168–69
Berdyaev, Nicolas, 218
Bergson, Henri, 273–75
Bhagavad Gita, 9, 50–51, 64, 110–11, 125–27, 178–79, 184–85, 192, 211–12, 223, 250–51, 276
Blake, William, 162
Boehme, Jacob, 207–8, 248–49
Boff, Leonard, 34
Boniface VIII, 89
Bonventure, 69–70
Borg, Marcus, 104–6
Borysenko, Joan, 77
Buber, Martin, 12–3, 18, 43, 94–97, 152–53, 215, 221
Bucke, Richard, 28
Buddha, ix, 9, 48, 65, 223–25, 238, 251–52

Cade, H. Emilie, 249
Campbell, Joseph, 77
Carmody, Denise, 224
Cassian, John, 243
Catherine of Genoa, 25, 51, 160, 183–84, 205, 248
Catherine of Siena, 72–73, 160, 185, 246, 277
Chardin, Pierre de, 11–12, 52, 54–55, 162, 249–250
Chittister, Joan, 250
Chopra, Deepak, 41–42, 65
Chuang, 139–140, 212, 225
Clare of Assisi, 159
Climacus, John, 67
Cloud of Unknowing, 218, 229, 258
Coles, Robert, 5–7
Confucius, 7, 133–35, 140, 179
Conn, Joann, 33
Conze, Edward, 252
Cordovero, Moses, 151, 214, 252
Cox, Harvey, 1
Cyprian, 88

Dalai Lama, 284–85
Day, Dorothy, 5, 280–81
Denys the Areopagite, viii, 66–67, 93, 159, 213, 226, 243–44, 256–57
Dhammapada, 65–66
Dyer, Wayne, 40

Eck, Diana, 132

Eckhart, Meister, 26, 45, 184, 218, 246, 258
Einstein, Albert, 2, 10–12, 278
El'azar of Worms, 152
Elizabeth de la Trinity, 278
Ellsberg, Robert, 293
Emerson, Ralph Waldo, 7–8, 42–43

Fisher, Robert, 16
Fox George, 99, 208
Fox, Matthew, 2, 26, 28, 45, 232–33
Francis of Assisi, 10, 40, 109, 159, 194, 277
Fromm, Erich, 13–14, 188
Fulghum, Robert, 19–20

Gamliel, Rabbi, 226
Gandhi, Mahatma, x, 25, 29, 131, 184, 186, 208, 253–54, 288–293
Ghazzali, Abu Hamid al-, 171–72
Ginsberg, Natalie, 153
Gluckel of Hameln, 152
Goode, William, 114
Griffin, Bede, 46, 239, 242
Guyon, Jeanne Marie, 262

Hadewijch, 194–95, 227–28
Hanha, Thich Nhat, 284
Hartmann, Thom, 16–17
Heschel, Abraham, 2
Hildegarde of Bingen, 248
Hilton, Walter, 246
Houston, Jean, 283–84
Hosea, 148
Huxley, Aldous, 19

Ignatius of Loyola, 161
Isaiah, 145
Israel ben Eliezar, 152

James, William, 43
Jeremiah, 147
Jesus, 9–10, 105, 154–57, 180, 192–93, 268, 270, 276–77
John, 158, 212–13, 225
John of Cross, 185, 187–88, 235–36, 261–62
Johnson, William, 67, 265

Jones, Rufus, 162
Judith, 149–50
Julian of Norwich, 4, 93, 97–99, 106–7, 213–14, 229–230, 246–48
Jung, Carl, 43

Kabbalah, 150, 252
Kabir, 28, 224
King, Martin Luther, Jr., 282
King, Ursula, 33–34, 67
Kishore, B.R., 240
Kobler-Ross, Elizabeth, 272
Kojiki, 141–42
Kook, Abraham Isaac, 152

Lao Tzu, 133, 136–39, 212, 250
Law, William, 262
Lawrence, Brother, 161–62
Lee, Matthew, 99–102, 108
Liebert, Elizabeth, 84
Lorde, Audre, 271

Maguire, Daniel, 272–73
Mahadevi, 128
Malcolm X, 175–76
Mandela, Nelson, 284
Marcaro, Juan, 14–15
Marie of Incarnation, 230
Maslow, Abraham, 43, 82–85, 91
Maximus the Confessor, 233–34
McKeever, S.G., 162, 198, 278–79
Mechthild of Magdeburg, 236–38, 245
Mencius, 7, 135–36
Merton, Thomas, 43, 294
Micah, 148
Miguel de Molinos, 158
Milton, John, 109
Mirabai, 128–29, 214
More, Gertrude, 93
Moses, 144, 180
Moses de Leon, 226
Mo Tzu, 270
Muhammad, 163–65, 167–69, 180,
Myss, Caroline, 77–78

Nasr, Seyyed Hossein, 165
Nicholas of Cusa, 90
Nihongi, 141–42

Nelson-Pallmeyer, Jack, 106

Oduyoye, Mercy Amba, 282
Origen, 66
Otto, Rudolf, 3, 15, 24, 31, 113

Palamas, Gregory, 234
Parrinder, Geoffrey, 15–16, 114
Patanjali, 64–65
Paul, 105, 157–58, 191–92, 277
Philokalia, 233
Plaskow, Judith, 154
Porete, Marguerite, 70–71
Prabhavananda, Swami, 63–64
Psalms, 148

Quran, ix, 67–68, 163–65, 193–94, 252–53

Rabi'a, 170
Radhakrishnan, Sarvepalli, 29, 185–86, 232
Ramakrishna, 129–131, 230–31, 240, 258
Robertson, F.W., 258
Rolle, Richard, 93, 159–160, 218, 245–46
Ruether, Rosemary, 86
Rumi, Jalal-id-Din, 30, 93, 173–75, 195–96, 227, 234, 277
Ruskin, John, 85–86
Ruysbroeck, Jan Van, 93, 221, 228–29, 277

Sartre, Jean Paul, 9
Schneider, Susan, 33
Schweitzer, Albert, 272
Shakespeare, William, 9
Shankara, 123
Shepland, H.P., 215–16
Smith, Huston, 93–94, 224
Soon, Cho Wha, 281–82
Spock, Benjamin, 22
Stephens, Carolyn, 258–59
Sufis, 168–170
Suso, Henry, 5, 220

Tagore, Rabindranath, 215
Talmud, 150
Tauler, John, 71
Taylor, Jill Bolte, 37–40
Templeton, John, 285–88
Teresa, Mother, 4, 87, 107–110, 182–83, 231–32, 241, 262–64, 279–280
Teresa of Avila, 33, 40, 73–76, 161, 187, 218, 234, 278
Theologia Germanica, 42, 228
Therese of Lisieux, 220–21
Thoreau, Henry David, 35
Thurman, Robert, 41
Tillich, Paul, 249
Tolle, Eckhart, 2–3, 11–12, 23, 44, 111–12, 254, 258
Tutu, Desmond, 162, 250

Underhill, Evelyn, viii, ix, 17–8, 23–4, 27–8, 32, 45–6, 79–81, 102, 183, 185–86, 207, 216–17, 219–220, 222, 233–35, 242, 254–56, 261–62, 264, 272, 282, 293
Upanishads, 121–22, 124–25, 210–11, 222–23, 250

Vatican II, 89
Vedas, 120–21
Vincent de Paul, 196

Wach, Joachim, 46
Walker, Alice, 18–19, 89
Walsh, Roger, 43–45
Wheatley, Margaret, 197–98
Whitney, Ruth, 79–81, 187–190
Wilber, Ken, 57–63
Williamson, Marianne, 198–200
Woolman, John, 196–97
Wordsworth, William, 253

Zoroaster, 179

www.ingramcontent.com/pod-product-compliance
Lightning Source LLC
Chambersburg PA
CBHW071229230426
43668CB00011B/1363